The Law of
Insurance Broking

The Law of
Insurance Broking

Christopher Henley
Solicitor, McKenna & Co

LONGMAN

© Longman Group Ltd 1990

ISBN 0851 21683 8

Published by
Longman Law, Tax and Finance
Longman Group UK Ltd
21–27 Lamb's Conduit Street
London WC1N 3NJ

Associated offices
Australia, Hong Kong, Malaysia, Singapore, USA

A CIP catalogue record for this book is available from the British Library

Phototypeset by Input Typesetting Ltd, London

Printed and bound in Great Britain by
Biddles Ltd, Guildford and King's Lynn

Contents

Part Two: The Contract of Insurance

Part Three: The Broker

Preface

This book considers those areas of the law which affect the professional life of an insurance broker and those legal relationships in which he is involved. It is aimed primarily at the broker's legal advisers, but also at the broker himself since any failure to understand or appreciate the relevant law means that the broker operates *in vacuo*; indeed, he must have a reasonable comprehension of the relevant law and must keep himself abreast of legal developments in his area of specialisation (*Park v Hammond* 1816 6 Taut 495). It is important that the broker understands both his rights and his obligations because he is regularly included in the increasing amount of litigation spawned by the contract of insurance, sometimes properly, sometimes for the sake of completeness, and sometimes on the basis that the greater number of defendants in any action, the more likely it is that each defendant will contribute to a settlement. (In *Wolff v Horncastle* 1 B & P 314, 321 Buller J commented that: 'Time was, when no underwriter would have dreamed of making such an objection: if his solicitor had suggested a loop-hole by which he might escape he would have spurned at the idea. He would have said is it not a fair policy? Have I not received the premium? and shall I not now when the loss has happened, pay the money? This would have been his answer, and he would have immediately ordered his broker to settle the loss'. Matters do not seem to have improved since his complaint in 1797.) Adding insult to injury, the broker is usually also joined by a co-defendant as a third party. From the point of view of the parties to an insurance contract, it is, therefore, axiomatic that the broker is always wrong. He operates in the middle of their conflict, and is fired upon by both sides.

Whilst it may only be for tactical reasons that the broker is often included in litigation, it is not necessarily a bad thing. The broker seeks to wear the hat of a professional and is now being treated as one, with its attendant obligations and liabilities. This should ensure that he provides a better service, but it is also a matter of public policy. The rules of insurance are relatively inflexible and apply equally to a layman wanting life insurance with minimum effort at the lowest possible premium, with no idea that the broker is actually his agent, as to a multi-national company with a risk management department well versed in the peculiarities of future warranties. When the layman is unable to recover for a technicality or breach, of which he may have been unaware and as to which his broker should have advised him, he should be able to obtain damages from his broker. The broker is not always liable today, but his liability has been considerably extended in recent years, both to the insured and to third parties. In reality all it means is that the broker's own liability insurers bear the insured's loss, rather than the insured's insurers. However, the insured himself does not suffer, which is a good thing.

Whilst this book is not intended to supplant those pillars of insurance law set out in Appendix 7 it should supplement them by drawing together the many threads of insurance law relevant to a broker's practice. Further, a consideration of several aspects of insurance law will be necessary to discharge properly the function of this book, since a broker must understand those aspects of the law which may impinge upon the discharge of his job — the construction of clauses, the effect of the slip or proposal form, or of a condition precedent, the principle of utmost good faith etc. Any failure by the broker to appreciate the extent and nature of the legal matrix within which he works may result in liability to others. I have selected for consideration those areas which I consider to be the most important; there are others which I have not been able to include for reasons of space.

I am grateful for the invaluable assistance of Julian Flaux of 7 Kings Bench Walk, Michael Nolan and Simon Kverndal of 2 Essex Court, John Powell QC of 2 Crown Office Row, and Tim Williams of CT Bowring. Any mistakes, however, remain my own and all comments will be gratefully received.

I am also grateful to the library staff of the Chartered Insurance Institute for their willingness and ability to help, and for their unfailing courtesy. Special thanks are also due to Christine Couzens for her care, co-operation and assistance throughout and to my long-suffering wife Sonia for her patience, forebearance and support.

The law continues to evolve rapidly. Judgment in *The Bank of Nova Scotia* v *Hellenic Mutual War Risks Association (Bermuda) Ltd, 'The Good Luck'* [1989] 2 Lloyd's Rep 238 should be available from the House of Lords later this year, as will that of *La Banque Financiere de la Cité SA* v *Westgate Insurance Co Ltd* [1988] 2 Lloyd's Rep. No book can hope to be prescient at its date of publication. The law is therefore considered as at 31 March 1990.

Christopher Henley
One Lime Street
London

Table of Cases

xiii

Table of Statutes

Table of Statutory Instruments

Table of Lloyd's Byelaws and Regulations

Part One

Agency

Chapter 1

The features of an insurance broker

An insurance broker is defined and regulated by the Insurance Brokers (Registration) Act 1977 and relevant Statutory Instruments but whose powers, rights and liabilities are otherwise controlled principally by the law of agency. An examination of the law of agency is therefore central to any consideration of the law and practice of insurance broking.

Agency is the legal relationship between two parties in which one is invested with power by the other to affect the other's legal relationship with third parties. Agency is consensual since the principal and agent must agree (by words or conduct) that the agent should act for the principal, and for legal purposes effectively as the principal. It is almost invariably contractual, because the agent is intended to be paid for his services by commission.

The lawyer's concept of agency is broad because it encompasses several varieties of the term. The three essential features are a service performed by the agent for the principal, the representation by the agent of the principal to other parties, and the valid subjection of the principal to rights, liabilities and obligations by the agent, to himself and to third parties. The insurance broker, however, should have identifying characteristics as follows.

(1) He is regulated mainly by the law of agency, which stands independently of the law of contract, although both usually operate to imply terms into the agent/principal relationship and delineate his *modus operandi*, and by statute in the form of the Insurance Brokers (Registration) Act 1977, and ensuing Statutory Instruments. He may only style himself as a broker if he complies with the qualifications for registration contained in s 3 of this Act.

(2) He is effectively a negotiator who attempts to obtain the best possible terms for a contract which is speculative in that the anticipated loss may not occur and is outside the control of the parties.

3

In fact his primary obligation is to introduce the party for whom he acts, the principal who will become the insured,[1] to another party who is able to provide the right type of insurance for the right price, period and terms.

(3) At no stage should the broker possess any goods or subject matter of the contract, and nor need he retain the policy, except where he has paid the premium and is exercising his general lien over it (implied by custom).

(4) The insurance broker is not just an agent, but is a 'professional'.[2] In particular he:

(a) uses specific mental skills within a specialised market;
(b) must have completed a specified course of training (unless exempted on the grounds of suitable experience under s 3(1) of the Insurance Brokers (Registration) Act 1977);
(c) will be accredited by a professional organisation known as the Insurance Brokers Registration Council which controls the entry of insurance brokers and regulates their subsequent performance, and probably another trade organisation of his choice;
(d) should be able to combine his integrity in relation to the market in which he deals with his duty and commitment to his client;[3]
(e) should maintain an efficient working infrastructure to enable him to provide a high standard of service to his principal.

(5) The broker is paid commission not by his principal but by the insurer. He may therefore be considered to be serving two masters, contrary to the primary tenet of the law of agency, which is to avoid any possible conflict of interest. In theory such a position

---

1 The broker's principal is the insured or proposed insured. In this book the principal and the insured or proposed insured are coterminous, unless otherwise indicated by the context.
2 See 'The Professions' by Sir Gordon Borrie in JBL March 1984 at p 111 and a letter in *Post Magazine* 7 December 1989 at p 10. A profession involves some advanced learning or education above that attributed to the man on the Clapham omnibus, which is distinguishable from the mere technical competence of other occupations.
3 SI 1978/1394, ss 3(A) and (B), and Lloyd's Byelaw No 11 of 1989. Aspect (d) may appear to an outsider to have been somewhat thinned as a result of the scandals of the insurance market in recent years, but no doubt holds good for the majority of insurance brokers. Certainly the examinations or requirement of experience should ensure a minimum standard of ability, competence and performance. In any event, the principal should always be protected from any lapse in standard which results in loss to himself since the broker is obliged to carry insurance to cover his professional negligence by the Insurance Brokers (Registration) Act 1977, s 12.

may give rise to a conflict, in that a broker may place business with an insurer after that insurer has offered the broker more attractive commission, which may not actually constitute the best or most suitable insurance for the principal. In practice, however, the principal should be able to evaluate the quality of the insurance obtained by the broker and can take his business elsewhere if it proves unsatisfactory or uncompetitive.

(6) A broker in marine business and (probably) at Lloyd's is responsible to the insurer for all premium, whether or not he has received it from the insured. Should the contract later be avoided after payment of premium by the principal to the broker, the insurer must return the premium to the principal, even though he may not have received it from the broker. This liability stems from a fiction in marine insurance that the underwriter has received the premium form from the insured and then loaned to the broker the premium, which the broker therefore owes directly to the underwriter (*Power v Butcher* (1829) 10 B & C 329), now enshrined in the Marine Insurance Act 1906. Section 53 renders the broker liable to the underwriter, and s 54 renders the underwriter bound by his acknowledgment of premium in the policy as against the insured, although not as against the broker. The position as regards non-marine insurance at Lloyd's is not so clear; it is arguable that the broker is directly liable to the underwriter for the premium, on the basis of market custom and practice, but the issue has not yet been settled. There is also the possibility that s 53 cannot apply to additional premium because 'this only becomes fixed when either agreed or in the last resort determined by arbitration, and so could never fictionally be deemed to have been paid or lent' (*The 'Litsion Pride'* [1985] 1 Lloyd's Rep 437, 510, 512).

(7) A broker may act as an agent before he has a principal to whom he can technically become an agent, since he may arrange reinsurance cover on a risk without a specific principal in mind. The rationale behind this curious proposition is that the broker who procures reinsurance cover before he has placed the original insurance does not act as a simple agent whose acts are later ratified by the insurer, but as a prospective agent who independently chooses whether or not to tender the benefit of the reinsurance to any particular insurer (*General Accident Fire & Life Assurance Corporation v Tanter, The 'Zephyr'* [1984] 1 Lloyd's Rep 58, 80 and [1985] 2 Lloyd's Rep 529).

(8) In some circumstances a broker may act in a dual capacity as agent for both the insurer and the insured, eg where the policy provides for notice of the claim to be given to the broker, who would owe a duty of care to the insurer to inform him of the claim,

or where the broker is entitled to issue cover notes for temporary insurance on the insurer's behalf. The broker may also owe other duties to the insurer, eg if an insurer relies upon the broker to introduce and monitor the activities of a coverholder in the context of a binding authority. However, the cardinal rule is that the broker is the agent of the party seeking insurance (or reinsurance) and he must not allow any other possible duty to conflict with his obligations to his primary principal. If such a conflict is perceived to exist, the broker must obtain the principal's fully informed consent to the broker acting in a dual capacity.[4]

(9) The insurance broker is not a party who is interested in the outcome of the contract, ie whether or not there is any loss or damage, and his commission is paid automatically by the insurer rather than under a cumbersome fee system by the principal, unless otherwise agreed. An insurance intermediary, however, may have a direct financial interest in the insurers whom he recommends, although such an interest must now be disclosed under the Financial Services Act 1986. The broker is obliged to provide independent impartial advice as to the most suitable insurance for his principal, and this is the reason for his existence.

(10) The insurance broker is employed under a contract for service, and his remit may extend beyond obtaining a quotation for a specific insurance to preparing a comparative survey of the insurances already in existence against the insured's needs. He will also usually be heavily involved in any claim made by the insured.

OTHER AGENTS

The categories of intermediary are limited only by the ability of insurance salesmen to invent new job descriptions. An insurance agent who does not register as a broker may call himself a financial consultant, financial management consultant, insurance consultant, insurance adviser, tax mitigation consultant or any combination of these, although he will of course be subject to the rigours of the Financial Services Act 1986. The essential difference between an agent and an insurance broker lies in their relative independence; an insurance broker must be independent and free from any influence which could affect his advice or judgement. In most cases

---

4 As to conflicts generally see *North & South Trust Co* v *Berkeley* [1970] 2 Lloyd's Rep 467; *Anglo-African Merchants Ltd* v *Bayley* [1970] 1 QB 311; *Eagle Star Insurance Co* v *Spratt* [1971] 2 Lloyd's Rep 116.

there is no presumption that a 'non-insurance' broker is the agent of the insured. The 'non-broker' categories can be broken down generally as follows:

Agents

Agents are usually independent, self-employed and work solely on a commission basis. They can therefore provide a wide range of policies to the consumer. They are similar to brokers but have not registered under the Insurance Brokers (Registration) Act 1977 either through choice or an inability to meet the relevant criteria. They generally have to comply with the codes of practice issued by the Association of British Insurers, which recognises them as independent.

Part-time agents

Part-time agents include solicitors, bankers, accountants and those who devote their time to other jobs or professions but who wish to provide an insurance facility to enhance their role and ability in serving their clients' needs. Some provide a 'cover at point of need' service, such as solicitors during a conveyancing transaction, or motor dealers, and their useful feature is a one-stop service to the client. Others may devote considerable resources to their clients' requirements, and may own brokers' firms as subsidiary companies. Usually, however, they provide only life and property insurance, and are connected with few insurance companies. Their role may vary; a solicitor will probably be a direct agent of the insurer, and a motor dealer may wear more than one hat during the contract. They should also reveal their commission to the insured, because it may otherwise constitute a secret profit in breach of their duties as agents.

Tied or appointed agents

Tied agents are restricted to selling the products of one insurance company for life business, or of mixed insurance companies for non-life business. Tied agents can therefore provide other companies' products if the company to whom they are tied cannot fulfil a particular client's needs.

Inspectors of agencies

An inspector does not sell insurance to the consumer, but rather sells his company's products to the agents; essentially he generates new business for the company which employs him.

Collecting agents

Collecting or canvassing agents are usually salaried employees of an insurance company or friendly society who visit clients without bank accounts to collect premiums in cash.

Own case agents

An insured person who requires large amounts of insurance and who can deal with the technical problems of insurance without assistance may place his own insurance direct with an insurer, and retain the commission normally payable to a broker, treating it as a discount.

Independent financial advisers

These intermediaries provide advice upon investments defined in the Financial Services Act 1986 and are therefore subject to formal authorisation and control.

Chapter 2

Relationship between principal and broker

FORMATION BY EXPRESS CONTRACT

The principal and broker must consent freely to the agency relationship, and there must be no misrepresentation, mistake, fraud, duress, incapacity to contract or other vitiating factor. The purpose of the contract must be lawful and capable of execution. There is no necessity for either party to sign any document relating to the agent's appointment.

FORMATION BY IMPLIED CONTRACT

The conduct of the parties may be such as to create by implication the relationship of agency without the specific details of a contract having been negotiated or agreed. An agency contract may be impliedly created where the circumstances show that the principal has given another party authority to act on his behalf, as happened in *Biggar* v *Rock Life Assurance Co* (1902) 1 KB 516, in which Mr Biggar as principal allowed the proposal form to be completed on his behalf by the agent, who was initially the agent of the insurance company. The agent inserted false information without Mr Biggar's knowledge, either due to the 'hurry of the game' of billiards which also required his attention (which was the excuse given by the agent in his evidence), or fraudulently to secure acceptance of the proposal and to obtain his commission. Mr Biggar failed to check the form and signed it, apparently taking a short break from his endeavours at billiards to do so. The insurance was accepted. Mr Biggar then lost the sight of one eye after a bottle of aerated water burst, and the policy was avoided by the insurer, an action upheld by Wright J on the basis that the insurer's agent was acting as the insured's agent because he was acting for the insured in filling the proposal form and because the insurer would not have authorised him to invent answers.

THE DUTIES OF THE BROKER

Duty to effect the specific agreement of agency

Duty to keep docs L + G Johnston 1995 LRLR

A contract containing express terms will set out the express rights and duties of the principal and agent.

If the agreement is clearly defined, the broker is under a duty to effect his duties in strict accordance with its terms. Therefore, if the broker agrees to obtain insurance for a specific risk for a specific period at a specific rate, he must attempt to do so. He cannot exercise any discretion unless specifically authorised. This situation is unlikely to occur, as the principal usually employs the broker to obtain the best insurance possible in his discretion, which involves balancing various competing aspects. If it did not, there would be no real benefit to the principal in using the broker, since he could place his own insurance without paying for the broker's services in any way (except at Lloyd's, where he is obliged to use a Lloyd's broker). If the broker is unable to perform the contract within a reasonable time or at all (*Cock, Russell* v *Bray Gibb* (1920) 3 Ll L Rep 71), he must inform the principal immediately so that the principal is in a position to protect his interests, and is not misled into believing that these interests have already been protected by the broker's performance of the contract.

If, however, the insurance is illegal or unlawful eg on purported insurance in which the 'insured' has no insurable interest but the parties agree that the policy is sufficient proof of interest, which is unenforceable owing to s 4(2) of the Marine Insurance Act 1906, or the principal cannot be informed of the lack of insurance in time to place it elsewhere, the broker's failure to inform the principal will not render him liable for breach of the agency agreement, since in the former case the contract could not have been enforced by the principal, and in the latter case the broker will not be liable in negligence, providing he has taken all reasonable steps to inform the principal.

Implied terms

However, it is unusual for the principal to express all relevant terms of his contract with his broker and many obligations are therefore implied by the law of agency. The mere appointment of an agent by a principal will engender a set of rules governing the conduct of the agent, as follows.

A duty to execute the purpose of the contract of agency
The broker must carry out the contract he has undertaken to perform. In most cases this will be initially to obtain quotations from various insurers, and, if acceptable to the principal, thereafter to effect contracts of insurance or reinsurance on behalf of the principal, to provide the relevant advice in the making of and administration of these policies, and to use the necessary infrastructure to assist the principal in the making of a claim against the insurer.

However, there is still some doubt as to the nature of the relationship between the broker and the principal, which can either be contractual or consensual; the distinction may be important as it can alter the duties owed by the broker to the principal during the initial stage of their relationship. Where the principal has agreed the broker's remuneration with him, either by express agreement or by accepting an implied term that the broker will earn his commission from the insurer, the relationship is contractual and the broker is obliged to fulfil this duty. Where, however, the broker is acting gratuitously, the relationship is not categorised as contractual, but as consensual. Thus a broker who agrees to execute the agency without consideration need not actually perform that agency provided that he informs the principal accordingly. However, if he does perform the agency he has a duty to do so with the same level of reasonable care and skill as if it were contractual. Similarly, when the insurance has been placed and the contract of agency discharged, any later action by the broker for the benefit of the insured must be properly carried out; any letter warning the insured as to the economic viability of his insurer, and suggesting that alternative insurance should be obtained, must be in clear terms, understandable by that particular insured (*Osman* v *J Ralph Moss Ltd* [1970] 1 Lloyd's Rep 313). The problem that arises in the non-contractual instance is in relation to the time of commencement of this duty, since the absence of a duty to perform the agency makes it conceptually difficult to state when any such duty arises, which will clearly be relevant to the liability of the broker for any breach. Further, the consensual broker is under no duty to complete the agency, although once commenced he is under a duty to inform his principal if he proposes to terminate the agency or is unable to complete it.

Another problem that may arise is that an insured may request the broker to insure an item, simultaneously sending a sum in respect of the premium or awaiting a request for premium. No contract exists, since the broker's silence cannot constitute an acceptance of the insured's offer, but the insured has requested that insurance be placed and will expect his instructions to be carried out. The position appears to be that a broker who holds himself out as able and prepared to obtain insurance is under a duty either to effect the insurance as promptly as the circumstances may dictate, or to inform the insured of his inability or unwillingness to do so by the fastest means of communication available (*Proudfoot* v *Montefiore* (1867) LR 2 511), so as to enable the insured to obtain insurance elsewhere. Thus whilst the broker's silence cannot complete the contract, it may give rise to an estoppel preventing him from denying that he has agreed to carry out the agreement. In *Smith* v *Lascelles* (1788) 2 TR 187 Buller J held that a request to insure must be effected in three instances. These are as follows:

(a) where the principal is abroad and the agent retains some of his assets in England, because the principal is entitled to payment by the agent in any manner he chooses;
(b) where the agent has always complied with previous requests for insurance from the principal, in the absence of a clear indication to the contrary; or
(c) if the request for insurance is intertwined with another of the principal's transactions involving the agent, the agent cannot effect the rest of the transaction and ignore the insurance element.

Any request for premium or further information by the broker, or an attempt by him to obtain the insurance (if known to the insured), would indicate to the insured that the broker was prepared to effect the insurance. Any failure to obtain the insurance or to inform the insured that the broker is not prepared to do so would result in liability in contract, in addition to a duty giving rise to liability in tort, once it had become intimated that the broker would earn commission, thereby satisfying the contractual requirement of consider ation (*Chaplin* v *Hicks* [1911] 2 KB 786). 'The duty in tort can include duties which could be described as assumpsit duties, that is to say, positive duties which are recognised by the law only because a party has voluntarily assumed them or voluntarily entered into a relationship to which they attach' (*per* Hobhouse J in *General Accident Fire & Life Assurance Corporation* v *Tanter The 'Zephyr'* [1984] 1 Lloyd's Rep 58, 85).

A duty to exercise reasonable skill and care and to act honestly

The broker is under a duty to use reasonable skill and care in the execution of the contract of agency, of a standard which is ordinarily exercised by reasonably competent insurance brokers. It should be emphasised, however, that the court will not uphold the performance of a contract by a broker which is broadly in line with the performance that other brokers would have executed if such a standard were considered by the court to be inadequate.

The payment of commission to the broker is to reward him for his expertise in placing the risk, since the insured usually leaves the broker to obtain the best terms at the best rate in the broker's discretion (*Moore* v *Mourgue* (1776) 2 Cowp 480). A broker may therefore be negligent if he recommends an insurer to an insured which any broker with a reasonable knowledge of the insurance market place might consider to be financially unsound. It might be thought that the existence of regulation of insurers by the Department of Trade and Industry should provide sufficient protection for a broker if an insurer appears unable to meet its liabilities, particularly in respect of UK business placed with UK insurers within the United Kingdom. However, brokers have found themselves using insurers who ultimately have turned out not to be licensed in the UK or regulated here, and this is particularly prevalent where a broker seeks commission terms which are not available from the 'normal' market or where he wants advantageous terms as to premium. If the insurer is unable to meet his liabilities, the insured may have a prima facie case against the broker for negligence.

The broker, in order to discharge his duty, should therefore ensure that any insurer to be used is licensed in the UK and regulated by the DTI. This information is easily obtainable from the DTI. Nevertheless, even if the insurer is licensed in the UK and properly regulated, it may be that some doubt may linger over its final ability to pay, particularly on long-tail business. There are professional analytical services available which will review the abilities of UK and worldwide insurers on an objective basis, but to their analyses the broker should add various subjective factors gleaned from his knowledge of the insurer's underwriting approach and the personalities involved. Many large brokers maintain detailed systems for reviewing the markets, involving public financial results with additional information about companies gathered by direct visits. The large international broker will probably have a special department (in addition to a security committee), whose sole occupation it is to vet the security of insurance companies.

The following items may be relevant in any assessment of an insurer.

(a) Its country of incorporation:

    (i) the degree of supervision by regulating authorities;

    (ii) the viability of its national economy;
    (iii) the political stability of the country;
    (iv) whether any foreign exchange problems exist;
    (v) inflation.

(b) Its capital:

    (i) whether it is fully or partly paid;
    (ii) whether it is adequate in relation to premium income.

(c) The quality of its assets:

    (i) whether its capital should be discounted for any intangible assets, such as goodwill;
    (ii) its liquidity;
    (iii) the debts of its parent company (if any);
    (iv) whether there is any shortfall in the market values of its security.

(d) The adequacy of its annual report:

    (i) the existence of an auditor's certificate, any audit qualification or notes to the accounts;
    (ii) the frequency of changes of directors;
    (iii) any significant change of management;
    (iv) its overall impression.

(e) Its premium income:

    (i) its rate of increase, and whether it has been a natural or sudden growth;
    (ii) whether it has been writing for income;
    (iii) the nature of the business, and in particular whether it is long or short tail;
    (iv) the amount of gross written premium income that is retained;
    (v) the quality of its reinsurance programme.

(f) Its technical reserves or provisions:

    (i) the adequacy of the claims provisions;
    (ii) the provision for claims which are incurred but not reported (IBNR) and IBNR as a percentage of premium income.

(g) The profitability of the insurer:

    (i) the extent of any underwriting profit in the absence of investment income;
    (ii) the amount of investment income in comparison with previous years;

(iii) the size of the dividends, and whether they are paid out of reserves.

(h) The ownership of the insurer:

    (i) the extent of the owner's long-term commitments to the insurance industry;

    (ii) any connections with cash-consuming companies;

    (iii) the domicile of the parent;

    (iv) the ultimate control of the insurer.

(i) The management:

    (i) the experience, character and integrity of the insurer;

    (ii) its reputation.

Osman v J Ralph Moss [1970] 1 Lloyd's Rep 313, is not an authority for the proposition that a duty is imposed upon the broker to obtain only the most secure and reliable insurance, or even that a broker must alert all his clients as to any impending insolvencies of insurers, but a court would hold a broker liable to his principal if he placed insurance with an insurer of doubtful integrity or ability to pay claims, since to do so is to fail to exercise reasonable care. Any doubts entertained by the broker at the time of placing should be brought to the attention of the insured, and full instructions sought. In *Dixon v Hovill* (1828) 4 Bing 665, Park J said 'It never was intended that the names of the underwriters should be submitted to the [insured] for previous approbation, but merely that they should be unexceptionable names; names of persons competent to pay in case of loss.' In fact the formal vetting of insurers is common practice by brokers and it will at some stage become accepted market practice. Brokers should therefore take steps to evaluate the probity of any insurer with whom insurance may be placed, and to record on the insured's file its points of evaluation, taking care to avoid any wording which may give rise to litigation instituted by the insurer for defamation.

A duty not to disclose any confidential information

The broker is under a duty not to disclose any information confidential to his principal. However, when he becomes aware that his principal is using his services for a fraudulent purpose, such as the placing of an insurance in which the subject matter does not exist or the collection of a claim which the broker knows to be fraudulent (as was alleged by the broker in the Savonita Affair), or inflating figures for stock in a fire policy (as was alleged against the insured in the dispute between the reinsurer and reinsured in *Insurance Co of Africa* v *Scor (UK) Reinsurance Co* [1985] 1 Lloyd's Rep 312) he must take any necessary steps to disassociate himself from the fraud. Failure to do so may result in civil and criminal liability, the latter under s 17(1) of the Theft Act 1968, s 14(1) of the Trade Descriptions Act 1968, and s 1 of the Prevention of Corruption Act 1906, breach of which can give rise to prison sentences. Clearly the broker cannot be required by the principal to incriminate himself in the course of his employment.

The Savonita Report (1978)[1] stated that:

In the board's view there is a continuing duty of disclosure on a broker in the presentation and negotiation of a claim. In the event of a broker becoming aware of circumstances which give rise to suspicions of fraud, that duty requires him to report his suspicions both to his client and to the underwriter. Thereafter he should pursue the claim against the underwriters, or inform his client that he is not prepared to continue to act and withdraw. Instead of taking one of the above two courses, [the broker] forebore from pursuing the matter and, indeed, actively mounted investigations for the purpose of persuading the reinsuring underwriters that the claim was fraudulent. . . . the board deeply regrets that a client should be effectively deserted by his Lloyd's broker without explanation.

The Fisher Report (1980) concluded to the contrary (at para 13.33):

If the Assured instructs the Broker to put forward a claim which the Broker knows or suspects to be fraudulent, it will be for the Broker to decide whether to comply with those instructions or to inform the Assured that he cannot do so (or cannot do so without disclosing his knowledge or suspicions to Underwriters).

The IBRC (Code of Conduct) Approval Order 1978 (SI 1978 No 1394) states that:

(A) Insurance brokers shall at all times conduct their business with utmost good faith and integrity.[2]

(B) Insurance brokers . . . shall place the interests of [their] clients before

---

1 The Savonita Report, reported at pp 2 and 3 of *Lloyd's List*, 8 December 1978. This is an extreme case, as the Report goes on to point out that 'After [the broker] had correctly reported his suspicions to the reinsuring underwriters and without notifying his client, he embarked upon a course of conduct . . . without regard for his responsibility to his client, . . . Instead of ensuring that his company either pursued the claim or withdrew, he set about collecting evidence to prove the alleged fraud, thereby acting contrary to the duty he owed to his client.'

2 Sir Gordon Borrie in JBL March 1984 at p 115 states that 'one essential attribute of a profession is a sense of obligation to the general good and a recognition that sometimes this obligation must prevail over the obligation owed to the individual client'.

all other considerations. Subject to these requirements and interests, insurance brokers shall have proper regard for others. . . .

(13) Any information acquired by an insurance broker from his client shall not be used or disclosed except in the normal course of negotiating, maintaining, or renewing a contract of insurance for that client or unless the consent of the client has been obtained or the information is required by a court of competent jurisdiction.

However, in *Weld-Blundell* v *Stephens* [1920] AC 956, 965, Viscount Finlay stated in the House of Lords that 'Danger to the State or public duty may supersede the duty of the agent to his principal.' This was a comment warmly endorsed by Bankes LJ in *Tournier* v *National Provincial and Union Bank of England* [1923] 1 KB 473.

In *Initial Services Ltd* v *Putterill* [1968] 1 QB 396, Lord Denning MR confirmed that the duty of confidence is subject to exceptions, not only 'where the master has "been guilty of a crime or fraud". It extends to any misconduct of such a nature that it ought in the public interest to be disclosed to others. Wood, VC put it in a vivid phrase: "There is no confidence as to the disclosure of iniquity".' Lord Denning MR extended the exception beyond the proposed or contemplated commission of a crime or civil wrong to 'crimes, frauds and misdeeds, both those actually committed as well as those in contemplation, provided always . . . that the disclosure is justified in the public interest'. The reason is that 'no private obligations can dispense with that universal one which lies on every member of the society to discover every design which may be formed, contrary to the laws of the society, to destroy the public welfare'. A crime may properly be disclosed to the police, to the relevant regulatory body[3] and to the party upon whom it is to be perpetrated.

The public interest was defined by Ungoed-Thomas J in *Beloff* v *Pressdram Ltd* [1973] 1 All ER 243 as including any matter in breach of national security, or in breach of law, including statutory duty, fraud or matters otherwise destructive of the country or its people. Thus the exposure of fraud will operate to override any individual's rights and constitutes a good defence to any claim for breach of the duty of confidence. This is not to say, however, that there is any

---

3 *Re A Company's Application* [1989] 2 All ER 248 at 252 where it was held that an injunction would not be granted to prevent disclosure to the Inland Revenue or FIMBRA of matters within their province, even though such disclosure may have been motivated by malice. Disclosure of confidential matters to the Inland Revenue which did not relate to fiscal matters would 'be as much a breach of the duty of confidentiality as the disclosure of that information to any third party'.

duty to expose fraud or disclose any suspicion, merely that to do so properly will not render the agent liable to the principal. May LJ stated in *The 'Good Luck'* [1989] Q Lloyd's Rep 238 at 265, 268 that:

Silence without a duty to speak, creates no rights against the silent party (*Mercantile Bank of India Ltd* v *Central Bank of India Ltd* [1938] AC 287). The law imposes no duty upon a person to report to the victim of fraudulent conduct that the fraud is being committed merely because that person has acquired knowledge of the fraudulent conduct. The law does not enforce any moral duty to inform the victim.

To speak improperly may render the agent liable for breach of duty and possibly for defamation or malicious falsehood for any damage caused (*Re A Company's Application* [1989] 2 All ER 248, 252). The Fisher Report acknowledged this by commenting (at para 13.33) that:

Where the *Broker* knows that the claim is fraudulent his duty will be clear; but where he merely *suspects* and cannot, despite all proper investigations, discover for certain whether or not his suspicions are wellfounded, he will be in a dilemma to which we see no easy answer. What is quite clear is that he has no duty or right to disclose his dilemma to Underwriters although they may draw certain conclusions if they hear that he has withdrawn.

At Lloyd's the position is now clear, as a result of Byelaw No 11 of 1989, which ensures that every person to whom the byelaw entitled 'Misconduct, Penalties and Sanctions' (No 5 of 1983) applies who:

(a) knows of any actual or proposed misconduct; or
(b) believes or has reason to believe that any misconduct (other than of a minor nature) is likely to occur or is likely to have occurred;

is under a duty to report the misconduct to the Deputy Chairman and Chief Executive of the Society of Lloyd's.

Under that Byelaw a person is guilty of misconduct if he:

(a) contravenes or fails to observe any provision of the Lloyd's Acts, or any verdict, order, award, penalty or sanction made or imposed, or any condition or requirement imposed, or any undertaking given, or any regulation or direction made, pursuant to Lloyd's Act 1871 to 1982 or any byelaw made thereunder; or
(b) conducts himself or itself in a manner which is detrimental to the interests of Lloyd's policyholders, the Society, members of

the Society, Lloyd's brokers, underwriting agents or others doing business at Lloyd's; or

(c) conducts any insurance business in a discreditable manner or with a lack of good faith or conducts himself or itself in any manner whatever which is dishonourable or disgraceful or improper.

A duty to execute the contract personally, and not to delegate

The broker must perform his role personally, since the relationship of principal and agent is confidential and fiduciary. The employment of a sub-agent by the agent will be in breach of this duty, unless permitted by statute, express agreement, or in the ordinary course of business. For example, a non-Lloyd's broker wishing to obtain insurance at Lloyd's must use a Lloyd's broker pursuant to s 8(3) of the Lloyd's Act 1982.

However, for practical purposes this general rule is of limited application because the authority of the principal to delegate can in many cases be implied, in particular where the principal is aware (or it may be presumed from the parties' conduct) that the broker intends to delegate his authority, where the performance of the contract cannot occur without delegation (such as to a Lloyd's broker, or in unforeseen circumstances as a result of business exigencies, or where the principal was a party to the appointment of the sub-agent, thus establishing privity of contract (*De Bussche* v *Alt* (1878) 8 ChD 286(310)), where the sub-agent's involvement is administrative and does not involve him in confidential matters or the exercise of judgement or discretion eg where he merely signs the policy (*Mason* v *Joseph* (1804) 1 KB 406), or where delegation is normal and acceptable in the ordinary course of business (*Coolee Ltd* v *Wing, Heath & Co* (1930) 47 TLR 78). It would be apparent, for example, that the appointment of a large firm of brokers would necessitate one or more employees within the firm carrying out the work, and this does not constitute 'delegation' in breach of duty. The specific appointment of an employee within a larger organisation does not preclude delegation by that person to others within the organisation, since that person would have accepted any task in his capacity as employee rather than on his own behalf, and the insured must be taken to have known that delegation would be likely to occur.

Further, delegation may be ratified by the principal.

As an extended example, the chain of agency could run from the US insured to the Lloyd's syndicates via a US local broker, US wholesale broker, London correspondent broker, specialist placing broker, and UK insurer, and thence through a reinsurance agent for a reinsurance pool, a treaty reinsurance broker and a Lloyd's broker.

Effects of delegation

It must be stressed that the dominant presumption is that the sub-agent is responsible to the broker and not to the principal, and that the authorisation of the creation of a sub-agency by the principal does not automatically create privity of contract. In *Calico Printers' Association* v *Barclays Bank* (1931) 145 SLT 51 at 55 Wright J commented that:

The agent does not as a rule escape liability to the principal merely because employment of the sub-agent is contemplated. To create privity it must be established not only that the principal contemplated that a sub-agent would perform part of the contract, but also that the principal authorised the agent to create privity of contract between the principal and the sub-agent, which is a very different matter requiring precise proof.

Privity of contract between a sub-agent and principal can therefore be created in two ways: by the principal conferring express or implied authority to do so upon the broker, or by ratification of the principal − sub-agent relationship. If privity can be established, it is unlikely that a court would hold a broker liable for the inadequate performance of obligations owed directly by the sub-agent to the principal, and directly enforceable by that principal against the sub-agent. However, even in cases of such privity, the broker could still be liable for his separate breaches of those obligations to the principal which survive the appointment of the sub-agency, eg allowing the sub-agent to set off sums due from him to the principal against sums due from the broker to the sub-agent.

Liability of broker for acts of sub-agent in the absence of privity

If privity between principal and sub-agent does not exist, then the broker should be liable for the sub-agent's breach of duty or failure to account, even if the appointment of the sub-agent was authorised by the principal (*Calico Printers' Association* v *Barclays Bank*). ' . . . it is trite law that for the purpose of accountability in respect of the receipt of money, receipt by a sub-agent is the same as receipt by the agent himself' (per Walton J in *Balsamo* v *Medici* [1984] 1 WLR 951, 957).

Liability of sub-agent in the absence of privity

The principal cannot sue the sub-agent for breach of obligations inherent in the sub-agency, since these are owed to the broker, and he need not remunerate or indemnify the sub-agent (*Schmaling* v *Tomlinson* (1815) 6 Taunt 147). Nor can the sub-agent be held responsible for monies had and received, even though these are ultimately intended to reach the principal. In *Balsamo* v *Medici* Walton J commented that an action for account by the principal against the sub-agent 'could not possibly have succeeded' owing to 'the fundamental principle that the action in account is one in contract'. There are, however, three possible methods by which redress could be sought from the sub-agent:

(a) an action for monies had and received if the sub-agent acknowledges that he is holding monies on behalf of or to the account of the principal, on the basis of *Griffin* v *Weatherby* [1868 LR 3 QB 753), *Shamia* v *Joory* [1958] 1 QB 448 and *IGI* v *Kirkland Timms* (Unreported);

(b) an action for secret profits made during the sub-agency, such as commission or brokerage, on the basis of the fiduciary relationship between principal and sub-broker, under the principle established in *Powell & Thomas* v *Evan Jones & Co* [1905] 1 KB 11. However, the Court of Appeal based their decision on the alternative ground of privity of contract and it is capable of criticism on other grounds. Nevertheless, it may still be argued that secret profits cannot be earned by sub-agents, whether or not any fiduciary duty exists;

(c) an action in tort on the basis that it is just and reasonable that a sub-agent should owe the principal a duty of care and that their relationship is sufficiently proximate. Although the courts are now seeking to enforce liabilities in contract in preference to those which may lie concurrently in tort, and may see no reason to allow the principal any alternative rights against the sub-agent to those which he may have in contract against the broker, an action in tort could fall within the current criteria. It is, for example, clearly within a sub-agent's reasonable contemplation that the principal will suffer the consequences of the sub-agent's negligence or breach of duty to the broker, and public policy does not appear to stand in the way; the extent of any liability will be known to the sub-agent at the outset, and since it is the sub-agent who has actually caused the loss, why should the principal be forced to sue his broker, who may have acted reasonably, or, more importantly, may have less errors and omissions insurance?

Against this argument lie the facts that the broker should be able effectively to pass on his liability to the sub-agent so that the broker does not suffer, that the broker had contracted with both parties in the knowledge that he would be liable to his principal (in any event) and that the sub-agent would be liable to him (which is simply a commercial risk that he could reasonably be expected to bear), and that the sub-agent would have to duplicate and perhaps exceed the broker's efforts in placing the insurance eg in preparing the presentation to the insurer, which might involve checking the information provided by the broker with the principal, thereby undermining the broker's commercial relationship with his principal.

The law as to the rights and liabilities between the sub-agent and principal is still unclear; for example, there may well be some liability in tort if the parties are sufficiently proximate, the law of restitution may supersede the accepted doctrine that monies received by the sub-agent cannot be claimed in contract owing to the lack of privity, and the right to an indemnity may now generally be considered to arise both in contract and independently.[4]

Duty to account

Declare monies received   A broker must pay his principal any sum obtained on the principal's behalf without delay. Any sums collected must be in a form authorised by or acceptable to the principal; cash and goods, or cash and set-off in another account will not be acceptable without the principal's consent.

It is anomalous that the broker need not disclose his commission to the insured, unless specifically requested to do so.[5] This lack of necessity to disclose the commission is curious because the insurer may have increased his rate of premium to reflect the broker's higher rate of commission, in which case the broker will make a profit at the insured's expense. It therefore runs contrary to the principles of agency law which state that the agent must make full disclosure of any personal interest to the principal and must account

---

4 *Craven-Ellis* v *Canons Ltd* [1936] 2 KB 403; *Robbins* v *Heath* (1848) 11 QB 257; *Sheffield Corporation* v *Barclay* [1905] AC 392; *Yeung Kai Yung* v *Hong Kong & Shanghai Banking Corporation* [1981] AC 787; *Leigh & Sillivan Ltd* v *Aliakmon Shipping Co Ltd* [1986] AC 795; *Yuen Kun Yeu* v *Attorney General of Hong Kong* [1987] 3 WLR 777; *Simaan General Construction Co* v *Pilkington Glass Ltd* [1988] 1 All ER 791; *Greater Nottingham Co-operative Society Ltd* v *Cementation Piling and Foundations Ltd* [1988] 3 WLR 396; and *La Banque Financiere de la Cite SA* v *Westgate Insurance Co Ltd* [1988] 2 Lloyd's Rep 513. However, such liability remains unclear.
5 *Great Western Insurance Company of New York* v *Cunliffe* (1874) LR 9 Ch Ap 525. Section 6 of the IBRC Code of Conduct; unless it is in respect of investment business and therefore disclosable pursuant to the rules of hard disclosure of FIMBRA or IBRC in force from January 1990.

for all sums received from any other party, unless specifically released from doing so by the insured.

There may also be some blurring as to the nature and extent of the commission. Pure brokerage clearly falls within this category. However, case law exists which indicates that items such as a discount for prompt payment, if usual in the market, need not be disclosed by the broker unless specifically requested. In *Baring* v *Stanton* (1876) 3 Ch 502, the broker was held entitled to retain 10 per cent discount for 'ready money' in addition to 5 per cent brokerage. This case did not follow *Turnbull* v *Garden* (1869) 38 LJ Ch 331 or *Queen of Spain* v *Parr* (1869) LJ Ch 73, which stated that discounts for prompt payment should be disclosed, but rather endorsed the comments of Mellish LJ in *Great Western Insurance Company of New York* v *Cunliffe* (above) who stated that:

'. . . it is quite obvious that they must have known, and they do not deny that they did know, that [the brokers] were to be remunerated by receiving a certain allowance or discount from the underwriters with whom they made the bargains. It was easy to ascertain by inquiry what was the usual and ordinary charge which agents who effect reinsurances are entitled to make. If a person employs another who he knows carries on a large business, to do certain work for him as his agent with other persons, and does not choose to ask him what his charge will be, and in fact knows that he is to be remunerated, not by him, but by the other persons — which is very common in mercantile business — and does not choose to take the trouble of inquiring what the amount is, he must allow the ordinary amount which agents are in the habit of charging.' That really seems to me to govern this case. It is quite clear that it was known to everybody connected with insurances that the insurance offices were in the habit of making allowances, by way of brokerage and otherwise, of 12 per cent of the profits, or 10 per cent discount, and also 5 per cent brokerage; so much so, that some of the documents produced actually contain the thing printed as common form. It is quite obvious that this is a recognised practice of the offices. That being so, it is very difficult to believe that [the insured] must not have known that [the brokers] were receiving from the offices such allowances as the offices were in the habit of making. Their dealings go on for years.

Both *Baring* and *Cunliffe* proceed on the basis that the insured in question must have been aware that allowances or discounts were obtained from the insurers, and that such allowances were both usual in the trade and reasonable. Both insureds are criticised for failing to make proper enquiries. Mellish LJ in *Baring* found that the discount for prompt payment was not a fraud on anyone and that the American insured should have become acquainted with the rules of the London market and could not later refuse to pay on the basis that he was unaware of its peculiar features. Nevertheless, he did not overrule *Turnbull* v *Garden* (above). In *Cunliffe* he also found that the 12 per cent gratuity paid by the insurer to the broker on the profits of a favourable year was an 'established remuneration' and perfectly proper. It is submitted that the discounts in these cases would today be held to constitute secret profits, for which the brokers would have to account; the gratuity in *Cunliffe* is an incentive to place either more business with the insurer, or more profitable work with the insurer, and clearly conflicts with the broker's duty to his client.[6] Certain aspects of these cases have already been overruled[7] and *Cunliffe* was partly decided on the insured's lack of objection for two years after the gratuity was discovered. Further, these old cases were often decided in a framework of the law then applying to factors, who were a prevalent part of the commercial scene, but are less relevant today. The solution to these divergent cases is that commission need not be disclosed unless requested by the insured, providing it consists of normal brokerage only, and that all other sums (however characterised) must be itemised. The propriety of the insured's claim to the sum alleged by the broker to be commission will rest on the knowledge that he had or should have had as to the nature of the broker's commission or reward, and the size of the commission; if substantially above market rates it should be disclosed (*Green & Son (Ltd)* v *Tunghan & Co* (1913) 30 TLR 64, and certainly must be disclosed upon request under section 6 IBRC of the Code of Conduct). Putting the insured on notice in any way is insufficient; he must be properly informed.

Secret profits   The broker will be entitled to receive as payment for

---

6 It could still be argued that Cunliffe's case is authority for the proposition that a purely consensual agent who is not party to any contract need not disclose any remuneration whatsoever, unless requested, on the basis that the agent is not being paid and is entitled to obtain and retain any benefit available, provided he keeps intact his fiduciary duties to the insured. James LJ stated that the agents 'were not paid servants to do the work, receiving remuneration for it, and they were left to make the profit which was incidental to the business itself. That was the character of their employment, otherwise it would have not been a profitable employment. The profit was not to come from the [insured] in the shape of any direct payment: it was to be profit which should enure to [the brokers] in the ordinary course of that kind of business. That was, the business of going to underwriters and getting the underwriters to accept the risks, paying them the premiums'.

7 The custom of a market cannot form part of a contract unless the party against whom it operates is aware of it and assents to it: *Stolos Compania SA* v *Ajax Insurance Co Ltd* [1981] 1 Lloyd's Rep 9.

his services either an amount agreed with the principal or a reasonable commission. He is not entitled to make any profit above this sum and any additional sums must be disclosed to his principal. Failure to do so will be a clear breach of his contract of agency and, if fraudulent, will prevent him from receiving his commission and may render him liable in the tort of deceit.

A secret profit is any sum above the amount he is entitled to receive from his principal, which he is paid as a result of the exercise of his authority. There need be no dishonesty or fraud, merely a financial advantage to the broker which accrues by virtue of his position. It does not matter that the principal would not have been able to obtain the same benefit, or even that the act occasioning the profit was not done strictly within the course of the broker's 'employment' (*Boardman* v *Phipps* [1967] 2 AC 46); the broker must account for all benefits or monies received, including gifts and any payment which the broker receives 'as a result of securing on behalf of that client any service additional to the arrangement of a contract of insurance', pursuant to para 11 of the IBRC Code of Conduct.

A secret profit becomes a bribe, and therefore capable of attracting civil and criminal liabilities, if it has come to the broker via a third party in order to ensure that the agent advises or takes action which is no longer impartial or disinterested, and may not necessarily be in his principal's best interests. There is an irrebuttable presumption that the agent is influenced by any bribe, and the motive for payment is irrelevant (*Hovenden & Sons* v *Millhoff* [1900–3] 11 All ER 848, 851). Millett J held in *Logicrose Ltd* v *Southend United Football Club Ltd* [1988] 1 WLR 1256, that the principal, upon discovering the proposed bribe, could elect to rescind the contract with the third party *ab initio* or, if it was too late to do so, to terminate it from that point onwards (*Panama & South Pacific Telegraph Co* v *India Rubber, Gutta Percha & Telegraph Works Co* (1875) LR 10 Ch App 515; *Armagas Ltd* v *Mundogas SA* [1986] AC 717, 742–3).

However, rescission is not confined to cases where a bribe or secret commission is agreed to be paid. It extends to any situation in which the agent puts himself in a position where his interest and duty may conflict (*Anangel Atlas Compania Naviera SA* v *Ishikawajima-Harima Heavy Industries Co Ltd* [1990] 1 Lloyd's Rep 167, 171), so that his principal does not necessarily obtain disinterested advice, and the other party to the transaction is aware of this. However, that other party must be aware either by actual knowledge or wilful blindness that the agent intended to conceal his conflict of interest from his principal. Constructive notice is insufficient since 'Parties to negotiations do not owe each other a duty to act reasonably, but only to act honestly'. (*Logicrose Ltd* v *Southend United Football Club*

Ltd (above), and the principal's right to rescind is for fraud, not negligence. This is, however, severely tempered by the rule (in *Panama & South Pacific Telegraph Co v India Rubber, Gutta Percha & Telegraph Works Co* (above)) that secret dealings between a principal and an agent of another principal constitute a fraud on the latter principal, and the former principal cannot claim that he thought that the agent would disclose the true position to the latter.

Whether the principal decides to affirm or rescind, he is entitled to recover the bribe from his agent, since it is regarded as a gift from the other principal. The bribe belongs to the principal in any event, which runs contrary to the usual rule of rescission whereby *restitutio in integrum* must be made, because such benefits do not constitute benefits under the contract or as part of the consideration, but are an independent secret profit. Upon affirmation, however, the principal is entitled to recover the bribe as money had and received to his own use, but he must give credit in any legal action for any sum recovered from his agent.[8]

The consequences of any failure to reveal that a secret profit has been made by any party to a transaction are serious, and may involve both criminal and civil liabilities, as an example will demonstrate. A discount may be paid by an insurer or a broker to a landlord with a large property portfolio, to secure his substantial book of business. The landlord may agree with his tenant that he will effect insurance in the landlord's name, the cost of which must be reimbursed by the tenant, or in their joint names, again upon reimbursement of the premium by the tenant. The tenant will pay the gross sum, and may not be aware that a discount or commission is being retained by the landlord. This is not in itself unfair, since the tenant pays the market rate and arguably should not benefit from his landlord's status or other business interests. The broker's involvement will include preparing debit notes and documents relating to premiums, which will probably be sent by the landlord to the tenant as evidence of the sum to be reimbursed, preparing any relevant insurance documentation which again will be sent to the tenant, and probably dealing directly with the tenant in connection with any problems or requests for information, which may include premiums.

---

8 *Mahesan v Malaysia Housing Society* [1979] AC 374, 383. The principal has two alternative claims: (1) for money had and received by the agent ie the bribe, as a restitutionary claim; or (2) damages for fraud ie the actual loss sustained by the principal as a result of the transaction, but not both.

Such documentation at best may state that the broker will be paid commission. It is unlikely to state that the landlord is obtaining a financial benefit, which may not be pecuniary but may, for example, consist of free valuations by the broker. Any attempts to colour or recharacterise the position will not succeed, however, since the real cost to the landlord remains less than stated on the documentation. Such a bald statement therefore may amount to a representation by the broker and the landlord that the gross premium is the amount payable by the insured party to obtain the insurance, which is clearly inaccurate and misleading.

Such non-disclosure may give rise to criminal liabilities under the following statutory provisions:

(a) Section 17(1) of the Theft Act 1968 which provides that 'Where a person dishonestly, with a view to gain for himself or another or with intent to cause loss to another, . . . (b) in furnishing information for any purpose produces or makes use of any account, or any such record or document as aforesaid [ie any record or document made or required for any accounting purpose] which to his knowledge is or may be misleading, false or deceptive in a material particular; he shall, on conviction on indictment, be liable to imprisonment . . . '. The insurer or broker has acted dishonestly (knowing of the misleading nature of the statement) with a view to gain for the landlord, and perhaps himself as a result of the greater flow of business;

(b) Section 14(1) of the Trade Descriptions Act 1968, which provides that: 'It shall be an offence for any person in the course of any trade or business: (*a*) to make a statement which he knows to be false; or (*b*) recklessly to make a statement which is false; as to . . . (i) the provision in the course of any trade or business of any services, accommodation or facilities'; and

(c) Section 1(1) of the Prevention of Corruption Act 1906, which provides that 'If any person knowingly gives to any agent, or if any agent knowingly uses with intent to deceive his principal, any receipt, account, or other document in respect of which the principal is interested, and which contains any statement which is false or erroneous or defective in any material particular, and which to his knowledge is intended to mislead the principal; he shall be guilty of a misdemeanour, . . . ' where the policy is in joint names so that the landlord acts as the tenant's agent in effecting the insurance. The insurer or broker must know that the policy will be shown to the tenant and will therefore mislead him, which may be enough to establish liability.

There is no requirement in s 1(1) for the payment to be made 'corruptly'.[9]

As to civil liability, the tenant would be able to avoid the policy upon discovery of the secret commission (*Alexander* v *Webber* [1922] 1 KB 642), or to sue the insurer, the broker and the landlord for any loss sustained as a result of the landlord's breach of duty to the tenant where the landlord has acted as the tenant's agent. This would probably be limited to the amount of the secret commission, which could be claimed in any event. If the tenant were to affirm the contract, he would not be entitled to be repaid the premium, and nor would he be able to obtain the commission paid by the insurer to the broker. This is partly because it is unclear whose liability it is to pay the broker, and partly because the broker would be entitled to receive his commission if he does not fall foul of the above statutes, because he did not practise any fraud upon the tenant (*Hippisley* v *Knee* [1905] 1 KB 1) ie if he was acting honestly in accordance with a trade custom, or if the tenant was aware of it and did not object. He will, however, be entitled to obtain the secret profit made by the broker. The tenant could also sue the insurer and the broker where the landlord's name only was on the policy, for a false representation as to the premium payable.

In short, therefore, the broker should not mislead the tenant in any way, and even stating on the documentation that the premiums are gross would not necessarily avoid the problem, since it does not provide the tenant with sufficient information to understand all relevant implications. Of course this may not apply where the lease entitles the landlord to retain the benefit of reasonable agency fees or discounts.

It is possible, however, to receive payments from both contracting parties as long as the insured is aware that the broker will be rewarded by the insurer in addition to receiving a fee from the insured (*Lord Norreys* v *Hodgson* (1897) 13 TLR 421).

A duty to advise the insured as to the adequacy of the insurance requested

The traditional view of the broker is that as an agent he simply effects the instructions of his principal, on the basis that his principal understands his own needs and instructs the broker to fulfil them.

---

9 Section 1(2), however, requires 'corruption', which may be difficult to establish unless the rate paid by the tenant was out of line with other market rates.

Thus where the broker failed to enquire as to whether additional insurance would be required to cover goods at the packers prior to transit (which was insured), he was not at fault or liable, because he was entitled to assume that the insured conducted his business prudently and had obtained the appropriate insurance (*United Mills Agencies* v *Bray* [1951] 2 Lloyd's Rep 631).[9] However, the broker is theoretically more proficient than a mere agent, since he has to fulfil certain requirements as to skill, ability and competence before using the appellation, and there seems to be no reason why he should not today have to satisfy a higher standard of care than in the past in ensuring that the insurance obtained meets the insured's requirements as precisely as possible.

Three factors substantiate this view. These are as follows:

(a) The overriding principles contained in the IBRC (Code of Conduct) Approval Order 1978 (SI 1978 1394) state that the broker shall conduct his business with utmost good faith and integrity, presumably both towards the insurer and insured, 'shall do everything possible to satisfy the insurance requirements' of his clients, and shall provide advice objectively and independently. Carrying out these principles will involve the broker dispassionately considering his principal's apparent wishes, and informing him of their adequacy or otherwise, taking care to ensure that his needs are adequately fulfilled.

(b) In *McNealy* v *The Pennine Insurance Co Ltd* [1978] 2 Lloyd's Rep 18) the broker failed to ascertain whether the insured fell within the category of an uninsurable part-time musician, which of course he did. Lord Denning MR said that 'It was clearly the duty of the broker to use all reasonable care to see that the assured . . . was properly covered'. Waller LJ said that 'It was clearly his [the broker's] duty, in my view, to make as certain as he reasonably could that the [assured] came within the categories acceptable to the [insurer]'. The Court of Appeal found that recording the insured's responses to the questions on the proposal form was not enough, and that a more active role should have been played by the broker. This case does not strictly support the proposition that a broker should advise upon his principal's insurance, except negatively to the extent that he should ensure that clearly inappropriate insurance should not be obtained. The obligation was, however, taken further by Hobhouse J in *General Accident Fire & Life Assurance Corporation* v *Tanter, The 'Zephyr'* [1984] 1 Lloyd's Rep 58, 67 where he commented that ' . . . It is the broker's duty to do his best to see that the assured's obligations of disclosure and absence of misrepresentation are fulfilled. The broker's skill and expertise extends beyond merely giving his client advice and complying with his client's instructions. He must make use of his knowledge of the market and use appropriate skills.'

(c) The requirements of the Insurance Brokers Registration Council (in its role as a Recognised Professional Body under the Financial Services Act 1986) and of the Financial Intermediaries, Managers and Brokers Association (a Self-Regulating Organisation under the Financial Services Act 1986) specify that brokers providing investment advice or executions must 'know their customer', provide the 'best advice' and only recommend investments which they believe to be suitable for that investor. A broker who is thus regulated may be subject to a higher duty of care in matters of insurance, particularly if he has discussed or executed matters of investment with the insured, on the basis that he must or should 'know his client'. Although the knowledge may have been gained in his capacity as investment adviser, there is no reason why it should not apply to him in his guise of insurance broker, given the similarity of function.

The problem with the application of a higher standard of care for a broker who has already advised his client on investment matters is that it may predicate a dual test of negligence, the IBRC or FIMBRA member owing a higher duty of care to the insured than a non-member. This argument could be eclipsed by stating that the 'higher' standard of care applies to all brokers, since the FIMBRA/I-BRC rules do no more than formalise and apply the standard of a reasonably competent broker, who should discharge his professional duties by knowing his client's requirements properly.

THE RIGHTS OF THE BROKER

Remuneration

Payment for broker's services

A broker is usually employed to obtain insurance for a specific period of a particular risk, on the best possible terms for the principal. Unless the contract of agency provides to the contrary, therefore, he is not entitled to any remuneration until a valid and proper contract of insurance has come into existence. If the contract cannot be placed with one insurer, or is to be placed at Lloyd's and/or in the companies' market, which invariably requires more time owing to the need to visit more insurers, and the risk intended to be insured against occurs before it has been fully insured, the individual insurers are liable for their share of the claim, and are entitled to their share of the premium (*General Accident Fire & Life Assurance Corporation v Tanter, The 'Zephyr'* [1985] 2 Lloyd's Rep 529). The broker will not be liable to the insured for his failure to obtain insurance for 100 per cent of the risk unless he was dilatory in carrying out his contractual duties, and he will be entitled to payment by commission from the individual insurers. If the broker cannot obtain the contract of insurance at all he will not be entitled to any remuneration unless the contract of agency specifically so provides, or unless it can be shown that it is necessary to imply such a term to give the contract business efficacy, which is unlikely. The fact that the broker has expended time and skill in attempting to place the insurance is irrelevant. He is paid by result.

The time for payment of commission to the broker is not upon the formation of a binding contract, which can exist without payment of premium or even agreement as to premium (as long as consideration passes in the form of agreement or liability to pay a premium to be fixed) but upon the payment of premium by the broker. The broker is invariably paid by commission, which is deducted by him upon receipt of the gross premium (ie including his commission) from his principal, prior to forwarding the balance to the insurer. However, in many cases premium is delivered by the principal considerably later than the date upon which the contract of insurance comes into force, which is why contracts may provide for the avoidance of the contract unless premium is received within a specified date after inception, or for a suspension of risk pending payment.

The broker is therefore paid by the insurer, to whom he has an opposing negotiating position in that any term agreed in the contract will usually be to the benefit of one party and at the expense of the other. The explanation for this apparent anomaly is that the premium agreed between the broker and the insurer will take into account the commission to be paid, and therefore, in reality, it is the insured who pays the broker for work done on his behalf (*Bancroft v Heath* (1901) 17 TLR 425). This practice is well established and fully sanctioned by the courts (*Great Western Insurance Co of New York v Cunliffe* (1874) LR 9 Ch App 525).

The basis for the liabilty to remunerate the broker is less clear. The British Insurance Brokers' Council has accepted (in its 1976 Consultative Document) that the broker's remuneration is paid by the insurer, and does not suggest that it should be paid directly by the insured to the broker. This would mean that where the insured pays the premium direct to the insurer, who is rendered unable to pass the commission therein to the broker, perhaps because the insurer becomes insolvent, the broker cannot recover from the insured. Further, where the insurer is liable to repay the premium eg on avoidance, he will pay the gross premium to the insured and seek to recover the commission direct from the broker.

Where, however, the broker himself is liable to pay the premium to the insurer, he can deduct his commission from the premium and pay the net sum to the insurer. He will then have to sue the insured for the gross sum (if unpaid), as representing monies paid on his behalf and effectively at his request both to the insurer and to himself, under his right to an indemnity, on the basis that the insured knew that the broker would have to pay the premium and effectively rendered him liable to do so when he instructed him, and that a payment of commission would be paid to or retained by the broker. The right to an indemnity will certainly extend to the net sum (ie premium less commission) paid to the insurer, and it should extend also to the commission. If it does not, the broker's right to commission will validate his claim for the balance over the net sum. The broker cannot, however, recover any sum paid voluntarily to the insurer, for which he was not liable (*DC Wilson v Avec Audio-Visual Equipment Ltd* [1974] 1 Lloyd's Rep 81).

Non-payment of commission
Although the insured is at liberty to terminate the contract of agency at any time, and that contract is not subject to any duty of good faith, it is arguable that he must compensate the broker for his time and skill if the principal prevents the broker from earning his commission. This may be on a *quantum meruit* basis, or in damages for breach of contract ie the commission that would have been earned. This may occur where the principal selects another broker to conclude the contract after the first broker had effectively arranged the contract by obtaining quotes on favourable terms ie the first broker has complied with his mandate and is really the direct and effective cause of the insurance contract. However, the broker must show that the principal was in default, and must prove wilful refusal or deceit (*Blake v Sohn* [1969] 3 All ER 133). In *Bareham v Christopher Moran & Co Ltd* (Unreported: May 1981) the reinsureds cancelled various reinsurance policies. The broker claimed damages for wrongful cancellation, since the cancellation would deprive him of his commission. Robert Goff J, as he then was, allowed the broker to deduct the commission due on the premiums after an application under Ord 14 RSC. On appeal Lord Denning MR clearly considered the broker's claim to be properly maintainable, but the matter was not decided. Most of the apposite case law involving the right of an agent to commission revolves around estate agents.

In *Alpha Trading Ltd* v *Dunnshaw-Patten Ltd* [1981] QB 290, 306 Templeman LJ in the Court of Appeal stated that a term could be implied into the contract to prevent the principal 'playing a dirty trick on the agent with impunity after making use of the services provided by that agent'.[10] And in *Luxor (Eastbourne) Limited* v *Cooper* [1941] AC 108, 128 Lord Russell in the House of Lords stated that 'In such contracts a term must, if not expressed, necessarily be implied that the principal will do nothing to prevent the agent from doing the work which the contract binds him to do'.

An insurance analogy would be for the principal to conclude the insurance contract direct with the insurer to preclude the broker taking his commission out of the premium, having availed himself of the broker's services up to the point immediately prior to the conclusion of a contract. However, this is unlikely to arise because insurers specify a gross premium (ie including commission), so there would be no benefit to the insured unless he could negotiate a reduced sum and persuade the insurer that he need not pay any sum direct to the broker.

Needless to say, this is exactly what happened in the case usually cited as authority for the proposition that the broker is entitled to obtain commission after use of his services and termination of his agency, *McNeil* v *Law Union & Rock Insurance Company Ltd* (1925) 23 Lloyd's Rep 314. The broker had placed the insured's insurance with the Law Union from 1912 until 1923. In 1924 the insured obtained quotations for lower rates of premium from other insurers and refused to insure with the Law Union unless it would accept a lower premium. The broker expended considerable effort to reconcile the parties' differences, but to no avail in monetary terms. The insured then suggested directly to the Law Union that the insured's company secretary be appointed or treated as agent for the renewal, with the commission nominally being paid to him but in fact being received by the insured. The Law Union agreed, concluded the renewal contract and accepted their quoted premium

---

10 Note, however, that the broker was not put on notice that the goods were uninsured prior to transit. McNair J said ' . . . I cannot appreciate why any insurance broker, unless he has that information conveyed to him in the clearest language, ought to assume that any merchant has been guilty of that omission [ie failure to insure]' at p 642. Confirmed in *George Moundreas & Co SA* v *Navimpex Centrala Navala* [1985] 2 Lloyd's Rep 515, 517. In Canada the broker may be able to sue the principal for his deceit, although not strictly for commission since commission technically would not have been earned: *Bradley-Wilson Ltd* v *Canyon Gardens Ltd* (1965) 52 DLR(2d) 717.

less commission. The broker sued them for his commission on the basis that he had been the 'efficient cause of the transaction', and succeeded before Branson J. Had the insurance been agreed on a 'completely fresh basis' or the broker's involvement limited to a mere 'introducer of the two parties' he would not have succeeded, but the judge fully accepted his role and that the allowance of the commission[11] to the insured's company secretary was 'a mere . . . pretence in order to enable the [insured] to get its insurance for a smaller sum than they would otherwise have done.'

This case may, however, be subject to criticism on account of the apparent moral censure against own case agency, disliked by the judge, the broker and the Brokers' Association, and the pretence used by the insured to obtain an effective lower rate of premium.

Legitimate conduct by the principal, such as instructing more than one broker to obtain insurance quotations, or agreeing insurance on better terms, will not entitle the disgruntled broker to payment. Whether the broker has any claim will depend on his contract with the principal. Where this contract contains the usual implied term that the broker will be paid commission out of his premium, he will have to arrange and effect a contract of insurance, and pay the premium himself (if authorised) or await it from his principal. The short, general answer is that the broker must bring about the conclusion of a contract of insurance to entitle him to commission. Further, he runs the risk of non-payment voluntarily; if he does not like it, he should specify an express contractual term to the contrary. Such a term will not be implied (*Luxor (Eastbourne) Ltd* v *Cooper* [1941] AC 108). Where more than one broker is competing for the same business, the payment of premium by one to the insurer indicates that the broker has been the cause of the business placed and is therefore entitled to commission.

There may be instances of two brokers paying premium to different insurers for the same risk, which may arise because the insured has (negligently) instructed both brokers to insure, in which case the insured is liable to both brokers for their premium (which includes their commission). However, if one broker has exceeded his actual authority (which may have been only to obtain a quotation

---

11 At p 316 the judge states premium but the meaning is clear. Except in cases containing estate agents eg in *Chesterfield & Co* v *Zahid Ansari The Times*, 13 February 1989 Garland J confirmed that the test for liability as to commission was whether the transaction had been effectively caused by the agent who had introduced the parties, or whether the original introduction could be regarded as spent.

for insurance), the insured is not liable to that broker for any premium paid, although he may be liable to the insurer (outside Lloyd's) if the broker effected a contract within his apparent authority. If the latter broker has made such a valid contract, the insured is liable to pay the premium to the insurer but can recover it from the broker. Conversely at Lloyd's or for marine insurance, where the broker is liable to the insurer for the premium, he cannot reclaim it from the insured.

Payment after termination of agency

A broker who can prove that he is the effective cause of the contract of insurance will usually be entitled to commission, as discussed above in *McNeil* v *Law Union*. This will usually be apparent by the tender of premium from the broker, who will have received it from the insured. However, a broker's authority may be terminated after a contract has been negotiated or agreed but before premium has been paid or after the initial premium has been paid but before any renewal premium has been paid. In *Gold* v *Life Assurance Company of Pennsylvania* [1971] 2 Lloyd's Rep 164), the broker claimed commission in respect of policies sold by him during his contract of agency, even though the premiums were paid or only became payable after the termination of the parties' agreement. Donaldson J, as he then was, quoted with approval *Halsbury's Laws of England* (3rd Edn) at p 167:

No remuneration is, as a rule, payable upon transactions between the principal and third persons introduced to him by the agent arising after the termination of the employment, whether such transactions are due to the agent's introduction or not. But remuneration may be payable in respect of such further transactions if they are in fact part of a transaction in which the agent was employed, or if there was an express term in the contract to that effect, or a clear intention to continue such remuneration after determination of the agent's employment can be discovered from the construction of the contract of agency; and in the latter cases it will be payable even though the agent was dismissed, and may be so though he was not the effective cause of the transaction.

He went on to say at p 170 that:

There is a very clear distinction between the first premiums and subsequent premiums if one looks at not only the realities of the situation, but also the contractual document. All the work is done in getting the insurance in the first place. That is why 40 per cent commission is payable on the first year's premium. Exactly the same position applies in English contracts. The rate of commission is about the same. Afterwards, once you have got the assured hooked, if I might use that expression, the problems are very much smaller and the thing runs itself. Hence, only a 2 per cent commission.

But all the work for which the 40 per cent commission is payable has been done and prima facie the agent is in those circumstances entitled to his commission for that work, even if it happens to be postponed in payment until after the end of the notice.

For those reasons, I am quite satisfied that [the broker] is entitled to the commissions which he claims, however much they may be.

Donaldson J made it clear that such a right would depend on the wording of the contract. However, in the absence of a clear delineation of the broker's continuing rights to commission after termination, a term may be implied into the contract of agency for commission to continue in respect of business completed between the insurer and insured. This seems eminently sensible. The position is not so clear on 'repeat' orders, where substantially the same contract enures for the benefit of the insured.

What happens if the contract of agency is terminated before any renewal premium becomes payable? Donaldson J addressed this possibility in *Gold* v *Life Assurance* (above, p 166), saying:

The [broker] does not, as perhaps he might have done, claim commission on renewal policies. When I say he might have claimed that, I do not think he would have been successful, but he might have advanced the claim.

Donaldson J clearly distinguished between original and renewal premiums and no further judicial comment has been elicited.

The curious aspect of *Gold* v *Life Assurance Company of Pennsylvania* is that *McNeil* v *Law Union* does not appear to have been cited or considered. *McNeil* v *Law Union* is authority for the proposition that commission will be payable to a broker whose efforts were the effective cause of the transaction, whether it is the initial transaction or a repeat. It does not state the number of repeats to which the principle applies; it logically should extend to all renewals on substantially the same terms as those negotiated by the broker, although it is arguable that he must contribute at each renewal to be considered as the effective cause of the contract. The practical solution appears to be that the insured should terminate the broker's agency and preclude him from the negotiations for renewal, and perhaps alter or introduce some terms that will enable a defence of a new contract to be put forward to any claim brought by the broker. Mr Justice Donaldson's comment, if upheld, will defeat the broker's claim to renewal commission, but it was obiter and he did not apparently consider *McNeil* v *Law Union*; the issue therefore remains live.

McNeil v *Law Union* may in many instances be capable of being distinguished on the basis that the incumbent broker contributed substantially to the placing of the contract, despite the fact that it was placed specifically on the basis of an own case agency, which was something that the incumbent broker was most unlikely to consider or agree. In most cases of renewal the incoming broker will handle the negotiations, ensconce himself as the effective cause, and rightly pocket the commission.

Some difficulties may arise following the transfer of agency by the insured from one broker to another, prior to the expiry of the policy, despite the dictat contained in para (12) of the IBRC Code of Conduct to the effect that 'Insurance brokers shall have proper regard for the wishes of a policyholder or client who seeks to terminate any agreement with them to carry out business.' 'Proper regard' presumably entitles the broker to rely upon and to enforce what he perceives to be his legal rights. Where the premium is adjustable at the end of the period of insurance, any adjustment made within the initial broker's account must be paid by him, and he will retain commission from any premium due or return commission on any return of premium to the insured (or to the insurer if the insurer settles direct with the insured). Any premium for alterations to the policy during the initial broker's contract will also be payable through the initial broker, and again he will retain commission. Alterations after the termination of the initial broker's contract will be payable through the second broker, and this will include any cancellation of the insurance. It has been suggested that any cancellation effected by the second broker will necessitate a refund of commission by that broker, even though he had never received it.[12]

The logical antidote would be for the second broker to obtain a specific indemnity from the insured to cover such an eventuality, or to ensure that the cancellation is effected by the initial broker during his tenure.

Where the original broker has been replaced with another who considers that he should receive the commission on future premiums, the new broker should have the contract formally terminated, and replaced with a new contract to avoid any dispute.

Long Term Agreements
Mention should be made at this point of Long Term Agreements (LTAs), which are arrangements by which an insurer offers a discount to the insured in return for his business over a specified period. The usual agreement is 5 per cent pa for three years in

---

12 See RL Peters: *UK Handbook of Retail Insurance Broking*.

property, liability and consequential loss insurance; LTAs are not available for motor insurance. The rationale behind an LTA is that the insured agrees to renew at each renewal date on the same terms, the consideration being the discounted premium, but the insurer is not bound to accept the offer. The insurer may alter the premium or terms of the insurance, in which case the insured is not required to renew. Breach of the agreement will probably result in a payment of damages equal to the discount allowed.

If the LTA runs smoothly the insurer receives a constant flow of business to his satisfaction, since he would not otherwise have written it in the first place, the insured receives a discount for no effort at all, and the broker receives the initial and renewal premiums, the latter again for a minimum of effort. The broker will not be pleased when his sinecure is displaced by the appointment of another broker. The principles set out in *McNeil* v *Law Union* (1925) Ll L Rep Vol 23 314 and *Gold* v *Life Assurance Company of Pennsylvania* (1971) 2 Lloyd's Rep 164 will apply. Thus the effective cause of the insurance will be entitled to commission, and not the incumbent broker by virtue of his original introduction.

However, trade organisations such as BIIBA have laid down certain principles to guide their members. These will not establish any rights between the brokers inter se, but may involve one broker in disciplinary action. Of course the contract of agency may obviate any consideration of the above by expressly specifying the consequences of termination.

Actions of the broker in excess of his actual authority

The broker is theoretically not entitled to remuneration for any contract made which exceeds his authority or which is in breach of his duties to his principal, or which is unlawful. If, therefore, a broker is asked to obtain employers' liability cover in respect of a business and he actually obtains contents insurance for goods stored at his principal's premises, even though the principal may be seeking such insurance elsewhere, he will neither be entitled to remuneration, nor indemnity for any premium paid (*Barron* v *Fitzgerald* (1840) 6 Bing NC 201, where the broker wrongly added an insured). The problem is that if the insurance is within the broker's apparent authority, the insured will be bound. If it is not, but the contract is ratified by the insured, it will be equally binding. As the broker's commission is contained in the premium, and is paid by the insurer, it will be difficult for the insured to prevent payment to the broker. The aspect of the broker exceeding his actual authority but remaining within his apparent authority was discussed in *Great Atlantic*

Insurance Co v *Home Insurance Co* [1981] 2 Lloyd's Rep 219 by Lloyd J, who considered that the broker would not be liable to the insured.

Similarly, a broker who places a 'tonner' policy at Lloyd's in breach of s 4 of the Marine Insurance Act 1906 will not be entitled to claim commission or indemnity.[13]

It is usually the case that any incapacity of an agent to act will prevent a successful claim for remuneration eg an unqualified person acting and holding himself out as a solicitor cannot recover anything for work done. An intermediary who styles himself an 'insurance broker' and thereby contravenes the Insurance Brokers (Registration) Act 1977 is, however, entitled to recover but subject to a fine of £2,000 under s 22 after conviction on indictment.

Indemnity from principal

The principal is liable to the broker in respect of all sums validly expended by the broker in the proper discharge of his duties, and in respect of any liabilities which the broker might incur on behalf of the principal within his apparent authority.[14] This right extends to authorised but gratuitous payments by the broker, but does not extend to acts outside his actual authority; or payments which could not be enforced but which the broker is pressurised to make (but not to premium which was paid by a non-marine broker outside Lloyd's, since it has not been established that the broker is liable to the insurer for premium (*DC Wilson* v *Avec Audio-Visual Equipment Ltd* [1974] 1 Lloyd's Rep 81); or for the broker's acts which are negligent, unlawful or in breach of duty, unless the broker can prove an alternative restitutionary right. The right to indemnity usually runs concurrently with the right to remuneration, and can continue to run after any authority has been determined in respect

---

13 A 'tonner' is an insurance policy in which the 'insured' has no insurable interest and is void by s 4 Marine Insurance Act 1906. It is so called after the practice of guessing the amount of marine tonnage to sink in any one period, and to place an insurance 'bet' on that basis, without having any insurable interest in the losses.

14 This is an implied term in the contract of agency; in a purely consensual arrangement the broker's claim is restitutionary (in quasi-contract) and may be limited to payments made by the broker under compulsion, the benefit of which is retained by the principal, if an independent contract to indemnify cannot be implied: see *Sheffield Corporation* v *Barclay* [1905] AC 392; *Yeung Kai Yung* v *Hong Kong & Shanghai Banking Corporation* [1981] AC 787.

of any matter capable of indemnification which arose before the contract was terminated.

However, many expenses incurred by the broker will not be reimbursed because they are considered to be included in his remuneration. If the broker can prove that it is the custom of the market in which he operates to reimburse all or specific expenses, and the custom was reasonable and not unlawful,[15] he would be entitled to claim. However, the parties should specify at the outset which expenses will be payable by the principal.

The right to an indemnity against liabilities incurred by him properly within the course of his agency and within his authority (or later ratified) is obviously important, since it provides the broker with a method of obtaining payment for any claims made against him, and for the recovery of sums expended by him in discharge of his liabilities, such as payment of premium to a Lloyd's syndicate by a Lloyd's broker, or payment of premium by a producing (ie non-Lloyd's) broker to a Lloyd's broker. The key is the agent's authority; if the agent could validly incur the expense, he is entitled to reimbursement. Thus payments in respect of transactions known by him to be unlawful, or void for being a wager, cannot be recovered.

Lien

Section 53(2) of the Marine Insurance Act 1906 states:

Unless otherwise agreed, the broker has, as agent of the assured, a lien upon the policy for the amount of the premium and his charges in respect of effecting the policy; and, where he has dealt with the person who employs him as principal, he also has a lien on the policy in respect of any balance on any insurance account which may be due to him from such person, unless when the debt was incurred he had reason to believe that such person was only an agent.

Marine insurance brokers have been held by the courts to have a general lien on all policy documents in their possession in respect of a general balance of account owed to them by their insureds (but

---

15 *Stolos Cia SA* v *Ajax Insurance Co* [1981] 1 Lloyd's Rep 9. A general knowledge of usages at Lloyd's may be presumed from any previous dealings at Lloyd's: *Bartlett* v *Pentland* (1830) 10 B & C 870, but an unreasonable usage of which the insured is unaware will not bind him, such as payment in account between the underwriter and broker. It must be 'known and notorious' to the parties: *Matveieff* v *Crossfield* (1903) 51 WR 365.

not in respect of contingent liabilities (*Hope* v *Glendinning* [1911] AC 419, 433), provided they have made no agreement inconsistent with the lien, or the policies were delivered to them for any purpose inconsistent with the lien (*Fisher* v *Smith* (1878) 4 App Cas 1). This will probably apply to non-marine brokers on the basis of custom and trade usage, and the words 'on any insurance account' in s 53(2) of the Marine Insurance Act 1906. This lien entitles the broker to retain any policy document until all liabilities in respect of the contract of insurance agency have been extinguished, but the broker cannot retain any policies for monies due for other services unconnected with the insurance (*Dixon* v *Stansfield* (1850) 10 CB 398) although he can exercise a lien on any policy in respect of any balance on any insurance account due to him from the principal (*Near East Relief* v *King, Chasseur & Co Ltd* [1930] 2 KB 40). The lien is lost if the insured pays the broker what he is owed, if the broker waives his right to the lien, if he validly parts with the possession of the policy document (subject to its revival if it returns to the broker's possession), or if he does any other act inconsistent with the continuing existence of the lien. The principle is restricted to policies in the broker's possession which belong to the insured, and apparently may not extend to money, so that a broker holding money may not be in a better position, subject to any claims in set-off or by counterclaim.[16]

Where privity of contract exists between a sub-broker and the insured, the sub-broker is an authorised agent of the insured and is therefore entitled to all remedies of such an agent, including a lien. Where such privity does not exist and the delegation was invalid, the sub-broker has no such right. Where the delegation was valid (in that it was within the broker's authority to delegate), the sub-broker will have a lien over policy documents in respect of any claim arising out of the duties delegated (*Fisher* v *Smith* (1988) 4 App Cas 1).

---

16 See note page 182 as to set off, and also *Fairfield Shipping & Engineering Co Ltd* v *Gardner, Mountain & Co* (1911) 104 LT 288 at p 289 where Scrutton J stated that 'I must not be taken as deciding that a lien on documents gives a lien on proceeds collected under them.' In contrast Lord Ellenborough commented in *Mann* v *Forrester* (1814) 14 Camp 60 that the brokers 'had a right to satisfy their general balance from the money received under the policy' which they held under a lien.

Chapter 3

Relationship between principal and third parties

ACTUAL AUTHORITY OF BROKER

A broker may be invested with actual authority to act on behalf of the principal when the principal orally or in writing expressly confers specific powers upon the broker to enable him to execute a particular task. The principal and the insurer are bound by any acts done by the broker which fall within such authority. The express authorisation of the broker to obtain a specific insurance will carry with it the implied authority of the principal for the broker to carry out any necessary or incidental acts to obtain such insurance, such as revealing all relevant information to the insurer.

OSTENSIBLE AUTHORITY OF BROKER

Usual authority

The appointment of a party by the insured as his 'insurance broker' entitles the broker to exercise any authority which an insurance broker would usually have in order to perform his duties. The insurer will be entitled to assume that the principal has invested the broker with any authority necessary to effect a contract of the type given to similar brokers, and usually found in that market, according to its reasonable customs.

Ascertaining such authority requires discussion of current practices with insurance brokers operating in the market, and considering the case law over the last two centuries. There is little case law relating to brokers in their capacity as agents for the insured, since there has been little dispute as to the nature of their authority. This is not true, however, of a broker when acting as an agent of the insurer, who:

(a) can grant temporary insurance if in possession of cover notes (*Stockton* v *Mason* [1978] 2 Lloyd's Rep 430) except where it is clear that his authority is limited (*Acey* v *Fernie* (1840) 7 M & W 151);

(b) cannot bind insurers to issue a policy in substitution of any temporary cover validly given (*Stockton* v *Mason* above);

(c) cannot contract on terms substantially different to those usually used by the insurance company (*Davies* v *National Fire & Marine Ins Co of New Zealand* [1891] AC 485)[1] especially if his authority is obviously limited by his position (*Wilkinson* v *General Accident* [1967] 2 Lloyd's Rep 182); (*Comerford* v *Britannic Insurance Co* (1908) 24 TLR 593);

(d) cannot give credit when employed to receive premiums (*Western Assurance Co* v *Provincial Insurance Co* (1880) 50 AR 190);

(e) cannot waive compliance with a condition where the policy makes it clear that such dispensation can only be authorised by the head office (*Brooks* v *Trafalgar Ins Co* (1946) 79 Ll L Rep 365);

(f) can waive a breach of condition if authorised to receive premiums and negotiate the terms of cover, provided a new contract is not formed and the insured is not on notice of any lack of authority (*Wing* v *Harvey* (1854) 5 De GM&G 265 (43 ER); (*Acey* v *Fernie* (1840) 7 M & W 151); (*Ayrey* v *British Legal* [1918] 1 KB 136);

(g) can receive notice of termination or loss (*Marsden* v *City & County Assurance Co* (1866) LR 1 CP 232; *Re Solvency Mutual Guarantee Co* (1862) 6 LT 574);

(h) cannot terminate the contract of insurance on behalf of the insured, since he does not act for him (*Hofmann* v *Economic Insurance Co* (1956) 4 SA 380(W). An independent broker acting for the insured will, however, probably have the authority to cancel.

Apparent authority

A broker may also be clothed with 'apparent' authority, which is his authority as perceived by others after his principal has

---

1 Unless the insurer has previously acquiesced in the granting of cover orally by the agent: *Murfitt* v *Royal Insurance Co* [1922] (10 Ll L Rep 191), or in any situation in which the agent's apparent authority has been extended by the insurer's conduct: *Brocklebank* v *Sugrue* (1831) 5 C&P 21.

represented in some way that the broker has authority to act for him. Apparent authority essentially arises by operation of law and complies with Ashhurst J's general proposition in *Lickbarrow* v *Mason* (1887) 2 Term Rep 63 at p 70 that 'wherever one of two innocent persons must suffer by the acts of a third, he who has enabled such third person to occasion the loss must sustain it'. Apparent authority will often coincide exactly with actual authority, but it may on occasion exceed it. It arises from words or conduct amounting to a clear and unequivocal representation (*Spiro* v *Lintern* [1973] 3 All ER 319)[2] to the third party, emanating from the principal (and not the agent), which may be express, or implied from previous dealings.

As long as the act done by the broker falls within his apparent authority, it does not matter whether or not the principal benefits, or that the broker acted purely in his own interests (*Hambro* v *Burnand* [1904] 2 KB 10), because an abuse of authority or trust by the agent is irrelevant.[3] However, the representation by the principal must have been made or communicated to the party with whom the broker contracted, or to those members of the insurance market likely to deal with the broker, and relied upon by that party (*Farquharson Brothers & Co* v *C King & Co* [1902] AC 325 at 343). The representation must be the proximate cause of the belief of the other contracting party that the broker was authorised to act as he did. Clearly if the contracting party was or should have been aware that the agent's authority was less than he thought or was represented, that notice of lack of authority will destroy the illusion of apparent authority. The representation must be such as to justify the inference that the insurer knew of and relied upon it in entering into the contractual relationship (*Farquharson Brothers & Co* v *King* [1902] AC 325). Further, the representation must have been made intentionally or recklessly, and even a representation made negligently may give rise to liability (*Hedley Byrne* v *Heller & Partners* [1964] AC 465).

---

2 Conduct of the principal which can be interpreted to indicate that the agent has no or limited authority will preclude a construction of apparent authority. The agent must act in a way in which an agent in his position would usually act, unless he is held out as having some additional authority: *Farquharson Bros* v *King & Co* [1902] AC 325.

3 The statement that acts done by the broker for his own benefit are irrelevant will be qualified by any knowledge of this practice acquired by the other contracting party which will defeat any argument based upon apparent authority, since that other party would have constructive notice of the agent's general untrustworthiness. See *Midland Bank* v *Reckitt* [1933] AC 1 Lord Atkin at 17 and 18.

A broker cannot confer authority or additional authority upon himself (*Overbrook Estates Ltd* v *Glencombe Properties Ltd* [1974] 3 All ER 511, 516.)[4]

TERMINATION OF BROKER'S AUTHORITY

[handwritten margin note: Duty to keep does continuous → Lorkin Godwin ✓ Johnston 1995 L RLR]

A broker's authority can be terminated at any moment by the principal, since the agency agreement cannot be enforced by either party. The principal-broker relationship is analogous to the position of employees employed under contracts of service, as to which public policy has dictated through the courts that such contracts cannot be enforced (*Frith* v *Frith* [1906] AC 254). In addition the fiduciary nature of the agency relationship cannot be enforced by specific performance or injunctive relief (*Denmark Productions Ltd* v *Boscobel Productions Ltd* [1969] 1 QB 699). The actual authority granted by the principal can be determined by agreement (orally, in writing or by conduct), by the inception of the contract of insurance, by the destruction of the subject matter of the proposed insurance contract prior to completion of the contract (which would negate a constituent of the contract, that of an insurable interest), by any event rendering the agency or proposed contract of insurance unlawful or frustrated (such as an outbreak of war turning either party into an enemy alien), by the death, insanity or bankruptcy of either party, or upon receipt of unilateral notice from the other party (by words or conduct) of an intention to determine the contract of agency.

The death (*Yonge* v *Toynbee* [1910] 1 KB 215, subject to ratification by the executors), insanity (*Drew* v *Nunn* (1879) 4 QBD 661) or bankruptcy (*Drew* v *Nunn* (1879) 4 QBD 661) of an individual principal, or the dissolution of a partnership, or the winding up of a company (*Babury Ltd* v *London Industrial plc* (1989) *The Independent*, 31 October), will deprive the agent by operation of law of a principal of any legal capacity for whom the agent can act. However, although a new partnership is formed upon death or retirement of a partner, or upon the inclusion of new partners, it may be that the contract

---

4 See also *Armagas Ltd* v *Mundogas SA* [1986] AC 717; *Polish Steamship Co* v *AJ Williams (Overseas Sales) Ltd* The 'Suwalki' [1989] 1 Lloyd's Rep 511, 514. However, such defective authority may be ratified or may, in exceptional circumstances, give rise to an estoppel against his principal eg *Pacol Ltd* v *Trade Lines Ltd* The 'Henrik Sif' [1982] 1 Lloyd's Rep 456; *Polish Steamship Co* v *AJ Williams Fuels (Overseas) Sales Ltd* The 'Suwalki' [1989] 1 Lloyd's Rep 511.

of agency is not personal to some of the partners but applies to all as a firm, in which case the authority of the agent would remain in force. Similar fates befalling the agent which vitiate his capacity to act will have the same effect on the contract. Bankruptcy of the broker, however, does not necessarily terminate his actual authority, which must be considered in the light of the agency agreement, although the Disciplinary Committee of the Insurance Brokers Registration Council may consider bankruptcy to constitute unprofessional conduct or to render the agent an unfit person to style himself 'broker', and erase his name from the register under s 15 of Insurance Brokers (Registration) Act 1977.

However, the apparent authority of the broker may continue after revocation of his actual authority (*Willis Faber & Co Ltd* v *Joyce* (1911) 104 LT 576), and academic considerations of authority have a practical application when the broker has purported to contract on behalf of his principal after the broker's actual authority has been determined. The death of a principal will terminate actual and apparent authority (*Blades* v *Free* (1829) 9 B & C 167). An insurance contract with a dead insured, if the contract has been completed when the principal was dead, is worthless to the insurer, who cannot sue for premium. Nor can the broker be liable on the basis that the lack of principal means that he contracted personally, although he may be liable for breach of warranty of authority, or under s 130 of the Companies Act 1989 in respect of an unformed corporate principal. The principal's insanity may in some circumstances be capable of maintaining the broker's apparent authority, if the principal remains capable of consenting to the continuation of the agency.[5]

Any contract of insurance entered into with an insurer after the termination of the broker's actual authority will be valid if the insurer does not have notice of the termination by the principal (*Willis Faber & Co* v *Joyce* (1911) 104 LT 576). The contract of agency is terminable at any stage unless there is an express contractual term which sets out the circumstances entitling the principal to determine the contract (*Martin-Baker Aircraft Co Ltd* v *Canadian Flight*

---

5 *Drew* v *Nunn* (1879) 4 QBD 661: the decision is one of public policy on particular facts. *Yonge* v *Toynbee* [1910] 1 KB 215 resulted in liability for the solicitors who warranted that they had the authority of their principal to defend an action brought against him. Before the action was commenced the principal became of unsound mind. Treitel at p 563 note 81, 6th Edn reconciles these two cases on the basis that the contract in *Drew* v *Nunn* could have been made, whilst in *Yonge* v *Toynbee* the insane principal had no capacity to contract at all.

Equipment Ltd [1955] 2 QB 556, 577), *Luxor (Eastbourne) Limited* v *Cooper* [1941] AC 108, 124–5), although even in the absence of these circumstances the personal and fiduciary nature of the contract will make such a provision unenforceable by the broker except in damages.

In some cases the broker's duties may extend beyond the termination of the contractual agency, in connection with contracts of insurance which he has previously placed. Such a consensual obligation occurred in *Cherry Ltd* v *Allied Insurance Brokers Ltd* [1978] 1 Lloyd's Rep 274, in which the insured became dissatisfied with the broker and requested him to cancel all insurances, to which the broker agreed. The broker wrote to the insurers to request cancellation and return of premium, and the insured arranged alternative insurance. However, two insurers refused to cancel the policies covering consequential loss, and the broker informed the insured accordingly. The insured therefore believed that he had double insurance for consequential loss, and cancelled the new policy. One of the apparently recalcitrant insurers then recanted and cancelled the policy. Unfortunately the broker failed to inform the 'insured' who suffered a disastrous fire eight days later. The court found that the broker had led the insured to believe that the consequential loss policy was and would remain in force, and that it would be sensible for the insured to cancel the new policy. The broker knew that his advice would be relied and acted upon, and should have informed the insured of any change immediately. The broker was held liable for the full amount of the original policy.

RATIFICATION

If an agent has no authority to bind his principal to a contract, but purports to do so, the principal can later ratify his agent's acts so as to validate the contract as if it had originally been authorised. Ratification can therefore give effect to the agreement intended to be made by the agent and third party (*Keighley, Maxsted & Co* v *Durant* [1901] AC 240, 263), and is 'equivalent to an antecedent authority' (*Koenigsblatt* v *Sweet* [1923] 2 Ch 314, 325). It operates ex post facto usually to smooth over technical or minor defects in the agent's authority.

The elements of ratification

Ratification can be expressly effected by the proposed principal confirming orally or in writing that he is treating the contract as valid, and he becomes the principal not when he so confirms, but at the date of the contract. Ratification can be implied where the proposed principal conducts himself in such a way that he is unequivocally adopting the contract (such as by paying or receiving premium, or by suing on the policy, or defending a claim on it (*Vershures Creameres Ltd* v *Hull & Netherlands SS Co Ltd* [1921] 2 KB 608) or retaining monies paid (*Hunter* v *Parker* (1840) 7 M&W 322), or manifesting in some way his assent, which could include silence or inactivity if this can be interpreted as the principal subjectively denoting his assent to the contract.[6] Indeed, the principal may be estopped from denying that he is bound if the other party is aware that the principal appreciates the position but takes no action to deny it (*Pacol Ltd* v *Trade Lines Ltd; The 'Henrik Sif'* [1982] 1 Lloyd's Rep 456; *Polish Steamship Co* v *AJ Williams (Overseas Sales) Ltd; The 'Suwalki'* [1989] 1 Lloyd's Rep 511). Ratification of part of the alleged contract will bind the parties to the entire contract, since to attempt to be bound or bind in part does not effect the contract originally anticipated and apparently agreed by the parties, unless the contracts are severable. In *Republic of Peru* v *Peruvian Guano Co* (1887) 36 Ch D 489 Chitty J said 'It is an attempt to affirm in part and disaffirm in part. A principal must act consistently; he cannot, as was stated by Lord Kenyon, blow hot and cold; or to approbate and reprobate at the same time: he must adopt entirely or repudiate entirely . . . the plaintiff could not avow the act as to part and disavow it as to the rest'.

Requirements

The agent must have purported to act for the principal

This rule precludes a party not associated either with the principal or agent later intervening to adopt the transaction. An undisclosed principal cannot ratify; the agent must contract for an identified or identifiable principal, and that person must later ratify (*Watson* v *Swann* (1862) 11 CB (NS) 756). The agent may intend to offer the contract to another intended principal, even though unnamed, but the only party able to ratify is the person believed by the insurer

---

6 *Bank Melli Iran* v *Barclays Bank* [1951] 2 TLR 1057 at 1064, 1065. A delay in repudiating the agent's act could ratify the agreement. '[The principal] is bound, if he dissents, to notify his determination within a reasonable time, provided he has an opportunity of doing so': *Prince* v *Clark* (1823) 1 B&C 186, 190. See also *Rust* v *Abbey Life Assurance Co Ltd* [1979] 2 Lloyd's Rep 334. *Spiro* v *Lintern* [1973] 3 All ER 319; *Waithman* v *Wakefield* (1807) 1 Camp 120; *French* v *Backhouse* (1771) 5 Burr 2727.

to be the agent's principal at the time of the purported contract. The exception to this rule occurs in cases of insurances of transit, where the specific identity of later principals is unknown at the time of the contract but such principals are properly contemplated at the date of the contract (*Tomlinson (A) (Hauliers) v Hepburn* [1966] AC 451; even though the agent intended to contract on his own account *Re Tiedemann & Ledemann Freres* [1899] 2 QB 66).

The agent must have had a competent principal when the act was done
Clearly the ratifying principal must have been in existence at the time the act was done by the agent (*Kelner v Baxter* (1866) LR 2 CP 174), either as a living person with full capacity to contract or as a juristic body such as a limited company. Any problems under this head usually arise out of a failure to incorporate or inability to trade or contract as intended. A contract made by a company not fully or properly incorporated cannot be ratified after incorporation. A new policy must be issued eg because the transaction is ultra vires. An act ultra vires the authority of a company cannot be ratified. There have also been instances of unratifiable contracts purportedly made on behalf of infants, or persons who become enemy aliens through circumstances over which they have no control (*Sovfracht v Van Udens Scheepvart* [1943] AC 203).

The principal must be legally competent to do the act himself at the time of ratification
Clearly the proposed principal must be legally competent to adopt the act done by the agent at the time of ratification, even though such ratification takes effect at the time the act was done.

The act must not be illegal
An act void in law cannot be ratified. Thus a company cannot ratify a contract made ultra vires (*Rolled Steel Products (Holdings) Ltd v BSC* [1982] 3 All ER 1057), and a forgery cannot be ratified (*Brook v Hook* (1871) LR 6 Ex 89). An unlawful act such as a tort can be ratified, for which the principal could be liable. ' . . . ratification, being the subsequent recognition of an unauthorised agent's authority to make the ratified contract at the time and place at which it had been made, put the ratifier in the same position as if the agent had had actual authority to make the contract . . . and the [principals], having authorised agents to make contracts in contravention of [an absolute statutory prohibition] were themselves guilty of offences under the Acts . . . ' (*Bedford Insurance Co v Instituto de Resseguros do Brazil* [1985] QB 966). 'It can be no defence to say that the act was committed by an agent in excess of his authority' (ibid, p 981).

A contract expressly prohibited by statute is therefore void *ab initio* (as well as being illegal), and cannot be ratified so as to enable the principal to recover, because he would have to rely on an illegal act to do so: ' . . . life cannot be given by ratification to prohibited transactions . . . ' (*Bedford Insurance Co* v *Instituto de Resseguros do Brazil*, at p 986). Voidable acts can be ratified, if the principal can be identified, and even though they would be void if unratified.

There may be a time limit

In addition, ratification may be subject to a requirement of execution within a certain time, or within a reasonable time (*Republic of Peru* v *Peruvian Guano Co* (1887) 36 ChD 489, 500), which may differ according to the circumstances (*Re Portuguese Consolidated Copper Mines Ltd* (1890) 45 ChD 16, 34). Ratification will not be allowed if it would unfairly prejudice any intervening right of the other contracting party. The principal can ratify, however, even after he has refused to do so, if that refusal has not been communicated to the third party (*Simpson* v *Egginton* (1855) 10 Exch 845) or if that third party has not relied on it in such a way as to estop the principal from relying on it. The principal can even ratify in the face of an attempted withdrawal from it by the third party (because the ratification is retroactive and dates back to the time of the agent's acceptance of the offer) (*Bolton Partners* v *Lambert* (1889) 41 ChD 295). However, notification to the principal of an intention to withdraw by the third party will force the principal to ratify the contract within a reasonable time or accept that it is not binding. Silence by the principal may amount to a withdrawal from the purported contract after a reasonable time (*Re Portuguese Consolidated Copper Mines Ltd* (1890) 45 ChD 16). The courts have also drawn a distinction between negotiating 'subject to approval' and contracting 'subject to ratification'; the former could bind the principal if the contract were later approved, but the latter could only bind if all the elements of ratification were satisfied (*Warehousing & Forwarding Co of East Africa Ltd* v *Jafferali & Sons Ltd* [1964] AC 1). Any intimation of any limitation of authority will suffice. Withdrawal of an offer which is accepted subject to ratification before ratification is proper and equivalent to the withdrawal of an offer before acceptance (*Watson* v *Davies* [1931] 1 Ch 455).

Non-marine insurance

Ratification by the proposed insured under an insurance contract after loss of or damage to the subject matter of the insurance clearly prejudices the insurer if it is valid. In non-marine insurance ratification cannot generally be effected after receipt of information of a loss (*Grover & Grover Ltd* v *Mathews* [1910] 2 KB 401),[7] except by those parties who are only identified generically and who are intended to be able to ratify, eg insurance effected on behalf of interested parties such as bailees (*Waters & Steel* v *Monarch Fire & Life Assurance Co* (1856) 5 E & B 870), (*Woolcott* v *Sun Alliance* [1978] 2 All ER 1253) or carriers (*London & North Western Railway Co* v *Glyn* (1859) 1 E & E 652) or hauliers (*Tomlinson (A) (Hauliers)* v *Hepburn* [1966] AC 451) or mortgagees (*Ebsworth* v *Alliance Marine Insurance Co* (1873) LR 8 CP 596), then the insurance may be ratified after loss by those parties. It is irrelevant that the party effecting the insurance owed them no duty to insure and/or was himself primarily responsible for the safety of the insured item, although he must have intended to insure their interests at the time of the contract (*Waters & Steel* v *Monarch Fire & Life Assurance Co* (1856) 5 E & B 870), and disclosed such intention to the insurer (*Tomlinson (A) (Hauliers) Ltd* v *Hepburn* [1966] AC 451), in accordance with the principle stated above.

Marine insurance

In marine insurance such ratification can be made by virtue of case law and s 86 of the Marine Insurance Act 1906, since the loss was as likely to occur before ratification as after, and the parties in this market accept as a custom that such ratification can be made (*Williams* v *North China Insurance Co* (1876) 1 CPD 757).[8] The anomaly is

---

7 This case may be subject to criticism on the basis that *Waters & Steel* v *Monarch Fire & Life Assurance Co* (1856) 5 E & B 870 was not cited; the case which most influenced the court was *Williams* v *North China Insurance Co* (1876) 1 CPD 757 which turned on another point, and one judge indicated that the marine rule should apply equally to all insurance. This rule has not been followed in Canada: *Goldschlager* v *Royal Insurance Co Ltd* (1978) 84 DLR (3d) 355.

8 *Hagedorn* v *Oliverson* (1814) 2 M & S 485; this custom derives from the marine market and in particular from the practice of underwriters prepared to reinsure any vessel reported overdue at Lloyd's, so that the direct insurers could lay off some of their risk for the ultimate total loss. This practice is, however, declining. The Lutine Bell is usually rung when there is news of an overdue vessel, but it has not been rung on the overdue market since 10 November 1981. However, in December 1988 the last known active overdue broker retired. This may perhaps be considered as merely a sign of the times; rarely do vessels vanish. Nevertheless, a 169,000 tonnes deadweight ore carrier named the *Derbyshire* vanished in 1980 without trace, the *Kronoss* vanished in February 1989, the *Mega Taurus* (30,413 tonnes with 30,000 tonnes of nickel ore) was the subject of a resolution of the Committee of Lloyd's in March 1989 after she had disappeared, and the *Marine* (1,397 tonnes) disappeared in the Bay of Biscay in late 1989.

that ratification is allowed even though the contract could not be made if the insurer was aware of the loss at the time of the contract.

Ratification must, according to Fry LJ in *Metropolitan Asylums Board Managers* v *Kingham & Sons* (1890) 6 TLR 217, be made within a reasonable time after the contract is made, which can never extend beyond the time at which the contract is to commence (or, presumably, beyond any specified time limit). However, Parker J in *Bedford Insurance Co* v *Instituto de Resseguros do Brazil* [1985] 1 Lloyd's Rep 210 stated that 'no authority was cited in support of this very wide statement and I know of no principle to sustain it'. In *Bedford* v *Instituto de Resseguros do Brazil* ratification was attempted after the contracts had taken effect and claims had been made. However, although the case involved marine insurance, Parker J's comments may be taken to indicate that the rule that contracts of marine insurance can be ratified after a loss applies equally to marine and non-marine, and that the requirement of reasonable time does not exist in either market. He does not refer to s 86 of the Marine Insurance Act 1906 to support his contradiction of Fry LJ's dictum, which one would expect if he were dealing exclusively with marine insurance. Nevertheless, it seems inequitable that a party's position can remain in limbo pending the decision to ratify and it seems logical that a reasonable time limit should be imposed by operation of law. This limit may be extended where the insurer has to ratify his agent's acts to validate the contract, and such ratification would not prejudice but instead benefit the insured.

Ratification intended when contract made

Ratification is actually a necessary constituent of those policies of insurance which designate the persons intended to benefit in general terms only, such as members of the insured's family and house guests in respect of a burglary or liability policy, or persons driving his car who cause or sustain injuries covered by his motor vehicle insurance. In these instances the insured who initiated the policy himself suffers no loss which requires an indemnity under the policy, and the policy is only enforceable to discharge any liability incurred by the person sustaining the loss or incurring the liability. Such persons are effectively insured as 'those whom the policy may concern', and the contract must be ratified by them after loss.

Effect of ratification

Once ratification has occurred, the contract becomes binding retroactively as from the date of its creation, and the rights and liabilities inter se of the insurer, broker and principal must be discharged in the normal way. The ratification is effectively an election to be bound by the contract, but the principal may not be held to have ratified if he is unaware at the time of ratification of all material facts so that he is unable to form an independent judgement (*Savery* v *King* (1856) 5 HL Cas 627), unless he fails to enquire properly as to the facts and assumes responsibility recklessly. 'The circumstances of the alleged ratification must be such as to warrant the clear inference that the principal was adopting the supposed agent's acts, whatever they were or however culpable they were' (*Marsh* v *Joseph* (1897) 1 Ch 213, 247). The contract is no more valid after ratification than when it was originally intended to be made, so that the insurer retains his right to avoid for non-disclosure if the insured has not complied with his obligations at the time of the attempted contract. The pre-contractual obligations arising out of the duty of good faith need only be discharged at the date of formation of the contract, so that any fact which was not material prior to the attempted contract but becomes material prior to ratification need not be disclosed (*Cory* v *Patton* (1874) LR 9 QB 577).[9]

Insurer—principal

The contract between insurer and principal can be enforced by each party in the normal way (*Wolff* v *Horncastle* (1798) 1 B&P 316), and subject to its terms eg non-payment of premium by the principal may terminate the contract if there is a date specified for such payment, or after a request for payment.

---

9 This case may be capable of criticism because the insurer initialled the slip subject to ratification, the loss occurring before ratification, and the court followed the standard rule of marine insurance to the effect that ratification was permissible, following *Hagedorn* v *Oliverson* (1814) 2 M & S 485. Whilst this is correct, it may be that the duty of good faith continues until ratification except in respect of marine losses.

Principal—broker

The contract of agency between principal and broker is extended to include the contract made by the broker in excess of his authority and ratified by the principal. This extension of actual authority carries with it the implied rights of the agent to remuneration via commission (*Keay v Fenwick* (1876) 1 CPD 745), reimbursement and indemnity (*Hartas v Ribbons* (1889) 22 QBD 254). But it does not authorise the broker to attempt to bind the principal to similar contracts in the future since it confers no additional authority except in respect of the previous contract. Ratification does not constitute the holding out of the agent by the principal to the effect that he is apparently authorised to act again in a similar manner on the principal's behalf (*Irvine v Union Bank of Australia* (1877) 2 App Cas 366), unless the situation occurs so frequently that it can constitute an extension by the principal of his broker's apparent authority, and indeed his actual authority.

The ratification of the contract should enable the broker to escape the consequences of his unauthorised act, in respect of both principal and insurer. However, in some instances the principal's ratification may not be fully voluntary, and may have been effected for commercial convenience or to protect his reputation, in which case he may be able to argue that he has not waived his broker's breach to the extent not only that commission should not be paid to the broker, but he may also have a claim in damages against the broker for the full amount of the premium. The former possibility is rendered tortuous by virtue of the fact that the broker is usually paid by the insurer, and the principal (theoretically) pays nothing in any event; no legal authority is known enabling the principal to obtain the broker's commission in such circumstances. The matter was touched on in *Great Atlantic Insurance Co v Home Insurance Co* [1981] 2 Lloyd's Rep 219 where Lloyd J commented that 'If the principal has held out his agent as having a certain authority, it hardly lies in his mouth to blame the agent for acting in breach of a secret limitation placed on that authority'. The inference is that a ratification which must be made by the principal must also negate any claim by the principal against the broker, even though it may have been involuntary owing to commercial pressure.[10] However, in principle there seems to be no reason why an agent with apparent power to bind his principal should not be liable to his principal if

---

10 See comment at (1982) 2 JBL 38.

his principal had forbidden him to use his apparent authority ie restricting his actual authority, and the same must be true of ratification out of commercial necessity.

Broker—insurer

The broker is technically liable to the insurer for his breach of warranty of authority, but effectively such liability is discharged by ratification since the insurer has not suffered loss and cannot therefore prove damage. However, if the insurer has suffered loss by relying on the broker's misrepresentation of his authority by, eg, issuing legal proceedings against the principal, the broker could perhaps be liable for legal costs and interest. Ratification may operate to render lawful an unlawful act perpetrated by the broker on the third party, for which the broker could be liable prior to ratification (*Whitehead* v *Taylor* (1839) 10 A & EL 210).

Chapter 4

Relationship between agents and third parties

RIGHTS AND LIABILITIES UNDER THE CONTRACT

The broker may be liable to the third party on the contract of insurance made between the principal and third party, or a separate, but related or collateral contract, or in tort. The most obvious example is by agreement, or by any custom or trade usage. Such liabilities usually arise in connection with the identity of the principal, or for breach of warranty of his authority, or from an obligation voluntarily assumed by the agent.

Undisclosed principal

Where the broker fails to disclose that he is acting on behalf of a principal, he leads the insurer to believe that he is contracting on his own behalf, and is liable accordingly (*HO Brandt & Co v HN Morris & Co Ltd* [1917] 2 KB 784, 793). Similarly, he may sue on the policy (*Sunderland Marine Insurance Co v Kearney* (1851) 16 QB 925). Thus where a broker signs an agreement in his own name without any qualification, he is liable unless any contrary intention appears in the agreement, which may often be difficult to establish (*Transcontinental Underwriting Agency v GUIC* [1987] 2 Lloyd's Rep 409). Given the fact that at Lloyd's all persons approaching underwriters have to be Lloyd's brokers, the possibility that an insurer would believe that a Lloyd's broker is a principal by virtue of such a principal not being disclosed is remote.

Unnamed principal

Where the broker discloses that he is acting for his principal but fails to reveal that principal's identity, he indicates clearly to the third party that he is not acting on his own behalf. The third party, in dealing with the broker on this basis, accepts that he is not contracting with the agent and that the broker should not be liable[1] and cannot be sued.

Where the broker is acting for insurers who are either named or whose existence has clearly been revealed to the insured, he cannot sue the insured for premium or be sued by the insurer for the premium (except in marine insurance or at Lloyd's), or by the insured for the loss (*Evans v Hooper* [1875] 1 QBD 45).

Warranty of authority

The principle in force during the first half of the 19th century was that any lack of liability on the part of the principal resulting from the broker's lack of authority resulted in liability on the part of the agent, who was held to have contracted personally. This form of liability was displaced by *Collen v Wright* (1857) EL & BL 622 which established that an agent acting without deceit or fraud who purported to incur liability on behalf of his principal, but actually failed to do so, was liable on an implied but separate warranty of authority. An agent acting fraudulently can be sued in tort for deceit or in contract for breach of warranty of authority (*Lewis v Nicholson* (1852) 18 QB 503, 511).[2] The latter course is usually more certain

---

1 But note that at Lloyd's the broker is liable for the premium in any case, and the producing broker is in turn liable to the placing (Lloyd's) broker: *Holmwoods, Back & Manson Ltd v Peel & Co Ltd* (1923) *The Times*, 27 January. However, Roche J found that the Lloyd's brokers had sued in the bankruptcy of the producing broker, had withdrawn their claim, and that their course of conduct evidenced an intention to look to the producing broker alone, rather than the insured (who had in fact paid the premium to the Lloyd's broker). Nevertheless, the expert evidence was that a Lloyd's broker always looked to the producing broker for premium, and he followed *Thomson v Davenport* (*Smith's Leading Cases* 12th Edn Vol II p 361). See also s 15 of Lloyd's Byelaw No 6 of 1988.

2 *Derry v Peek* (1889) 14 App Cas 337. The contractual position may be that the 'offer' of warranty of authority by the agent is based upon the consideration of the third party entering into the contract with the principal, and accepted by such a contract. In *v/o Rasnoimport v Guthrie & Co Ltd* [1966] 1 Lloyd's Rep 1, 13 Mocatta J developed a contractual relationship out of a promissory estoppel by the agent to the effect that he had any necessary authority. However, it is more likely to be a quasi-contractual implied obligation arising by operation of law rather than any agreement between the agent and third party. Buckley J in *Yonge v Toynbee Ltd* [1910] 1 KB 215 did say, however, that the agent's liability depended upon an implied contract. The warranty has been categorised as contractual for historical reasons (ibid, p 228).

since the burden of proof is lower, and is therefore to be preferred, although an action founded in deceit may be better rewarded, since a finding in deceit may carry with it some moral obloquy and censure in the form of higher damages.

The liability for breach of warranty of authority is strict and does not depend on deceit or negligence. In the absence of another's negligence, deceit or fraud, it is only right that the liability should fall on the party who represents his authority as being complete, and that he is capable of rendering his principal liable to the third party, if such representation is incapable of being sustained and therefore occasions a loss on the part of the third party. It may not be his fault, but then neither is it the fault of the third party, who may be worse placed to confirm such authority and is under no duty to enquire as to the extent of the authority. The fact that it is warranted is sufficient. The immutability of strict liability may give rise to legal decisions which appear to be harsh, in that the broker may not be negligent, but then neither is the third party. Thus, a broker who warrants that he is capable of negotiating an agreement on behalf of his principal to give rise to a binding contract must warrant that the principal is competent to contract. In the absence of such capacity on the principal's part, eg for insanity (*Yonge* v *Toynbee* [1910] 1 KB 215), death (*Smout* v *Ilbery* (1842) 10 M&W), lack of juristic capacity (eg after dissolution of a company (*Salton* v *New Beeston* [1900] 1 Ch 43)), the broker breaks his warranty of authority. Negligence is, however, not required to found an action against the agent (*Yonge* v *Toynbee* [1910] 1 KB 215).

It is even possible that liability for breach of warranty of authority could exist in respect of a representation that another party has authority[3] when he has not.

As with all representations, the warranty will not give rise to legal liability if it is one of law unless it is made in the knowledge that it will be acted upon and is wrong, in which case it may give rise to a claim in the tort of deceit. However, distinguishing between representations of fact and law is not always easy.

Ways around the warranty

A disclaimer by the broker or sufficient action by words or conduct by the broker or another should negative the warranty, although one wonders why an insurer should attempt to agree a contract with a broker without authority, unless the broker agrees to obtain

---

3 See Bowstead 460 and illustrations 4&9.

authority (*Halbot* v *Lens* [1901] 1 Ch 344).[4] Ratification by the principal will usually mean that the third party suffers no loss and therefore that no claim for breach of warranty can be made against the broker. Similarly, the principal cannot make any substantive claim against the broker, having ratified his action (*Home* v *Great Atlantic Insurance Co* [1981] 2 Lloyd's Rep 219, 277).

DAMAGES

The general rule is that damages for breach of contract must compensate the claimant by placing him in the same financial position as if the main contract had been properly and successfully performed, provided the lack of authority is a sufficiently proximate cause of the loss, there is no supervening event, and the loss was within the reasonable contemplation of the parties (*C Czarnikow Ltd* v *Koufos* [1969] 1 AC 350). The damages payable for breach of warranty are wider, and extend to recovery of any loss or damage which actually flowed from the breach, and which were a foreseeable consequence of the breach. However, the breach of warranty of authority cannot give rise to a better claim against the broker than it would against the principal, because, if the warranty had been true, the third party would have had to sue the principal. Thus limited damages will be awarded if the principal is insolvent, in which case the third party's position would be that of mere creditor unless, for example, the presence of a valid authority would have placed the third party in a better position eg with rights to debenture stock which would not be affected by any insolvency (*Firbank's Executors* v *Humphreys* (1887) 18 QBD 54).

Similarly, a transaction which is unenforceable against the principal even if the broker were authorised precludes a successful claim against the broker (*Heskell* v *Continental Express Ltd* [1950] 1 AER 1033).

The cost of legal proceedings initiated by the third party prior to ratification may be recovered from the broker. Such litigation could be brought initially against the principal for breach of any contract alleged to have been agreed by the broker under his apparent

---

4 However, a broker need not even have a specific principal in mind when obtaining reinsurance cover, but technically this is not ratified by the insurer; rather the broker decides whether to tender the benefit of any reinsurance to any particular insurer: *General Accident Fire & Life Assurance Corporation* v *Tanter; The 'Zephyr'* [1985] 2 Lloyd's Rep 529.

authority, although a court would be more likely to award costs against the third party if it continued with the litigation after it had become clear that the broker was not held out as authorised, since the likely unsuccessful result would be known.

Part Two

The Contract of Insurance

Chapter 5

Principles of insurance

A contract of insurance is a legally enforceable agreement by which an insurance company or active underwriter representing other underwriters ('the insurer') agrees to pay to another person ('the insured') a sum of money or provide its equivalent on the happening of a specified event not within the control of the insurer, provided that the insured has complied with any obligations imposed by the agreement, and in respect of which contract the insured has agreed to pay a sum of money to the insurer (*Prudential Insurance Co v IRC* [1904] 2 KB 658, 663). No statutory definition of insurance exists, despite the strict statutory regulation of insurance business.

THE RELEVANT PRINCIPLES

Insurable interest

An interest capable of being insured by the insured is necessary. This is required as a matter of public policy to prevent gambling or attempts by a beneficiary to hasten the demise of a person whose life was to be insured. Lawrence J defined it in *Lucena* v *Craufurd* (1806) Bos & PNR 269, 302 as:

A man is interested in a thing to whom advantage may arise or prejudice happen from the circumstances which may attend it . . . and whom it importeth that its condition as to safety or other quality should continue: interest does not necessarily imply a right to the whole or part of a thing, nor necessarily and exclusively that which may be the subject of privation, but the having some relation to, or concern in the subject of the insurance, which relation or concern by the happening of the perils insured against may be so affected as to produce a damage, detriment, or prejudice to the person insuring; and where a man is so circumstanced with respect to matters exposed to certain risks or damages, or to have a moral certainty of advantage or benefit, but for those risks or dangers, he may be said to be interested in the safety of the thing. To be interested in the preservation of a thing, is to be so circumstanced with respect to it as to have benefit from its existence, prejudice from its destruction. The property of a thing and the interest devisable from it may be very different; of the first the price is generally the measure, but by interest in a thing every benefit or advantage arising out of or depending on such thing may be considered as being comprehended.

In essence the insured has an insurable interest in a physical object owned by him or as to which he may have contractual or other rights and obligations, if he will suffer prejudice by its damage eg as a bailee, consignee or mortgagee. Similarly an insurable interest exists in any situation in which the insured will suffer prejudice as a result of his actions which give rise to liability to others. The interest need only be present at the time of the loss or damage (s 6 of the Marine Insurance Act 1906). The absence of an insurable interest will render the contract of insurance invalid and unenforceable.

Uberrima fides

The doctrine of *uberrima fides* applies to all contracts of insurance and is codified in s 17 of the Marine Insurance Act 1906:

A contract of marine insurance is a contract based upon the utmost good faith, and, if the utmost good faith be not observed by either party, the contract may be avoided by the other party.

The problem inherent in contracts of insurance is that the insured knows considerably more about the subject matter of the insurance than the insurer, and in many cases has more control over it. Lord Mansfield in *Carter* v *Boehm* (1766) 3 Burr 1905, 1909 put it thus:

Insurance is a contract upon speculation. The special facts, upon which the contingent chance is to be computed, lie more commonly in the knowledge of the insured only: the underwriter trusts to his representation, and proceeds upon confidence that he does not keep back any circumstance in his knowledge, to mislead the underwriter into a belief that the circumstance does not exist, and to induce him to estimate the risque as if it did not exist. The keeping back of such a circumstance is a fraud, and, therefore, the policy is void. Although the suppression should happen through mistake, without any fraudulent intention; yet still the underwriter is deceived, and the policy is void; because the risque run is really different from the risque understood and intended to be run at the time of the agreement . . . The governing principle is applicable to all contracts and dealings. Good faith forbids either party by concealing what he privately knows, to draw the other into a bargain, from his ignorance of that fact, and his believing the contrary. . . .

Similarly it was said in *Rozanes* v *Bowen* (1928) 32 Ll L Rep 98, 102

It has been for centuries in England the law in connection with insurance of all sorts, marine, fire, life, guarantee and every kind of policy, that, as the underwriter knows nothing and the man who comes to him to ask him to insure knows everything, it is the duty of the assured, the man who desires to have a policy, to make a full disclosure to the underwriters without being asked of all the material circumstances, because the underwriter knows nothing and the assured knows everything. That is expressed by saying that it is a contract of the utmost good faith — *uberrimae fides*.[1]

NON-DISCLOSURE

It is the duty of the insured to disclose to the insurer all material facts or circumstances which he knows (or ought in the ordinary course of business to know), so that the insurer is given as accurate and fair a presentation of the risk as possible. The duty of good faith is extra contractual (*La Banque Financiere de la cité SA* v *Westgate Insurance Co Ltd* [1988] 2 Lloyd's Rep 513), and the duty to disclose applies to all contracts which are *uberrimae fidei* (*March Cabaret Club & Casino Ltd* v *London Assurance* [1975] 1 Lloyd's Rep 169). The duty thus extends beyond facts actually known to the insured or his agent (even where the information is deliberately concealed by the agent (*Proudfoot* v *Montefiore* (1867) LR 2 QB 511)), to facts presumed to be within his (or their) knowledge, which he ought to have known in the ordinary course of business; that he was unaware of a fact in this category where it was capable of discovery by reasonable enquiry will still render the contract voidable at the insurer's option. The rationale behind this is that an insured could carelessly or recklessly decide not to enquire, when he ought to do so (*Blackburn, Low & Co* v *Vigors* (1887) 12 App Cas 531, 537).

MATERIALITY

Section 18(2) of the Marine Insurance Act 1906 states:

Every circumstance is material which would influence the judgment of a prudent insurer in fixing the premium, or determining whether he will take the risk.

---

1 Actually it should be *uberrima fides*, or *uberrimae fidei*.

The materiality of the fact to the underwriter in question is irrelevant; it is the prudent underwriter who is the yardstick (*CTI* v *Oceanus Mutual Underwriting Association (Bermuda) Ltd* [1984] 1 Lloyd's Rep 476). This test applies equally to non-marine insurance (*Lambert* v *Co-operative Insurance Society Ltd* [1975] 2 Lloyd's Rep 485). The materiality of any fact will be assessed by reference to the date by which it should have been communicated to the insurer ie by the date of the conclusion of the contract (*Canning* v *Farquhar* (1886) 16 QBD 727). Later proof of immateriality or untruth will not assist the insured; similarly, a fact which is immaterial at the relevant date but which later becomes material will not enable the insurer to avoid. Such material facts are broadly divisible into two areas: those aspects which affect the subject matter of the insurance, and those which relate to the insured. The following facts are usually material:

(a) facts indicating that the subject matter of the insurance is exposed to greater risk than would normally be the case, such as its condition, nature, surroundings, history, occupation or hobbies or habits;

(b) facts indicating that the insured is a 'moral hazard'. These include the following.

Previous convictions within a reasonable period prior to the claim

The seriousness of the offence, its bearing upon the insurance, and its age are all factors which a court will consider in evaluating whether a conviction was relevant and constituted a material fact (*Woolcott* v *Excess Insurance Co Ltd and Miles Smith Anderson & Game Ltd* (No 2) [1979] 2 Lloyd's Rep 210); the court will also apply the Rehabilitation of Offenders Act 1974 which enables certain convictions to be considered 'spent', again according to their seriousness and age, thereby obviating the need for their disclosure.

Outstanding criminal charges

The insured should logically reveal those charges as to which he knows he is guilty since they will be material but there seems to be no logical reason as to why he should reveal those in regard to which he may be innocent.[2] The balance of court decisions is narrowly in favour of disclosing such charges.[3] Charges not pursued or resulting in acquittal need not be disclosed, but a verdict of 'Not Proven' in a Scots court may present a problem. Such a verdict may be considered material;

Nationality

This is not strictly a moral hazard. The Race Relations Act 1976 requires that discrimination should not occur on the grounds of race, colour, nationality or ethnic or national origins, and the insured's duty of disclosure does not include these aspects;

Previous encounters with insurers

Previous claims are generally considered to be material in non-marine insurance, since they produce the only empirical basis for estimating future claims and may reflect upon the insured's predilection for claiming regularly, or his honesty, or his ability to avoid claims. Where the insurance is for similar subject matter the claims' record is clearly relevant (*Rozanes* v *Bowen* (1928) 32 Ll L Rep 98). Where the insurance is different the duty to disclose could become unduly extensive, since all claims under all insurances could be relevant, and the courts have therefore limited the duty to aspects of other insurance claims which could indicate that the insured is likely to make claims under the new contract of insurance (*Ewer* v *National Employers Mutual General Insurance Association Ltd* [1937] 2 All ER 193, 200).

Previous refusals to insure constitute material facts, which must be disclosed, whether such refusals relate to similar (*Re Yager and Guardian Assurance Co* (1913) 108 LT 38) or unconnected subject matter (*Locker & Woolf Ltd* v *Western Australian Insurance Co* [1936] 1

---

2 But it is not for the insured to assess his guilt. He may believe that he is culpable, but (a) a jury may not, and (b) his guilt must be determined by the law, in which he may have a suitable defence which is unknown to him at the date of the proposal or insurance.

3 *March Cabaret Club* v *London Assurance* [1975] 1 Lloyd's Rep 169 obiter at 177; *Inversiones Manria SA* v *Sphere Drake Insurance Co plc: The 'Dora'* [1989] 1 Lloyd's Rep 69; against: *Reynolds & Anderson* v *Phoenix Assurance Co Ltd* [1978] 2 Lloyd's Rep 440.

KB 408),[4] except in marine insurance which applies the rationale that each insurer must independently evaluate the risk without reliance on the subjective foibles of others (*Glasgow Assurance Corporation Ltd v William Symondson & Co* (1911) 104 LT 254). There does not appear to be any sensible reason for this distinction between marine and non-marine practice.

Overvaluation of the subject matter of insurance

Valued policies

The valuation is conclusive between the insurer and insured (*Bousfield v Barnes* (1815) 4 Camp 228) but is subject to the duty of good faith in its assessment. Thus submitting an excessive valuation is a breach of this duty of good faith and renders the policy voidable at the insurer's option (*Inversiones Manria SA v Sphere Drake Insurance Co plc: The 'Dora'* [1989] 1 Lloyd's Rep 69). However, where the insured has actually paid the amount submitted as the true value of the subject matter, the fact that it is worth considerably less will not constitute a material fact entitling the insurer to avoid (*Inversiones Manria SA v Sphere Drake Insurance Co plc: The 'Dora'* (see above)).

Unvalued policies

Unvalued policies offer more leeway to the insured and the courts are loathe to find that overvaluations are material. The insurer must show that the overvaluation is material and must satisfy a heavy burden of proof to enable him to terminate. A wilful misrepresentation of value for a claim may amount to fraud (*Britton v Royal Insurance Co* (1866) 4 F & F 905).

Facts considered material by the insurer and known to be so by the insured

Facts considered material by the insurer and known to be so by the insured include the following:

---

4 Although the decision was made on the primary basis that the insured specifically stated in the proposal form that no other insurance had been declined, in response to a question requesting information as to other requests for insurance.

Life and accident insurance

Examples include: age of insured (*Keeling* v *Pearl Assurance Co* (1923) 129 LT 573); residence (*Grogan* v *London & Manchester Industrial Assurance Co* (1885) 53 LT 761); medical history (*Life Association of Scotland* v *Foster* (1873) 11 MacPh 351), and anything affecting life expectancy; potentially harmful activities and habits; drug use or abuse; sexual activities and history; occupation;[5] hobbies (*McNealy* v *Pennine Insurance Co* [1978] 2 Lloyd's Rep 18); and height and weight (*Levy* v *Scottish Employers Insurance Co* (1901) 17 TLR 229).

Fire insurance

Examples include: immediate environment if capable of 'inducing' fire (*Bufe* v *Turner* (1815) 6 Taunt 338); age and condition of the property; and use of the property (including temporary or occasional storage of flammable items (*Hales* v *Reliance Fire* [1960] 2 Lloyd's Rep 391)).

Motor insurance

Examples include: storage of the car (*Dawsons Ltd* v *Bonnin* [1922] 2 AC 413); previous accidents of any proposed driver (stated with accuracy) (*Dent* v *Blackmore* (1927) 29 LlL Rep 9); age of proposed drivers; previous 'losses' of the car (*Farra* v *Hetherington* (1931) 40 LlL Rep 132); and cancellations of other policies (*Norman* v *Gresham Fire & Accident Insurance Society Ltd* (1935) 52 LlL Rep 292).[6]

Burglary and property insurance

Examples include: location, age, use and condition of the property.

---

5 Curiously this may not be material to personal accident insurance: *Woodall* v *Pearl Assurance Co Ltd* [1919] 1 KB 593. But the Court of Appeal found as a fact that there had not been any misdescription since the description was not misleading or substantially incorrect, although their comments do give rise to a presumption that they would have found a way around this problem. Bankes LJ says on p 602 that he was unable to accept the contention that the insured had misdescribed his occupation because (a) if it succeeded it would turn policies into 'mere traps to catch the unwary'; and (b) the description of occupation was as understood in the district.

6 This postulate could apply to all types of policy. The concept that the insured should confirm that his other policies were not cancelled for non-payment of premium was put forward, since it would also confirm that the insured was financially capable of taking all necessary steps to retain the vehicle in good condition. The court did not decide the case on this ground, but Lewis J held at p 301 that the cancellation of previous policies was a material fact.

MISREPRESENTATION

Section 20(1) of the Marine Insurance Act 1906 states that:

Every material representation made by the assured or his agent to the insurer during the negotiations for the contract, and before the contract is concluded, must be true. If it be untrue the insurer may avoid the contract.

Any statement of fact made by the insured which induces the insurer to contract with him on the terms agreed must therefore be accurate, and any change in accuracy before the contract is formed must be communicated to the insurer (*Canning* v *Farquhar* (1886) 16 QBD 727). A failure to complete an answer on the proposal form may constitute a misrepresentation by way of negative inference (*Roberts* v *Avon Insurance Co Ltd* [1956] 2 Lloyd's Rep 240), as may a statement literally true but nevertheless misleading (*Condogianis* v *Guardian Assurance Co* [1921] 2 AC 125). Statements of law are irrelevant, and any statement of opinion carries with it only the representation that the opinion is sincerely and honestly held (*Irish National Insurance Co and Sedgwick* v *Oman Insurance Co* [1983] 2 Lloyd's Rep 453). Statements as to intention are similarly relieved of liability if the intention was honestly held when the statement was made, even though altered after the contract was formed (s 20(3) of the Marine Insurance Act 1906). Section 20(4) of the Marine Insurance Act 1906 excepts minor omissions if a statement is true but has false implications, or is partially untrue, if those implications or untruths are effectively immaterial.

Usually representations are made by the insured. However, where the insurer induces the insured to contract by the former's representations, the duty of good faith also applies to require that such representations are accurate. Thus there is a misrepresentation by the insurer as to the effect of a document if it is made with knowledge that it has a different meaning eg that the insured need only pay a fixed amount premium when the premium will increase with the age of the insured (*Molloy* v *Mutual Reserve Life Insurance Co* (1906) 22 TLR 525, 527).

Proposal forms usually include a warranty that the insured's answers are correct, which effectively converts the answers into warranties. Any inaccuracy becomes a breach of warranty, enabling the insurer to avoid the policy, whether the answer is material or not (*Dawsons Ltd* v *Bonnin* [1922] 2 AC 413). Equally, there may be a clause making the accuracy of all answers or representations during negotiations a condition precedent to the contract. The effect of any untruth will be harsh for the insured, unless he can expressly qualify the form by stating that they are only true to the best of his belief, so that an innocent misrepresentation will not be fatal to his position (*Macdonald* v *Law Union Insurance Co* (1874) LR 9 QB 328).

FACTS WHICH NEED NOT BE DISCLOSED

Section 18(3) of the Marine Insurance Act 1906 states:

In the absence of enquiry the following circumstances need not be disclosed, namely:
(a) Any circumstance which diminishes the risk;
(b) Any circumstance which is known or presumed to be known to the insurer. The insurer is presumed to know matters of common notoriety or knowledge, and matters which an insurer in the ordinary course of his business, as such, ought to know;
(c) Any circumstance as to which information is waived by the insurer;
(d) Any circumstance which it is superfluous to disclose by reason of any express or implied warranty.

Any circumstance which diminishes the risk

This part of s 18(3) enshrines in statute the words of Lord Mansfield in *Carter* v *Boehm* (1766) 3 Burr 1905 to the effect that:

The underwriter needs not be told what lessens the risque agreed and understood to be run by the express terms of the policy . . . If he insures for three years, he need not be told any circumstances to shew it may be over in two; or if he insures a voyage, with liberty of deviation, he needs not be told what tends to shew there will be no deviation.

Any circumstance which is known or presumed known to the insurer

Information acquired in any way by the insurer or his agent need not be disclosed by the insured (*Woolcott* v *Excess Insurance Co Ltd, and Miles, Smith, Anderson & Game* [1978] 1 Lloyd's Rep 633, (No 2) [1979] 2 Lloyd's Rep 210), except perhaps where it is of a specific nature and involves a subject matter of no interest or concern to the insurer at the time of its acquisition (*London General Insurance Co Ltd* v *General Mutual Marine Underwriters' Association Ltd* [1921] 1 KB 104). The insurer is presumed to be aware of all relevant commercial matters, such as the practices affecting the subject matter to be insured (*Noble* v *Kennoway* (1780) 2 Doug 510 eg stowage on deck or lengthy unloading periods) but in *Carter* v *Boehm* (1766) 3 Burr 1905 it was said that the underwriter

needs not to be told general topics of speculation: as for instance — the underwriter is bound to know every cause which may occasion natural perils; as, the difficulty of the voyage — the kind of seasons — the probability of lightning, hurricanes, earthquakes etc. He is bound to know every cause which may occasion political perils; from the ruptures of States from war, and the various operations of it. He is bound to know the probability of safety, from the continuance or return of peace; from the imbecility of the enemy, through the weakness of their counsels or their want of strength, etc.

In *Bates* v *Hewitt* (1867) LR 2 QB 595, 610 the underwriter

. . . is not bound to communicate things which are well known to both. He is not bound to communicate facts or circumstances which are within the ordinary professional knowledge of an underwriter. He is not bound to communicate facts relating to the general course of a particular trade; because all these things are supposed to be within the knowledge of the person carrying on the business of insurance, and which, therefore, it is not necessary for him to be specially informed of.

At p 605 of the same report, it is stated that

. . . when a fact is of public notoriety, as of war, or where it is one which is matter of inference, and the materials for informing the judgment of the underwriter are common to both, the party proposing the insurance is not bound to communicate what he is fully warranted in assuming the underwriter already knows. Short of these things, the party proposing the insurance is bound to make known to the insurer whatever is necessary and essential to enable him to determine what is the extent of the risk against which he undertakes to insure; . . . if the insurer chooses to neglect the information which he receives, he can take advantage of his wilful blindness or negligence; if he shuts his eyes to the light, it is his own fault: provided sufficient information, as far as the assured is concerned, has been placed at his disposal . . . If indeed, the insurer knows the fact, the omission on the part of the assured to communicate it will not avail as a defence in an action for a loss; not because the assured will have complied with the obligations which rested on him to communicate that which was material, but because it will not lie in the mouth of the underwriter to say that a material fact was not communicated to him, which he had present to his mind at the time he accepted the insurance . . .

And at p 610 in regard to the underwriter it is commented that:

It is not enough that the underwriter be furnished with materials from which, by a course of reasoning and an effort of memory, he may be induced to suspect that the vessel is a dangerous risk. The matter must not be left to speculation or peradventure.

Thus the insured or his broker cannot assume that the insurer has read or retained information contained in Lloyd's List (*Morrison* v *Universal Marine Insurance Co* (1872) LR 8 Exch 40).

Any circumstance as to which information is waived by the insurer

An insurer does not often intentionally waive his right to information concerning the risk. He may, however, in some circumstances be held to have done so. Where, for example, the insurer asks specific questions he may alter the insured's duty of disclosure, since the questions asked may indicate the extent of the information required. Thus asking about one particular area and ignoring another may give rise to a presumption that the insurer is not interested in the latter area, even though the general duty of disclosure of all material facts should override the semantics of the form (*Arterial Caravans* v *Yorkshire Insurance Co* [1973] 1 Lloyd's Rep 169). However, insurers should not rely on this catch-all statutory and common law requirement and should be wary of the potentially limiting nature of their questions.

In *Hair* v *Prudential Assurance* [1983] 2 Lloyd's Rep 667, 673 Woolf J took the view that a waiver could be implied from a failure to ask specific questions on the basis that 'if it was intended that an assured should answer matters even though he is not questioned about them . . . I would have expected something to be said which clearly indicated to a proposer that, although they had not been asked any specific question about the matter, if there was something relevant to the risk which they knew of, but which was not covered by the questions, they should still deal with it, and leave a space for them to do so'. In practical terms this ratio is limited to the particular facts and wording, but it does illustrate consumer-orientated judicial thinking to the effect that a proposer need not concern himself with legal precepts as to which he may be unaware, but need only 'fill in the form'. Another example of this limiting effect is *Jester-Barnes* v *Licenses & General Insurance Co Ltd* (1934) 49 Ll L Rep 231, 237 where an obiter comment indicated that a question requesting information arising within a specified period obviated the need for the insured to provide relevant information outside that period.

Waiver may also be effected where the insured's answer does not provide all the information which an insurer might require but rather puts him on notice that further information is available, but this may depend on the extent of the information provided. In

Container Transport International Inc and Reliance Group Inc v Oceanus Mutual Underwriting Association (Bermuda) Ltd [1984] 1 Lloyd's Rep 476 the Court of Appeal decided (pp 498, 530) that putting the insurer on enquiry was inadequate to discharge the duty of disclosure, and that waiver of disclosure could only apply when the insurer affirms the contract after he is in possession of the material facts. The issue of a policy after such notice does not constitute a waiver of the breach unless it constitutes an election or rights are prejudiced (*Morrison v Union Marine Insurance Co* (1873) LR 8 Ex 197). A complete failure to answer the question cannot constitute an inaccurate statement but does not put the insurer on notice that further relevant information may exist (although an inference may be drawn that the answer is intended to be negative). It is the duty of the insured to disclose all material facts, and not for the insurer to elicit those facts (*Arterial Caravans v Yorkshire Insurance Co* [1973] 1 Lloyd's Rep 169). Where the only answer available to the insured would have elicited an unfavourable response by the insurer there may be a concealment of a material fact.

The situation may be further distinguished by the agreed status of the answers given by the insured on the proposal form. Such forms usually state that the veracity of the answers is important and relevant to the insurer in assessing the risk, and constitutes a condition precedent to the contract. The clause attempting to effect this must be clear in both respects: the answers must be warranted true and their importance made obvious. Where the condition precedent is effective, the answers must be complete and correct, and any untruth will give rise to a right of the insurer to avoid for non-disclosure, whether the fact is strictly material or not (*Dawsons Ltd v Bonnin* [1922] 2 AC 413).

Where the proposal form does not contain a clause making its contents the basis of the contract, the effect of any untruth has a lesser effect in that it does not automatically entitle the insurer to repudiate liability, unless the untruth can be considered to constitute non-disclosure of a material fact or a misrepresentation.

The usual rules of construction apply to documents used in the making of any insurance contract. The following tenets have particular application:

(a) The document must be considered as a whole. Minor omissions or trivial mistakes do not operate to render the document inaccurate since it must be considered as a whole. Any answer may be qualified by another, even in another proposal if two or more proposal forms refer to each other (*McGugan v Manufacturers & Merchants Mutual Fire Insurance Co* (1879) 29 CP 494).

(b) A fair and reasonable construction must be placed on the contents of the proposal form, and the words used will be construed as if interpreted by ordinary men of normal intelligence and average knowledge of the world (*Yorke* v *Yorkshire Insurance Co Ltd* [1918] 1 KB 662, 668). For example questions requesting information about illnesses are limited to serious illnesses (*Connecticut Mutual Life Insurance Co of Hertford* v *Moore* (1881) 6 App Cas 644), and may also be limited to the context of the insurance; an insured's eyesight which is slightly defective but nevertheless satisfactory for the purpose of driving will not require specific disclosure in a proposal for motor insurance. Similarly, other insurance unconnected with the insurance in question need not be disclosed, unless clearly requested. Thus a question in a fire insurance proposal form as to whether the insured is or has been 'insured in this or any other office' does not include all property ever occupied by the insured, but refers only to the particular premises to be insured, unless other premises are distinctly referred to (*Golding* v *Royal London Auxiliary Insurance Co Ltd* (1914) 30 TLR 350).

In general a question which may be ambiguous or has been wrongly misinterpreted (without recklessness) which elicits a truthful but incomplete answer from the insured will be construed '*contra proferentem*' against the insurer. Thus in *Yorke* v *Yorkshire Insurance Co Ltd* (1914) 30 TLR 350 the answer to a question as to the temperate habits of the insured which correctly represented his lack of alcoholism but failed to include his capacity for certain drugs did not entitle the insurer to rescind. The courts have, however, also decided against the insured in instances of honest mistake (*Glicksman* v *Lancashire & General Assurance Co* [1927] AC 139) and whether or not there is a right to rescind will depend on the facts.

(c) The insured must disclose the whole truth of any answer. Supplying an answer which is literally true but does not provide all the information requested will enable the insurer to rescind the contract. Thus supplying a correct answer such as identifying one claim, without identifying all other relevant claims, is inadequate, since the clear inference is that there are no other claims (*Condogianis* v *Guardian Assurance Co* [1921] 2 AC 125).

(d) Inconsistencies apparent from the face of the document operate to waive the insurer's rights to rescind, since the insurer has the option prior to the formation of the contract of declining to accept the risk, or obtaining additional information, or charging a higher premium (*Keeling* v *Pearl Assurance Co Ltd* 129 (1923) LT 573).

BURDEN OF PROOF

The burden of proof is clearly on the insurer alleging that there has been non-disclosure, since the fact that a policy exists gives rise to the presumption that all obligations have been satisfied (*Elkin v Janson* (1845) 13 M&W 655). Such a presumption is, of course, rebuttable. However, ' . . . the universal rule in professional or any negligence, [is] that he who alleges must prove' *Insurance Co of the State of Pennsylvania* v *Grand Union Insurance Co* [1990] 1 Lloyd's Rep 208, 224). Facts which are clearly material do not require evidence to substantiate their materiality (*Glicksman v Lancashire & General Assurance Co* [1927] AC 139) but facts less obviously so will require the testimony of an expert witness, who will usually be someone well known in the relevant market, to demonstrate the matters that are material to the 'prudent insurer' (*CTI v Oceanus Mutual Underwriting Association (Bermuda) Ltd* [1984] 1 Lloyd's Rep 476). Thus in cases in which brokers are sued for negligence in failing to transmit specific information to the insurer, where their defence is that the insurer would either not have accepted the risk, or would have been entitled to avoid it for another reason, the insurer should be invited to state whether he would have pursued either course to the detriment of the insured.[7]

The absence of expert evidence enables the court to draw on its experience of materiality, and it will not apply the standard of the ordinary businessman, who knows little of insurance, but rather its own judgment from such knowledge as it has (*Glasgow Assurance Corporation Ltd* v *William Symondson & Co* (1911) 104 LT 254, 257). It will not, however, jump to the conclusion that a fact is material where any substantial doubt exists.

EFFECT OF BREACH OF DUTY OF GOOD FAITH

The remedy for a pre-contractual breach of good faith is rescission under s 17 of the Marine Insurance Act 1906, which serves to dissolve the contract as though it had never existed, at the option of

---

7 *Fraser v B Furman (Productions) Ltd* [1967] 2 Lloyd's Rep 1; *Dunbar v AB Painters Ltd* [1986] 2 Lloyd's Rep 38.

the insurer.[8] The 'default necessarily strikes at the very basis of the contract itself' and the insurer must elect to ignore the defect or avoid *ab initio*. The insured is entitled to repayment of his premium under s 84(1) of the Marine Insurance Act 1906, unless there is fraud on his part or unless the contract contains a term denying the insured's right to such return of premium. In the latter case, there is a chicken and egg quality concerning the concept of a right to retain premium which was paid under a contract which is deemed never to have existed. Nevertheless, a court may uphold such a clause (*Thomson* v *Weems* (1824) 9 App Cas 671).

The remedy for a post-contractual breach, such as a failure to provide all relevant information under a 'held covered' provision or non-disclosure in respect of a claim, is again rescission or avoidance at the insurer's option. However, ' . . . the underwriters were fully entitled to defend the claim on grounds of bad faith and to reject the claim simpliciter while leaving the policy intact . . . fully in accordance with the modern approach that the remedy should be proportional to the breach — eg *Hongkongfir Shipping Co Ltd* v *Kawasaki Kisen Kaisha Ltd* [1962] 2 QB 26 . . . s 17 . . . did no more than confer upon the insurer, or the assured in appropriate circumstances, a right to avoid. It did not therefore follow that the insurer was required or bound to avoid, at all events for post-contract breach, particularly since s 91(2) of the [Marine Insurance] Act specifically preserved the rules of common law save insofar as they were inconsistent with express provisions of the Act'. (*The 'Litsion Pride'* [1985] 1 Lloyd's Rep 437, pp 514, 515).

Where the breach is effected by a positive misrepresentation, the court theoretically has power to refuse to allow rescission and to substitute damages in place of the insurer's right, under s 2(2) of the

---

8 'Rescission' has been regularly regarded as coterminous with 'termination', a usage described as 'misleading' by Diplock LJ in *Photo Productions Ltd* v *Securicor Transport Ltd* [1980] AC 827. Rescission for misrepresentation arises from a defect in the formation of the contract, entitling the insurer to avoid *ab initio*. Rescission for breach arises from a defect in the performances of the contract, giving rise to a right to claim damages for breach; the difference is that damages are not available for breach of a non-existent contract. So a breach of the duty of good faith after inception in theory should give rise to a right to damages. But the duty of good faith starts when negotiations commence for the contract, and continue until complete expiry of all its aspects; breach at any time is retroactive to the inception of the duty ie *ab initio*. The effect is that damages cannot be available for a breach of the duty of good faith, as confirmed by the Court of Appeal in *La Banque Financiere* [1988] 2 Lloyd's Rep 513 and *The Bank of Nova Scotia* v *Hellenica War Risks Association (Bermuda) Ltd The 'Good Luck'* [1989] 2 Lloyd's Rep 238.

Misrepresentation Act 1967. A court would no doubt be sympathetic where the misrepresentation is innocently made and immaterial to the cause of the insured's claim, but Steyn J in *Highland Insurance Co v Continental Insurance Co* [1987] 1 Lloyd's Rep 109 stated that:

Avoidance is the appropriate remedy for material misrepresentation in relation to marine and non-marine contracts of insurance . . . the rules governing material misrepresentation fulfil an important 'policing' function in ensuring that the brokers make a fair representation to underwriters. If Section 2(2) were to be regarded as conferring a discretion to grant relief from avoidance on the grounds of material misrepresentation the efficacy of those rules would be eroded. This policy consideration must militate against granting relief under Section 2(2) from an avoidance on the grounds of material misrepresentation in the case of commercial contracts of insurance.

Waiver

The insurer must remain alive to the possibility that his conduct in dealing with any claim could constitute a waiver of his right to avoid the policy, after he has become aware of any breach of duty by the insured. The relevant principles were considered in *Liberian Insurance Agency v Mosse* [1977] 2 Lloyd's Rep 60 to be that the insurer had to have full knowledge of the facts and that being put on inquiry was insufficient; he was entitled to a reasonable time in which to decide whether to affirm the contract, and 'he will be deemed to have affirmed the contract if either so much time has elapsed that the necessary inference is one of affirmation or the assured has been prejudiced by the delay in making an election or rights of third parties have intervened' (ibid at p 565).

Where the insurer satisfies the criteria for affirmation outlined in *Liberian Insurance Agency v Mosse* he cannot later attempt to avoid the contract eg by giving notice of cancellation in accordance with the policy, rather than attempting to avoid for non-disclosure (*Mint Security Ltd v Blair* [1982] 1 Lloyd's Rep 188), he will be deemed to have affirmed and will be unable to rely on the non-disclosure at any time. Accepting premium and issuing a policy after notification of a material variation of the risk constitutes an affirmation of the contract by the insurer (*Hadenfayre Ltd v British National Insurance Society Ltd* [1984] 2 Lloyd's Rep 393). If he affirms a pre-contractual breach of the duty of good faith, he must also meet any claim. The insurer can waive his right to avoid for a post-contractual breach, and affirm the policy, but he can still refuse to admit the claim (*The 'Litsion Pride'* [1985] 1 Lloyd's Rep 437). However, the insurer need not avoid for a pre-contractual breach if the non-disclosure in breach of the duty of good faith can be construed in the light of the proposal form as a breach of a term resembling a warranty, which enables the insurer to state that the 'warranty' takes effect not as a full-blooded warranty but as a phrase which delimits and/or is descriptive of the risk and is not promissory in nature, entitling him to reject the claim and retain the policy on foot, rather than avoid the entire policy (*CTN Cash & Carry Ltd* v *General Accident Fire & Life Assurance Corporation* [1989] 1 Lloyd's Rep 259). A court may also characterise a minor default in the insured's activities as a casual non-observance, where the warranty is that the insured's procedures will not be varied, rather than as a strict variation of procedure (*Mint Security* v *Blair* [1982] 1 Lloyd's Rep 188).

Implied affirmation

The insurer may affirm the contract by failing to demonstrate that he intends to avoid the policy, particularly if he does nothing at all. Under the principle of *Liberian Insurance Agency* v *Mosse* a total failure to act will result in affirmation of the contract, at the end of a 'reasonable time'. The insurer may also take a step consistent with the contract without meaning to affirm it, such as issuing a policy without a protest after becoming aware of a non-disclosure by the insured. *Morrison* v *Union Marine Insurance Co* (1872) LR 8 Ex 197 states, after a fashion, that such an act does not constitute an affirmation of the contract since it is an administrative act, particularly where the insured is not prejudiced by a failure to disaffirm the policy. The insurer is entitled to a reasonable period in which to consider his position. However, *Bawden* v *London, Edinburgh and Glasgow Assurance Co* [1892] 2 QB 534 and *Stone* v *Reliance Mutual Insurance Society Ltd* [1972] 1 Lloyd's Rep 469 may be authorities for the proposition that the issue of a policy constitutes affirmation of the contract, although these situations may be more properly categorised as acceptances of the offers rather than affirmation.[9]

---

9 In *Elkin* v *Janson* 13 M & W 655 at 663 Parke B appears to accept that the issue of the policy is an affirmation of the contract on the basis that no prudent man possessed of the relevant information would execute a policy unless he intended to waive a non-disclosure of a material fact, but the case is not clear.

DURATION OF THE DUTY

The pre-contractual duty of good faith by definition does not extend beyond the date at which the contract is formed ie when offer and acceptance have occurred, in whatever form. The nature of the duty then becomes less onerous upon the insured; he need not disclose any aspects that may have been irrelevant prior to the contract but have since become relevant, since the risk has attached and the premium agreed, as pre-contractual materiality is assessed primarily in these contexts.

The relevant date can, however, be postponed by the insurer until receipt of the initial premium. Where the contract is not complete until such payment, the duty of disclosure continues until payment has been effected. Any material fact arising before receipt of payment should be disclosed (*Harrington* v *Pearl Life Assurance Co Ltd* (1914) 30 TLR 613). Alternatively the insurer's obligations may not attach until the policy has been issued (*Alliss-Chalmers Co* v *Fidelity & Deposit Co of Maryland* (1916) 114 LT 433). The duty includes informing the insurer or his agent that any previous statement has been discovered to be or has become inaccurate (*Golding* v· *Royal London Auxiliary Insurance Co Ltd* (1914) 30 TLR 350), and extends to the date of the contract even where the risk incepts previously (*Sillem* v *Thornton* (1874) 3 E & B 868).

The duty should be rigidly observed upon the renewal of the insurance and all material facts which have become relevant during the policy period disclosed, except for a life policy which is not, for obvious reasons, an agreement capable of renewal every year, so as to enable the insurer to reject a new proposal. So too does the duty of disclosure reattach when the insured proposes to modify the contract, but only insofar as such information specifically relates to the alteration. Facts which may have become material since the contract need not be disclosed if irrelevant to the modification, although such information should be disclosed upon renewal (*Lishman* v *Northern Maritime Insurance Co* (1875) LR 10 CP 179, 182; *Cory* v *Patton* (1874) LR 9 QB 577).

The post-contractual duty of good faith was considered by Hirst J in *Black King Shipping Corporation* v *Massie, The 'Litsion Pride'* [1985] 1 Lloyd's Rep 437, in which a warranty that information relating to the entry of the vessel into a war zone must be relayed as soon as practicable was held to be subject to a continuing duty of good faith, and the culpable failure of the insured to communicate the duration of increased risk and the nominated discharge port were held to be highly material in order to enable the insurers to fix the premium and to consider reinsurance. The insured must notify any relevant information available from time to time under such a notification procedure; even if only one notification is required, the insured must include within it all relevant information available to him at the time he gives it (ibid p 512). The general principle of utmost good faith also applies to claims, enabling the insurer to avoid the entire policy not only for a fraudulent claim but also for culpable misrepresentation or non-disclosure.

The definition of materiality for claims extends to 'Any fraudulent statement which would influence a prudent underwriter's decision to accept, reject or compromise a claim' (ibid p 513). The extra-contractual duty of good faith could also on particular facts become an implied contractual term in accordance with 'legal principle and sound policy' (ibid p 519).

The position therefore seems to be that the post-contractual duty of good faith applies between the insurer and insured, encompassing all aspects which could influence the insurer's judgment in his consideration of a claim or other circumstances such as increasing the premium under a 'held covered' clause, and breach of which entitles the insurer to avoid the policy in toto (so that any unsettled claims need not be paid and paid claims should be repaid).[10] The duty applies, in slip insurance, to each underwriter; a breach of good faith by the insured in his contract with the lead underwriter will entitle that underwriter to avoid, but not the following market without a breach for each individual underwriter.

OPEN COVERS, FLOATING POLICIES AND THE DUTY OF UTMOST GOOD FAITH

An open cover is an agreement between the insurer and the broker or insured by which the insurer agrees that he will accept any risks falling within specific categories. It is not itself a contract of insurance but an agreement by the insurer to provide insurance if certain conditions are met. Nevertheless, it is subject to the duty of good faith (*Glasgow Assurance Corporation Ltd v William Symondson & Co* (1911) 104 LT 254) and all relevant information must be provided

---

10 The British Columbia Court of Appeal considered a fraudulent claim in *Gore Mutual Insurance Co v Bifford* (1987) 45 DLR (4th) 763. The Court held that the effect of a fraudulent claim under common law was to allow the insurer to treat the policy as repudiated as from the date of the fraud, so that restitution of sums paid before the fraud need not be made.

by both parties prior to the conclusion of the agreement for open cover.

A floating policy is similar to an open cover and is an agreement between the same parties whereby the insurer will provide insurance for specified categories of risk, but it usually refers only to a particular subject matter of insurance, such as a cargo or warehoused goods, which change during the period of cover but remain within the same category, in contrast to the open cover which provides insurance for a selection of individual risks.

During an open cover the broker or insured will allocate a risk within the specified categories to the cover, and the contract of insurance comes into existence at that date. Provided that the relevant conditions of the cover are met, no further information needs to be provided by the broker or insured and the placing of the specific contract of insurance is not subject to a continuing duty of disclosure, although it is of course subject to a duty of good faith insofar as claims are involved (*The 'Litsion Pride'* [1985] 1 Lloyd's Rep 437). A floating policy is similar except that post-contractual declarations of information must be provided — in marine policies they must include the cargo, its value and the name of the vessel — but again, provided the subject matter falls within the relevant category, the insurance will incept at the date that such conditions are fulfilled. The declarations need not necessarily be made before the loss has occurred, and the duty of good faith continues in that the insured or broker must make honest declarations, although s 29(3) of the Marine Insurance Act 1906 provides that 'An omission or erroneous declaration may be rectified even after loss or arrival, provided the omission or declaration was made in good faith'.

It is arguable that the duty of utmost good faith under an open cover continues after formation of the contract of open cover, as Kerr J decided in *Berger & Light Diffusers Pty Ltd* v *Pollock* [1973] 2 Lloyd's Rep 442, on the basis that the open cover had been granted to the broker, thus preventing any enforcement of the cover by the insured. Although the broker was clearly the agent of the insured, the insured at the time of the contract was not in the contemplation of the broker so that he could not ratify the broker's act. He also held that the agreement was not obligatory upon the insurers so that they could refuse to accept risks if they so wished. The rule as to ratification is capable of criticism since it could be argued that the insured is one of a class of potential future insureds under the policy, and the case turns on its facts since an open cover without obligations upon the insurers is effectively meaningless. Where the agreement is obligatory the continuing duty of utmost good faith does not exist beyond the agreement of open cover since any increases in risk are immaterial, provided the subject matter of the insurance falls within the specified areas. In fact this decision was reached by the judge because he was faced with what he perceived to be a clear injustice, which he would have to uphold unless he could find some way around it. The fact that was not disclosed was plainly irrelevant to the underwriter, but it would have been material to a prudent underwriter. *Container Transport International Inc v Oceanus Mutual Underwriting Association (Bermuda) Ltd* [1984] 1 Lloyd's Rep 476 has since made the position clear.

Berger v *Pollock* was distinguished in *The 'La Pointe'* (1986) Lloyd's Rep 513, 522 (reversed on other grounds [1989] 2 Lloyd's Rep 536) on the basis that the open cover under consideration by Kerr J was very narrow, and matters had been reserved to the underwriters. It may therefore be of limited value. Indeed, Kerr LJ (as he was to become) commented in *Citadel Insurance Co v Atlantic Union Insurance Co SA* [1982] 2 Lloyd's Rep 543 that each declaration under an open cover did not give rise to a new duty of disclosure, but merely to a new obligation of the insurer.

ALTERATION OF THE RISK

The premium and terms of any insurance policy are calculated by the insurer upon his estimation of the probability at the date of the contract that the risk insured against is likely to occur. The insurer will therefore be most unhappy at any increase in the risk during the currency of the policy. Nevertheless, it is permissible for the insured to increase the risk after the date of inception provided there has been no breach of the duty of good faith and the facts as represented or warranted to the insurer at the date of the contract were correct or believed to be correct at that time.[11]

However, there is a distinction between an alteration of the risk and an alteration of the subject matter insured. In the latter case the identity of the subject matter does not constitute an alteration of risk but a substitution of a new risk, and the premise upon which the insurance was founded is nullified. Thus a failure to comply with any warranty relating to, or a description of, the subject matter at the date of the contract renders the contract void, irrespective of materiality (*Sillem* v *Thornton* (1854) 3 E&B 868). An alteration of the subject matter insured after inception will depend upon the terms

---

11 *Pim* v *Reid* 1843 6 Man & G 1; *Shaw* v *Robberds* 1837 6 AD & EL 75; *Tyson* v *Gurney* 1789 3 Term Rep 477.

of the policy: if there is no specific term or continuing warranty, it is for the insurer to show that the alteration has changed the subject matter of the insurance to something other than was agreed. In *Shaw* v *Robberds* (1837) 6 Ad & EL 75 the gratuitous drying of bark on one occasion by the insured who had cover only for corn-drying was held not to constitute an alteration of business because it was not permanent or habitual, although Denman CJ mentioned that payment to the insured could affect the position.

In fact the issue invariably concerns the construction of the policy. Where the policy contains no term at all as to any increase of risk, the risk can be increased provided the subject matter is not altered. Whether an express term as to the description of the subject matter may also impose an obligation not to increase the risk is a matter of construction of the term in question, which may be a represen-tation of an intention honestly held at the date of the contract (which will of course enable the insured to change his intention and alter the risk), or it may be a warranty which continues into the future so that the description must prevail throughout the cur-rency of the policy, or it may be a term merely delimiting the risk so that the insurer need not pay any claim made whilst the warranty is not complied with.

THE INSURER'S DUTY OF GOOD FAITH

It has never been doubted that the duty of good faith cuts both ways, but no case on point had gone to term until *Banque Keyser Ullman SA* v *Skandia* which became *La Banque Financiere de la Cite SA* v *Westgate Insurance Co Ltd* [1988] 2 Lloyd's Rep 513 in the Court of Appeal. The initial problem concerned the definition of materiality, which had to be framed on the basis of the Marine Insurance Act 1906, and which appeared to be identical with the insured's duty, but in reverse eg those circumstances which rather than increase the risk serve to decrease it. The Court of Appeal rejected the test of 'good faith and fair dealing', and held that the insurer need not disclose all those facts which might influence the insured, stating that a fact would be material if it was material to the risk sought to be covered or to the recoverability of a claim. This decision will no doubt generate considerable litigation as to its extent. For example, it is arguable that the insurer probably need not disclose to the insured the meaning of each clause in the policy under his duty of good faith, but should disclose any unusual term.

KNOWLEDGE IMPUTED TO THE PARTIES

The presence of a broker between the contracting parties has engendered litigation arising out of his failure to pass on information in his possession to one party which that party would wish to have. There is a rule in the law of agency that the knowledge of an agent is imputed to his principal, and vice versa, whether or not the knowledge is actually passed on. The principal will therefore be estopped from denying that he was aware of the information, provided that the broker obtains the information in his capacity as broker for the principal during the relevant transaction; it is his duty to inform the principal, and the insurer is not aware that the information has not been passed on to the principal. The status of the broker when he acquires the information is therefore important.

If the broker obtains information material to the risk whilst acting as agent for the insured, and prior to the conclusion of a contract of insurance, it is his duty under s 19 of the Marine Insurance Act 1906 to disclose it to the insurer (*Blackburn* v *Haslam* (1888) 21 QBD 144). Any failure to do so will enable the insurer to avoid, and the broker's reason for not disclosing it is irrelevant.

If the broker is acting for the insurer, any knowledge acquired by him within his authority to acquire such knowledge will be imputed to the insurer. Knowledge acquired prior to his employment by the insurer or in another capacity is irrelevant. In *Wilkinson* v *General Accident Fire & Life Assurance Corp Ltd* [1967] Lloyd's Rep 182 the agent acquired knowledge of the sale of a car as a car dealer and not as agent for the insurer, and therefore the knowledge could not be imputed to him as agent. However, an exception was outlined in *Taylor* v *Yorkshire Insurance Co Ltd* (1913) 2 IR 1, 21 where the agent's position and relationship with his principal enabled previously obtained information to be imputed where the agent was 'an agent to know'. A proper disclosure of all material facts by the insured to the broker will discharge his duty to the insurer (*Joel* v *Law Union & Crown Insurance Co* [1908] 2 KB 863) and the broker's actions thereafter will not affect the insured eg if the broker fails to communicate all material facts to the insurer.

There is, however, a divergence in the authorities as to the imputation of knowledge between the disclosure of material facts generally and the broker's completion of the proposal form. The first view proceeds on the basis that any inaccuracy in the answers on the proposal form is to be regarded in the light of any information acquired by the broker, which will therefore temper the insurer's position, since the knowledge acquired by the broker is imputed to the insurer. In *Bawden* v *London, Edinburgh, & Glasgow Assurance Co*

[1892] 2 QUB 534[12] the broker completed a proposal form for a one-eyed illiterate insured, which warranted that the insured had no physical deformity. The insured's luck changed for the worse; not only did he use a broker who failed to do his job properly, but he also lost the sight of his other eye. The insurer was held liable to him because the broker's knowledge was imputed to the insurer.

The other view is that the role of the broker changes from that of the insurer's agent to the insured's agent if the broker completes the proposal form, particularly since the proposal form may be the only document used by the insurer to evaluate the risk. The insured, by signing the proposal form, accepts and endorses the broker's answers, and his failure to verify them, whether he reads them or not, or even whether he has had an opportunity to read them eg by signing a blank form and leaving everything to the broker (*Parsons v Bignold* (1846) 15 LJ Ch 379; *Biggar v Rock Life Assurance Co* [1902] KB 516), should not prejudice the insurer. This view was accepted by the Court of Appeal in *Newsholme Bros v Road Transport & General Insurance Co* [1929] 2 KB 346[13] on the basis that the agent had completed the form at the insured's request and therefore must have acted as his agent, and that additional evidence should not be introduced to vary the terms of a written contract. Curiously, though, the Court emphasised the agent's lack of actual authority to complete proposal forms, ignoring the principles of apparent authority.

Nevertheless, the rule is that a person is bound by his signature, and everything to which that signature relates, and *Newsholme* therefore appears to govern this situation. The Court of Appeal did, however, in *Roberts v Plaisted* [1989] 2 Lloyd's Rep 341 criticise the position on the basis that a lay insured believes that all information placed in the broker's possession, one way or another, will be transmitted to the insurer, and does not regard the broker as his agent. Paragraph 14 of the IBRC Code of Conduct states that the broker must ensure that the proposed insured understands the importance of the accuracy of the answers on the proposal form.

---

12 *Bawden v London, Edinburgh & Glasgow Assurance Co* [1892] 2 QB 534; followed in *Thornton-Smith v Motor Union Insurance Co* (1913) 30 TLR 139; *Keeling v Pearl Assurance Co Ltd* [1923] All ER 307; *Ayrey v British Legal & United Provident Assurance Co* [1918] 1 KB 136.

13 *Newsholme Bros v Road Transport & General Insurance Co* [1929] 2 KB 346; followed in *Facer v Vehicle & General Insurance Co Ltd* [1965] 1 Lloyd's Rep 113 but subject to the adverse decision of *Stone v Reliance Mutual Insurance Co* [1972] 1 Lloyd's Rep 469.

The position is slightly different where the broker has properly completed the proposal form and no aspect is inaccurate, but further information should have been disclosed. If the broker has become aware of the additional information but has failed to communicate it to the insurer, the insurer will not be able to avoid, because the broker is the insurer's agent, provided the fault lies solely with the broker (*Woolcott* v *Excess Insurance Co and Miles, Smith, Anderson & Game Ltd* [1979] 2 Lloyd's Rep 210). An insured cannot rely on the broker's default if the proposal form states that the broker is his agent, although he could of course sue the broker for any defective performance.

Chapter 6

Formation of the contract

THE OFFER

The usual principles of contract law apply to the formation of any contract of insurance, the only major peculiarity being the imposition of an extra-contractual duty of good faith. An analysis of certain other distinguishing factors is necessary, however, to complete the picture, and in practice a strict and formal analysis is often crucial to determine the rights and obligations of the parties, particularly since the date of formation of the contract serves to conclude the pre-contractual duty of good faith.

Thus an offer must be made which contains all material terms, which is certain, intended to constitute an offer, and communicated to the other party who accepts it without alteration whilst it remains valid and capable of acceptance. Usually it is the insured who makes the offer, initially at least, either directly (where possible) or through his or the insurer's agent; and the offer is made on the insurer's proposal form. The offer is made on the insurer's usual terms, and these will bind both parties if the insurer accepts, unconditionally (*Browning v Provincial Insurance Co of Canada* (1873) LR 5 PC 263), even though the insured may not know their extent or nature (*Parker v SE Rly* (1877) 2 CPD 416, 422), they are not contained or referred to in the proposal form, or that any uncontentious term has not been brought to the insured's attention at any time (*Re Coleman's Depositories Ltd and Life & Health Assurance Association* [1907] 2 KB 798). In many cases there is little negotiation between the parties: the insurer will accept the offer if it appears to be a reasonable risk, or he may impose additional terms or restraints upon the insured. Negotiation will occur, however, where the value of the contract is high for both parties, or where the risk is of an unusual nature, and the position of the parties will change according to which made the last counter-offer. This can occur even when a proposal form is used if the insurer introduces an unusual term or a term which is not contained in his usual general terms, and which categorises him as offeror, making a new offer on different terms. Even charging a higher (or lower) premium may constitute a fresh offer, where the rate is outside the insurer's standard rate. The two most obvious examples of offers made by insurers are renewal notices and open covers/floating policies. The former is usually considered to be an offer to insure the same risk on the same terms, and as a new offer it is subject to the pre-contractual duty of good faith; the latter is a standing offer which each declaration accepts, giving rise to an independent contract in each case.

THE ACCEPTANCE

The contract is complete where the offer is accepted without amendment or condition. Such acceptance by an insurer may take the following forms.

Formal acceptance

Communication in any way is sufficient. If written and sent by post, the contract is formed at the date and place of posting. If telexed or telefaxed or mailed electronically so that communication is instantaneous, the date of formation is where and when it is received by the offeror (*Entores Ltd* v *Miles Far East Corporation* [1955] 1 Lloyd's Rep 511; *Brinkibon Ltd* v *Stahag Stahl* [1982] 1 Lloyd's Rep 217).

Acceptance of the premium

Receipt and retention of the premium by the insurer will raise the presumption that the contract is complete (*Canning* v *Farquhar* (1886) 16 QBD 727, 731). In the absence of a satisfactory explanation the insurer is liable to issue a policy (*Bhugwandass* v *Netherlands India Sea & Fire Insurance Co of Batavia* (1888) 14 App Cas 83), and in damages for any loss.

Issue of a policy

The insurer will crystallise the contract in a policy. At Lloyd's the Lloyd's broker will draw up the policy, as will a reinsurer in reinsurance contracts. The issue of a policy is prima facie confirmation by the insurer that all necessary steps and conditions to complete the contract have been fulfilled. Theoretically it is a binding crystal-lisation of the position, and should reflect all amendments agreed since the original offer. At Lloyd's the policy must be considered in conjunction with the slip, which is the primary evidence of the contract, and if the policy does not accurately reflect the slip, it is subject to rectification. Where the insurers have authorised a leading underwriter to agree a policy wording on their behalf, that wording sets out the rights and obligations of the parties and reflects their agreement (subject to any argument that the leading underwriter has exceeded his authority (*Barlee Marine Corporation* v *Mountain The 'Leegas'* [1987] 1 Lloyd's Rep 471). The slip cannot then be used as an aid to the construction of the policy in the absence of a claim for rectification, since to do so would be to defeat the object of the policy (*Youell* v *Bland Welch* Lloyd's List 23 February 1990).

If the insurer is on notice of any fact but proceeds to issue the policy without demur or protest, this action does not constitute a prima facie election to be bound (even though it is a positive act), but it may create an estoppel which can be relied on by the insured, since he will effectively have been deprived of the opportunity to obtain alternative insurance (*Morrison* v *Universal Marine Insurance Co* (1873) LR 8 Exch 197, 205). A policy made under seal need not be delivered to the insured to complete the contract; its execution is enough and further communication to the insured is unnecessary (*Roberts* v *Security Company Ltd* [1897] 1 QB 111).

Conduct of the insurer

Where such conduct shows that the insurer has completed the contract, a binding contract exists, rendering the insured liable for premium and the insurer liable for loss, and also subject to an obligation to issue a policy and accept any premium.

Can silence be deemed acceptance?

Silence by the insurer cannot constitute an acceptance of the insured's offer, since silence clearly does not fulfil the requirement as to communication of acceptance. Silence can, however, perfect a contract. In *Rust* v *Abbey Life Assurance Co Ltd* [1979] 2 Lloyd's Rep 334 the insured retained a life policy for seven months before disput-ing that she was bound by it. The Court of Appeal found that her offer had been accepted by the insurer's issue of the policy, but considered that the issue of a policy could constitute an offer which was accepted by the insured's conduct after its receipt. Where the insured's conduct manifests an intention not to be bound, presumably within a reasonable time so as not to constitute deemed acceptance by laches, or the insurance is not relied on eg by attempting to obtain alternative insurance, then silence does not bind the insured (*Taylor* v *Allon* [1966] 1 QB 304).

Suspensory clauses

Such clauses can be divided into two types: those suspending the commencement of the risk, and those which suspend the contract itself. The former usually require the insured to fulfil a condition, such as placing a vessel at a specified port, or payment of the premium. In the absence of a warranty requiring premium to be paid within a specified time, premium must be tendered within a reasonable time (*Kirby* v *Cosindit SpA* [1969] 1 Lloyd's Rep 75, 80), and even after loss, so as to circumvent any objection by the insurer. In the absence of payment a recital in the policy that premium has been paid may prevent the insurer from relying on a suspensory clause (*Roberts* v *Security Co Ltd*). There is also a possibility that the issue of a policy overrides the requirement that premium be paid, on the basis that it is waived. Conversely, acceptance of premium will override a requirement that a policy be issued before the contract is binding, and the insured could compel the insurer to issue the relevant policy by specific performance.

A clause suspending the contract itself ensures that no contract exists prior to the satisfaction of that clause. The insurer will not be liable for any loss occurring before such satisfaction. The distinction between these categories will depend in each case upon the wording used.

THE COVER NOTE

The proposal form will be considered by the insurer and further information required or terms imposed before any contract of insurance is concluded. This process takes time. Temporary insurance may therefore be issued to the insured in the form of a cover note, which provides fully effective cover from the date of application, and is particularly useful in cases of compulsory insurance, such as motor. In some forms of insurance, however, such as marine (and many forms of non-marine), a broker's cover note has no contractual effect and is no more than a representation by the broker that he has obtained cover on certain terms. If he has not, he will be liable to the insured.

Doctrine of ostensible authority

Although the broker is the agent of the insured, he may be authorised to grant temporary cover on behalf of the insurer if he obtains
the insured's consent to his dual agency and a conflict of interest
does not (and cannot) exist. The extent of such authority is sometimes called into dispute. Where the broker has actual authority, no
problem will exist. Where the broker is held out to be properly
authorised, or is of a class whose usual authority includes the issue
of temporary cover, the doctrine of ostensible authority will serve
to make the insurer liable for loss. Entrusting an agent with blank
cover notes will confer on him implied or ostensible authority, even
though the insurer may have discontinued that area of business
from its operations (*Mackie* v *European Assurance Society* (1869) 21 LT
102). However, an agent may be authorised in the absence of cover
notes where he has previously bound insurers by temporary contracts made orally with their consent, which had subsequently been
ratified. The position of an insurance broker is stronger. In *Stockton*
v *Mason* [1978] 2 Lloyd's Rep 430 Diplock LJ held that any broker
with a pre-existing arrangement to act as an agent for an insurer is
impliedly authorised to issue cover notes. Although the broker may
issue the cover note as a binding contract, he is not in any way
liable upon it unless he is not properly authorised so that the insurer
is not bound, in which case he will be liable to the insured for
breach of warranty of authority.

The terms of the temporary contract of insurance

No formal document is required; the contract may be made orally in
informal, colloquial language (*Stockton* v *Mason*). Usually the insurer
impresses his usual terms into the contract by so providing on the
cover note, or by issuing the cover note after completion of a proposal form which makes the position clear, but it is generally
assumed that the contract contains the insurer's standard terms,
provided they are reasonably available to the insured and are not
unusual or inappropriate.

Where the terms of the temporary cover note have not been
specified in detail or at all, the insured may have a problem in
complying with his obligations under the contract. This situation
can be demonstrated in the area of claims, particularly in liability
policies which require an assessment of the position by the insured
as to possible liability, and contain specific requirements as to notification. In *Re Coleman's Depositories Ltd Life & Health Assurance Associ-*

ation [1907] 2 KB 798 a company completed a proposal form for employer's liability insurance on 28 December, and contemporaneously received a cover note (without conditions). A policy was issued on 3 January, to run from 1 January, and delivered to the insured on 9 January. An employee was injured on 2 January but the injury did not appear to be serious. Notice was given to insurers on 14 March, by which date the illness clearly was serious: the employee died on 15 March. The insurer refused to pay on the grounds of failure to comply with the immediate notification provision. Contrary to apparently accepted law a majority Court of Appeal held the insurer liable since the condition was not precedent to liability, and the insured could not have complied with it at the relevant time since he was then unaware that it existed. The decision is fair (to the insured) but odd, its main hurdle being the accepted practice that the insured's application is for a contract on the insurer's usual terms.[1] This can easily be shown to be applicable to the facts of this case by asking what information the insurer would have provided to the insured had he required details of the terms of the temporary and intended future cover when the cover note was issued, or prior to the accident.

One explanation is perhaps that the insured should not be bound by terms requiring positive action on his part until he is capable of complying with them.[2] But even this would have required notice immediately after receipt of the policy on 9 January. Another is that the insurer's duty of good faith required him to disclose any unusual[3] material or other term which requires action by the insured, particularly since it is the insurer who drafts them and

---

1 Earlier authorities such as *Adie & Sons* v *Insurance Corporation Ltd* (1898) 14 TLR 544 and *General Accident Insurance Corp* v *Cronk* (1901) 17 TLR 233 were not cited to the court, but have since been approved by the Court of Appeal in *Rust* v *Abbey Life Assurance Co Ltd* [1979] 2 Lloyd's Rep 334 at 339: 'It is clear that in ordinary insurance cases a policy may become a binding contract between an insured and insurers even though the insured has not seen or expressly assented to all the detailed terms of the policy, provided always that such terms are the usual terms of the insurers'.

2 This will also dispose of the implied point to the same effect as *Re Coleman* in *Mayne Nickless* v *Pegler* (1974) 1 NSWLR 228 where a binding contract was concluded before the insured became aware of its terms.

3 *Charlesworth* v *Faber* (1900) 5 Comm Cas 408 which held that a reinsurance policy was not invalidated by the non-disclosure of a clause in the primary insurance policy because that clause was usual. The claim was contested on the basis that the (re)insured should have disclosed any unusual clause to the reinsurer, and there is no reason why this principle should not apply to insurance.

knows their effect. Merely informing the insured on the cover note which refers to the insurer's (unspecified) general conditions, or states that they may be inspected at the insurer's offices, hardly constitutes adequate disclosure of a material term. The only proviso to this is that the broker may already be aware of any such terms and that such knowledge will be imputed to the insured, by the broker as his agent. The case can, however, effectively be disregarded as insurers have since always stipulated that the temporary cover is on their usual terms, provided these terms are readily available.

The duty of good faith

There is no logical reason why the duty of good faith should not apply to temporary contracts of insurance. There is, however, a conceptual problem. A cover note constitutes a separate contract which is not considered by the insurer himself, although it will be read by the broker acting as the insurer's agent. Whether or not the relevant details are brought constructively to the attention of the insurer, the fact is that the broker will not evaluate the risk in detail, but will simply charge according to a standard tariff. Thus the question of materiality does not arise until the proposal form is evaluated by the insurer, after the contract has been completed. So how can an insured comply? The answer may be that all relevant details must be brought to the broker's attention, as agent for the insurer. The Australian case of *Mayne Nickless* v *Pegler* (1974) 1 NSWLR 228 supports the view that the duty of utmost good faith applies. The insured bought a car and the vendor simultaneously arranged insurance by telephone. The insured later received a cover note dated for the day of purchase and incorporating the insurer's usual terms. The insured had failed to disclose previous losses on the proposal form and the insurer successfully avoided the contract on the basis of a breach of good faith. The court made no distinction between temporary and final contracts of insurance.

Duration of the cover note

The temporary cover will expire after a specific period, or when the policy is issued or cover refused, or when revoked. The defined period will be construed exactly, and *contra proferentem* in case of doubt (*Cartwright* v *MacCormack* [1963] 1 WLR 18). The policy will replace the cover note but only if the insurer wishes to contract; the date of the insurance will usually be retroactive to the inception of the insurance in the cover note, but the cover note will remain in force until the policy is issued so that any claim arising in the period prior to its issue will be determined according to the terms of the cover note.

Where the cover note imposes an additional duty on the insurer of specifically rejecting the proposal, the insurer must actually ensure that the insured is so informed and the cover continues until he has been informed (*Hawke* v *Niagara District Mutual Fire Insurance Co* (1876) 23 Grant 139). An extra requirement of return of premium similarly retains the cover in force until compliance, although some premium may be kept by the insurer in respect of the insurance benefit derived by the insured, depending on the wording (*Mackie* v *European Assurance Society* (1869) 21 LT 102, 105).

THE POLICY

Commencement

The fact that a policy has been issued does not automatically ensure that the risk has commenced, since the inception of the risk may be expressed not to commence until the premium is paid, or a particular time and date, or until a particular state of facts has come into being, such as a vessel arriving at a specific port, or as to the condition of the subject matter of the insurance. The insurer will therefore not be liable for any loss or damage prior to the fulfilment of the requirements of the policy.

The policy may be backdated in order to replace a cover note. A loss arising during the tenure of the cover note will prima facie be governed by its terms, rather than those of the policy, although there is no reason why the parties cannot seek to enforce their subsequent agreement, which they have specifically retrodated to cover the period of the cover note.

Duration

Most policies state precisely the period of cover granted to the insured, specifying the relevant times and dates. In the absence of absolute clarity, such as a provision that the insurance run from noon on 1 January to noon on 31 December, the courts apply the rule that the first day is excluded from cover, but the last day is included, until midnight (*Cartwright* v *McCormack* [1963] 1 WLR 11). Where the policy states that the duration is for a specific period, the words 'beginning with' ensure that the first day is included.

Termination

If the duration of the insurance is specified in the policy, the insurance ends at that intended date. A life policy continues whilst premium is paid, and the insurer cannot terminate during its currency. The parties may agree, however, to terminate any insurance contract by consent, provided they do so clearly. The policy may even contain a clause entitling the insurer to cancel the policy unilaterally during the policy period, the extent of such a power being determined by the wording. Thus an absolute power will enable the insurer to disregard his obligations by cancelling when he perceives that the loss insured may occur (*Sun Fire Office* v *Hart* (1889) 14 App Cas 98), which tends to vitiate the concept of insurance. In fact such absolute clauses are not in current use, although versions do exist which provide the insurer with the right to cancel in limited circumstances. The insurer must notify the insured of his decision, and return the premium for the period not to be covered (*Bamberger* v *Commercial Credit Mutual Assurance Co* (1855) 15 CB 676).

The policy will be terminated where the insurer goes into liquidation, leaving the insured with the right to prove in the liquidation for the balance of his premium and for any loss that has occurred. In *Re Cavalier Insurance Co Ltd* [1989] 2 Lloyd's Rep 430 the insured was able only to recover his premiums because the insurer was not authorised to write that class of insurance.

A breach of warranty entitles the insurer to avoid from the date of the breach even if it is immaterial to the risk. Thus a warranty as to the condition of the subject matter at the date of the contract may render it void ab initio, whilst a breach of a continuing warranty will be void when it occurs, which may be some time into the policy period. Such a later breach renders the insurance voidable at the insurer's option.

A breach of condition does not necessarily confer such a right, unless it is a condition precedent to the policy, in which case the risk would not have run. Where the condition is precedent to liability, such as notification within a fixed time, then the policy remains valid but unenforceable by the insured in respect of any claim which fails to comply with that term. A later loss which complies can therefore be enforced.

Breach of a condition subsequent will result in the entitlement of the insurer to avoid the policy from the date of the breach, unless the wording allows the policy to become reinstated when the condition is satisfied. Any claim arising before the breach can be enforced (*Bamberger* v *Commercial Credit Mutual Assurance Co* (1855) 15 CB 676).

Renewal

Unless otherwise agreed the contract ends at the expiry of the specified period, unless determined earlier, or extended (which is not a renewal but is a variation of a contractual term). Any later contract will therefore be a new contract, attracting a new duty of disclosure for satisfaction by the insured, which the broker should draw to the insured's attention. Thus a fact such as an increase in risk after the inception of the expiring policy must be disclosed prior to the conclusion of the new policy.

The contract usually provides for renewal:

(a) upon the agreement of the parties;
(b) at the option of the insured;
(c) upon a withdrawal of notice of cancellation by the underwriter at the anniversary date ('NCAD');
(d) in the absence of notification by one party that he does not wish to renew; or
(e) it may be silent.

Agreement of the parties

An agreement must by definition be mutual, so that either party can refuse to renew. A renewal notice from the insurer constitutes an offer to renew, which may be accepted by the insured tendering the renewal premium. Some form of positive action appears to be required by both parties, but the usual rules of contract law apply, so that an insured who rejects the insurer's offer on a higher premium cannot later remedy the position by tendering that increased premium, even during the days of grace (*Salvin* v *James* (1805) 6 East 571). The renewal is considered to be a new contract and all material facts must therefore be disclosed (*Pim* v *Reid* (1843) 6 M & G 1). Representations made prior to the original contract are deemed repeated unless altered (*Re Wilson & Scottish Insurance Corporation* [1920] 2 Ch 28).

Absolute right to renew

An absolute right to renew entitles the insured to renew in perpetuity. However, the insurer usually prevents such longevity by judicious wording in the policy so that the right is construed as a standing offer made by the insurer which can be withdrawn by him before its acceptance by the insured. The insurer must notify the insured (usually on reasonable notice) of his intention to determine the policy at the end of the current period (*Salvin* v *James* (1805) G East 571).

Automatic cancellation of a policy

The policy may be limited to the period stated on the slip or wording by a provision stating that notice of cancellation is automatically given at the anniversary date (NCAD), and the policy will expire unless otherwise agreed. This clause is used when the insurer requires the annual provision of contract statistics by the broker, together with an argument from the broker to satisfy him that cover should be continued.

Automatic continuation of a policy

The policy may continue automatically unless either party notifies the other of his intention to terminate their agreement. Whether this option gives rise to a perpetual cycle of renewals will depend on the wording; the contract may only be renewable for a specified number of times (*Salvin* v *James* (see above)).

Silence in regard to renewing a policy

Silence as to renewal gives rise to a new contract since there is no provision for continuing the old policy. The parties can renegotiate all terms at will.

Methods of renewal

The sending of a renewal notice by an insurer constitutes an offer to renew on the terms of the notice. Payment of the premium constitutes an acceptance. Payment of the premium in the absence of any indication or offer from the insurer is an offer made by the insured.

Duty of the broker to warn insured of the renewal

The relationship of the broker to the insured will determine his duty to warn the insured of the renewal. *Cherry* v *Allied Insurance Brokers* [1978] 1 Lloyd's Rep 274 indicates that the broker is under a duty to notify the insured as to renewal dates, and *Fraser* v *B Furman (Productions) Ltd* [1967] 2 Lloyd's Rep 1 and *Dunbar* v *AB Painters Ltd* [1986] 2 Lloyd's Rep 38 indicate that a broker should monitor the insured's insurance requirements continuously, ensuring that they are adequate and up to date, perhaps as part of the recognised 'professional' status that now lies upon insurance brokers. Certainly professional indemnity insurers have indemnified brokers who have overlooked renewals, or more particularly who are unable to prove that they have discharged their duty of care to their insured (eg *United Marketing Company* v *Hasham Kara* [1963] 1 Lloyd's Rep 331, in which the brokers were held liable for failing to renew, having apparently agreed to do so by their previous conduct). Further, the broker should take the opportunity at renewal of updating all insurances, or at least warning the insured that he may not be properly insured. Finally, if the renewal has not been effected in substantially similar terms to the expiring insurance, the broker must inform the insured (*Mint Security Ltd* v *Blair* [1982] 1 Lloyd's Rep 188).

Rectification

Methods of rectification
The parties may agree to rectify the policy to reflect the contract. In the absence of such agreement an application must be made to the court, which will presume that the policy is accurate until proven otherwise. The party seeking to rectify must show that an agreement was concluded in terms differing from those contained in the policy. If the court is unable to establish an agreement between the parties either on the policy or on the alternative terms, so that they are at cross-purposes, it will declare that neither party is bound because the mistake operates to negative consent to the contract. The court may refer to any relevant document to assist it in determining the terms of the agreement, such as the proposal form or slip, correspondence or evidence of representations and negotiations between the parties or their agents. Section 89 of the Marine Insurance Act 1906 specifically provides for the availability of the cover note or slip in any legal proceeding involving the policy.

Effect of policy containing terms not agreed
The parties are bound by the original agreement which is contained in and evidenced by the slip, and the delivery of a 'wrong' policy does not affect their rights or obligations, unless it is relied upon or affirmed. The insurer (or Lloyd's broker) is responsible for issuing the correct policy, and cannot obviate any agreed liability by producing a document which fails to reflect that agreement (*Griffiths* v *Fleming* [1909] 1 KB 805) unless the parties have failed to reach a consensus *ad idem*, so that a contract never existed. In *Pindos Shipping Corporation* v *Frederick Charles Raven* [1983] 2 Lloyd's Rep 449 a claim for rectification of the slip and the policy failed because the parties had not reached a consensus over a warranty. If the insured decides not to have the policy rectified and sues on it without demur, he affirms that the policy reflects the contract and cannot later rely on the original agreement, or apply for rectification (*Baker*

v *Yorkshire Fire & Life Assurance Co* [1892] 1 QB 144). However, until rectification the policy is considered to contain the contract. A positive step by the insured will constitute a waiver of his rights to amend the policy and an election to be bound, provided he is aware of all relevant facts. Unreasonable delay may estop him from rectifying the policy as long as he was aware of any defect in the policy. A requirement that the insured notify the insurer of any inaccuracy may also create an estoppel, so that he is later unable to rectify (*Rust* v *Abbey Life Assurance Co* [1979] 2 Lloyd's Rep 334).

JURISDICTION

Insurance is a multi-national affair. In the absence of clear agreement this may give rise to problems of jurisdiction. The contract of agency is governed by the law of the country in which the contract is made; if concluded in different countries the court will examine the contract and consider its essential features, and particularly where it is to be effected, before nominating its proper law.

Other factors to be taken into account in deciding the proper law include the residence or domicile of the parties, any inference that can be drawn as to the intention of the parties (*Armadora Occidental SA* v *Horace Mann Insurance Co* [1972] 2 Lloyd's Rep 406), such as the state of development of insurance law in any alternative forum (*Amin Rasheed Shipping Corporation* v *Kuwait Insurance Co* [1983] 2 Lloyd's Rep 365), where the contract was negotiated and signed, whether the contract contains a clear choice of forum clause (*Atlantic Underwriting Agencies Ltd* v *Compagnia di Assicurazione di Milano SPA* [1979] 2 Lloyd's Rep 240), where the books and accounts were kept, where the calculation of balances and resulting remittances were made, with which system of law (or commercial market) the obligations in question have their closest and most real connection, and where the centre of gravity of the contract is located (*Citadel Insurance Co* v *Atlantic Union Insurance Co SA* [1982] 2 Lloyd's Rep 543; *Berisford* v *New Hampshire Insurance Co* [1990] 1 Lloyd's Rep 454).

If one party then requests that the action be stayed because there is an alternative forum in which to hear the action, the English court will consider the place of the incident giving rise to the dispute, and the availability of factual and expert witnesses and documentation and other general advantages of efficiency accruing to the parties in litigating in England ie it will apply the doctrine of *forum non conveniens*. It will identify the most suitable forum for the interests of the parties and for the ends of justice (*Spiliada Maritime Corporation* v *Cansulex Ltd* [1987] 1 Lloyd's Rep 1), except in connection with parties domiciled in countries subject to the Civil Jurisdiction and Judgments Act 1982 which enacts the Brussels Convention 1978.

A written agreement involving one or more such domiciliaries specifying a choice of law or forum must be upheld by the Court. Otherwise art 2 specifies that:

persons domiciled in a Contracting State shall, whatever their nationality, be sued in the courts of that State.

Articles 7–12A deal with jurisdiction in insurance matters, but are not applicable to reinsurance (*Arkwright Mutual Insurance Co* v *Bryanstone Insurance Co Ltd* [1990] *Financial Times* 26 February 1990). Article 8 provides that:-

an insurer domiciled in a Contracting State may be sued:
(1) In the courts of the State where he is domiciled, or
(2) In another Contracting State, in the courts of the place where the policyholder is domiciled, or
(3) If he is a co-insurer, in the courts of a Contracting State in which proceedings are brought against the leading insurer.

Article 8 goes on to extend the meaning of 'domicile' by deeming a party to be domiciled in a country if the dispute in question arises from the operations of its 'branch, agency or other establishment' in that country. In *Berisford* v *New Hampshire Insurance Company* [1989] 1 Lloyd's Rep 454 Hobhouse J applied art 8 to a contract of insurance issued by the London branch of an insurer incorporated and domiciled in New Hampshire, USA, to deem the insurer domiciled in the United Kingdom. However, the insured, who wanted to sue in the UK, was not domiciled in the UK (or any convention country) and therefore could not rely upon art 8 to sue in the place of his domicile. Hobhouse J held that art 2 required his court to accept exclusive jurisdiction owing to the defendant insurer's deemed domicile in the UK.

Articles 9 and 10 deal with liability insurance and render the insurer capable of being sued in the courts of the place where the harmful event occurred, or being joined in proceedings which the injured party has brought against the insured. The plaintiff has the option of suing in the place where the damage occurred or the place of the event giving rise to that damage.

Article 11 entitles an insurer to bring proceedings only in the courts of the contracting state in which the defendant is domiciled, irrespective of whether he is the policyholder, insured or a beneficiary.

An English domiciled broker who has acted as an insurance

broker only, in England, should be subject to English law and jurisdiction whether he has had the foresight so to specify before-hand in the contract of agency, or under the proper law of the contract, or under the doctrine of *forum non conveniens*, or under art 2. Nevertheless, the Act has provided more jurisdictional options than had previously been the case, in addition to a considerable degree of complexity, and it is clear that the broker could now be sued in several countries depending on the domicile of the parties. Article 21 provides that the court first seised of any litigation will retain jurisdiction in preference to later proceedings elsewhere, and thus a broker wishing to have a dispute heard in London should not hesitate to issue proceedings promptly.

Chapter 7

The classification of terms in a contract of insurance

The obligations of the parties are contained in the contract. Some of those obligations will be more important than others, a breach of which will affect the rights and liabilities of the parties more radically. The classification of the contract terms is therefore important to determine the effect of a breach of any term.

The terms can broadly be divided into three categories:

(a) conditions;
(b) warranties;
(c) stipulations, or clauses delimiting the risk.

CONDITIONS

Any term may be classified as a condition if the parties so intend, and that intention is clearly shown. The insurers usually expressly specify that a term is to have the effect of a condition, the satisfaction of which is necessary to their liability. These conditions are categorised as follows.

Conditions precedent to the validity of the policy, or to the attachment of risk

These conditions must be fulfilled before the contract itself can exist and, if not fulfilled, the contract fails to incept so that the insurer cannot be on risk and the insured is entitled to return of his premium in full for failure of consideration. The insurance is void *ab initio*. These typically involve payment of premium, truth of statements during negotiations, and that the item insured is properly decribed.

Conditions precedent to the liability of the insurer

These do not affect the validity of the contract but rather define areas of compliance by the insured, necessary to the insurer's liability. Usually they relate to the conduct of the insured after a loss, particularly as to the claims process. Thus compliance with a requirement for notification within a specified time is necessary before the insurer can become liable. The distinction between this form of condition and a condition precedent to the validity of the policy, or to the attachment of risk, is that the policy remains in existence whether or not the condition has been discharged; the insured will not, however, be able to claim for the particular loss, although he will be able to claim for later losses if the condition is properly satisfied.

Conditions subsequent to the liability of the insurer

These conditions are agreed to be necessary for the contract to continue in force and any breach avoids the contract from the date of the breach. The insurer, however, remains liable for loss to the date of breach and may only have a right to claim damages for breach if the wording is imprecise. Thus a failure to comply with a condition will not legally incapacitate the insured if the condition is a mere condition, and only entitles the insurer to damages, if the insurer can show loss or damage. Such conditions may relate to alteration in risk, additional insurance or alienation of insurable interest.

Defining the term condition

A condition is a condition if it is so capable of determination by the court from a construction of the document in which it is contained, using the ordinary rules of construction. Subjective evidence of the intention of the parties is not relevant, since such intention is to be construed from the words specifically selected to express it, although the court will seek to enforce what it believes to be their intention.

The two commonest methods of conceiving a condition are to specify the consequences of a breach of that term, or to specify in clear language that compliance with that term is precedent to the validity of the contract or to liability.

Any wording which provides for an avoidance of the policy or a preclusion of liability in the absence of compliance will be a condition precedent (*Stoneham* v *Ocean Railway & General Accident Insurance Co* (1887) 19 QBD 237; *Re Coleman's Depositories Ltd & Life & Health Assurance Association* (1907) 2 KB 798. No specified form of words is necessary provided the intention is clear, and it is the insurer's duty to make it clear if he intends to rely on it (*London Guarantie* v *Fearnley* (1880) 43 LT 390).[1] Curiously the nomination of any clause as a condition precedent is not necessarily conclusive (*Stoneham* v *Ocean Railway & General Accident Insurance Co* (1887) 19 QBD 237), and may be ousted if it is not capable of being treated as a condition precedent as happened in *Re Bradley and Essex and Suffolk Accident Indemnity Society* (1912) 1 KB 415. This is surprising because 'It is competent to the contracting parties, if both agree to it and sufficiently express their intention so to agree, to make the actual existence of anything a condition precedent to the inception of any contract; and if they do so the non-existence of that thing is a good defence. And it is not of any importance whether the existence of that thing was or was not material; the parties would not have made it a part of the contract if they had not thought it material, and they have a right to determine for themselves what they shall deem material' (*Thomson* v *Weems* (1884) 9 App Cas 971).

Re Bradley remains valid law but may be capable of being distinguished, since the disputed condition was one of several stated to be precedent by a heading, and may not apply to a clause individually expressed to be a condition precedent. This may be taken to extremes by individually expressing each term to be precedent, but the court may treat such stipulations as semantics rather than specifically agreed conditions precedent (*London Guarantie* v *Fearnley* (1880) 43 LT 390). The term must bite at the root of the contract. Nevertheless, some insurers continue to express all clauses as conditions precedent (eg *Aluminium Wire and Cable Co Ltd* v *Allstate Insurance Co* [1985] 2 Lloyd's Rep 280).

WARRANTIES

A warranty in a contract of insurance is equivalent to a condition in other contracts. Warranties outside insurance are effectively collateral to the main contract, breach of which give rise only to a right to damages; in insurance contracts any breach gives rise to a right to repudiate liability from the date of the breach.

---

1 *Re Bradley* comments on this case at [1912] 1 KB 427, 428 and 433. See also *The 'Litsion Pride'* [1985] 1 Lloyd's Rep 437, 469.

Section 33(1) of the Marine Insurance Act 1906 defines a warranty as something 'by which the assured undertakes that some particular thing shall or shall not be done, or that some condition shall be fulfilled, or whereby he affirms or negatives the existence of a particular state of facts.'

Warranties can therefore be divided into present warranties, which refer to circumstances in force at the time the warranty is made, and future warranties, which continue throughout the period of insurance. The distinction is often fine, but nevertheless important.

A warranty in non-marine insurance must be express. In marine insurance ss 36–41 of the Marine Insurance Act 1906 imply certain warranties into every contract, but otherwise marine warranties must also be express. Under s 35(2) of the Marine Insurance Act 1906 marine warranties must be incorporated into the policy either by inclusion in the policy itself or by incorporating another document by reference (s 35(2) of the Marine Insurance Act 1906), but otherwise a warranty may be contained in an independent document. It can even be oral, and need not be referred to in the policy, provided it does not contradict any express term of the policy, or fall foul of the parol evidence rule (*Anglo-Californian Bank Ltd* v *London and Provincial Marine & General Insurance Co (Ltd)* (1904) 20 TLR 665). No specific wording is necessary to create or incorporate a warranty provided the intention is clear; the courts will look at the body of the term rather than its description, and will describe the term in another way if it is incapable of construction as a warranty (*De Maurier (Jewels) Ltd* v *Bastion Insurance Co* [1967] 2 Lloyd's Rep 550).

The usual method by which insurers infuse a term with the status of a warranty is to obtain a signed declaration on the proposal form to the effect that the information contained in the proposal is warranted correct. This deletes any requirement of materiality or reliance by the insurer on the truth of the representation, since s 33(3) of the Marine Insurance Act 1906 states that strict compliance with every warranty is necessary to render the insurer liable. Thus any breach of warranty entitles the insurer to refute liability, even though the breach is immaterial to and unconnected with the loss, and even though the breach actually benefits the insurer eg by diminishing the risk (*Dawsons Ltd* v *Bonnin* [1922] 2 AC 413). Adding possible insult to injury, s 34(2) provides that a temporary breach renders the contract voidable, even though remedied prior to any loss.

However, the insured's duty extends no further than strict compliance, and warranties are sometimes construed by the courts to produce the effect specifically required to discharge them, even though the real effect may be to nullify the result intended. Thus a warranty that mills would be worked by day only was not held to be broken by the working of part only of the mills at night (*Mayall* v *Mitford* (1837) 6 A & E 670).

The varieties of warranty

The distinction between the types of warranty will be important in determining the date of breach, and therefore the effect of the breach on the contract. It is often fine and some legal decisions may appear somewhat arbitrary.

Present warranties

Such a warranty represents that a particular state of affairs exists at the date the warranty is made. If it changes prior to formation of the contract the insured is obliged to inform the insurer.

In many cases this will be capable of objective proof eg where a vehicle was garaged, or its condition.

Problems arise where the warranty is phrased so as to be capable of indicating an element of futurity. The insurer would benefit from such a construction because the insurance can be avoided from the date of breach. A present warranty as to the intention of the insured can later be changed by the insured with no ill effect; if it is a future warranty then such change will be a breach. Statements appearing to ensure that a warranty continues must therefore be carefully phrased. Thus in *Woolfall & Rimmer* v *Moyle* [1942] 1 KB 66 an insured who confirmed that the machinery was properly guarded and in good condition was not warranting that this state would enure throughout the contract. Lord Greene MR did not consider that the insurer had appropriately phrased the wording to extend any element of futurity into the answer, which would have been easy to do had the insurer so intended, and that the value of the question to the insurer was that it enabled them to ascertain the type of person with whom they were dealing. Breach of a present warranty (in that the situation warranted did not exist at the date of formation of the contract) entitles the insurer to avoid *ab initio*, so that the insured is entitled to a return of premium.

Future warranties

Such a warranty requires the insured to comply with it during the policy period and the insurer is not liable after breach, although he remains liable up to the breach. A representation or intention evinced by the insured cannot amount to a future warranty without clear wording. Any ambiguity will be construed in favour of the insured.

These two types of warranty can also be sub-divided into warranties of fact and warranties of opinion. Any breach of a warranty of fact is capable of determining the insurance, even though the insured was not at fault or even aware of the breach. A warranty of opinion may prove to be incorrect, but produces no adverse consequence for the insured if it was honestly held. The distinction is again fine, which allows the court some latitude in its decisions, according to the merits of the case rather than adherence to firm rules which could produce injustice. The court may thus interpret apparently subjective answers which depend on the opinion of the insured not as warranties of opinion but as statements of fact, or refuse to accept subjective statements which simply could not be justified on the facts (which in reality imposes an objective standard). A warranty that the insured knows no adverse facts is tempered by its interpretation as including only those facts known to be adverse by a reasonable man, and not those facts which would not be recognised by the reasonable man as adverse but which turn out to be so (*Kelsall v Allstate Insurance Co Ltd* (1987) *The Times* 20 March 1987). In *Thompson v Weems* (1884) 9 App Cas 671 the affirmative response to a question as to whether the insured was and had always been temperate was held to be a warranty of fact, which was broken by the alcohol related death of the insured.

Clauses delimiting the risk

The courts have expressed their dislike of the rule that a warranty must be strictly satisfied to the cost of the insured, particularly where the warranty broken is immaterial to the loss that occurred. The Law Commission have also made known their dissatisfaction, in their Report No 104 in October 1980 (CMND 8064). The anticipated Insurance Law Reform Bill appendixed to the Report did not materialise and on occasion the courts have therefore construed potential warranties as clauses describing or delimiting the risk which have the effect of removing the insurer from liability whilst the term is not discharged, rather than enabling him to terminate the contract. Section 34(2) of the Marine Insurance Act 1906 is also thereby emasculated because the risk re-attaches as soon as the term is complied with.

Thus in *Farr v Motor Traders Mutual Insurance Society* [1920] 3 KB 669 it was warranted that two taxis would be driven for one shift only in 24 hours. Repairs to one taxi necessitated a double shift for the other taxi. The warranty was then complied with. The insurers were held liable for a later accident because the term merely described the risk, although they would not have been liable for any loss or damage which occurred during any double shift.

Similarly the Court of Appeal held in *Roberts v Anglo-Saxon Insurance Co* (1927) 27 Ll L Rep 313 that a term specifying that the insured vehicle would only be used for commercial travelling was not a warranty, though the insured could not recover for any loss incurred during domestic use. In *Provincial Insurance Co Ltd v Morgan* [1933] AC 240 Buckmaster and Blanesburgh LJJ refused to construe a term specifying that a lorry would only be used for carrying coal as a warranty. Thus carrying timber at any time would not entitle the insurer to repudiate liability, although any loss which occurred while timber was carried would obviously not be covered. Russell and Wright LJJ took the view that the term simply specified the occasions upon which the insurer would be on risk.

In *De Maurier (Jewels) Ltd v Bastion Insurance Co* [1967] 2 Lloyd's Rep 550 a term which 'Warranted road vehicles fitted with locks and alarm systems approved by underwriters and in operation,' entitled the insurer to come off risk during any period of non-compliance. The rationale for this decision and that of *Farr v Motor Traders Mutual* appears to be that the wording did not clearly extend the term through the policy period, but it seems that the courts will continue to provide justice where the breach has been remedied and is not of a substantially deleterious effect to insurers. The appellation and effect of a term delimiting the risk was also conceived by the court in order to enable the insurer to refute liability for any loss incurred whilst the insured was in breach of the requirement, instead of avoiding or affirming the contract in toto as they may be required to do so by the decision in *West v National Motor & Accident Insurance Union* [1955] 1 WLR 343, where the insurer attempted to reject a claim made after the insured had incorrectly valued the subject matter insured, and then proceed to arbitration under the policy. The court held that the insurer had affirmed the contract by waiver and could not reject the claim. The argument is that if the breach is fundamental to the validity of the contract, eg where it is a case of non-disclosure, a claim cannot be denied on the basis of that breach without avoiding the contract. To affirm the breach is to affirm the entire contract. The point is logical, and prevents an insurer denying all claims on the basis of a breach entitling him to avoid, whilst retaining the premium. This decision should not slavishly be upheld because the wording could have been construed as entitling the insurer to reject the claim without terminating the contract, but this point was not properly argued as it was irrelevant for the insurer's purposes.

However, whilst the Law Commission's recommendation that this case be statutorily reversed has not yet been implemented, the effect of *West v National Motor & Accident Insurance Union* has been eroded. In *Mint Security v Blair* [1982] 1 Lloyd's Rep 188 the wording was construed as enabling the insurer to terminate the policy for breach or reject only the claim and allow the policy to continue. In *The 'Litsion Pride'* [1985] 1 Lloyd's Rep 437 the distinction between pre-contractual and post-contractual breaches was confirmed by Hirst J (p 515) when he stated that

> . . . 'avoidance' in s 17 means avoidance *ab initio* . . . Section 17 provides that the policy may be avoided, not that it must be avoided. In the pre-contract situation . . . the assured's default necessarily strikes at the very basis of the contract itself, so that when, as in West's case, the underwriter affirms the contract, it necessarily follows that he is electing not to rely on default, but the same considerations do not apply in the case of post-contractual default . . . in the case of post-contract breach it is open to the underwriter simply to defend the claim without avoiding the policy.

In *The Bank of Nova Scotia v Hellenic War Risks Association (Bermuda) Ltd The 'Good Luck'* [1989] 2 Lloyd's Rep 238 the Court of Appeal confirmed that a breach of warranty does not automatically avoid the contract, but rather entitles the insurer to elect to avoid or repudiate from the date of breach. The breach itself without more does not bring the contract to an end, but merely gives the insurer the option to terminate.

Occasionally it is the insurer who will argue that an apparent warranty is in fact a term delimiting the risk. In *CTN Cash & Carry Ltd v General Accident Fire & Life Assurance Corporation plc* [1989] 1 Lloyd's Rep 259 a term stating that 'It is warranted that the secure cash kiosk shall be attended and locked at all times during business hours' was held only to delimit the risk when the kiosk was not attended. The insurer therefore successfully denied liability for the loss which occurred when the kiosk was not attended, without necessarily repudiating the policy. If the term had been a full-blooded warranty, the insurer would have had to affirm or repudiate the contract, such affirmation requiring the insurers to pay the claim. The distinction may not always be easy to draw; the key appears to be the relationship between the clause and the rest of the contract, and the warranty argument will succeed where the clause is 'so basic and so much at the root of the contract'.

Waiver

A breach of any term may be waived by the party entitled to rely on that term provided it is in possession of all relevant information. There are two types of waiver.

Waiver of a breach already committed An express waiver in writing should be clear enough, but reducing a waiver to writing is not necessary unless required by the policy. Where any term of the policy is relied on after breach, evidenced by a positive act inconsistent with the avoidance of the policy, and without any reservation of rights, there is a waiver by conduct (eg *Yorkshire Insurance Co* v *Craine* [1922] 2 AC 541). Thus accepting premium (*Wing* v *Harvey* (1854) 5 De GM & G 265) or proceeding to arbitration (*West* v *National Motor & Accident Insurance Union* [1955] 1 WLR 343), or requesting a post-mortem (*Donnison* v *Employers' Accident & Life Stock Insurance Co Ltd* (1897) 24 Rettie 681) amounts to a waiver. However, mere lapse of time does not constitute a waiver unless there is prejudice to the insured, or to the rights of third parties, or it is so long that a waiver must be presumed (*Allen* v *Robles* [1969] 1 WLR 1193). In fact such inactivity is not so much a waiver as an estoppel, and where the doctrine of estoppel can be applied, it may be available to circumvent the effect of a failure to waive a breach expressly in writing, where the policy so requires. The insured or his agent must be aware of the facts evidencing the waiver, so that they can be relied upon.

Waiver of future performance A term coming into effect simultaneously with and as part of the contract can be nullified if it can be shown to have been waived. Thus a term suspending liability until payment of premium may be waived by a recital in a policy issued under seal that the premium has been paid (*Roberts* v *Security Co Ltd* [1897] 1 QB 111). Similarly, the use of 'held covered' clauses suspends the breach of a warranty provided the breach is remedied immediately so that additional premium and alternative terms may be agreed. Otherwise the insured may rely on the continuation of the policy if the insurers indicate by words or conduct that breach of any term will not affect the contract.

Waiver can be effected by the insurer's agent provided the waiver is within his authority. An agent able to accept premiums or settle claims will have ostensible authority to waive any breach, though a canvassing or mere 'commission' agent will not (*Brook* v *Trafalgar Insurance Co* (1946) 79 Ll L Rep 365).

In the case of a renewal of the policy, which contains a term in respect of which the insurer has waived discharge, the insurer will be able to insist on compliance with the term since the further agreement produces a new contract. Waiver of a breach of an expired contract should not be imported into a fresh contract, which clearly stands by itself.

INTERPRETATION AND RULES OF CONSTRUCTION

Where the meaning of a word or set of words, or substantially similar words, has previously been decided by the court, the meaning will not be altered by the court, which will apply that previous construction (*Andersen* v *Marten* [1908] AC 334, 340). It is for this reason that words which appear archaic or incongruous in today's fast changing mercantile world are still used: they are 'hallowed' because they are capable of one meaning only. Nevertheless, the court's function of construction continues to be important and certain rules will be applied to its discharge of that function.

Meaning attached to the words used

The words must be given their ordinary and natural meaning. A contract of insurance is subject to the same rules of interpretation as any other contract and the words used to express the intentions of the parties are to be construed in their plain, ordinary and popular sense, as would be understood by ordinary men of normal intelligence and average knowledge of the world according to the accepted rules of grammar.[2] There are several qualifications to this rule:

(a) any words will be given their technical meaning where they have acquired such a meaning by a known usage of the trade. Thus the word 'average' in the context of marine insurance refers to a partial loss, whilst in property insurance it refers to under-insurance;

(b) any technical legal words will similarly be construed. Thus the word 'riot' is not accorded its popular meaning of an insurrection or an occasion for boisterous merriment, but rather according to its strict legal definition (*London and Lancashire Fire Insurance Co* v *Bolands* [1924] AC 836). The word 'theft' will likewise be defined (*Grundy (Teddington)* v *Fulton* [1983] 1 Lloyd's Rep 16). Loss caused by plunder by an armed vessel in the Amazon of the insured's goods intended for Bolivian troops did not fall to be indemnified by the insurer (under the 'piracy' clause of the policy) because it was not indiscriminate plunder for private gain and therefore did not constitute piracy, but was

---

2 *Robertson & Thomson* v *French* (1803) 4 East 130. *Yorke* v *Yorkshire Insurance Co Ltd* [1918] 1 KB 662, 668. *The 'Alexion Hope'* [1988] 1 Lloyd's Rep 311.

done for the political purpose of resisting the Bolivian Government (*Republic of Bolivia* v *Indemnity Mutual Marine Assurance Company Ltd* [1909] KB 784). Interestingly these rules of technical interpretation may not apply where the risk insured is situated out of the English jurisdiction so that the English law, and particularly that of construction, is inapplicable to define the risk, which may be given a broader meaning. 'The policy is obviously to be construed as if it related to a loss by crimes or misdemeanours perpetrated in that foreign country, and to be punished . . . according to the laws of the foreign country' (*Algemeene Bankvereeniging* v *Langton* (1935) 40 Comm Cas 247, 260). The wording in this case was accompanied by phrases not having any technical significance in English law, and therefore capable of a sensible commercial construction);

(c) the word(s) in dispute must be considered in context. This rule extends to a consideration of the policy as a whole and words in one clause may be altered by those in another (*Roberts* v *Plaisted* [1989] 2 Lloyd's Rep 341, 347), and also where the context gives rise to the clear intention of the parties to use the word in dispute in a specific sense (*Robertson* v *French* (1803) 4 East 130). Similarly, the word(s) may be limited by the context, where the word in dispute is normally used broadly but follows a series of words which are confined to one area or aspect or genus. The *eiusdem generis* rule applies to limit the meaning of the 'wider' word to the narrower context of the earlier, specific terms. Even the heading may be relevant (*Youell* v *Bland Welch and Co Ltd* (Unreported: Judgment 27 March 1990).

The intention of the parties

The intention of the parties must prevail, where it can be ascertained. Reference may be made to the circumstances of the contract and the wording will be construed as liberally as possible. A literal construction leading to a capricious or absurd result will not be upheld, although the courts will not rewrite the policy to reflect what they think the policy should mean, since this would effectively constitute speculation by the court. Thus in the case of inconsistent words or clauses the court will disregard the section apparently inconsistent with the parties' intention (*Western Assurance Co of Toronto* v *Poole* [1903] 1 KB 376). *Forbes* v *Git* [1922] 1 AC 256 is authority for the proposition that the earlier of two clauses inconsistent with each other will be upheld, but this case will not be followed where the relative importance of each clause is clear, even though some inconsistency results (*Insurance Co of Africa* v *Scor* [1985] 1 Lloyd's Rep 312) except where the earlier clause is open to an alternative interpretation and the later clause is clear (*Yien Yieh Commercial Bank Ltd* v *Kwai Chung Cold Storage Co Ltd* 25 July 1989). The Privy Council also stated that the rejection of one clause in a contract which was inconsistent with another involved a rewriting of the contract, which was only justified where the two clauses could not be reconciled. The court will apply the construction which does least violence to the language, even though upholding one clause will emasculate the other (*Insurance Co of Africa* v *Scor*, ibid p 331).

Ambiguity in the wording

Verba chartarum fortius accipiuntur contra proferentem, or, any ambiguity will be construed against the party in whose favour it is purported to be drawn and who seeks its protection. Thus an insurer who has drawn up the wording without sufficient care cannot rely on any ambiguity therein. At Lloyd's any ambiguity in the slip may be construed against the insured, since they are 'by their brokers . . . the proferentes of the slip' (*American Airlines Inc* v *Hope* [1973] 1 Lloyd's Rep 233, 250). Hobhouse J commented in *Abrahams* v *The Mediterranean Insurance and Reinsurance Company Ltd* (Unreported: 29 June 1988) that ' . . . a contract which was presented by the broker to the relevant underwriter for him to accede to . . . is therefore a document which has to be construed resolving any ambiguities against the broker and his client [the insured]'. Any amendments inserted by the insurer will be construed against him (*Jaglom* v *Excess Insurance Co Ltd* [1971] 2 Lloyd's Rep 171, 177). However, it is only relevant to ambiguities and should not be considered as a universal panacea for poor draftsmanship; language will not be strained to produce an ambiguity to the detriment of the insurer (*Jason* v *British Traders Insurance Co Ltd* [1969] 1 Lloyd's Rep 281, 290).

Further, the court will apply as reasonable a construction as possible to any ambiguity (*Victor Melik & Co Ltd* v *Norwich Union Fire Insurance Society Ltd* [1980] 1 Lloyd's Rep 523).

Precedence of express terms

Any term specifically made express will take precedence over others. This means that:

(a) express terms override inconsistent implied terms;

(b) written words override printed words.

Insurance contracts may contain implied terms, whose effect will be denied by any intention of the parties which is specifically expressed. Similarly, any amendments to the printed terms of the standard form policy are intended to express the parties' intentions and override any inconsistency with other printed terms.

Extra-contractual extrinsic evidence

Other evidence may be considered by the court where the slip or policy contains an ambiguity, such as a proposal form (if not already incorporated), later documentary confirmation of the agreed meaning of any words) (*Smith & Son v Eagle Star and British Dominions Insurance Co Ltd* (1934) 48 Lloyd's Rep 67, 69), or any explanation provided orally by their agent (*Bawden v The London, Edinburgh, and Glasgow Assurance Co* [1892] 2 QB 534). Such evidence merely confirms the intention of the parties by preventing one party resiling from his stated position. Evidence of negotiations are not usually admissible to assist the court in its construction of a document thought to constitute the contract, but direct evidence of the parties' intentions (which can be shown by their negotiations) is admissible in an action for rectification, or for rescission for mistake or misrepresentation.

Where the entire contract is contained in a slip or policy, oral evidence cannot usually alter the apparent meaning of the contractual wording. However, such evidence may be called to substantiate one of several premises, including:

(a) that the policy is void or has not commenced. The contract is not altered in any way but evidence may be called to confirm or disprove its binding effect, eg as to the accuracy of answers in the proposal form where that form is stated to be the basis of the contract but no wording to this effect appears in the policy (*Rozanes v Bowen* (1928) 32 Ll L Rep 98). Evidence may be called as to incapacity, mistake, *non est factum* and other invalidating factors, or to show that the risk or contract would not incept until fulfilment of a certain requirement, which has not occurred (*Mann v Nunn* (1874) 30 LT 526);

(b) that the policy does not reflect the agreed terms. Preliminary documents may be considered by the court to assist it in assessing whether the contract was concluded, and its terms. However, the slip may not be used as an aid to the construction of the policy where the slip provided for the policy wording to be agreed by the leading underwriter, in the absence of a claim for rectification, since the rationale of the policy is that it replaces the slip (*Youell* v *Bland Welch* (1990) *Lloyd's List*, 23 February). Evidence of representations made by the insurer or his agent upon which the insured relied in agreeing the contract may be considered by the court. Evidence may also be called to add collateral terms running parallel with the contract which are not inconsistent with it;

(c) Once again, in regard to the occurrence of ambiguity in a policy, evidence may be called to confirm that a word or phrase has a specific meaning other than its usual meaning, when used peculiarly to a geographical locality or trade which uses it in that different sense (*Woodall* v *Pearl Assurance Company Ltd* [1919] 1 KB 593) eg 'average' in a marine policy. Such evidence will not be applicable where the purported usage is inconsistent with any express policy wording, and the rule exists to give effect to the presumed intention of the parties. Such evidence is admissible to prove custom, provided it does not contradict any express term.

Chapter 8

Subrogation

DOCTRINE OF SUBROGATION

The doctrine of subrogation exists to prevent the unjust enrichment of the insured at the insurer's expense by enabling the insurer to stand in place of the insured in order to enforce any of the insured's claims against third parties to diminish the loss covered by the insurance (*The Sea Insurance Co v Hadden & Wainwright Ltd* (1884) 13 QBD 706), and also to recover from the insured any benefits received by him in diminution of that loss (in accordance with and to the extent of the insurer's interest) (*Young v Merchant's Marine Insurance Co Ltd* [1932] 2 KB 705). Thus, a hull insurer is not entitled after damage caused by a third party to be subrogated to his insured's claim for loss of freight, since these are two different interests (*The Sea Insurance Co v Hadden & Wainwright Ltd*). In *Castellain v Preston* (1883) 11 QBD 380, 388 Brett LJ said that

. . . as between the underwriter and the assured the underwriter is entitled to the advantage of every right of the assured, whether such right exists in contract, fulfilled or unfulfilled, or in remedy for tort capable of being insisted on or already insisted on, or in any other right, whether by way of condition or otherwise, legal or equitable, which can be, or has been exercised or accrued . . . .

The insurer is entitled to be subrogated to the insured's rights without express contractual provision because it is in every case applicable either as an equitable principle or as an implied contractual term. There has been some judicial dispute as to the basis of the doctrine but the legal scales currently seem weighted in favour of equity.[1] This should give rise to the application of discretion by

---

1 MacGillivray and Parkington think not: see paras 1133–1143.

the court as to whether or not the insurer should be allowed to pursue a subrogated claim, but in fact such discretion has not been recognised, except by Denning LJ in *Morris v Ford Motor Co* [1973] 1 QB 792. One reason for the lack of judicial recognition of a discretionary element may be that in marine insurance, s 79 of the Marine Insurance Act 1906 does not consider discretion, and also the Marine Insurance Act 1906 was intended to restate the common law, which did not distinguish between marine and non-marine rights of subrogation (*H Cousins v D&C Carriers Ltd* [1971] 2 QB 230). The distinction may become important in practice where the policy contains an express provision for subrogation but the insurer seeks to rely on a wider, implied term (provided there is no contradiction), in which case a juristic base in equity would favour him, or where the insurer has paid the insured on an *ex gratia* basis (in the absence of illegality or considerations of public policy) because the loss fell outside the terms of the policy: as a matter of equitable principle the insurer could utilise the insured's rights after indemnity, but an implied term would only apply to payments made within the contract of insurance, so that the insurer could not recover.

Insurer's right of subrogation

The insurer's right of subrogation is a strict corollary of the insured's right of indemnification, as well as that of contribution, and is ancillary only to policies of indemnity. It is not applicable to life or accident insurance.[2] The right comes into existence when the parties conclude a contract of indemnity insurance but remains contingent in that it cannot be effected until the insurer has indemnified the insured (*John Edwards & Co v Motor Union Insurance Co* [1922] 2 KB 249, 254). However, the insured is unlikely to receive payment in full, either because there is an excess clause or he is underinsured. It is not yet settled whether the insured must be indemnified up to the policy limit for the insurer to be able to take action, or whether

---

2 Unless perhaps they contain indemnity provisions which give rise to a right of subrogation such as a specified amount for the insured's loss of earnings during a period of disablement: *Orion Insurance Co Ltd v Hicks* (1972) 32 DLR (3rd) 256. The authors of Insurance Contract Law suggest, however, that the inability of subrogation to apply to life and accident policies is too well established to be capable of justified or sustainable dissent; *Commercial Union Assurance Co v Lister* (1874) LR 9 Ch App 483; and *Andrews v The Patriotic Assurance Company* (1886) 18 LR Ir 355.

the insured must be fully compensated for his loss. Clearly indemnification under the policy is the minimum payment upon which to base a right of subrogation (*Page* v *Scottish Insurance Corporation* (1929) 98 LJ 308). Some support for the view that full compensation is necessary can be derived from the rationale of subrogation, which is to prevent the unjust enrichment of the insured. He cannot be unjustly enriched until he has been fully compensated for his loss. In reality the point does not arise because the insurance policy will expressly state that the insurer's subrogation rights will become exercisable upon indemnification under the policy.

The insured can be compelled by the insurer to institute proceedings against the party causing the loss (*Mason* v *Sainsbury* (1782) 3 Doug KB 61). The insured is entitled to control these proceedings until he has been fully indemnified (subject to any express clause in the policy) and after any payment may retain any initial balance beween the insured sum and his loss, holding any additional sum on trust for the insurer (up to the limit of his indemnity) (*Re Miller Gibb & Co Ltd* [1957] 1 WLR 703). He may also settle the claim without incurring liability to the insurer if effected *bona fide*, taking the insurer's interest into consideration eg where the claim is weak or the third party likely to become insolvent (*Commercial Union Assurance Co* v *Lister* (1874) LR 9 Ch App 483).

The dominant feature of the doctrine is that the insured must not prejudice any rights of the insurer by his behaviour. Thus issuing proceedings against a third party for uninsured losses only instead of the full potential liability of the third party will render the insured liable to the insurer for all monies paid, if judgment has been given and cannot be set aside, eg on the ground that the third party has purposefully submitted to judgment in default for uninsured losses only in the knowledge that a subrogated claim for the full potential liability was pending. An insurer may remedy the position only if he acts before judgment (*Buckland* v *Palmer* [1984] 3 All ER 554), because the principle of *res judicata* precludes the insurer from any recovery against the third party.

The rule that the insured must not prejudice any of the insurer's rights of recovery thus reaches back prior to any payment by the insurer, who may be able to protect his position at any stage by forcing the insured to take any steps that appear necessary, such as obtaining a Mareva injunction or Anton Piller order against a third party. The insured is 'compelled to give all the assistance which is required' (*Dufourcet & Co* v *Bishop* (1886) 18 QBD 373, 379). Any failure by the insured to comply may render him liable in damages for prejudicing the insurer's right to subrogation. The only justification for a refusal by the insured to assist would be where there are two alternative courses of action and he follows the one that is least prejudicial to his own commercial interests. In *Normid Housing Association Ltd* v *Ralphs* [1989] 1 Lloyd's Rep 265 the Court of Appeal overturned the Mareva injunction granted at first instance, which prevented the defendant (insured) from reaching a settlement with his insurer. The plaintiff argued that a compromise which was considerably less than his claim against the insured and the payment of that claim by the insurer constituted a dissipation of the insured's assets. The Court of Appeal found that it was possible that the insured might have received nothing at all from his insurer if the insurer's allegation that the policy was voidable for material non-disclosure could be susbtantiated, that the settlement was neither inexplicable nor unreasonable, and that it was in the ordinary course of business. Had the settlement been so disadvantageous as to have been made in bad faith, or the evidence had shown any collusion between the insurer and insured, Mareva injunctive relief could have been granted (ibid 277, 278).

The insurer may also be able to insist that the insured issue and serve any proceedings before they become time barred. However, it is not clear whether the insured must take any such steps without a request to do so from the insurer; the insurer is entitled to stand in the insured's shoes but prior to payment the insured should not have to walk in the absence of instructions to do so. The converse argument is that the insurer is entitled to insist that the insured takes such action to protect his rights and implicitly therefore that the insured should protect these rights in any event. The issue has yet to be settled. There does not appear to be any reason why the duty of good faith should not extend to subrogation and therefore the insured should pass on to the insurer any information that may be relevant to the recovery.

Where the insured has obtained additional insurance on the same subject-matter and risk, he is able to proceed against either insurer to the limit of his indemnity, and he does not prejudice any subrogation rights by so doing since the insurer who has been selected by the insured to indemnify him can proceed against any third party in full, though it can only recover the amount of its payment, holding any balance on trust for the insured, who in turn may hold the balance over his loss on trust for the other insurer, if he also contributes.

Bringing an action without an assignment

The insurer cannot bring an action in his own name (in the absence of an assignment) but must use that of the insured, who may be compelled by the court to accede to the insurer's demand that he do so, provided the insurer indemnifies the insured against the costs to be incurred (*Wilson* v *Raffalovich* (1881) 7 QBD 533, 558). The action against the third party will usually be at common law for damages but the insurer may apply in equity for an order compelling the insured to lend his name, or institute proceedings naming the insured as co-defendant who will hold any payment on trust for the insurer. The insurer will only obtain full control after complete indemnification of the insured, and will obtain no better rights against third parties than can vest in the insured. The insurer may therefore be subject to certain limitations imposed by the position of the insured. These are outlined as follows.

The insured cannot sue himself
This is inherent in the contract of insurance, which would be pointless without it. In *Simpson* v *Thompson* (1878) 3 App Cas 279 the House of Lords refused to allow the insurer of two ships owned and insured by the same owner under one policy to offset his right to proceed against the insured for the damage caused to one ship by the master of the other against the amount payable for the damage caused. It will also be relevant where there are two parties named as the insured under one policy eg bailor/bailee, mortgagor/-mortgagee.

Any proceedings instituted by the subrogated insurer of one co-insured against another will not succeed on the principle that such litigation represents circuity of action (*Petrofina (UK) Ltd* v *Magnaload* [1984] QB 127) provided that the parties have insured the same interest eg under a joint or composite policy. However, such proceedings may be capable of institution under a composite policy (ie where the parties retain different interests in the same property or goods eg landlord/tenant or bailor/bailee) where one insured is guilty of wilful misconduct and the insurer is subrogated to the other; under a joint policy any wilful misconduct by one co-insured is attributed to the other so that the insurer need not indemnify either.

An action time-barred

The action against the relevant third party may be time-barred (*London Assurance Co* v *Johnson* (1737) West T Hard 266, 269).

Third party may benefit from an agreement with insured

The third party is entitled to the benefit of any agreement with the insured which exempts that third party from liability (*State Government Insurance Office (Qld)* v *Brisbane Stevedoring Pty Ltd* (1969) 123 CLR 228). Any such agreement which is in force before the formation of the insurance contract is binding on the insurer, but he may be able to avoid the policy *ab initio* for non-disclosure of a material fact (*Tate & Sons* v *Hyslop* (1885) 15 QBD 368). The presence of any factor which restricts the right of the insurer to proceed by way of subrogated recovery seems clearly material in that it would influence the judgment of a prudent insurer when fixing the premium, since he would probably charge more if it were obvious at that time that he would always be unable to offset recoveries against claims.

A third party may also seek the advantage of such an agreement where it is not express but he can prove that the insured and third party intended that he should have the benefit of the insurance. Thus in *Mark Rowlands Ltd* v *Bernie Inns Ltd* [1986] 1 QB 211 the tenant defeated a claim made by his landlord's subrogated insurers against him on the basis that it was implied in the landlord's agreement to insure the premises on their joint behalf that the landlord would not later sue him. Similarly the insurer of an employer, who was liable for the actions of another employer's employee working under an agreement between the employers on the former employer's premises, was found not to be entitled to be subrogated to that employer's claim against the employee because it was either inequitable or because his subrogation rights were impliedly excluded by the employer's agreement.[3]

Any agreement, express or implied, precluding an action against the third party by the insured which is made after loss or payment will similarly preclude a subrogated claim unless the third party is aware that the insured had been paid by the insurer and therefore

---

3　*Morris* v *Ford Motor Co* [1973] 1 QB 792. However, in *University of Western Toronto* v *Yanush* (1988) 56 DLR (4th) 552 two students set fire to paper piled on another student for a lark. Extensive damage was caused both to the student and the hall of residence, and the plaintiff's insurers sued the students. The court found that the plaintiff's insurers had rights of subrogation against the students, because they did not fall within the category of 'named waived subrogees'. *Morris* v *Ford Motor Co* conflicts with *Lister* v *Romford Ice & Cold Storage Co* [1957] AC 555 but reflects the current state of play because the insurance industry agreed with the Government in 1965 that it would not seek to enforce its subrogation rights in such circumstances. This agreement is not legally binding.

that the release clearly compromised the insurer's rights (*Haigh* v *Lawford* (1964) 114 LJ 208). The insurer will have to show that it would be unjust and inequitable for the judgment to stand eg by showing that the defendant or his insurer had deliberately acted to exploit the misunderstanding between the insured and the insurer. Fully contesting the claim does not satisfy this criterion (*Hayler* v *Chapman, The Times* 11 November 1988). This is, however, subject to the entitlement of the insured who has not received a full indemnity to control the litigation and reach a bona fide compromise, which will be binding even though the third party is aware of the insurer's interest.

Third party defence

The insurer may also be confronted by a defence of the third party which does not apply to the insured but only to the insurer, such as the fact that the insurer is an enemy alien or has agreed with the insured that he will not pursue any subrogated action against the third party.[4] However, it is arguable[5] that the authorities for these propositions are obiter and therefore that this is still in issue. Certainly the third party cannot claim as his defence that the insured, who technically brings the action, has suffered no loss because he is insured, and nor can the third party claim that the insurer has voluntarily assumed the liability eg where he did not exercise any right to avoid the contract, as long as the insurers provided the indemnity honestly (*King* v *Victoria Insurance Co* [1896] AC 250).

---

4 *The Palm Branch* (1916) 115 LT 557. In *Thomas & Co* v *Brown* (1899) 4 Com Cas 186 the insurer tried to pursue a subrogated claim against a lighterman who had caused damage to the insured. The slip stated that 'This policy to pay any claim or loss irrespective of any other insurance, and without recourse to lightermen'. The insurer effectively argued that this clause did not protect the third party owing to the absence of contractual privity between them, and the third party successfully showed that his contract with the insured contained an implied term that he would not be liable for any insurable risk, or unless he was negligent, and that the policy reflected this market practice.
5 *Subrogation in Insurance Law*; SR Derham (1985) Law Books Co Ltd p 90. Presumably the third party's defence (based on an agreement to which it is not a party) could succeed if the insured lent its support, by enforcing the term or refusing to lend its name to the insurer.

Allocation of sums received

Any sums received by the insured from a third party are subject to allocation according to established principles, to the effect that:

(a) the insurer is only entitled to recover what it has paid the insured in respect of the insured loss or liability, together with interest (*Yorkshire Insurance Co v Nisbet Shipping Co* [1962] 2 QB 330). Thus any sum recovered by the insured in excess of the sum paid by the insurer may be retained by the insured, save for the amount of interest due to the insurer from the date of settlement. The insured can retain interest payable from the date of loss (or shortly afterwards) until the date of payment by the insurer (*H Cousins v D & C Carriers* [1971] 2 QB 230);

(b) the insured is entitled to receive a full indemnity in respect of its losses before any sum recovered becomes payable to the insurer. Thus payment up to a specified limit by the insurer which leaves the insured less than indemnified will enable the insured to retain the shortfall before the insurer becomes entitled to payment. If the sum recovered exceeds the payment by the insurer and the shortfall, the insured may keep the balance;

(c) any policy subject to average will transform the insurer and insured into co-insurers where the policy limit is less than the loss, so that any subrogated recovery must be apportioned according to their respective liabilities.

There are, however, certain payments upon which the insurer's rights of subrogation will not attach. These include damages payable to the insured for consequential loss since these do not diminish the loss insured, or payable for any claim which is additional to and independent from the loss insured, or for any sum paid to discharge a loss which is clearly not insured (*Horse, Carriage & General Insurance Co Ltd v Petch* (1916) 33 TLR 131). Similarly an ex gratia payment by a third party to the insured will not be subject to subrogation if it was intended as personal compensation for the insured rather than in diminution of the loss. However, clear proof will be necessary to rebut the presumption that any payment is made to diminish the loss (*Stearns v Village Main Reef Gold Mining Co Ltd* (1905) 21 TLR 236). The insurer has no right to such gifts (where they are intended to benefit the insured personally), and particularly where the insured has no right to demand compensation from the third party (*Castellain v Preston* (1883) 11 QBD 380, 391). The courts will also refuse to uphold any insurance contrary to public policy, such as wagers or honour 'contracts' (*John Edwards & Co v Motor Union Insurance Co Ltd* [1922] 2 KB 249).

Part Three

The Broker

Chapter 9

The premium

GENERAL PRINCIPLES

The premium is the amount payable by the insured as consideration to the insurer in exchange for which the insurer accepts certain specified future liabilities, usually to pay an amount up to a certain limit if the event insured against occurs. In fact premium need not be paid if good consideration passes, as a matter of general contract law. In mutual insurance the consideration is constituted by the insured's liability to contribute towards his members' losses and s 85(2) of the Marine Insurance Act 1906 specifies that those sections of the Act relating to premium do not apply to mutual marine insurance.

The amount of premium is agreed by the insurer and insured, usually as a percentage of the sum insured, and in non-marine insurance must either be determined or made subject to a mechanism for its determination before a contract can exist, since a failure to agree the amount of premium may render the contract void for uncertainty.[1] In some classes of insurance, such as liability, the parties may agree that some premium is to be paid immediately and an adjustment made at the end of the policy period to reflect the risk actually incurred by the insurer, or they may agree that the premium should be reduced either during the currency of the contract or upon renewal to reflect a diminution of the risk, or to reflect

---

1 In *American Airlines Inc* v *Hope, Banque Sabbaq SARL* v *Hope* [1973] 1 Lloyd's Rep 233 the Court of Appeal held as a matter of construction that the risk had not attached until the additional premium for war risks had been agreed, the slip having been marked 'tba l/u' (to be agreed by leading underwriter) in respect of the geographical limits and additional premium. These limits were never agreed, and the premium could not be agreed until the geographical limits had been clarified.

the fact that the insured has not made a claim under the policy — the familiar 'no claims bonus'.

In marine insurance a failure to agree the amount of premium is remedied by statute. Section 31 of the Marine Insurance Act 1906 provides:

(1) Where an insurance is effected at a premium to be arranged, and no arrangement is made, a reasonable premium is payable.

(2) Where an insurance is effected on the terms that an additional premium is to be arranged in a given event, and that event happens but no arrangement is made, then a reasonable additional premium is payable.

Payment of premium

The premium may be paid by the insured or any connected party, such as his agent or personal representative, but payment by a stranger will not constitute good payment unless ratified by the insured (*London & Lancashire Life Assurance Co* v *Fleming* [1897] AC 499).

Mode of payment

The premium should be paid in cash (*Sweeting* v *Pearce* (1861) 6 CBNS 534) and an insurer, according to the old cases, need not accept any alternative mode of payment.[2] However, alternative methods of payment will give rise to proper payment if the insurer has expressly so agreed, such as the crediting by the broker of a running account (*Prince of Wales Life Assurance Co* v *Harding* (1858) EB & E 183). The usual modes are by cheque or by settlement in account, with many of the old cases turning on payment by bill of exchange or promissory note, both of which effectively allow credit to the insured (as does a post-dated cheque), which is outside the power of an agent in the absence of specific authority. Thus, whilst in theory a cheque need not be accepted by an insurer, his agent will probably have apparent authority to accept a cheque on his behalf because this is a usual method of payment.

Payment is deemed to have occurred on the date the cheque was

---

2 Thus a cow in payment is not good payment unless specifically agreed, but a cow with writing on its hide which complies with the Bills of Exchange Act 1855 is good payment as a cheque, if a cheque is agreed payment. See AP Herbert's 'Misleading Cases'.

received by the insurer or his agent, rather than the date of payment by the bank, but this presumption will be rebutted by any later dishonour of the cheque provided that the cheque was not accepted as absolute payment, rather than being conditional upon being honoured (*Charles* v *Blackwell* (1877) 2 CPD 151). It is a question of fact whether the delivery of a cheque constitutes conditional or absolute payment, and this depends upon the parties' intentions (*Goldshede* v *Cottrell* (1836) 2 M & W 20). It is considered unlikely that an insurer would expressly or impliedly authorise the acceptance of a cheque as an absolute settlement of the debt owed as premium, and therefore the general rule must be that such payment is conditional. The Court of Appeal held in *Re Charge Card Services Ltd* [1988] 3 All ER 702 that payment by a 'credit' card was accepted by the creditor as an unconditional discharge of the debt in substitution for payment by cash, but this decision revolved around three separate bilateral contracts which regulated the parties' relative rights and obligations, and assumed that the debtor's liability would be extinguished by payment by card. It should not affect the payment of premium by cheque. In a running account the premium is held to have been paid when debited to the account, rather than the date of actual payment of any balance to the insurer (*Prince of Wales Life Assurance Co* v *Harding* (1858) EB & E 183).

Where the premium is payable periodically the insurer will not be liable if they fail to remind the insured that it is due, unless they have agreed to do so. However, most policies extend the time for payment by providing days of grace, which do not extend the period of cover but may enable the insured to recover in the event of a loss occurring before the days of grace expire (*Stuart* v *Freeman* [1903] 1 KB 47).

Days of grace
Any right of the insurer not to renew will not be affected by the tender of renewal premium (*Tarleton* v *Staniforth* (1794) 5 TR 695), unless it is accepted. Any right of the insured to continue the insurance could fall into one of two categories. It may be a continuing contract of insurance until the insured effectively terminates it himself by non-payment, in which case the last day of grace is the last day that the insured is covered. Thus the insured may obtain several days of insurance for which he has not paid and he will be paid by the insurer should the loss envisaged by the insurance occur during that time (*Stuart* v *Freeman* (ibid). If no loss occurs, the insured has had free cover. If a loss occurs, the premium must be paid to the insurer). The policy usually provides for such payment even though the premium has not been paid, so that there

can be no argument that the second category applies, which is that the policy is renewable only by payment of an additional premium during the days of grace. A loss which occurs before the premium has been paid will not be covered.

Time for payment

Although the premium can theoretically be paid within a reasonable time, commercial and economic necessity dictate that it be paid as soon as possible, since insurers build into their offers of insurance the fact that investment income is obtained from premium received. The financial equation is such that a loss can sometimes occur without preventing the insurer from making a profit. It is therefore important to the insurer that premium be paid without delay, and to minimise loss insurers often specify in the contract that the policy will not come into force before the premium is paid, or that it will lapse if the premium is not paid within a specified period.[3] Usually the insurer will specify that the contract is in force but that they are not to become liable until the premium has been paid. Faulty drafting can also give rise to the possibility that the contract is in force and that after payment of the premium the insurer will be liable from the date of inception of the policy period, which will entitle the insured to payment of a claim, even though the loss occurs prior to payment of the premium. The amount of premium can properly be deducted from the claim in non-marine insurance outside Lloyd's.

A refusal to insure until the premium is paid means that payment

---

3 Obviously this can only apply to certain types of insurance; it cannot apply to contracts where the nature and extent of risk can only be estimated at inception, because the amount of cover cannot be known until the end of the year. Thus premiums will be adjusted for wage expenditure in employers' liability, or for stock values per month in fire insurance on stock. The insurers and brokers contract on specific terms of trade eg payment within X days, depending upon the nature of the risk and the country of residence of the insured. Usually the clause entitles the insurer to cancel the policy, and is often used in the Lloyd's Market where the broker is liable for the premium. This clause is therefore incorporated at the Lloyd's broker's request to ensure that he need not provide the premium himself in the absence of payment to him by the insured, although the clause does not do more than enable the underwriter to cancel. Whether he does so will depend upon his relationship with the broker, who will have to make any request himself. Premium warranties may also be found in reinsurance contracts, although not in surplus or excess of loss treaties where the amount due to the reinsurer will not be known until advised by the reinsured. However, initial deposit premiums may be required under excess of loss business to ensure prompt payment.

is a condition precedent to liability under the policy, and payment activates the policy from its date of inception (*Ocean Accident & Guarantee Corporation Ltd* v *Cole* [1932] 2 KB 100).

Section 52 of the Marine Insurance Act 1906 states:

Unless otherwise agreed, the duty of the assured or his agent to pay the premium, and the duty of the insurer to issue the policy to the assured or his agent, are concurrent conditions, and the insurer is not bound to issue the policy until payment or tender of the premium.

On the one hand the marine insurer need not issue the policy until the premium has been paid, and a contract of marine insurance must be embodied in a marine policy under s 22 of the Marine Insurance Act 1906, but the contract will nevertheless come into force (although the risk may not attach retrospectively until any premium stipulation has been satisfied); on the other hand the insured need only tender the premium (within time) to entitle him to enforce the contract.

Non-payment by the insured

There are two situations where non-payment of the premium does not affect the insured's right to payment in the event of loss. These are as follows.

Policy made under seal reciting payment of premium The insurer can be potentially estopped from denying pre-payment where the policy is made under seal and recites that the premium has been paid. The strength of the recital must be balanced against any conflicting proviso stating that the insurer would not be liable prior to payment. The insurer will be liable when the policy has been executed if the recital carries more weight than the proviso (*Roberts* v *Security Co Ltd* [1897] 1 QB 111), but not when the proviso makes it clear that liability cannot arise until 'actual' payment, particularly where the receipt clause was a matter of 'common form' (*Equitable Fire & Accident Office Ltd* v *The Ching Wo Hong* [1907] AC 96). Further, a necessary ingredient of estoppel — actual reliance by the party later seeking to rely on it — is missing. Even if the insured attempted to rely on it, it is clearly inconsistent with his knowledge that premium has not been paid, so that it is not an unequivocal representation. In policies which are not made under seal the apparent confirmation of receipt in the policy does not amount to a waiver of any stipulation for payment prior to liability, and the insurers can rely upon non-payment to avoid liability.

Every Lloyd's policy states that the premium has been paid and is treated as so paid at the completion of the contract. The insurer cannot rely upon non-payment to avoid liability because s 53 of the Marine Insurance Act 1906 makes the broker directly responsible to the insurer for premiums, and s 54 states:

Where a marine policy effected on behalf of the assured by a broker acknowledges the receipt of the premium, such acknowledgment is, in the absence of fraud, conclusive as between the insurer and the assured, but not as between the insurer and the broker.

Thus the policy is valid even though the premium has not been paid by the insured to the broker, or accounts settled between insurer and broker.[4] The rule that the broker is liable to the underwriter is established in all business at Lloyd's[5] and marine business outside Lloyd's, although the issue is not fully resolved insofar as it concerns non-marine business outside Lloyd's. Unfortunately the leading case of *Wilson* v *Avec Audio-Visual Equipment Ltd* [1974] 1 Lloyd's Rep 81[6] is a decision of limited value, since the judgments of the Court of Appeal make it clear that they had no option other than to reach the conclusion that the broker in non-marine business outside Lloyd's is not liable to the insurer for premium. The broker had operated under the mistaken belief that he was liable to the insurer, and had paid him the premium. Edmund Davies LJ commented that 'It requires clear and precise evidence of a very special relationship before an agent can be rendered personally liable in respect of a contract entered into on behalf of his principal . . . The Plaintiff [broker] was not within 1000 miles of establishing that there were any special circumstances in this case which entitled him to

---

4 In *Universo Insurance Co of Milan* v *Merchants Marine Insurance Co* [1897] 2 QB 93 and *Power* v *Butcher* (1829) 10 B & C 329 the court enunciated the basis for this rule, which is the fiction that the broker paid the insurer when the policy was effected, the underwriter then lending it back to the broker and becoming his creditor.

5 However, an action came before Saville J in the summer of 1989 on the liability of non-marine brokers at Lloyd's to pay premium to underwriters. It was compromised after three days, so the position remains arguable. Lord Denning MR commented in *Bareham* v *Christopher Moran and Co Ltd* (unreported: May 1981) that 'the point is open to question . . . There is no reason whatever for drawing any distinction between the two classes of business', with which Sir Denys Buckley agreed.

6 Upheld by the High Court of Australia in *Con-Stan Industries of Australia Pty Ltd* v *Norwich Winterthur (Aust) Ltd* (1986) 160 CLR 226. One argument in this latter case concerned an estoppel by convention or mutual assumption that only the broker was liable to the insurer for the premium. The court placed emphasis on the distinction between an assumption of law and an estoppel by fact, and chose not to follow apparent precedents in analogous areas. This case has been criticised, notably in *Eslea Holdings Ltd* v *Betts* (1986) 4 ANZ Ins Cas 60–78.

be treated in any way different from the general run of agents.' And that ' . . . there is no certainty that the rights and liabilities of a broker dealing with a company are the same or are co-existive with the rights and liabilities of a broker dealing with a Lloyd's underwriter'. Scarman LJ put it plainly when he said that 'This case should not be taken, in my judgment, as any indication as to the nature of the duties and liabilities of an insurance broker vis a vis the insured when a premium has not been paid.' He also commented that 'I do not exclude the possibility that had the Plaintiff [broker] fully divulged the facts of the situation he might have established an implied authority to pay these two premiums on behalf of the Defendant company . . . ' since he had 'in mind the general rule of law that every agent has implied authority to act in the execution of his express authority according to the usages and customs of the business in which he is employed'. Thus, in the absence of proof of a usage to pay the insurer (which must also be known to and accepted by the insured), the broker could perhaps obtain payment under his implied right to an indemnity. He should be entitled to assume that his principal does not intend to default on the premium or that he has authority from his principal to pay as a necessary part of his function, and if he pays it he may be able to recover it.

No specified time limit on payment   Where the insured does not have to comply with the condition of payment within a specified time, because the insurer has agreed to accept a later payment of premium, the insurer waives the condition of payment and cannot avoid liability to the insured by relying on the insured's non-payment. However, the necessary conditions must be present to enable the insured to prove that the insurer has waived his rights, which invariably depend upon the circumstances. The insurer must be aware of all relevant facts, and intend to waive. Thus waiver will be implied where the insurer agrees to give credit to the insured (*Prince of Wales Life Assurance Co v Harding* (1858) ElBl & El 183) or to accept a negotiable instrument (*London & Lancashire Life Assurance Co v Fleming* [1897] AC 499), but not from mere delivery of the policy to the insured (*Equitable Fire & Accident Office Ltd v Ching Wo Hong* [1907] AC 96) or perhaps because prompt payment had previously been waived (*Redmond v Canadian Mutual Aid Association* (1891) 18 OAR 335). Where the insurer wrongfully refuses to accept premium, he is in breach of contract and liable in damages accordingly for the occurrence of any insured risk (*Honour v Equitable Life Assurance Society of United States* [1900] 1 Ch 852).

Finally, the insurer can sue for the premium even though the policy provides that the risk cannot attach until payment.

Payment to the insurer's agent

Payment to the insurer's agent constitutes valid payment to the insurer if that agent had sufficient authority to accept payment in the manner in which it was made. The agent must have usual or apparent authority to receive the premium, which may be implied from the insurer's conduct. Thus payment to the agent who originally effected the insurance on behalf of the insurer usually constitutes valid payment (*Wing* v *Harvey* (1854) 5 De GM & G 265). Similarly, an agent with authority to provide a cover note has authority to accept premium, as does a sub-agent (*Rossiter* v *Trafalgar Life Assurance Corporation* (1859) 27 Beav 377).

If the policy stipulates a particular method of payment and the insurer's agent accepts premium in another way, the insured cannot argue that the agent had authority to accept the premium, because he knows of the agent's lack of authority. Authority to accept payment in the manner tendered by the insured must be proved by the insured for such payment to be binding upon the insurer, for example where the insured can prove that the insurer had previously accepted the insured's manner of payment, and therefore waived his contractual right to payment in a particular manner; the general rule, however, is that payment can only be made in money (*Pape* v *Westacott* [1894] 1 QB 272).

An agreement by the agent to accept payment in full by the insured at a later date — such as a post-dated cheque — is not within an agent's authority since it amounts to the supply of credit. Where, however, the agent agrees to provide credit to the insured and to pay premium to the insurer on behalf of the insured, the agent becomes the agent of the insured as regards payment of premium, and can sue him for the debt thereby created (*Newcastle Fire Insurance Co* v *Macmorran & Co* (1815) 3 Dow 255, 264).

More usual is settlement in account between the insurer and the insured's agent, where the agent is simply debited with the premium less his commission. In fact actual settlement need not occur; the agent need only debit himself with the premium in his account to constitute valid payment (*Prince of Wales Life Assurance Co* v *Harding* (1858) EB & E 183).

Return of premium

The premium is returnable by the insurer to the insured where the risk contemplated by the parties is never run by the insured, so that he obtains no benefit from the contract. Put simply, 'the insurer shall not receive the price of running a risk if he runs none' (*Stevenson* v *Shaw* (1877) 4R (Ct of Sess) 1076), and the whole of the premium should be returned, subject to any agreement to the contrary. Similarly, any agreement as to the return of all or part of the premium will override any statutory stipulations, which are contained in ss 82–84 of the Marine Insurance Act 1906. Section 82 states that:

Where the premium or a proportionate part thereof is, by this Act, declared to be returnable
(a) If already paid, it may be recovered by the assured from the insurer; and
(b) If unpaid, it may be retained by the assured or his agent.

Section 83 states that:

Where the policy contains a stipulation for the return of the premium, or a proportionate part thereof, on the happening of a certain event, and that event happens, the premium, or as the case may be, the proportionate part thereof, is thereupon returnable to the assured.

Section 84 stipulates that:

(1) Where the consideration for the payment of the premium totally fails, and there has been no fraud or illegality on the part of the assured or his agents, the premium is thereupon returnable to the assured.
(2) Where the consideration for the payment of the premium is apportionable and there is a total failure of any apportionable part of the consideration, a proportionate part of the premium is, under the like conditions, thereupon returnable to the assured.
(3) In particular:
   (a) Where the policy is void, or is avoided by the insurer as from the commencement of the risk, the premium is returnable, provided that there has been no fraud or illegality on the part of the assured; but if the risk is not apportionable, and has once attached, the premium is not returnable;
   (b) Where the subject-matter insured, or part thereof, has never been imperilled, the premium, or, as the case may be, a proportionate part thereof, is returnable;
Provided that where the subject-matter has been insured 'lost or not lost' and has arrived in safety at the time when the contract is concluded, the premium is not returnable unless, at such time, the insurer knew of the safe arrival.
   (c) Where the assured has no insurable interest throughout the currency

of the risk, the premium is returnable, provided that this rule does not apply to a policy effected by way of gaming or wagering;

(d) Where the assured has a defeasible interest which is terminated during the currency of the risk, the premium is not returnable;
(e) Where the assured has over-insured under an unvalued policy, a proportionate part of the premium is returnable;
(f) Subject to the foregoing provisions, where the assured has over-insured by double insurance, a proportionate part of the several premiums is returnable:

Provided that, if the policies are effected at different times, and any earlier policy has at any time borne the entire risk, or if a claim has been paid on the policy in respect of the full sum insured thereby, no premium is returnable in respect of that policy, and when the double insurance is effected knowingly by the assured no premium is returnable.

Thus the premium may be recovered in whole or in part.

Recovery of the entire premium

This is allowed where the consideration has totally failed, under s 84(1) above, and where:

(a) there has been a failure to agree so as to negative consensus ad idem;
(b) the policy is void because its issue was ultra vires the insurer (*Re Phoenix Life Assurance* (1862) 2 J & H 441);
(c) the policy is illegal; or
(d) the insurer has been fraudulent.

A contract which is illegal when it incepts gives neither party any rights under it, if both parties are equally guilty. Thus any guilt of the insured will operate so as to prevent him reclaiming any premium. So the absence of an insurable interest in life insurance which is known to the 'insured', or the absence of authorisation on the part of the insurer, of which the insured is aware, will ensure that the premium remains with the insurer (*Re Arthur Average Association for British, Foreign and Colonial Ships, ex parte Hargrove* (1875) 10 Ch App 542). There are, however, certain exceptions which operate in favour of the insured:

(a) where the insurer fraudulently represented the position and such fraud induced the insured to contract with the insurer eg as to the legality of the contract, eg where the insurer represented that an insurable interest was unnecessary under a life policy, knowing that this was untrue (*Hughes* v *Liverpool Friendly Society* [1916] 2 KB 482; *Tofts* v *Pearl Life Assurance Company Ltd* [1915] 1 KB 189). An innocent misrepresentation as to legality will not entitle the insured to a return of premium (*Harse* v *Pearl*

Life Assurance [1904] 1 KB 558). The rationale for this is that whilst ignorance of the law is not usually a defence, the parties are not expected to be experts in insurance law and where both parties are innocent, the situation is simply frozen;

(b) where the insured contracted under a mistake of fact, such as an ignorance that war has broken out and the insured has become someone who cannot validly contract, eg an enemy alien, or that a life is insured in the belief that the *cestui qui vie* is alive, when he is not;[7]

(c) perhaps where there is *locus penitentiae*. This is literally a chance of repentance and can be exercised by the insured whilst the contract remains executory and the risk has not attached.[8] It is not clear whether the insured actually has to repent or can simply state that he does not want to continue;

(d) breach of the duty of good faith by the insurer may also entitle the insured to recover his premium, because damages are not available for breach of the duty (*La Banque Financiere de la cité SA v Westgate Insurance Co Ltd* [1988] 2 Lloyd's Rep 513), so that avoidance is the only remedy, giving rise to a right to premium. The insured can elect to waive the insurer's breach, in which case he will not be entitled to any return of premium.

Misrepresentation or non-disclosure The policy is avoided by the insurer for misrepresentation or non-disclosure by the insured. This may occur:

(a) if the misrepresentation or non-disclosure was innocent. The insurer can avoid the contract ab initio, in which case the premium must be returned because the consideration has wholly failed, the risk never attaching (*Anderson v Thornton* (1853) 8 Ex 425); or

(b) if the insured has acted fraudulently. Fraudulent behaviour by the insured disentitles him to sue for the recovery of any premium paid, since to allow him to do so would be to condone his fraud. Curiously, though, a court may not grant the equitable remedy of rescission to an insurer on his application in such a

---

7 *Oom v Bruce* (1810) 12 East 225; *Pritchard v The Merchant's and Tradesman's Mutual Life Assurance Society* (1858) 3 CB(NS) 622, 644, 645; *Strickland v Turner* (1852) 7 Ex 208. These examples apply the general principle that money paid under a (common) mistake of fact is recoverable, since the contract is void.

8 *Lowry v Bordieu* (1780) 2 Dougl 468; *Busk v Walsh* (1812) 4 Taunt 290; *Howard v Refuge Friendly Society* (1886) 54 LT 644.

situation unless he effectively repays any premium, on the basis that 'he who seeks equity must do equity'.[9]

Subject matter of contract is unidentifiable   The subject matter of the contract of insurance is incapable of identification so as to render the contract void for uncertainty, or it has been destroyed (except in marine insurance where the risk has attached retrospectively), or the insured has no insurable interest in the subject matter (except where a marine policy is effected by way of gaming or wagering).

The policy does not accord with the contract   Premiums will be refundable because they were paid under a mistake (*Fowler v Scottish Equitable Life* (1858) LJ Ch 225), except where the insured is entitled to rectification of the policy (*General Accident Insurance Corporation v Cronk* (1901) 17 TLR 233).

Breaking a warranty   In certain circumstances where the insured has broken a warranty, the insurer may elect to avoid. Examples of this include the following situations:

(a) where the insured warrants that a particular state of affairs exists at inception, such as that his habits are temperate, when in fact they are intemperate (*Thomson v Weems* (1884) 9 App Cas 671 (682)), or that the subject matter is in a specified location or condition when that is not in fact the case, the risk does not attach with the effect that the premiums are not due. They should be refunded as money paid without consideration (*Dawsons Ltd v Bonnin* (1922) AC 413);

(b) where a continuing warranty or future warranty is broken after inception, premiums paid prior to the breach will not be returned to the insured because the insurer has been on risk. However, premiums paid after the breach may be recovered, and after a renewal of the contract, since there is a new contract of insurance which falls into (a) above: the risk does not attach as the breach takes place before (re)inception (*Sparenborg v Edinburgh Life* [1912] 1 KB 195, 204). However, this entitlement to recover may be negatived by agreement by a term providing for forfeiture of premiums if the insured breaches any warranty.

---

9 *Barker v Walters* (1844) 8 Beav 92, 96; *London Assurance v Mansel* [1897] 11 ChD 363, 372. However, it may be arguable that there is no equity against the insurer, where it is blameless. Wright J did not decide this point in *Biggar v Rock Life Assurance Company* [1902] 1 KB 516, at 526. See MacGillivray & Parkington p 419.

The insurer is not avoiding the policy but rather is repudiating it by relying on its terms, subject to any argument that such a clause is a penalty (*Kumar* v *Life Insurance Corp of India* [1974] 1 Lloyd's Rep 147).

Recovery of part of the premium

By agreement   An agreement to return premium can often be found in marine policies, but it is less usual in non-marine. Partial return of premium may occur when the policy is cancelled by agreement or the risk is reduced, or upon the exercise of a clause by which the insurers can unilaterally cancel upon return of unearned premium (on a pro rata basis).

In reinsurance treaties it is usual for the reinsured to set aside and retain a proportion of the premium (up to a specified total), known as a premium reserve deposit. This provides the reinsured with security for the termination of the contract, against the risk exposure to primary insureds, which may leave it exposed for many years. There may also be a local statutory requirement which may require the imposition of this term by a foreign reinsured, which may sometimes be satisfied by the provision of Letters of Credit. In this way unearned premium ie premium for the period after termination until the end of the risk, calculated on a pro rata basis, can be allocated by the reinsured either to pay claims against him or as premium for other reinsurance.

Section 84(2) of the Marine Insurance Act 1906, which applies to marine and non-marine insurance   Where the risk can be apportioned, a proportionate part of the premium will be returnable if there is a total failure of any apportionable part of the risk. This will only be effective where the insurance covers several subject matters, or where a clear division of risk can be made eg where a voyage is subject to different warranties for different sections. Failure to comply with a warranty will mean that the risk will not attach for that part of the voyage, and a proportionate part of the premium will be refundable (*Stevenson* v *Snow* (1761) 3 Burr 1237). The success of any attempt to apportion a risk will always depend on the construction of the policy (*CT Bowring Reinsurance Ltd* v *Baxter* [1987] 2 Lloyd's Rep 416). Where the liability to pay premium accrues on a monthly basis, rather than globally at the outset, premiums need not be paid after any frustrating event.

Over-insurance   The principle allowing for return of premium in over-insurance is that some of the premium has been paid for the balance of the over-insurance, ie over the amount that the insured would be entitled to claim. Thus part of the premium is paid without consideration, since the insurer would not have to pay the full amount of the insurance in the event of loss. This principle was enunciated in *Fisk v Masterman* (1841) 8 M & W 165, 168 as being 'on the ground of short interest'.

Unvalued policy In non-marine insurance the premium is not apportionable and is therefore not recoverable under the above principle (*Wolenberg v Royal Co-operative Society* (1915) 84 LJKB 1316). Marine insurance under s 84(3)(e) provides for a proportionate return of premium.

Valued policy The parties have agreed the value of the subject matter, and overinsurance cannot therefore occur. But where the extent of insurance provided to the insured cannot be fully ascertained until the policy period has expired, the premium cannot be properly quantified in any event.

Double insurance This is a form of over-insurance, in circumstances where more than one policy has been taken out on the same subject matter, and the total amount recoverable is in excess of the true value of the subject matter. The overriding principle is that, since the contract of insurance is generally one of indemnity, the insured cannot therefore recover more than he has lost. Each insurer must have been on risk in order for the insured to be able to recover under either policy. That being so, the premium cannot be apportioned in non-marine insurance and the insurers can therefore retain the premium.

However, for marine insurance s 84(3)(f) of the Marine Insurance Act 1906 provides that a proportion of the premium is returnable, depending on the dates upon which the policies were effected. These are as follows:

(a) policies effected on the same day are treated as one insurance, and therefore neither insurer will bear the risk in full. The insured may recover premium in proportion to the amount each insurer has agreed to pay (*Fisk v Masterman* (1841) 8 M & W 165);

(b) policies effected on different dates must mean that the earlier insurer was on risk in full, and would be liable if a loss had occurred before further insurance was effected. Therefore, as the consideration has not failed, no premium need be returned by the 'earlier' insurer. But the later policies occasion the over-insurance and may have to return premium on a pro rata basis, in proportion to the sums insured. Where a claim is made on one policy for the full sum, no premium will be returned, nor when the double insurance is knowingly effected by the insured.

Where the insurer goes into liquidation Liquidation of a corporate insurer will result in termination of the policy. The consideration will therefore have failed for the remainder of the policy after the date of liquidation and the insured will be entitled to a partial return of premium. Of course any loss prior to the date of liquidation occasions liability on the part of the insurer, although there may be insufficient funds to pay in full. Where the insurer was not authorised to make the contract of insurance, and it is thus illegal, the insured (who could not enforce any claim in the insurer's liquidation) could recover his premium in full if he was unaware of the lack of authorisation (*Re Cavalier Insurance Co Ltd* [1989] 2 Lloyd's Rep 430).

The amount recoverable will be assessed under ss 53–59 of the Insurance Companies Act 1982 if applicable, and the Insurance Companies (Winding-Up) Rules (SI 1985/95) as amended (SI 1986/2002).

'Cooling-off' period The insured may decide that he does not wish to continue with the policy of insurance during the statutory period for 'cooling off' (eg Insurance Companies Act 1982 ss 75–77) and is therefore entitled to return of his premium.

Chapter 10

The claims process

The contract of insurance can be considered effectively to fall into two parts. The offer and acceptance lead to a binding and executed contract for the payment of a sum on the happening of an event, but the contract remains executory in the sense that neither party need do anything further (save comply with continuing warranties) except await that event. The event, when it happens, then gives rise to a prima facie liability on the insurer to pay, but initially it triggers an additional set of rights and obligations which fall on the insured, through which he must tread warily if he is to succeed.

DUTY OF BROKER

The insured should already have established whether he will be able to retain the broker as his guide. In insurances effected at Lloyd's the assistance of the broker in steering claims through underwriters may be implied into the contract of agency by custom, market usage and the fact that the Lloyd's underwriter is not accessible to the insured, except through litigation (because he is directly liable to the insured under s 53 of the Marine Insurance Act 1906). However, outside Lloyd's the broker's obligation to assist may not be specified in any written contract of agency and the insured will therefore have to prove that it is implied, or was otherwise agreed. Brokers in personal motor insurance usually specify the extent of their claims service, mainly owing to the small amount of the business and its value to them, and will only render their services if the insured pays them a fee. Life and pensions practice differs between brokers, with either the insured or the broker dealing with all aspects. In *Anthony Gibbs, Sage Limited* v *Euro Afro Traders Limited* (Unreported: October 1981) the Court of Appeal was faced with the insured's argument that a 'broker who agrees to negotiate the formation of a contract of insurance thereby undertakes the shadowy obligation to pursue a claim if it comes to his notice that the adventure the subject of the insurance contract has met with a catastrophe so that a claim is on foot', and that the broker should be liable for failing to inform the insured of the correct procedure for making an insurance claim following a loss. In the light of an earlier comment that this 'interesting' implied term was shadowy, Lord Justice Cumming-Bruce commented that 'the shape of the shadow is so obscure that the greater the attempts that are made to discern what the edges of the shadow are, the more difficult it is to convince oneself that there is a shadow at all'. Lord Justice Templeman agreed, stating that the possibility that 'the duty of a broker extends in some respects to pursuing a claim which falls due under the policy' was an 'interesting and startling proposition'.

It is therefore clear that the party should agree the extent of the broker's duties prior to the execution of those duties, although whether a broker acts would depend mainly on the size of the claim and the likelihood of future business; a refusal to act will probably result in the absence of future business, since there may be plenty of other brokers available who are not only willing to act, but who also view an efficient claims service as the best advertisement of their abilities.

Upon receipt of information as to a loss and instructions from the insured to activate and pursue a claim on his behalf, the broker should consider whether he is already contractually bound to execute the wishes of the insured, and if not, whether he is prepared to do so. It seems reasonable that a broker who holds himself out as able and prepared to obtain insurance also holds himself out as able to carry out all ancillary aspects of that insurance, which would include claims, although he would not be under any duty to do so in the absence of agreement (*Xenos v Wickham* (1867) LT 2 HL 296, 320).[1] Whilst a unilateral request by the insured to the broker to pursue a claim cannot constitute a contract in the absence of acceptance by the broker, it would appear that the broker should inform the insured immediately of his inability or unwillingness to act on his behalf, so that the insured will not be prejudiced by any delay and so as to enable the insured to obtain assistance with his claim elsewhere. In *Jameson v Swainstone* (1809) 2 Camp 546 Note 3

---

1 In *Minett v Forrester* (1811) 4 Taunt 542 Mansfield CJ stated at p 544 'that [the broker] is the agent of the insured, first, in effecting the policy, and in every thing that is to be done in consequence of it;' but this latter clause appears to relate to any administrative requirements rather than claims. He had earlier

the insured successfully showed that he had been led by the two-year silence of the broker to believe that the claim had been settled and that he had therefore been deprived of the opportunity to enforce his policy. The broker should also clarify the extent of his assistance with the insured, and in particular the remuneration to be paid whether the claim is successful or not. In the absence of a previously agreed contractual retainer, any acceptance by the broker of the insured's instructions will constitute a new agency.

Without delay the broker should consider the policy in detail to confirm that the loss should give rise to a liability upon the insurer to pay, and to ascertain the framework within which the route to payment is set. Having also satisfied himself that the premium has been paid, the first step is notification of loss. However, the initial obligation to fall upon the insured is that of mitigation of loss.

MITIGATION

It is a principle of English law that the party who suffers from the other's breach of contract must mitigate the effects of that loss.[2] An insured is subject to this doctrine in respect of an insured event because an action on an insurance contract is one for unliquidated damages for breach of contract, rather than in debt (*Edmunds* v *Lloyd Italico* [1986] 2 All ER 249). The duty to mitigate stipulates that the insured must take all reasonable steps to avert or minimise his loss,

---

commented during argument that 'The assured might have taken the policy from the broker who effected it, paying him what he owed him at the time of taking it, and might have placed it in the hands of another broker to be adjusted,' at p 543, thus appearing to accept the divisibility of the broker's possible obligations. The position may be different where the broker has retained the policy because 'he shall be presumed to promise, that he will collect the sums due from the underwriters upon a loss happening, in consideration of the commission he receives for effecting the insurance. Here, [the broker], if he chose to part with his lien, might have handed over the policy to the assured as soon as it was effected, and his responsibility would then have been at an end; but as he retained it, he was bound to use all reasonable diligence to bring the underwriters to a settlement of the loss, according to the usage of the trade in this respect': *Bousfield* v *Creswell* (1810) 2 Camp 545. In *Bell* v *Kinmouth* (1988) 53 DLR 4 731 the Court of Appeal in British Columbia held that as an agent 'his duty was to exercise a reasonable degree of skill and care to obtain policies in the terms bargained for and to service those policies as circumstances might require'.

2　McGregor on Damages breaks down the 'duty' to mitigate into three rules: the insured cannot recover for any loss which he could have avoided; he can recover for any loss incurred in reasonable attempts to avoid loss; and he cannot claim for any benefit to the insurer.

and must avoid taking unreasonable steps that increase his loss. The test is that of a reasonable man intent on preserving his own property, as opposed to claiming on the insurer (*Integrated Container Service Inc* v *British Traders Insurance Co Ltd* [1984] 1 Lloyd's Rep 154, 158), the question as to what is reasonable depending on the circumstances. For example, it is unreasonable for an insured knowingly to spend more money mitigating a loss than the loss is worth. The insured must reasonably believe that mitigation was necessary owing to his perceived imminent danger of loss to the insured subject matter, but can only recover if the expense was properly incurred and the loss would have been caused by a risk insured against. The insurer will not be able to rely on evidence showing that the insured risk did not later materialise if the 'anticipatory' mitigation was reasonable when effected.[3].

Section 78(4) of the Marine Insurance Act 1906 states that:

It is the duty of the assured and his agents, in all cases, to take such measures as may be reasonable for the purpose of averting or minimising a loss.

Marine policies usually contain a 'sue and labour clause' which specifies that the insured must mitigate his loss and that the insurers will contribute in proportion to their cover.

As the duty to mitigate is applicable throughout contract law, the statutory obligation imposed by s 78(4) upon marine insureds simply restates the obligations owed by marine and non-marine insureds alike. A failure to mitigate will result in the insurer pleading a reduction of the claim in his Defence for the amount of loss in monetary terms that could and should have been avoided by the insured. Phillips J assessed this at 20 per cent in *Youell* v *Bland Welch & Co Ltd* (Unreported: Judgment 27 March 1990) where he also commented that:

In my judgment the significant distinction between failure to mitigate and negligence on the part of the Plaintiff which intervenes between wrong and loss, is that failure to mitigate bars recovery in the situation where the Plaintiff deliberately acts in a manner which is unreasonable. It seems to me that an essential part of the rationale underlying the bar to recovery where there has been a failure to mitigate is that the loss in question is caused by the Plaintiff's voluntary conduct, not by the Defendant's wrong. The test of unreasonable conduct is thus not objective, but involves

---

3 Ibid ' . . . there is obvious justification for a "stitch in time" approach . . . The risk of loss was therefore not too remote, at the time the expense was incurred by the plaintiffs, to warrant activity under the sue and labour clause' at p 163.

consideration of the Plaintiff's knowledge . . . where a Plaintiff is unaware of the breach, the implications of his conduct fall to be determined, not according to the specific doctrine of mitigation but according to the general principles of causation. If it is not reasonably foreseeable that the Plaintiff will remain in ignorance of the breach and fail to react to it so as to avoid loss, the loss may be too remote. If the Plaintiff negligently fails to discover the breach, so that he takes no steps to mitigate its effect, the normal consequences of negligence will follow including, where appropriate, the application of the 1945 Act.

Recovering costs of mitigation

Having mitigated his loss for the benefit of the insurer, whose subsequent payment to the insured may be substantially smaller as a result, the insured will want to recover his costs of mitigation. He may be able to do so on the basis that the contract contains an implied term to this effect; the insured is insured against the loss in question, and it is not for his benefit that he has incurred costs. *Emperor Goldmining Co Ltd* v *Switzerland General Insurance Co Ltd* [1964] 1 Lloyd's Rep 348 is an Australian authority in favour of the recovery by the insured of his proper costs of mitigation in marine insurance, in the absence of a sue and labour clause, which would appear to be applicable also to non-marine insurance in England.

However, this case was not followed by Neill J ('with great diffidence') in *Integrated Container Service Inc* v *British Traders Insurance Co Ltd* [1981] 2 Lloyd's Rep 460, 465) because 'it is not necessary to imply an obligation on the insurers to reimburse the insured for any expenses incurred in carrying out the duty imposed by statute . . . '. Further, the implied term was not thought necessary to give business efficacy to the contract. However, Neill J and the Court of Appeal on other grounds held that the expenses of mitigation were reasonable upon the construction of the policy, the latter without reference to *Emperor Goldmining* although Eveleigh LJ stated, in the context of s 78(4), that 'the right to recover expenses is a corollary to the duty to act'. The argument therefore remains open partly because *Emperor Goldmining* was distinguished by Neill J on the basis that it did not contain a sue and labour clause, and partly because Neill J was in a difficult position; having already rejected the right to recovery expressed in the contract, he could not then imply a similar right. He also made it clear that his views were strictly obiter. Finally, he was essentially construing s 78(1) which only attaches when a sue and labour clause exists in the policy, and the effect of Clause 9 of the Institute Container Clauses and s 78(4) on the sue and labour clause, rather than the duty of mitigation imposed solely by s 78(4). On the other hand, if upheld *Emperor Goldmining* would render all sue and labour clauses otiose since the insured could recover any sum provided it was reasonably incurred. It is therefore arguable that the costs of mitigation can be recovered in the absence of a sue and labour clause (which invariably makes any expenditure an indemnifiable loss), perhaps provided that the total sum payable by the insurer does not exceed the limit of insurance cover under the policy.

Incurring an increased loss or 'secondary' liability

The insured, whilst attempting to mitigate, might actually increase the loss, or incur a 'secondary' liability to a third party. Provided the insured's actions were reasonable and the secondary loss or liability was not too remote to be excluded by the doctrine of proximate cause, he can recover a sum in respect of his loss in addition to his costs of mitigation (*Lloyds & Scottish Finance Ltd* v *Modern Cars & Caravans (Kingston) Ltd* [1966] 1 QB 764). Problems may arise where the insured's actions give rise to loss from an uninsured risk. In this case the court will apply the doctrine of proximate cause and consider whether the secondary loss can be directly linked to the insured risk or whether the steps taken by the assured give rise to a *novus actus interveniens*. Thus damage caused by water used to douse goods on fire will be considered as damage caused by fire (*Stanley* v *Western Insurance Co* (1868) LR 3 Exch 71), and even loss caused by theft of the insured's goods after their removal from burning premises was held to be recoverable under a fire policy (*Levy* v *Baillie* (1831) 7 Bing 349). Negligence by an insured may, however, preclude recovery, if it is a *novus actus interveniens*.

Further, the commencement of the insured risk will enable the insured to take whatever steps he considers necessary to mitigate without breaking the chain of causation from the risk, so that 'any loss resulting from an apparently necessary and bona fide effort to [minimise the risk] . . . , every loss that clearly and proximately results whether directly or indirectly, from the [risk], is within the policy' (*Stanley* v *Western Insurance Co* (1868) LR 3 Exch 71, 74). However, where the risk appears to have commenced but in actuality has not, for example smoke emanating from a cargo hold which comes not from a fire but from a defective valve, then the damage caused by mitigation will not be recoverable by the insured (*Watson & Sons* v *Firemen's Fund Insurance Co of San Francisco* [1922] 2 KB 355), a principle reflected in s 78(3) of the Marine Insurance Act 1906 which states:

Expenses incurred for the purpose of averting or diminishing any loss not covered by the policy are not recoverable under the suing and labouring clause.

NOTIFICATION OF LOSS

The insured is under no duty to give immediate notice of any loss (*The 'Litsion Pride'* [1985] 1 Lloyd's Rep 437) to the insurer in the absence of a term requiring such a prompt reaction. Such terms are usually phrased 'as soon as possible' or 'as soon as reasonably practicable' and are subject to the usual rules of interpretation, which take all relevant circumstances into account, including the availability of knowledge of a loss or events giving rise to a claim to the party responsible for bringing a claim. These clauses are, however, construed objectively in that delay which could have been avoided, or which ought to have been avoided in the circumstances, will operate to defeat the claim. 'Forthwith' or 'immediately' require stricter compliance, not only within a reasonable time and without unjustifiable delay, but also probably at the first available opportunity.[4]

It is arguable, however, that the absence of a term requiring immediate notice will not absolve the insured from giving notice as quickly as possible after a loss or event for two reasons. First, the contract of insurance is subject to an extra-contractual duty of good faith (*La Banque Financiere de la cité SA* v *Westgate Insurance Co Ltd* [1988] 2 Lloyd's Rep 513) which is at its most important prior to the formation of the contract but which continues to apply to all aspects of the contract, including claims (*The 'Litsion Pride'* [1985] 1 Lloyd's Rep 437). The contract period may have expired and the claim may have occured during any run-off period, but the duty should still apply. It would appear logical that any notification should be provided timeously. Secondly, the insurer is entitled to be subrogated to the rights of the insured and could be prejudiced in his ability to claim against offending parties if notification is late.

---

4 *Re Williams and Lancashire and Yorkshire Accident Insurance Co* (1902) 19 TLR 82. However, Nourse J held in *PS Refson & Co Ltd* v *Saggers* [1984] 3 All ER 111 that there was no difference in meaning or effect between 'forthwith' and 'as soon as reasonably practical'. 'Immediately' was held in *Re Coleman's Depositories Ltd and Life & Health Assurance Association* [1907] 2 KB 798 at 807 to mean 'with all reasonable speed considering the circumstances of the case', and was followed in *Farrell* v *Federated Employers Insurance Association Ltd* [1970] 3 All ER 632 at 635. The fact is that the meaning of any limiting phrase will be determined by the wording.

It is therefore arguable that a term requiring timeous notification is implied into every contract, since the very purpose of prompt notification is to enable the insurer to take such steps as he may consider necessary to ameliorate the position. Whether or not the notice must be given as promptly as possible, Lloyd J endorsed Professor Hardy Ivamy's view (at p 398) that notice must be given within a reasonable time, in *Hadenfayre Ltd* v *British National Insurance Society Ltd* [1984] 2 Lloyd's Rep 393, 402).

Although the insured need not exercise any right to claim under the policy, and is entitled to pursue the offending party for recompense for his loss, the obligation to notify does not arise when he decides to claim under the policy, but at the date of the relevant event giving rise to the loss.

A condition precedent

A more difficult problem of interpretation from the view of the insured is whether or not the term is a condition precedent, with which he may have been unable to comply. A condition precedent demands its discharge before the insurer can be liable, whilst an ordinary condition entitles the insured to claim even when in breach. Breach of an ordinary condition entitles the insurer to claim damages but these will be minimal where the notice provision has been complied with as soon as practicable, or where the insurer has not suffered prejudice. The courts tend towards holding that a condition is not a condition precedent unless it is very clearly expressed, since the rules of construction dictate that the clause relied upon to preclude liability is construed *contra proferentem*, and will only do so where the clause is specifically expressed to be a condition precedent, or where it is clearly stated that compliance with it is of fundamental importance to the insurer.

Nevertheless, conditions expressed to be precedent may be held not to have that effect. In *Re Bradley and Essex and Suffolk Accident Indemnity Society* [1912] 1 KB 415) several conditions stated to be precedent to liability were not upheld because some of the clauses could not be so appropriately described. The case was decided in 1912 but seems to have anticipated recent trends favouring the consumer (the insured) in that factors such as the size of print, the insurer's failure to indicate the inclusion or nature of the terms in the policy, and their general unsavoury nature operating against the insured, were all held to be relevant in a decision which was distinctly contrary to what was agreed by the parties. This decision is outside the English contractual doctrine of laissez-faire and may not be upheld today; there did not appear to be any great inequality of bargaining power between the parties, and the insured may have been able to obtain less onerous insurance elsewhere. Nevertheless, extreme care should be taken by the insurer to specify the nature of conditions precedent and their importance to him if he is to enforce them.

However, *Pioneer Concrete (UK) Ltd* v *National Employers Mutual General Insurance Association Ltd* [1985] 2 All ER 395 may serve to redress the balance. Bingham J adopted a strict technical approach to hold that breach of a clearly expressed condition precedent was an absolute defence by the insurer, and that the fact that the insurer was not prejudiced by late notification was irrelevant. He also commented that if prejudice were necessary, relatively little prejudice would be sufficient eg any weakening of the insurer's position in that they were unable to negotiate or put the claimant to proof, or apply their minds as to the tactics of litigation.

Absolute terms

A time specified by the insurer in absolute terms (ie 'within 14 days') which is also a condition precedent requires absolute compliance, even though the loss claimed for does not arise until well after the event giving rise to that loss (*Cassel* v *Lancashire and Yorkshire Accident* (1885) 1 TLR 495). However, any such condition may require to be drawn specifically to the attention of the insured and would, no doubt, be considered with disfavour by the courts where the insured has not complied but has not been at fault. Thus in *Re Coleman's Depositories Ltd and Life & Health Assurance Association* [1907] 2 KB 798 there was a departure from the rule that an insured's offer to pay premium is accepted by the insurer on his usual terms, and that the contract is made when the offer is accepted, in respect of which both parties are bound, although this perhaps may be distinguished on the grounds that the insurance was provisional, the cover note being a contract distinct from any later contract of insurance, and the conditions usually inserted by the insurer were not expressly incorporated into the cover note. One other explanation which was not canvassed by the Court of Appeal was the proposition that the insurer must draw attention to any strict or onerous requirement upon which he will insist, under his obligation of good faith. Perhaps more relevant today is the court's dislike of such exclusion clauses generally.

Failure to comply with a strict notification period

The fact is that a failure to comply with a strict notification period contained in a condition precedent, where the insured is clearly unable to comply, which apparently justifies non-payment by the insurer (and retention of the premiums), is an absurdity, since such a clause enables the insurer to have his cake and eat it. It wholly defeats the purpose of the insurance. It has, however, been ameliorated by the change of wording in fraud policies where the time for notification does not begin to run until the insured becomes aware of the fraud, and not when it occurred or when the insured ought to have become aware of it. This is laudable, particularly since the nature of fraud is such that its existence is unlikely to be discovered until well after the event. But it should apply across the board. Statutes such as the Latent Damage Act have gone some way to redress the balance in other fields, but the Unfair Contract Terms Act 1977 was excluded from insurance contracts on an understanding between the insurers and the Government, later contained in a 'Statement of Practice' dated 1981 and revised in 1986.[5] Unfortunately this currently has no legal effect, in the absence of a court decision stating that the Code delineates the insurer's obligations of good faith, and the only sanction in the face of any unreasonable behaviour by insurers is to legislate. The 'better' insurers do, however, carefully heed the Statement of Practice.

Time limits in liability policies
It is accepted, however, that time limits in liability policies require a higher level of compliance. A liability policy enables the insured to obtain payment up to a specified limit in respect of any liability considered or found to be owing by the insured to a third party, and the keystone for such payment is the event giving rise to the alleged liability. Insurers usually insist on becoming involved with the resolution of the claims following events which may lead to liability, to the extent of appointing their own loss adjusters or investigators to look into the event as quickly as possible after it happens, and notification provisions are therefore important to liability insurers. The insured must therefore draw a line between constantly advising his insurers of every event which could in some way lead to a claim, however unlikely, and notifying his insurers only of events which will clearly give rise to claims. Nevertheless, however tedious it may be, he should err on the side of excessive advice and should request insurers to inform him whether they require further information in each case. A failure by insurers to

---

5 See 'the Legal Status of Non-Statutory Codes of Practice' 1988, JBL 12.

follow up such requests may lead to an estoppel operating against their later denial of liability.

Temporary cover

The other problem that may occur concerns temporary cover, which does not specify or necessarily incorporate any terms of the policy intended to be issued. Any claim by the insured will be under the contract as evidenced by the cover note, and the comments above should apply to this situation. However, the insured may be in a stronger position than he would have been had a policy been issued, in that he may not be penalised if he is not made aware of any term as to notification, as in *Re Coleman* (above). Where the cover note states that it is subject to the proposal form, which in turn states that it is subject to the usual conditions of the insurer's policy, the insured will be bound by the insurer's usual terms (*Wyndham Rather Ltd* v *Eagle Star and British Dominions Insurance Company Ltd* (1925) 21 Ll L Rep 214).

Notice to a party competent to receive it need not be in writing unless specified by the policy. As has been noted, the purpose of giving notice to the insurer is not only to enable the insured to initiate formally the claims process, but also to enable the insurer to consider the loss and take such steps as may be necessary to minimise it so far as they are capable. Thus blithely and vaguely informing the insurer that events have occurred which may give rise to a claim may not constitute good notice, even though it would probably lead to proper notice if the insurer took further steps or investigated it further. Essentially the notice must bring 'home to the mind of a reasonably intelligent and careful recipient such knowledge as fairly, and in a business sense amounts to notice of' the relevant event or loss.

In *Thorman* v *New Hampshire Insurance Co and Home Insurance Co* [1988] 1 Lloyd's Rep 7 the developers of a building, which had suffered damage as a result of the architects' negligence, wrote to the architects in terms that 'Serious problems have arisen in this development, inter alia, with regard to cracking and defective brickwork, for which we must hold you responsible' in June 1982. The Court of Appeal held that this letter constituted a general claim which included defective brickwork, as a result of the words inter alia, so that later claims would fall under the policy in force at the date of notification, even though the detail would not become known until much later.

Policies specifying the extent and depth of notice

Some policies specify the extent and depth of the notice. 'Full particulars' means 'the best particulars which an assured can reasonably give' (*Mason* v *Harvey* (1853) 8 Ex 819, 820). Compliance with such clauses generally requires the insured to provide sufficient particulars to enable the insurer to understand the nature, ambit and essence of the loss. Since particulars are by definition more detailed than notice, a longer time for their provision will be allowed in the absence of a term to the contrary. However, the insured must still take all possible steps to comply. Thus a failure to comply with a provision requiring the insured to provide a detailed account of the loss within 15 days 'as the nature and circumstances of the case will permit', in that the insured could have provided a more detailed account than he did, will justify non-payment by the insurer (*Hiddle* v *National Fire & Marine Insurance Co of New Zealand* [1896] AC 372).

What constitutes good notice

Notice to any party with apparent authority to accept such notice will constitute good notice and may be given by any party authorised by the insured. There is some judicial dispute as to whether notification of an event or loss under the policy to the insurer by a third party is capable of discharging an obligation in the policy that notice of loss must be given by the insured. The current law is embodied in *Lickiss* v *Milestone Motor Policies at Lloyd's* [1966] 2 All ER 972 in which Denning MR and Danckwerts LJ held that the notification proviso had been discharged by the provision of notice of loss by the third party to whom the insured was (or would become) liable and by the police. The insurer had not suffered any prejudice by the insured's failure to notify under the policy, and the rationale of the notification clause had been effected since the insurer was in a position to take whatever steps he deemed necessary, and indeed was in the identical position to that in which the insured had given notice. Salmon LJ, however, adopted the view that the obligation to notify was personal to the insured as a matter of construction. *The 'Litsion Pride'* ([1985] 1 Lloyd's Rep 437) may support this latter view, on the basis that the notification clause is subject to a continuing duty of good faith by the insured, which cannot be discharged by notification by a third party.

However, the decision of the majority in *Lickiss* v *Milestone* may be sustainable on the basis that the obligations inherent in the duty of good faith do not change from those prior to the formation of the contract, where the insured need not disclose information 'known or presumed to be known' by the insurer under s 18(3)(b) of the Marine

Insurance Act 1906. The most acceptable solution would seem to be that information known by the insurer which constitutes clear notice of loss or an event which may give rise to liability will not enable the insurer to disclaim liability on the basis of breach of condition, but this is subject to the qualification that the parties' rights and obligations will depend on the construction of the wording in each case.[6] Where the notice provision is a condition precedent such a claim may not be sustained, and the burden of proof on the insured to show that the insurer was fully aware of the position, and able to protect himself accordingly, will be high. Thus a failure to notify in the case of, say, a major disaster which is well reported, may not be justifiable unless the insured can prove that the insurer knew; the insurer may have been on holiday and not reading newspapers, or have failed to realise that he has insured a line.

Notice must be given to competent authority

The notice must also be given to a party sufficiently competent to accept it and thereby discharge the insured's notification obligation. Most policies specify the address to which notice must be sent, often a firm of solicitors in reinsurance policies, or the insurer's head office. The broker is not competent to receive notice on behalf of the insurer unless expressly authorised, but a failure to forward the notice by the broker where he is the insured's agent will render him fully liable if the insurer would have been liable for the claim.

It should be noted that any condition imposed by the insurer in the contract need not be discharged by the insured if the insurer waives his right to insist on performance of that condition. Any waiver must have originated from a party authorised to waive compliance with a contractual term and the action giving rise to the waiver must have been capable only of the interpretation that the insurer intended to waive compliance by the insured. Waiver will be easier to prove if the insured would be prejudiced by the insurer's later allegation that the condition breached should be or should have been complied with, or where the insured is unable to comply with the condition as a result of the position adopted by the insurer (*Lickiss* v *Milestone* [1966] 2 All ER 972). Any failure by the insurer to take action or confirm that he will rely on the breach of notification clause to avoid or reduce liability (eg by set-off if the

---

6 See *The 'Mozart'* [1985] 1 Lloyd's Rep 238 and *Valla Giovanni & C Spa* v *Gebr van Weelde Scheepvaartkantor BV The 'Chanda'* [1985] 1 Lloyd's Rep 563 for further examples and confirmation of the 'futility principle'.

condition is not precedent) will not by itself amount to waiver, but waiver by silence may be sustained if the insured had suffered prejudice, or where third parties' rights would be affected, or where the delay in processing a claim made out of time by the insured was sufficiently long to give rise to a presumed intention by the insurer that he would accept liability (*Allen* v *Robles* [1969] 2 Lloyd's Rep 61).

The next stage is to ascertain the amount of the loss.

QUANTIFICATION OF LOSS

The insurer's liability to the insured must be identified before any payment can be made, since the insurer can only discharge its liability by pecuniary payment (or reinstatement). Such liability has already been established in the case of a valued policy which specifies the sum to be paid in the event of the loss, and is conclusive except in the case of fraud or mistake. An unvalued policy merely specifies the limit of indemnity of the insurer and the insured must prove the extent of indemnity to be paid by the insurer. If the insured's loss exceeds the value of the policy, he is only entitled to the sum insured.

Section 28 of the Marine Insurance Act 1906 states:

An unvalued policy is a policy which does not specify the value of the subject-matter insured, but, subject to the limit of the sum insured, leaves the insurable value to be subsequently ascertained, in the manner hereinbefore specified.

In the case of liability insurance, the liability of the insured to a third party must be established before the insurer need pay anything.

Clearly, in any liability insurance, the insured is in a better position to determine the extent of any payment to a third party by the insurer. Nevertheless, the insurer has to investigate the position to satisfy himself as to the amount of payment. There is therefore a duty upon the insured to co-operate with the insurer. This general duty continues from the duty to notify the insurer of the loss, to providing details of the loss so that the insurer can determine the amount he should pay the insured, or a third party in liability policies, and beyond into assisting the insurer in any subrogated claim.

Usually a formal proof of loss or claim form is completed with the assistance of the broker in as much detail as reasonably practical. There is some dispute as to the level of information required, and whether it is to be a reasonable level when objectively viewed or whether it may be subject to the insurer's unreasonable requirements. In *Welch* v *Royal Exchange Assurance* [1939] 1 KB 294 the insured refused to provide information requested by the insurer which was not relevant to the loss, and did not justify the insurer's repudiation of the claim. He was held to be in breach of a condition precedent which stated that he was to produce all information 'as may reasonably be required', partly because the term was a condition precedent, and partly because the arbitrator found that production of the information was 'reasonably required' since the insurer had reason to consider the information requested as being material. There are, however, earlier cases which impose a requirement of reasonableness on the insurer to ensure that he does not act capriciously or unjustly[7] but the position is not clear. Whether the insured has provided sufficient information is determined by the circumstances: commercial loss through a warehouse fire will require a higher standard of verification through stock records etc than other damage which may be capable of more accurate, independent assessment.

Further information can be provided at any stage, but care must be taken to comply with the specified time of a condition precedent. The insured is also under a post-contractual duty of good faith to disclose all material facts to the insurer when submitting a claim (*The 'Litsion Pride'* [1985] 1 Lloyd's Rep 437).

Burden of proof

The insured must prove (on the balance of probabilities) that he has suffered a loss payable by the insurer by adducing sufficient evidence to show that it is covered by the policy (*Munro, Brice & Co* v *War Risks Association Ltd* [1918] 2 KB 78). Thus, in marine insurance, where the insured is attempting to recover under a marine policy for a peril of the sea, he must prove that the peril was fortuitous (*The 'Alexion Hope'* [1986] 1 Lloyd's Rep 311). Where he cannot do so, the court is entitled to find that the insured's case is insufficiently proven, enabling the claim to be rejected (*Rhesa Shipping Co SA* v *Edmunds, The 'Popi M'* [1985] 2 All ER 712).

---

7 *Moore* v *Woolsey* (1854) 4 EL & BC 243, 256. *Fearnless Braunstein* v *Accidental Death* (1861) 1 B & S 782.

Proximate cause

The insured can only recover those losses whose dominant or operative causes are covered by the contract of insurance (*Leyland Shipping Co Ltd* v *Norwich Union Fire Insurance Society Ltd* [1918] AC 350). Thus where damages are actually caused by an explosion but that explosion is initiated by a fire, and fire is covered by the policy, the insured can recover. The loss or damage must be the necessary consequence of the peril insured against, and it must be a necessary consequence of that peril: the result must be the logical imperative of the cause. Disputes arise where the loss is caused by more than one peril and it is difficult to state which cause constituted the proximate cause. If both perils may be said to be proximate causes, the insured may be entitled to recover on the basis that either one would have caused the loss. Disputes may occur where the insured takes action to avoid a loss or in mitigating damage, and the loss that occurs is not proximately caused by an insured peril. Thus putting a ship into port to avoid any risk of being captured cannot constitute a loss by capture (*Becker, Gray & Co* v *London Assurance Corporation* [1918] AC 101) and the removal of goods from insured premises when there is no prospect of fire will not be covered. The risk insured against must occur (*Moore* v *Evans* [1918] AC 185).

Of course the policy must be carefully considered to determine whether the insured is covered. The exclusions or excepted perils clause may affect the insurer's liability, since what appears to be covered may not be. Thus in *Coxe* v *Employers' Liability Insurance Corporation* [1916] 2 KB 629 an officer was inspecting sentries along a railway line during the Great War. He was killed by a train and his death was clearly caused by this accident. However, he could not recover under his life policy because it excluded death caused directly or indirectly by war. He would not have been near the railway line had it not been for the war, which was therefore an indirect cause of his death.

Reduction of claim

Having established the insured's liability (where necessary) and the amount payable by the insurer, there are several ways in which the payment by an insurer may be reduced, as follows:

Pro rata contribution by other insurers concurrently liable to the insured
This will depend on the terms of the policies and, in the absence of an express term, the insured can claim from either insurer. An

express term will ensure that the insured must proceed against the insurers for their respective contributions, up to the amount of loss suffered (and no more), rather than request payment in full from one (*North British & Mercantile Insurance Co* v *London, Liverpool & Globe Insurance Co* [1877] 5 ChD 569).

Problems may arise owing to conflicting contractual terms. Thus in *Gale* v *Motor Union Insurance Co Ltd* [1928] 1 KB 359 each policy excluded liability if alternative insurance existed and contained a 'contribution by rateable proportion' clause. The court held that both insurers should each pay half the loss. The policy may also require the discharge of other policies before any payment under it can be made (ie an excess policy) but this too may be subject to other contribution clauses under similar policies.

An excess clause or right to contribution from the insured

An excess clause specifies that the insurer's duty to pay only comes into force after a specified level of pecuniary loss has been reached, and the insured effectively pays for the claim up to this sum. Thus any settlement of the insured's liability paid by the insurer to a third party (where the insurer is entitled to conduct and settle the claim) enables the insurer to repayment from the insured of the excess (ie the deductible) (*Beacon Insurance Co Ltd* v *Langdale* [1939] 4 All ER 204). The clause might also specify that the insured must retain a proportion of any loss; an insurance of this retention elsewhere will avoid the policy, as a breach of a continuing warranty (*Traill* v *Baring* (1864) 4 DeGJ & S 318). Alternatively the policy may specify that the insurer will only be liable for a specified portion of the loss, in which case the insured can obtain insurance elsewhere.

A clause limiting payment in certain circumstances

This is simply an ordinary term of the contract specifying the conditions in which the insurer will be liable.

An average clause

An average clause ensures that an insured who is not fully insured bears a rateable proportion of any loss he suffers by making him a co-insurer. It does not apply to a total loss, for which the insurer is fully liable even if the insured is underinsured, since the insured automatically bears the uninsured balance, but simply ensures that the insured suffers a proportionate reduction in respect of the uninsured section of any partial loss. Sections 67(2) and 81 of the Marine Insurance Act 1906 are relevant.

Section 67(2) states that:

Where there is a loss recoverable under the policy, the insurer, or each insurer if there be more than one, is liable for such proportion of the measure of indemnity as the amount of his subscription bears to the value fixed by the policy in the case of a valued policy, or to the insurable value in the case of an unvalued policy.

Section 81 states that:

Where the assured is insured for an amount less than the insurable value or, in the case of a valued policy, for an amount less than the policy valuation, he is deemed to be his own insurer in respect of the uninsured balance.

Section 81 ensures that marine insurance is subject to average, but under a non-marine policy the insured bears no part of a partial loss until the limit of indemnity is surpassed (*Sillem* v *Thornton* (1854) 3 E&B 868, 888).

For a non-marine insurance to be subject to average, a specific condition must be incorporated, and this will not be implied.

Where the insured has more than one contract of insurance containing an average clause, he cannot claim the loss from one insurer, but effectively will have to obtain from each insurer their rateable proportion of the loss (*Acme Wood Flooring* v *Martin* (1904) 20 TLR 229).

An 'event' clause

These are usually phrased in terms of 'accidents' or 'occurrences' and operate to limit the insurer's liability by imposing a limit of payment where the insurer is potentially liable to pay out several times as a result of liability flowing from any one incident, which may amount to payment above the policy limit. Such a limit operates to aggregate all loss and naturally occasions litigation to determine what constitutes an 'event'.

'Any one accident' refers to each loss or damage suffered by third parties, and does not entitle the insurer to aggregate claims and limit his liability, but means that he must pay each claim in full up to the policy limit (*South Staffordshire Tramways Co* v *Sickness & Accident Assurance Association* [1891] 1 QB 402). The word 'occurrence' is the subject of judicial dispute but will probably be interpreted as meaning that the occurrence is not the loss or damage suffered but is the act giving rise to that loss or damage (*The 'Alexion Hope'* [1986] 1 Lloyd's Rep 311, 316). In *Forney* v *Dominion Insurance Co Ltd* [1969] 3 All ER 831, 835, the court clearly distinguished between 'accident' and 'occurrence', and stated that the word 'occurrence' had been specifically included in the policy to exclude the *South Staffordshire* interpretation of 'accident'. Thus 'occurrence' operates in favour of the insurer to limit the total amount payable by the insurer to the policy limit. *Philadelphia National Bank* v *Price* [1938] 2 All ER 199 is an opposing decision in which the Court of Appeal held that a fraud perpetrated on the bank over six years under one agreement entitled the insurers to avoid payment by relying on the excess (which exceeded each fraudulent payment), and therefore that the occurrence was not the overall fraud by instalments on one agreement, but a series of individual incidents.[8]

Betterment by the insured

Section 69(1) of the Marine Insurance Act 1906 codifies the rule in marine insurance that any insurance monies owed can be reduced where the insured is placed in a better position by virtue of the loss. The amount is subject to negotiation by experts but may be subject to exclusion by prior agreement. The principle of betterment cannot apply to liability insurance and must be irrelevant in replacement policies on goods in which the insured may be charged a higher premium for any potential betterment, the quid pro quo for which is that the insured is entitled to replace his stolen or damaged goods with new ones. The principle of betterment can be implied in non-marine insurance in the absence of an express term excluding it (*Reynolds & Anderson* v *Phoenix Assurance Co* [1978] 2 Lloyd's Rep 440, 453).

A franchise clause

The insurer is not liable to pay any sum below a specified figure, but is liable to pay for the amount of the loss when that figure is reached ie there is no deductible amount.

Fraud

'Fraud is proved when it it shown that a false representation has been made knowingly or without belief in its truth or recklessly, careless whether it be true or false' (*Derry* v *Peek* (1889) 14 App Cas 337). Proving fraud is of course the problem. *Hornal* v *Neuberger Products Ltd* [1957] 1 QB 247 stated that 'a charge of fraud will naturally require for itself a higher degree of probability than that which it would require when asking if negligence is established. It does not adopt so high a degree as a criminal court, even when it is considering a charge of a criminal nature; but still it does require

---

8 The authors of Insurance Contract Law comment that this case should not be relied on mainly because there was insufficient distinction drawn between 'loss' and 'occurrence', which seems to be correct.

a degree of probability which is commensurate with the occasion'. Stephenson LJ cited in *ICA* v *Scor* [1985] 1 Lloyd's Rep 312 the standard of proof in *Naranayan Chettiar* v *Official Assignee, Rangoon* (1941) All India Reporter 93 Privy Council, to the effect that 'fraud of this nature, like any other charge of a criminal offence whether made in civil or criminal proceedings, must be established beyond reasonable doubt'. Leggatt J had already commented at first instance that fraud has to be established with 'a higher degree of probability than would otherwise be requisite' (*ICA* v *Scor* [1983] 1 Lloyd's Rep 541, 553). A claim tainted in any way by fraud is a breach of the insured's duty of good faith and may entitle the insurer to treat the policy as void ab initio, or to reject the claim and continue with the policy, retaining the premium (*The 'Litsion Pride'* [1985] 1 Lloyd's Rep 437). If treated as void ab initio, the policy never came into effect and therefore any claims paid must be repaid as must any premium. A fraudulent claim by one insured will not affect another insured provided the policy is composite (in the names of more than one insured) for their separable respective rights and interests (*Woolcott* v *Sun Alliance & London Insurance Ltd* [1978] 1 All ER 1253, where a fire policy was avoided against a non-disclosing mortgagor but not against the mortgagee building society also named as an insured).

The concept that a fraudulent claim is capable of rendering the policy void ab initio is somewhat harsh, since it involves repayment of all premiums and claims, and may be considered disproportionate to the breach. The position is not yet clear. Hirst J in *The 'Litsion Pride'* [1985] 1 Lloyd's Rep 437 cited with approval (at p 514) Lord Trayner's decision in *Reid* v *Employers Accident* (1899) 1 F 1031, 1036[9] that 'a fraudulent claim would not have avoided the policy. The fraudulent misdescription, when discovered, would have been an answer to that particular claim, or to that part of the claim which was fraudulent, but it would have left the policy as a current obligation untouched'.[10] However, in *The 'Captain Panagos DP'* [1986] 2 Lloyd's Rep Evans J stated (obiter) that:

. . . fraud . . . also breaks an implied term of the contract . . . which entitles the insurer to avoid the policy ab initio . . . and so give(s) him the

---

9 Hardy Ivamy believes this Scottish case to be out of kilter with English authorities, at p 408 note 1.

10 However, there is a passage later in *The 'Litsion Pride'* which endorses the view that the policy can be avoided ab initio, despite Hirst J's clear acceptance of Lord Trayner's dictum.

right to elect whether or not to accept the breach as discharging him from further performance of the contract . . . there would be force in [counsel's] submission that fraud in the making of one could only release insurers from liability in the other if insurers exercise their right to avoid or terminate the contract, subject always to prior affirmation with full knowledge of the facts. Here, however, the two claims are closely connected, notwithstanding their technical separation for the purposes of alternative partial loss claims, and on the present hypothesis the one claim is defeated by connivance by the assured. In these circumstances, in my judgment, the plaintiffs' fraud in relation to one entitles the defendants to refuse liability in respect of both.

The position remains capable of judicial clarification.

Varieties of fraud   The commonest fraud is an overestimate of the loss. This may be based on one of two premises: either that the overestimate is clearly fraudulent in that it is made with the intention of obtaining payment of the claim in full (*Dome Mining Corp Ltd* v *Drysdale* (1931) 41 Ll L Rep 109); or that it is made as a bargaining factor and takes into account the almost inevitable reduction upon which the insurer will insist, so that the insured will be paid what he considers to be his true loss. The former is clearly fraudulent; the latter may not be. The insured, when faced with evidence of his exaggeration, will state that it was made in order to bargain. The insurer will either have to prove that the insured intended to act fraudulently, or show that the exaggeration is so excessive as to refute any intention of honesty (*London Assurance Co* v *Clare* (1937) 57 Ll L Rep 254). The difference between a bargaining factor (which the insured does not intend to recover in full) and fraud is one of degree. Any fraud in relation to any part of the claim will nullify the whole claim, and perhaps the entire contract (*'Captain Panagos DP'* at p 511).

Other varieties include destruction of the subject matter which as wilful misconduct cannot be recovered owing to s 55(2)(a) of the Marine Insurance Act 1906, the absence of any loss, adding further subject matter to the insured subject matter in the claim, or incorrect statements as to the cause of loss, particularly where the actual loss is an event not covered by the policy. However, the insured is allowed some leeway in his information, provided that any inaccuracy is not material to the insurer's decision as to payment (*Cox* v *Orion Insurance Co* (1982) RTR 1, obiter) and as long as it was made in good faith (*The 'Litsion Pride'* [1985] 1 Lloyd's Rep 437).

Settlement and payment

In liability insurance the claim against the insured will almost invariably be handled by the insurer who will pay to the claimant the sum agreed by way of settlement, or the amount found due by the court from the insured, subject to policy limits. Settlements are a matter for negotiation between the insurer and insured and have no legal effect until they fulfil the usual requirements of contract law — any offer made must be unconditionally accepted, and the settlement replaces and discharges the insurer's obligations to the insured under the policy, at least in respect of that claim (*Kitchen Design & Advice Ltd* v *Lea Valley Water Co* [1989] 2 QB 221). Of course the insured can claim for as many events or losses that take place during the policy period, subject to any term limiting the number of claims either to an aggregate value or during a specified period. The insurer may, however, by injudicious wording in the settlement agreement lose his rights of subrogation where, for example, he makes a part payment only and the insured later receives greater compensation from a third party than the insurer was prepared to pay to the insured (*Brooks* v *MacDonnell* (1835) 1 Y & CEx 500).

Payment must be made by the insurer in cash (*The 'Admiral C'* [1981] 1 Lloyd's Rep 9; *The 'Okeanis'* [1986] 1 Lloyd's Rep 195) to the insured or to his authorised agent (broker, assignee, personal representative, trustee or even judgment creditor); in case of doubt the insurer should seek a declaration of the court. The court has the power to award payment in a foreign currency. Where the currency of a policy is specified, payment in that currency is a good discharge of the insurer's liabilities. Payment in Sterling in respect of a loss or liability expressed in a foreign currency will require calculation at the exchange rate applicable when payment becomes due (*Sturge* v *Excess Insurance Co Ltd* [1938] 4 All ER 424). Interest will not be payable unless expressly provided in the contract (The *'La Pintada'* [1984] 2 Lloyd's Rep 9). It is, however, within the discretion of the court to award interest under s 35A of the Supreme Court Act 1981, provided that proceedings were commenced prior to the acceptance of any payment of the principal sum due (*Edmunds* v *Lloyd Italico* [1986] 2 All ER 249). Interest will not be payable until a suitable time has elapsed, in order to enable the insurer to investigate the loss (*Burts & Harvey* v *Vulcan Boiler & General Insurance Co* (1966) 1 Lloyd's Rep 354).

Interim payments   In the absence of agreement the insured can apply to the court for an interim payment under Ord 29 r 11 of the Rules of the Supreme Court, where it is clear that the insurer will be found liable and the outstanding litigation relates largely to quantum. If the insurer can establish that it is not liable at all, the insured can apply for an interim order against the broker. The insured cannot, however, sue both (in the alternative) and obtain an interim payment order against either since it will not be apparent who will be liable (*Ricci Burns Ltd* v *Toole* [1989] 3 All ER 478).

Effect of mistake upon payment of insurers   At common law any payment by the insurer is irrecoverable unless paid whilst the insurer was labouring under a mistake of fact which is so fundamental to the agreement and in whose absence the agreement as negotiated would not have been reached (*Bell* v *Lever Bros* [1932] AC 161). Equity has been used by the courts to widen this principle and will grant rescission more easily, even to mistaken inferences drawn from known facts, which could be categorised as mistakes of fact, or fact and law. In *Solle* v *Butcher* (1950) 1 KB 671 Denning LJ held that the contract could be set aside in equity if the parties were under a common misapprehension either as to the facts or their relative rights, as long as the misapprehension was fundamental to the later contract and the party seeking rescission was not at fault. A mistake only of law, however, will not entitle the insurer to recoup his payment (*Kelly* v *Solari* (1841) 9 M & W 54, 58). Where the insurer has paid under a mistake of fact, payment to the insured's agent will entitle the insurer to recover, provided that the agent has not paid it to the insured (*Holland* v *Russell* (1863) 4 B & S 14), either in cash or by way of settled account (*Trinidad Lake Asphalt* v *Commissioners of Income Tax* [1945] AC 1). If it has been paid over to the insured, the insurer will have to sue the insured for monies had and received, and will have no claim against the broker. This doctrine can also operate in favour of the insured, eg for premium paid by mistake (*CT Bowring Reinsurance Ltd* v *Baxter* [1987] 2 Lloyd's Rep 416).

The distinction between mistake of law and fact is not always easy to make and some settlements may be predicated on a combination of mistaken law and fact. In such circumstances the insurer will have to prove that the mistake of fact dominated over the mistake of law in persuading him to settle on the terms agreed (*Home & Colonial Insurance Co Ltd* v *London Guarantee & Accident Co Ltd* (1928) 43 TLR 134). The most common areas of dispute are as follows:

(a) The absence of a valid contract of insurance, which covers the loss claimed for — this will entitle the insurer to repayment since the payment was based on his belief that a policy existed. This does not constitute a mistake of law ie that he was under an obligation to pay, but is a mistake of fact ie that a physical contract existed which satisfied the relevant requirements — offer, acceptance, consideration etc (*Kelly* v *Solari* (1841) 9 M & W 54). Where, however, the insurer is aware of all facts occasioning the loss but is ignorant of the law, so that the loss or damage was not covered by the insurance, the insurer will not be entitled to repayment. Thus where an insurer agrees to pay under a contract of insurance for marine perils for damage to a cargo of fruit after a collision but the real cause of loss was their ripening, he was entitled to recover since his factual belief was that the collision was the cause of loss, which was fundamental to his decision to pay (*Norwich Union Fire Insurance Society Ltd* v *Price* [1934] AC 455).

(b) The voidability of the contract occasioned by a misrepresentation or non-disclosure of a material fact of which the insurer was not aware at the date of settlement may cause this dispute. This was the case in *Bilbie* v *Lumley* (1802) 2 East 469 where the court held that the insurer could not rely upon a non-disclosure of a letter at the date of the formation of the contract of insurance to set aside a later settlement, if the letter had been submitted to him before the settlement was agreed. The mistake did not relate to the non-disclosure but to the insurer's right to rely on non-disclosure. In *Magee* v *Pennine Insurance Co Ltd* [1969] 2 Lloyd's Rep 378 the Court of Appeal held that a material misrepresentation in a proposal form, the truth of which was unknown both to insurer and insured at the time of settlement, was a fundamental common mistake which categorised the contract as voidable. Although rescission requires *restitutio in integrum*, the premium in this case was not ordered to be returned. It is difficult to understand why such disputes should reach court, except as a result of inconsistencies between the definitions of a mistake of law and a mistake of fact. It seems clear that an insurer would prefer not to pay out money under a liability which he may not have, and therefore that any facts which may vitiate that liability are clearly fundamental to any agreement he may reach. It is not a question of mistake of law, but a mistake of fact inducing a mistake of law. Any mistake of fact which engenders a mistake of law should give rise to a right of the insurer to avoid the policy, and will entitle him to repayment of sums paid under a liability assumed and founded on the apparent truth of the mistake, provided the insurer was not and could not have been aware of the mistake of fact. Where the insurer has paid in full knowledge of the facts but in ignorance of the law, or could have investigated the facts but declined to do so (*Kelly* v *Solari* (1841) 9 M & W 54), he will be unable to recover. Where, however, he once knew the facts but had forgotten them at the date of settlement, he may be able to recover. The knowledge, or decision not to enquire, apparently must exist at the date of payment.

(c) A breach of contract by the insured may occur. Where the insurer is aware of the breach but does not realise that such breach entitles him to refuse to pay, then the insurer is aware of the facts and the mistake can only be categorised as a mistake of law; repayment need not be made.

(d) The insured has no insurable interest at the inception of the insurance ie where the lack of insurable interest is sufficiently fundamental to render the insurance illegal, void or unenforceable, the mistake will justify repayment to the insurer, since it is one of fact. A mistake is similarly characterised where it concerns the extent of the insurable interest (*Irving* v *Richardson* (1831) 2 B & Ad 193). But where the insurer is aware of the nature of the interest and fails to recognise that he need not pay as a matter of law, the mistake is of law and will not engender repayment.

(e) The insured has suffered no loss. Such a situation brings to mind cries of fraud or misrepresentation. However, it can occur without either. Where the insurer has paid under an indemnity policy he is entitled to take possession of the insured subject matter, even though it may later be found that no loss has occurred. Payment for a partial loss under an indemnity policy must be returned since there is no right to salvage. Similarly, no such right exists in non-indemnity policies, eg life assurance: beneficiaries cannot retain payment if the 'deceased' subsequently reappears. Such return of payment would appear properly predicated on the basis that the insured had died, and that his death was fundamental to the payment. However, it has been argued successfully in America that the insurer has waived his rights to a return of payment since he has assumed the risk that the event occasioning payment has occurred, and should have investigated the position more thoroughly (*New York Life Insurance Co* v *Chittenden* 112 NW 96 [1907]). A change of position by the beneficiary will also serve to refute any claim for repayment eg where the money has been spent, or where the beneficiary can argue that the consideration for the settlement is an avoidance of litigation with the insurer, presumably in the absence of collusion between the beneficiary and the insured.

(f) The value of the loss is actually less than the payment. The insurer has no right to repayment after payment under a valued policy. In the event of a disagreement which cannot be proved one way or the other (ie literally a value judgement) under an unvalued policy, then any later increase or decrease in the settlement sum will not affect it. The rule as to mistake does not apply to a negotiated settlement between insurer and insured particularly where the insured has misrepresented the position or was fraudulent in connection with the settlement (*Herbert* v *Champion* (1809) 1 Camp 134), or the insurer has effectively waived enquiry (ie where he is on notice but still agrees to settle) or the payment is expressed to be ex gratia. Thus where none of the other situations capable of affecting the settlement arises, the parties are bound. A properly negotiated settlement can then only be impeached by the insured proving duress, where the insurer has threatened an unlawful act eg breaking the contract in circumstances where the insured has no real choice other than to accept. The right to repayment in the light of excessive claims by the insured depends on the amount of exaggeration suffered by the insurer. In cases of extreme optimism by the insured, he may be liable to return the entire sum paid, as happened in *Assicurazione Generali de Trieste* v *Empress Assurance Corp Ltd* [1907] 2 KB 814 where the reinsurer recovered monies paid to the reinsured after the latter had recovered the monies it had paid to the insured, as a result of the insured's fraud. Otherwise he may have to return the balance between the sum received and the amount due under the policy (*North British & Mercantile Insurance Co* v *Moffatt* (1871) LR 7 CP 25, where the excess was simply not covered by the policy).

(g) There has been fraud or misrepresentation. A fraudulent claim is a breach of the continuing duty of good faith and may entitle the insurer to avoid ab initio, recovering all payments made to the insured in return for all premiums paid. Any non-fraudulent misrepresentation inducing a settlement, and relied on by the insurer, will render the settlement voidable and any payment will be returned in the event that it is avoided by the insurer (*Livesey* v *Jenkins* [1985] 1 All ER 106).

Recovery of payment to brokers

Where an insurer has paid money to a broker pursuant to a settlement but then ascertains that one of the above exceptions is applicable, the broker is obliged to return that money (*Kleinwort, Sons & Co* v *Dunlop Rubber Co* (1907) 97 LT 263) if he has not already paid it to the insured (*Holland* v *Russell* (1863) 4 B & S 14), unless the broker has become aware that the settlement is voidable (and known to be so by the insurer) but pays nevertheless (*Oates* v *Hudson* (1851) 6 Ex 346).[11] Such payment need not be physically transferred to the

---

11 But the broker may be under no duty (outside Lloyd's, and subject to the application of the insured's duty of *uberrima fides*) to inform the insurer as to the true position; if he knows that he has wrongly been paid money, is he then to hold it indefinitely? The solution may be to pay it to the insured subject to an agreement with the insured to indemnify the broker in the event that the broker is later forced to repay the money.

insured; the relevant debits and credits effected by the broker in his account with the insured will be sufficient provided that account is clearly in existence.

Ex gratia payment

An ex gratia payment is one made by insurers in their alleged absence of liability, which does not bind them in later similar situations, so that they can then dispute liability without having estopped themselves from so doing by any earlier compromise. They are offers made for commercial reasons where the insured's future business is sizeable, and operate to both parties' advantage, since it obviates the insured from proving:

(a) the loss; and

(b) that it falls within the policy,

whilst heightening the insurer's business reputation.

They cannot be recovered except where characterised as a loan which is to be returned if the insured fails to establish the insurer's liability.

DISPUTE DOCUMENTATION

It is often the case that the broker holds documentation which may be of assistance to one party, and detrimental to the other, particularly since the insurer rarely retains a placing file. The insurer will want to re-evaluate the information provided by the broker on behalf of the insured and upon which the risk was accepted, the drafts of the slip or policy wording as evidence of the parties' intention, evidence as to the extent and nature of the insurance expected by the insured and whether that is inconsistent with the insured's current stance, evidence as to any admission of the insured, and evidence of the broker's negligence. However, the insurer has no right to see the file where it clearly relates to work done by the broker as agent for the insured, and if the broker hands it over without authority to do so from the insured, he will not be fulfilling his duty of confidence. The only documents to which the insurer may have access in the placing file are the initialled slip and policy wording. The insurer will, in the absence of the insured's consent, have to wait until discovery before seeing other documentation. The exception to this rule will occur where the broker has acted for the insurer in any capacity eg where he holds a binding authority from the insurer, in which case the documents are the property of the insurer, or there may be a claims file containing information obtained by the broker for or on behalf of the insurer which is the property of the insurer, such as loss adjusters' or solicitors' reports. If such documents exist, the broker is placed in an invidious position largely of his own making, and he must minimise any conflict of interest, either by ceasing to assist the insurer in the handling of the claim or removing himself altogether where he has obtained confidential information as agent for the insurer which should be disclosed to the insured but cannot, since to do so would be to break the duty of confidence which he has assumed to the insurer. Such documents should not be sent to the insurer via the broker where the information contained is detrimental to the insured, particularly at Lloyd's since this will be in breach of Lloyd's Byelaw No 5 of 1988.

The insured will have a strong prima facie case to the production of all documents held by the broker on the basis that the broker is his agent and that the documents therefore belong to the insured. In principle this is correct. The insured is entitled to see the placing file of his broker, although he may not have a right to its entire contents; attendance notes of conversations or meetings, internal memoranda, draft slips and wordings, and internal accounting documents are deemed to be the broker's own documents, made for the benefit of the broker 'in carrying out his expert work' (*Leicestershire CC v Michael Faraday & Partners Ltd* [1941] 2 KB 205, 216). They need not be handed over (unless perhaps they formed part of the broker's presentation to the insurer), although they may be subjected to a subpoena *duces tecum* for production at trial.[12] Documents provided to the broker by the insured, and carbon copies of letters to third parties or the insured belong to the insured. Potentially the most useful single item will be the report prepared by a loss adjuster, which will set out the known facts, liability and recommended strategy for the insurer.

The practice used to be that the insurer would instruct the broker who placed the insurance to obtain a report from an adjuster or assessor, which would be passed to the insurer via the broker, who would retain a copy on his file. However, the broker would not disclose the report to his principal, the insured. Megaw J in *Anglo-African Merchants Ltd v Bayley* [1970] 1 QB stated that:

---

12 Provided that they are sufficiently particularised and are not merely conjectural (unless evidenced in some way). A compendious description of the documents will suffice provided that evidence can be produced to satisfy the court that the documents do exist or had existed: *Re Asbestos Insurance Coverage Cases* [1985] 1 All ER 716. See also *Sunderland Steamship P&I Association v Gatoil International Inc* [1988] 2 Lloyd's Rep 180.

In the absence of such express and fully informed consent . . . it would be a breach of duty on the part of the insurance broker so to act . . . Such a relationship with the insurer, inevitably, even if wrongly, invites the suspicion that the broker is hunting with the hounds whilst running with the hare . . . a custom will not be upheld . . . if it contradicts the vital principle that an agent may not at the same time serve two masters — two principals — in actual or potential opposition to one another: unless, indeed, he has the explicit, informed consent of both principals.

The insured was therefore entitled to see the broker's file. However, in *North & South Trust Co* v *Berkeley* [1971] 1 WLR 470 Donaldson J held that such a breach of duty did not entitle the insured to insist that the brokers were bound to disclose any information obtained in breach of duty, including information which had been obtained by the brokers on terms that it be kept confidential from the insured, or information for which the brokers would not have been accountable to the insured, or not acquired in the service of the insured or in discharge of the broker's duty to the insured. The insured had a legitimate complaint and could claim damages, but could not see the documentation held by the brokers. Donaldson J fitted his analysis in with that of Megaw J in '*Anglo*' on the basis that the documents in '*Anglo*' included much material to which the insured was plainly entitled.

If the insured is unable to obtain an assessor's report from the broker, he may be able to obtain it on 'Discovery' in any litigation with the insurer if the report does not attract legal professional privilege. Often it will, since the dominant purpose of the insurer in commissioning the report will have been for the purpose of obtaining legal advice (*Waugh* v *British Railways Board* [1980] AC 521) or to assist in the conduct of litigation which must have been 'in reasonable prospect' at the time the report was commissioned or produced. It is equally arguable that any report may have been commissioned in order to provide the insurer with information to consider and settle the claim, rather than on the basis that the insurer intended to litigate with the insured.[13] Where the report is commissioned for two purposes, such as, on the one hand, the continuing operation of the insured's business and its safety, and on the other hand, the obtaining of legal advice, the court will only

---

13 It will depend entirely on the facts in each case. Where the insured and insurer can be the only two parties to litigation, any report would appear more likely to be privileged. Where other parties are involved eg in liability insurance, a report commissioned for litigation between the insurer and a third party may not attract privilege in respect of later litigation between the insurer and insured.

uphold a claim of legal professional privilege if the latter is the dominant purpose.

An insurer may also wish to claim privilege in respect of documents passing between the insured (or his agent) and the insurer, if the insurer later pursues a subrogated recovery claim, such as a letter from the insured giving notice of a claim against him. In *Guinness Peat Properties* v *Fitzroy Robinson Partnership* [1987] 2 All ER 716 the Court of Appeal held that such a letter was privileged since the insurer almost invariably obtained legal advice as to whether to pay or not, and therefore that there was a reasonable prospect of litigation when the letter was written.

Chapter 11

Accounting

PROCEDURES

Lloyd's, the insurance companies, the Institute of London Underwriters ('ILU') and Policy Signing and Accounting Centre ('PSAC') have developed systems whereby balances between intermediaries and underwriters are settled in accordance with the central accounting records of these bureaux and by means of central settlement systems. The effect of these arrangements is to enable a complete set-off of all transactions involved in the settlement irrespective of the underlying contractual relationship.

As a result of these settlement arrangements, brokers treat each of the bureaux as single entities and disclose only the ultimate balance due to or from each, regardless of the fact that the net balance may represent numerous transactions and regardless of whether the members of those bureaux were acting as principals or as agents.

Lloyd's Policy & Signing Office

Although the Lloyd's Policy & Signing Office ('LPSO') originally evolved for the purposes of policy signing of all Lloyd's policies, it became apparent that the parties' accounting requirements could be satisfied by a parallel system of accounting, which evolved into a centralised accounting method in 1961. In 1970 the two aspects were separated in order to accelerate premium settlement and today the broker must not delay the accounting procedure by pleading that he is awaiting production of the policy. The current procedure is initiated by the submission of the signing slip to the leading underwriter, together with the original slip for his approval and initials. The initialled signing slip is then sent with the completed premium advice note to the LPSO, who check the relevant details and allocate a signing number and date to the closing. The signing slip is then returned to the broker whilst the LPSO retain the premium advice note for entry in their central accounting procedure. The LPSO computer will then print out the signing table (of the syndicates subscribing the policy) for attachment to the policy.

The broker then arranges for his collection of the premium from the insured, but must not allow any delay in his submission of the accounting documents to the LPSO, ensuring that they are submitted within the limits prescribed by the terms of credit scheme in force. The period of credit relates to the month of the settlement statement in which the relevant policy appears, rather than the date of submission of the accounting documents to LPSO. There are several periods of credit, which vary according to the type of risk and the countries from which the premium emanates. Of course the parties can agree alternative periods of credit; the periods of credit expressed in the *Lloyd's Policy Signing & Central Accounting Manual* are maximum limits, but brokers can apply and obtain the approval of a tribunal for different periods of credit. In fact the Terms of Credit Scheme (introduced in 1972) was intended to provide a monitoring system of the performance of brokers so that appropriate action could be taken to ensure that late payers paid properly. Statistics of late settlements are provided on a monthly basis to the broker, the chairman of broking firms, underwriters and brokers' associations. Penalties are not imposed for late payment but underwriters are kept informed so that they can take any action they consider appropriate with regard to future negotiations with the brokers in question.

Institute of London Underwriters

The Institute of London Underwriters ('ILU') is a formal association of marine and aviation company insurers in London, which provides the insured with a single policy for all its members participating in any one risk whilst retaining the independent liability of those members for their share. It is also a trade organisation, perhaps best known for its development of standard clauses, which are well known and used by other markets.

The ILU deals with the checking of the policy and closing documents submitted by the broker and also operates a single monthly market settlement system whereby the net balance owed by the participating brokers and underwriting companies is calculated and paid. Brokers are considered liable for the premiums, and cheques must be produced by specified accounting dates. Premiums are paid by brokers two months after they have provided the relevant documentation, but claims are paid one month after their request, which enables brokers to fund claims out of the premiums due to the underwriters. The underwriters consider that the Institute policy is as secure as a Lloyd's policy and are therefore concerned about non-payment of claims by their co-insurers, and thus they accept fully the necessity for close mutual supervision of all aspects of their business. Each member is responsible only for its share, and there is no central guarantee fund available in the case of any default, so each member recognises the need for good individual security, and continuing scrutiny.

Policy Signing and Accounting Centre

Policy Signing and Accounting Centre ('PSAC') provides a facility for broker-produced non-marine insurance companies which encompasses standardised accounting procedures, terms of trade for the insurers (ie settlement terms for the payment of accounts between the insurer and broker on the placement of business), daily advices of premium and claims processed, weekly central settlement of balances direct to participants' bank accounts, together with checking and signing policies on behalf of insurers.

PSAC also provides a claims scheme for loss advices and settlements, which includes the first electronic claims scheme in the London Market, weekly central settlement in nine foreign currencies, and central settlement of special payments (usually for premiums). It is linked to the London Insurance Market network (LIMNET), which provides access to the PSAC database (which includes a record of every transaction since 1977), and co-ordinates with Lloyd's, London Insurance Brokers Committee and Reinsurance Offices Association and aims to improve the efficiency of the market by eliminating unnecessary duplication and reducing paperwork.

The system

The running account is prevalent throughout the insurance market, usually to the benefit of all. The system is relatively simple: the insured's claim (when proven payable) appears in the central account as a credit to the broker opposite any debit items for premiums. A balance will be due on this account. There will be many others, for other insureds. All these accounts will be netted off at the end of the week, and the balance paid or rolled over into the following week. Such a multi-programmed system is generally efficient and convenient, but in legal terms it may also create problems.

A broker authorised to receive payment of claims from the insurer is not thereby authorised to set-off the insured's claim against a debt owed by the broker to the insurer. The insured must specifically authorise such set-off. In the absence of specific authority and where the insurer knows that the broker is acting only as agent, the insurer may not set off any personal or other liability of the broker to him, since the insurer would be aware that the broker is not using his own funds to discharge his liability, and the insurer would remain liable to pay the insured if the broker did not pay the insured the claim due. The broker is operating outside his actual and apparent authority.

Right to receive payment in cash
The insurer would argue that such setting-off is a valid and binding custom of the market. This argument will fail unless the insured knows of and has specifically consented to this operation.[1] The custom is contrary to another established rule: the insured is entitled to payment of claims in cash (*Sweeting* v *Pearce* (1861) 9 CBNS 534). The principle is that the insured is more likely to receive his claims money if he is paid in cash. This is reasonable, from the insured's view, since it is unreasonable to expect him to rely on the broker's credit when he has contracted with a blue chip insurance company or Lloyd's syndicate — indeed, the record of a syndicate with respect to claims may have influenced the insured in renewing his policies or placing all new business with that syndicate. There is also the possibility of fraud or collusion arising out of set-off between broker and Lloyd's underwriter (*Bartlett* v *Pentland* (1803) 10 B & C 760, 764).

Payment by cheque does not satisfy this rule, except by agreement or where the insured cashes it and the money is duly credited. Crediting the insured's bank account with the claim is acceptable eg inter-bank transfers between broker and insured.

Thus where the insurance policy provided for claims 'to be collected' by the broker, setting-off was held not to apply because the

---

1 Which he may do in respect of his own claims and premiums, but which he is unlikely to do in respect of those of other insureds represented by the broker. The courts will not impose such an agreement without express consent, or a clear acceptance and acquiescence by the insured of the position, and sometimes not even then.

insured had not agreed to it; 'collected' meant its natural and ordinary meaning of 'collected in cash', not bringing 'into account between brokers and insurers in the manner customary in the market' (*Stolos Compania SA* v *Ajax Insurance Co Ltd* (*The 'Admiral C'*) [1981] 1 Lloyd's Rep 9, 10). Even where the insurance policy stated that 'all claims and losses hereon are to be recoverable only according to the customs and usages of Lloyd's unless otherwise stipulated', the insured company was not bound by the set-off or central accounting unless it actually knew of the custom (*McCowing Lumber & Export Co Inc* v *Pacific Marine Insurance Co Ltd* (1922) 38 TLR 901). This is particularly true at Lloyd's because it is such a specialised and restricted market.

The fact remains, however, that the workings of the insurance market would be extremely and unnecessarily cumbersome if the insured were to insist that all claims be paid in cash. Nevertheless, the law will not succumb to the convenience of the market, though it usually encourages contractual set-off where it can. The only occasion when the central accounting procedure can be by-passed is when urgent settlement of a claim is required, usually in respect of a large claim, eg after a disaster. Speedy settlement reflects well on the insurance market. The approval of all subscribing insurers is required to initiate the 'special settlement' procedure.

Further, particularly in the case of reinsurance, the (re)insured may himself maintain a consolidated rolling account with the broker. If the broker credits the (re)insured with the claims monies in account and this is accepted in payment, the sums are balanced in the account and the broker's lack of authority to receive claims in account will not matter since the (re)insured has been paid.

FUNDING

Funding is the name given to the practice whereby a broker pays claims to the insured before the broker has himself been paid by the insurer, or premiums to the insurer before the broker has received any premium for the insured. It is usually done for sound commercial reasons: apparently prompt settlement of claims will raise the insured's perception of the broker's ability and also his choice of insurer (just as the opposite applies), and will serve to delay any claim by the insured against the broker for his negligent choice of insurance security eg *Moore* v *Mourgue* (1776) 2 Cowp 479. The broker may pay in the hope that the insurer will recommence paying. Informing the insured of the position may result in an immediate claim against the insurer, and also against the broker in the alternative. By funding, however, the broker runs the risk of further liability to the insured for failing to inform the insured that the insurer is not paying claims promptly or at all, which is clearly a relevant fact to the insured since it would enable him to replace the insurance elsewhere.

By funding the broker discharges the liability of the insured to the insurer for premium, or of the insurer to the insured for claims. The issue to be considered is the extent to which the discharge of that liability by voluntary payment can be reversed or mitigated.

Premiums

The broker is liable to the insurer for premium under s 53 of the Marine Insurance Act 1906 for marine insurance, and by custom at Lloyd's for all insurance. The insured is liable to the broker under s 53(2) and the broker's implied right to an indemnity. Any payment of premium by the broker cannot be recovered by the broker from the insurer unless made under a mistake of fact eg an overpayment, or perhaps if the policy is avoided and the premium (wrongly) returned by the insurer to the broker. The insurer must return the gross premium to the insured pursuant to s 53(1), even though the broker may himself have paid the net premium to the insurer, without receipt of premium from the insured. The practice at Lloyd's is for the insurer to pay the gross premium (ie including commission) into an escrow account, pending any decision to avoid the policy. If the insurer then avoids, he will pay the gross premium and any interest earned to the insured, and recover the commission from the broker. He need not pay the interest but usually does so as a matter of goodwill.

Claims

The broker is not liable to pay any claim made by the insured. Such payment is inadvisable from a legal point of view, but brokers sometimes pay for commercial reasons, or the fear of admitting either that the security chosen by themselves is inadequate, or that the brokers' claims service is incompetent, whether this is true or not.

Having paid a claim, the broker may be able to recover it in one of two ways: either by requesting its return from the insured, or from the insurer.

The almost unavoidable result of funding is to conceal the true position from the insured. He will therefore probably be unaware that it is the broker paying his claims, and not the insurer; if he is aware, he must choose between hoping that the broker will continue to pay, and 'coming clean' so that he can terminate the contract for breach and place the insurance elsewhere. If the insured is unaware, the broker will be unable to obtain repayment on the ground that the claim was really a loan or an advance, made on the basis that it would be repayable if the insurer failed to pay within a reasonable time. Clearly no such agreement could exist without any *consensus ad idem*, which would be difficult to prove if the insured were unaware that the broker was funding. The broker would be estopped by his conduct from reclaiming any money, and the insured could go further by claiming damages for the broker's misrepresentation that the insurers were paying, on which he relied to his detriment if the broker stops funding and the insurer continues to fail to pay. Thus undisclosed funding will hold no joy for the broker against the insured. Nor will the broker encounter much joy vis a vis the insurer. He cannot utilise the doctrine of subrogation which can only apply to the situation in which a payment is made pursuant to a legal obligation to pay. The broker has no obligation to pay any claim to the insured and cannot sue the insurer on this basis, because the amount of any claim is owed by the insurer to the insured, not by or to the broker.

Right of insured to sue in his own name

He may, however, be able to sue the insurer for his own benefit and in his own name. The earliest authority for this proposition is *The Provincial Insurance Co of Canada* v *Leduc* (1874) LR 6 224 PC) in which the party insuring was a part owner of half of the vessel, who had been authorised to insure the other half and to recover in full to discharge a debt owed by his co-owner, and thus was not actually a broker. Nevertheless, Sir Barnes Peacock stated that 'It is clear that an agent who insures for another with his authority may sue in his own name'. In *Lloyd's* v *Harper* (1880) 16 ChD 290 James LJ said that 'nobody ever supposed that a broker could not sue on the policy for the benefit of persons interested', in which case he would (presumably) hold any proceeds on trust for those interested persons, rather than for his own benefit. *Woodar Ltd* v *Wimpey Ltd* [1980] 1 WLR 277, 293–4 explained the principle alleged to have been set out by *Provincial* v *Leduc* on the basis that the party suing has suffered loss, or is suing in a fiduciary capacity, as did Hirst J in *Transcontinental Underwriting Agency* v *Grand Union Insurance Co* [1987] 2 Lloyd's Rep 409 and *Pan Atlantic Insurance Co Ltd* v *Pine*

Top Insurance Co Ltd [1988] 2 Lloyd's Rep 505. The brokers successfully claimed a return of premiums as plaintiffs in *CT Bowring Reinsurance Ltd* v *Baxter* [1987] 2 Lloyd's Rep 416 and their right to sue does not appear to have been questioned by the insurers or Hirst J, presumably on the basis that they were liable for the payment of premiums as marine brokers at Lloyd's and were properly suing on their own behalf. However, even though the issue tried as a preliminary issue, it was framed in terms that it was the insured who was entitled to a return of premium, not the broker, because s 53 of the Marine Insurance Act 1906 specifies that the insurer is directly responsible to the insured for the return of premium.

Broker suing in his own name

However, these cases do not provide authority for the broker who has funded a claim to sue in his own name and for his own benefit. *Provincial* v *Leduc* states that there is a custom entitling the broker to sue the insurer after funding, but the broker will encounter difficulty in proving such custom, which is not substantiated by any dicta and is of a personal rather than fiduciary nature. A broker seeking to rely on *Lloyd's* v *Harper* (above) would not, in the case of funding, be suing on the policy for the benefit of the persons interested, but rather for his own benefit. Similarly, in *Pan Atlantic* v *Pine Top* (above) the plaintiff who sued as trustee also had a clear interest in the reinsurance contracts as a party thereto. The plaintiff managing agents of the reinsurance pool in *Transcontinental Underwriting Agency* v *GUIC* (above) were not brokers and stood in the position of agents who had signed the contract on behalf of their principals without disclosing their status as agents by any qualification; a broker will rarely stand in this position, and will usually have acted as disclosed agent only. Thus, the chances of the broker successfully reclaiming in this manner from the insurer any sums paid by the broker are doubtful.

The alternative method is to obtain the authority of the insured to sue in his name, or to obtain an assignment of his name (or of the debt) to the broker. This will be viable if the insured consents, such consent being given in the former case in exchange for a suitable indemnity as to damages and legal costs. If the insured refuses, the broker will have to argue that he is entitled to sue on either basis, on the premise that the funding gave rise to such right. This would probably succeed if the insured requested the broker to fund the claim, since a court may imply that the insured would assist the broker as necessary to recover the funded claim from the insurer. Where the insured is unaware of the funding there is no such agreement and therefore cannot be any implied term.

An assignment by the insured of his name may give rise to a valid set-off by the insurer of premiums due from that insured, and the broker should carefully phrase the contract of indemnity that the insured will require to ensure that he does not become liable to pay out more than he receives, in addition to paying the insurer's legal costs if he is unsuccessful!

One other possibility is that the insurer may acknowledge his indebtedness for the claim to the broker in his accounts, giving rise to a right to the broker to sue the insurer. This position occurred in *The 'Okeanis'* [1986] 1 Lloyd's Rep 195 in which the broker and insurer were alleged by the insured to have agreed an account which included a claim. Bingham J found that the claim had not been agreed and the broker's right to sue the insurer was not considered.

Right of the insurer to sue the broker

The corollary of the above proposition is the right of the insurer to sue the broker which was fully considered by Hirst J in *IGI* v *Kirkland Timms* (Unreported), in which he held that the brokers had unfortunately rendered themselves liable to pay premium by sending out statements of account to the (non-Lloyd's) insurers which acknowledged their liability. The claims evinced by the insurers succeeded for three reasons.

Agency
The brokers stood as intermediaries (ie as agents for both parties) between the insurers and the holders of a binding authority (who were agents of the insurers) and sent premium advice notes which constituted advice that premium was due from the brokers to the insurers, having been properly processed through the brokers' books, and which supported the proposition that they acted under an agency obligation to the insurers. This finding was commercially convenient.

Accounts stated
The principle behind an account stated is that the parties have agreed that certain items will be offset against other items and that the balance only should be paid (*The 'Okeanis'* [1986] 1 Lloyd's Rep 195, 200). The evidence was that the balances stated in the accounts were final, that the title 'premium advice note' connoted a premium

already received, a deduction of commission predicated the exist-ence of premiums in the brokers' hands, and notification of an exchange rate predicated a payment or credit at that rate and date, rather than a future payment in respect of which the exchange rate had not been assigned.

Premiums credited

The brokers' internal accounts credited premiums to the cover holder, and their external accounts showed that they were (at the very least) holding premiums for the use of the insurers. There was therefore a good claim for monies had and received. Hirst J upheld the principle in *Griffin v Weatherby* (1868) LR 3 QB 753 and *Shamin v Joory* [1958] 1 QB 438[2] so that:

> where a person transfers to a creditor on account of a debt, whether due or not, a fund actually existing or accruing in the hands of a third person, and notifies the transfer to the holder of the fund, although there is no legal obligation on the holder to pay the amount of the debt to the transferee, yet the holder of the fund may, and if he does promise to pay to the transferee, then that which was merely an equitable right becomes a legal right in the transferee, founded on the promise; and the money becomes a fund received or to be received for and payable to the transferee, and when it has been received an action for money had and received to the use of the transferee lies at his suit against the holder.

Thus the insurer could obtain payment of those debts due from the broker to the coverholder, if the coverholder notified the broker to pay the insurer and the broker agreed to do so. A deemed payment on account is sufficient to constitute a fund necessary for this principle to apply.

The position is, therefore, that brokers should be extremely careful in their choice of wording on any communication sent to insurers, if they are to avoid liability by estoppel. The insured may force the broker to fund a claim from the insurer by deducting it from pre-mium due to the broker. Such involuntary funding entitles the broker to recover the sum in full from the insured if payment is not forthcoming from the insurer.

---

2 See Goff and Jones *The Law of Restitution*, Sweet and Maxwell (1986) p 404.

SET-OFF

The doctrine

The law of set-off is complex[3] and compounded by the insertion of the broker into the various sets of equations.[4] In matters of insurance any dispute usually revolves around payment of premium, claims and commission, the equations differing according to the (in)solvency of the parties.

The essence of set-off is that where two parties have reciprocal monetary or proprietary obligations, the larger obligation can be discharged to the extent of the smaller obligation, resulting in satisfaction of both obligations to that lesser extent, leaving a balance payable. The key to the doctrine is mutuality. Thus a party will not be allowed to set off another's debt to discharge his own personal liability unless otherwise agreed; each party must be the beneficiary of the debt owed to him and personally liable for the debt owed by him.

One might consider that debts of premium owed by the insured and claims owed by the insurer were sufficiently mutual to enable set-off to be applied, but the broker's involvement may invalidate such mutuality owing to s 53(1) of the Marine Insurance Act 1906 in respect of Lloyd's business and non-marine insurance outside Lloyd's. It will be recalled that the broker is liable to the insurer for premiums, and the legal fiction applied in *Power* v *Butcher* (1829) 10 B&C 329 ensures that the insured is not liable to the insurer because

---

3 Set-off is capable of many fine distinctions, of which the most important are: *legal* which includes independent set-off of debts unconnected with the same transaction and is mainly exercised as a judicial remedy because the party claiming set-off is unable to do so unilaterally; *equitable* which includes set-off of debts occasioned by the same or closely connected transaction and can be exercised unilaterally. Neither claim need be liquidated; *contractual* which can be anything the parties want. It includes the possibility of unilateral action, unliquidated claims, unconnected claims and even unmatured claims; *judicial* which cannot be exercised unilaterally but can be enforced by a court, and can be assessed by a court if unquantified; *insolvency* which is a creature of statute only. It ensures reciprocity of claims on a *pari passu* basis only.

4 There are many varieties, many of which are irrelevant to this book. The distinction for example between legal and equitable set-off will not be considered in detail because the differences are minimal and the House of Lords has stated that the distinction is only of academic interest because equitable defences are available in the common law courts: Salmon LJ in *The 'Aries'* [1977] 1 All ER 398, 408.

the insurer has already been paid by the broker, who originally borrowed the amount from the insurer.

However, claims payable by the insurer are debts payable to the insured and the insurer cannot therefore set off sums due from the broker as premiums, since the insured is not liable to the insurer to pay the premium (*DC Wilson* v *Avec Audio-Visual Equipment Ltd* [1974] 1 Lloyd's Rep 81). The insured may already have paid the broker who is liable to the insurer; why should he be forced to pay twice? The insurer will have to pay the claim in full to the insured and seek to recover his premium from the broker, who in turn will sue the insured. Similarly, the broker can retain any premium returns from the insurer against premiums due or paid by the broker to the insurer.

In non-marine insurance outside Lloyd's a broker cannot set off premiums owed by the insured against claims monies owed by the broker to the insured because the insured owes those premiums to the insurer, not the broker, and mutuality is therefore not present.[5] Similarly, premiums paid to the broker for transmission to the insurer cannot be set off by the broker against claims monies owed by the insurer since these are owed by the insurer to the insured.

However, mutuality between the broker and insured may arise by the operation of a lien, giving the broker the necessary beneficial interest in claims or returns of premium. The broker will retain a general lien over the policy to secure payment of the premiums, which confers on the broker a sufficient proprietary interest in the insured's claim to establish mutuality between that claim and the broker's liability to the insurer to the extent of the amount secured, which will usually be the premium owed. Thus where the broker is liable to pay the premium, and has a lien on the policy, and the insured is liable to pay the broker, the broker can set off the premium against the claim.[6] However, such a lien can only operate

---

5 Subject to a court finding that by custom *all* brokers are liable to pay premium to the insurer. *DC Wilson* v *Avec Audio* states that the broker is not liable but the case is riddled with doubt because it was badly presented. It was, however, effectively upheld in *Con-Stan Industries of Australia Pty Ltd* v *Norwich Winterthur Insurance (Australia) Ltd* [1986] 64 ALR 481.

6 *Davies* v *Wilkinson* (1824) 4 Bing 573. See also: *Parker* v *Beasley* (1814) 2 M & S 423; *Greater Britain Insurance Corporation Ltd* v *Bowring & Co (Insurance) Ltd* (1925) 22 LlL Rep 540; *Koster* v *Eason* (1812) 2 M & S 112. Note, however, that in the old cases brokers sometimes paid claims to the insured as *del credere* agents, entitling the broker to sue under the doctrine of subrogation or restitution, rather than under a lien.

when the debt is due and where the lien remains capable of enforcement eg the broker has not sent the policy to the insured.[7]

Alternatively, the insurer and broker could be personally liable to each other for losses and premium, where the broker is effectively the principal because he has some clear beneficial ownership in the insured's claim, as a result of an assignment or, as above, because the broker is enforcing his lien against the underwriter (*Grove* v *Dubois* (1786) 1 TR 112). However, the broker's authority to sue the underwriter does not necessarily mean that he is beneficially entitled to the claims monies, which he will hold on trust for the insured (*Transcontinental Underwriting Agency* v *Grand Union Insurance Co* [1987] 2 Lloyd's Rep 409), subject perhaps to deduction of any premium paid by him to the insurer but not yet paid to him by the insured.

Set-off by agreement

The parties are of course at liberty to agree that the larger liability can be reduced by the smaller, leaving a net balance to pay, and the contract to do so is governed by the general law of contract. Thus a contractual set-off may be implied or arise by custom; there is no required form, and it may be vitiated in the usual way by lack of authority, illegality, misrepresentation etc. Contractual set-off may be used to consolidate the many contracts of insurance concluded every day, through a central multi-lateral netting scheme such as PSAC, specifically to balance out non-mutual claims.

Such an agreement can be evidenced by the accounts thereafter produced. Mutual set-off in the accounts after agreement constitutes valid payment, and the party whose cash entitlement is reduced cannot argue that such payment is invalid because it was not made

---

7 It is arguable that the lien extends beyond the policy document, which is the physical representation of a chose in action, into the intangible chose itself — the debt. As a solicitor may have a lien over a client's judgment to secure costs owing by that client, there seems to be no reason why a broker should not have a lien over claims monies and premiums payable by the insurer to the insured, to secure monies paid by the broker. See paras 16–195 of Wood on 'English and International Set-Off'. In *Fairfield Shipbuilding & Engineering Co Ltd* v *Gardner, Mountain & Co Ltd* (1911) 104 LT 288 the extent of the lien and its grasp over the claims monies was not decided. The analogy, however, is not exact; the debt owed by the solicitor's client to the solicitor is mutual in that it is owed in payment of work carried out by the solicitor. The lien itself is required in insurance disputes to provide the mutuality to enable monies to be set off.

in cash (*Trinidad Lake Asphalt* v *Commissioners of Income Tax* [1945] AC 1, 11). Such accounting entries amount to actual payment and receipt of the parties' indebtedness. Where no agreement has been reached, an acceptance of clear records without demur may give rise to an estoppel or to a waiver of the right to accept payment in cash (*The 'Okeanis'* [1986] 1 Lloyd's Rep 195); *IGI* v *Kirkland Timms* (Unreported); the accounts should therefore be as clear as possible.

Insolvency

The Insolvency Act 1986 and Insolvency Rules 1986 are automatically imposed upon the parties' relationship in the event of any party becoming insolvent. In particular, any contract providing for non-mutual set-off will not be upheld, as the imposition of the insolvency set-off clause is mandatory, which requires mutuality between debts.

Insolvency of insured
The insured's liquidator may obtain payment from the broker of claims paid by the insurer into the central accounting system, in his account with the broker, although monies held by the broker may be subject to set-off for any premiums paid by him. The extent of the broker's claim may prove to be critical, since if it exceeds the sum held by him the liquidator may recover the claims due in full from the insurer, who is unable to set off the premiums due to him. This can only be effected where the broker was not authorised by the insured to deal in account with the insurer. The broker will have to prove in the liquidation for premiums paid by him to the insurer. The broker can retain any premiums paid to him by the insured if the broker is personally liable to the insurer. Where he is not personally liable, the broker will have to repay the premium to the liquidator because he holds it merely as agent for the insured, and the insurer will have to prove in the liquidation.

Insolvency of insurer
The insured has two options: to prove in the insurer's liquidation, or to accept payment from the central accounting system. He would inevitably adopt the latter course, by ratifying the broker/insurer account if necessary, and receive money from the broker. The insured cannot complain if the sum paid equals claims less premium on the claims in question. Where the broker has received a lesser payment because the insurer has set off premiums on other claims, the broker may be liable because he has accepted the risk of the insurer's insolvency, and because the insured may not have authorised him so to act.

In the case of premium, the broker must pay it to the insurer's liquidator where he is personally liable for premium, but need not do so where he is not personally liable, since he is holding it only as agent for the insured. The broker is liable to pay the insurer's liquidator where it was previously agreed that he would hold any premium as agent for the insurer.

Insolvency of broker

The right of the insured to payment in cash is considered above; it is a difficult premise to overcome. Where payment in cash is not made, and in the absence of any agreement to the contrary, the insurer has not discharged his obligation to the insured and remains liable to him even though he may have paid money into the central accounting system.

Alternatively the insured can pursue the other members of the central accounting system where the net payment has not actually been made, under the principle in *British Eagle International Air Lines Ltd v Compagnie Nationale Air France* [1975] 1 WLR 758.[8] The clearing agreement which there provided for multi-lateral netting out was held void in respect of the provision for payment of debts which conflicted with the insolvency law stating that debts must be paid pari passu. Therefore all claims stand alone and cannot be affected by an agreement to net off. Sums which were not netted off prior to the presentation of a winding-up petition against the broker can be recovered, even if the insured authorised the operation by the broker of the central accounting system.

In cases of premium held by the broker, it will be retained by the liquidator as an asset whether the broker is liable to the insurer or not. The insured can prove for this premium in the liquidation, on the basis of money had and received by the broker for the use of the insured;[9] the insurer can also sue in respect of any personal liability of the broker to him.

---

8 Similarly in *Greater Britain Insurance Corporation Ltd v CT Bowring & Co (Insurance) Ltd* (1926) 24 Ll L Rep 6, 9 set-off was held effective before the date of insolvency even though the arithmetic of the actual netting had not occurred, because unliquidated damages could be included in 'mutual dealings' and because their identity had become indistinct so that only a balance was due.

9 Unless it can be shown to be held by the broker in trust: *Re Multi Guarantee Co* (1987) BCLC 257; *Re Eastern Capital Futures Ltd* (1989) 5 BCC 223. There must be an intention or agreement to create a trust: *Vehicle & General Insurance Co Ltd v Elmbridge Insurances* [1973] 1 LLoyd's Rep 325 and one will not be implied because an 'Insurance Broking Account' exists pursuant to the IBRC Accounts & Business Rules SI 1979 No 489 or Lloyd's Byelaw No 5 of 1988.

Statutory authority for set-off

RSC Order 18 Rule 17 states that:

Where a claim by a defendant to a sum of money (whether of an ascertained amount or not) is relied on as a defence to the whole or part of a claim made by the plaintiff, it may be included in the defence and set off against the plaintiff's claim, whether or not it is also added as a counterclaim.

Section 49(2)(a) of the Supreme Court Act 1981 stipulates that:

Every court . . . shall so exercise its jurisdiction in every cause or matter before it as to secure that, as far as possible, all matters in dispute between the parties are completely and finally determined, and all multiplicity of legal proceedings with respect to any of those matters is avoided.

4.90 of the Insolvency Rules 1986 (SI 1986/1925) states that:

(1) This Rule applies where, before the company goes into liquidation there have been mutual credits, mutual debts or other mutual dealings between the company and any creditor of the company proving or claiming to prove for a debt in the liquidation.
(2) An account shall be taken of what is due from each party to the other in respect of the mutual dealings, and the sums due from one party shall be set off against the sums due from the other.
(3) Sums due from the company to another party shall not be included in the account taken under paragraph (2) if that other party had notice at the time they became due that a meeting of creditors had been summoned under section 98 or (as the case may be) a petition for the winding up of the company was pending.
(4) Only the balance (if any) of the account is provable in the liquidation. Alternatively (as the case may be) the amount shall be paid to the liquidator as part of the assets.

The setting-off of reciprocal claims which are not connected, say premiums and claims in non-marine insurance outside Lloyd's in respect of different contracts of insurance, is now possible under the above provisions. Thus the court will enforce an independent cross-claim of the debtor when this is raised by the debtor as a defence to judicial proceedings instituted by the creditor. It is not available as a self-help remedy (except where there is a lien) and a tender of the balance by the debtor does not constitute valid tender of payment to the creditor. However, the court will penalise the creditor by awarding costs against him if he fails to give credit for the debtor's claim. In The 'Nanfri' [1978] 2 Lloyd's Rep 132, 139 (CA) Lord Denning MR said ' . . . the distinction between set-off and cross-claim is crucial. When the debtor has a true set-off it goes in reduction of the sums owing to the creditor. If the creditor does not allow it to be deducted, he is in peril. He will be liable in damages if he exercised his contractual right of withdrawal wrongly. But when the debtor has no set-off or defence properly so called, but only a counterclaim or cross-action, then the creditor need not allow any deduction to be made. He can exercise his contractual right without fear; and leave the debtor to bring an action for damages on his counterclaim'.[10] Nevertheless, the debtor must be careful not to trigger any default provision in the event of his failure to tender valid payment eg a premium warranty which renders the insurance void.

Thus in *Simpson* v *Accidental Death* (1857) 2 CB (NS) 257 premiums had to be paid within 21 days of expiry, although the insurer was not obliged to renew. The premium was due on 22 January and the insured died on 1 February. Premiums were not paid (by mistake) and the policy expired. The insurer was not held liable and did not have to apply the monies that would have been payable to discharge the payment of premium, paying the balance to the insured. The position may be different where the insurer cannot refuse to renew.

Liquidated sums

Both claims sought to be applied in the set-off must be liquidated or ascertainable with certainty at the time of pleading. Clearly credit cannot be given by a party if the sum to be credited is not quantifiable, and such a cross-claim will only be heard if it is a proper counterclaim for determination by the court.

Claims will be liquidated if the policy is valued, eg life insurance, but claims for indemnity are usually unliquidated and therefore

---

10 Lord Denning's comments related specifically to non-payment of freight in 'The Nanfri'. There is no real defence to a claim for freight and therefore no entitlement to set-off. The nature of the debt is different to premium, but there is no apparent reason why the principle should not also apply to premium.

incapable of being set off, unless they have already been judicially determined and remain unpaid, or arbitrated and incapable of reassessment (*Williams* v *British Marine Mutual Insurance Association Ltd* (1886) 57 LT 27). A partial loss under a valued policy may be considered unliquidated (*Castelli* v *Boddington* (1852) 1 EL 7 BL 66), as is a claim for indemnity even after adjustment of the loss, which apparently is of no more value than to enable the court more easily to arrive at the proper estimate of damages (*Luckie* v *Bushby* (1853) 13 CB 864).

Claims under contracts of reinsurance are for indemnity and would appear to be liquidated in that they have usually been ascertained and paid by the primary insurer, and are payable by the reinsurer unless there are grounds of impugnment such as a failure by the insurer/reinsured to take all proper and business-like steps to ensure that the *quantum* of the loss was fairly and carefully ascertained (*Insurance Co of Africa* v *Scor* [1985] 1 Lloyd's Rep 312), or that the claim was outside the primary policy, or fraud or lack of good faith. However, in the absence of payment by the reinsurer, such claims are for damages for breach of contract and are therefore unliquidated (*Edmunds* v *Lloyd's Italico* [1986] 2 All ER 249).

The policy of insurance may provide for set-off by the insurer of unliquidated claims against premiums, either in respect of amounts owed under that particular policy ('transaction' set-off) or against all such contracts between the parties ('independent' set-off). The extent of any rights to set-off will clearly be governed by the policy if defined therein. Where the reciprocal claims arise out of one policy, an unliquidated claim can be set off. Where the reciprocal claims arise from different policies and are independent, the claim for unliquidated damages may not be set off either unilaterally or in court proceedings, subject to the court's overriding discretion, although the claim may form the subject of a counterclaim and subsequent judgment (*Baker* v *Adam* (1910) LT 248).

It should also be remembered that the withholding of payment by one party to force the other party to pay a reciprocal debt is frowned upon by the court, perhaps paradoxically in the light of the extent of 'judicial set-off', which operates to pull all claims into the same arena. The effect of unilateral set-off was considered in *The 'Kostas Melas'* [1981] 1 Lloyd's Rep 18 by Robert Goff J who commented at p 26 that:

. . . it is to be remembered that although a right of set-off is a defence, with all the legal consequences which follow from it, in practice the exercise of a right of deduction or set-off is essentially a provisional act. It decides nothing finally. Its exercise simply operates as a temporary retention of an economic asset by the party exercising the right, and the temporary deprivation of the other party of that asset. For the exercise of the right does not prevent either party from subsequently proving his claim or cross-claim, and so does not affect the final resolution of the fundamental dispute. It affects the question of the identity of the plaintiff; it affects the economic security of the parties, if the plaintiff so identified cannot obtain security for his claim; and it affects cash flow. But it is, as I have said, essentially a provisional act. Furthermore, the exercise of a right of deduction or set-off is essentially an act of self-help; it requires no order of the Court or arbitrators for its enforcement. If a party exercises it, however, he must have justification for doing so; and in theory he should be able to prove, at the time of its exercise, that he has that justification. But, as I have already indicated, the full facts may not be known to him, or the full evidence may not be available to him at that time. Even so, bearing in mind the characteristics of the right, it is my judgment implicit in its very nature that it should only be exercised in good faith on reasonable grounds, and furthermore, if the other party considers that it is not being so exercised, he should be able to obtain a rapid adjudication upon that question.

Defence or counterclaim

Set-off is essentially a defence. If not it may, however, fall within the provisions of RSC Ord 15 r 2 as a counterclaim, which will produce the same result for most practical purposes. The counterclaim may be independent and unliquidated, but will not be allowed if unduly complicated or capable of delaying or embarrassing the trial of the main action, in which case a separate trial will be ordered.

Reinsurance

Reinsurance is more fully considered in Chapter 14, to which reference should be made. However, it is necessary for the purposes of this chapter to deal with it briefly.

Liability for premium

The most important difference between the contracts of insurance and reinsurance is that the liability of the broker for payment of the premiums to the reinsurer under a reinsurance treaty has not yet been established by statute or common law, and the broker is not liable in the absence of prior agreement. There is no reason why the broker should be liable; the parties to the agreement are both professionals operating in a specialised market and are subject to solvency controls, thereby reducing the apparent risk of default by the parties. In practice brokers do not usually render themselves liable to pay reinsurance premiums, subject of course to the Lloyd's custom that a Lloyd's broker is personally liable to the Lloyd's underwriter,[11] that s 53 of the Marine Insurance Act 1906 applies to facultative marine reinsurance, and that the broker may foolishly incur liability by sending out accounts stating his liability, or as a principal under the terms of the reinsurance contract.

Some of these aspects appeared in *Grand Union Insurance Company Limited* v *Evans — Lombe Ashton & Company Limited* (Unreported: June 1989) where the Court of Appeal heard the reinsurance brokers' argument during an appeal from a summary judgment against them under Ord 14 of the RSC, to the effect that their undisputed liability for premium under s 53 for marine facultative reinsurance was displaced by the universal practice in the reinsurance market known as net accounting. The reinsurers argued that the brokers owed them the premiums and could not set off any claims monies due from the reinsurers to the reinsured, because the reinsurers were directly liable to the reinsured, unless the reinsured's contract was made in the name of the broker. The Court allowed the brokers' appeal to enable them to go to trial in order to establish the existence of the alleged universal practice. A decision on this point is still awaited.

Agent for reinsured

The broker acts as agent for the reinsured. Thus, any premium paid by the reinsured to the broker does not constitute a discharge of the reinsured's debt until passed on to the reinsurer. There are often several brokers in the reinsurance chain, and a broker passing on money to another should ensure that he is authorised by the reinsured to do so. The broker is liable to account for it as an agent holding money had and received to the use of the reinsured. The insolvency of the broker will mean that the reinsured must prove as an unsecured creditor in the liquidation, either for unpaid premium or as a debtor for claims received from the reinsurer.

---

11 Customs are notoriously difficult to establish. A case on the liability of brokers to pay premium to non-marine underwriters at Lloyd's actually reached trial in 1989 but was settled without a decision of the court. The fact that this issue remains arguable must also mean that the reinsuring non-marine underwriter cannot unquestionably recover premium from the broker.

Mike Harris (of J. Archer). Settled half-way thru case, negociations were better. the parties + both sides were dissatisfied. Lloyds pressure?

Non-payment of premium

Payment of premiums in treaty reinsurance is unlikely to be a condition precedent, although non-payment could eventually constitute a breach, entitling the reinsurer to treat the contract as terminated.

Payment by the reinsured to the broker in cash or by setting off premiums due to the reinsurer against claims due from the broker are irrelevant to the reinsurer. He does not necessarily obtain payment from the broker personally, as in marine and Lloyd's insurance, but may look to the reinsured for payment. Similarly, the reinsurer cannot set off premium alleged to be owed from the broker against claims because the broker is not the creditor of the reinsurer for claims monies, which are owed direct to the reinsured.

Intermediary clause

The term 'intermediary' is found throughout the insurance world, particularly in reinsurance. However, the concept of the intermediary was frowned upon by Megaw J in *Anglo-African Merchants Ltd v Bayley* [1970] 1 QB 311, since it involved conflicting duties and interests. Thus, although the general rule is that the broker acts for the insured or reinsured, nevertheless the parties can agree that payment to the broker constitutes good payment to the other party. The parties can therefore set off sums due to them on the contract of reinsurance, but not on others without a wider agreement to do so, since the connection will not be close enough to constitute 'mutuality', there being no mutuality of liability in the first place. The usual insurance position remains in force in respect of the entitlement of the broker to act in his personal capacity: he cannot sue for premiums or claims since he owes and is owed neither. These debts exist solely between the reinsurer and the reinsured. The reinsured can of course sue the broker where the broker has received claims monies from the reinsurer but has failed to pass them on.

Liability of reinsurer to pay insolvent reinsured

A reinsurer may argue that he is not liable to pay a reinsured where the reinsured is unable to pay the insured in full. This issue was considered in *Home & Overseas Insurance Co Ltd v Mentor Insurance Co (UK) Ltd* [1989] 1 Lloyd's Rep 473 when the reinsurers applied for summary judgment for a declaration that they were not liable because the insured had not been paid in full by the reinsured. The Court of Appeal decided that the action would be stayed as a result of the arbitration clause, but considered that the question was not capable of a quick, unequivocal answer. The issue would depend upon the wording used between the parties.

Set-off

A broker in a strict legal analysis should not need to set off. He is not liable for premium, and therefore need only act as a pure agent, without personal liability, subject to the proviso that he may be liable for premium in marine and Lloyd's facultative contracts of reinsurance. In reality, however, he funds claims. His entitlement to sue personally or otherwise recover has been considered above, from which it will be seen that his chances of success are slim, unless he receives assistance from the reinsured.

He is also at risk in respect of any central system of multilateral netting-off without the reinsured's consent, since again there is no mutuality. The broker is obliged to receive payment in cash and cannot set off claims against premium without the reinsured's consent. The broker may attempt to establish a market usage for netting off, but it would probably go no further than premiums and claims in one account between the reinsured and reinsurer; a reinsured would be unlikely to accept netting off between unrelated contracts. The broker would, however, point out that the reinsured is a professional who is fully cognisant of the accounting position, and therefore that he has consented to the custom. A court decision is awaited with interest, to enforce the comments of Bingham J in *The 'Okeanis'* [1986] 1 Lloyd's Rep 195, 200.

The view of the Council of Chartered Accountants

It is the present practice of insurance intermediaries to show in their accounts debtors and creditors relating to insurance business. Although this practice does not generally reflect the intermediaries' legal obligations and rights, it usually accords with the commercial substance of the underlying transaction. The Council of the Institute of Chartered Accountants therefore consider that the inclusion of such debtors and creditors in the accounts will usually be justified in order for the accounts to show a true and fair view, provided a suitable note is included in the accounts to explain the position.

As the purpose of this practice is to reflect the commercial substance of the transaction, they recommend that the accounts of insurance debtors and creditors should reflect the normal method of settlement of those balances to or by the intermediary, so that where there are a number of accounts with a third party, they should be set off as a net debtor or creditor if it is the intermediary's practice to make or accept such set-off when settling those accounts. The debtors and creditors appearing in the balance sheet will be the aggregation of the individual net debt and credit balances respectively after making such set-off as is appropriate. In arriving at the constitution of debtors and creditors, they do not consider it necessary to have regard to the ultimate principals where these are not parties with whom the accounts are directly settled.[12]

---

12 Statement of Council of Chartered Accountants: Accounting by Insurance Intermediaries under the Companies Act 1985, September 1986.

Chapter 12

The broker's professional liability

An insurance broker is usually instructed at the beginning of his legal relationshipwithhisprincipaltoobtainquotationsforintendedcontracts of insurance, or to procure the best possible insurance, which he must do by using his best endeavours and exercising reasonable skill and care. This is an implied term of his contract both at common law and by s 13 of the Supply of Goods & Services Act 1982. A failure by the broker to do so will result in a claim against him, which may be founded on breach of contract, or upon a failure to discharge the concurrent duty of care in tort owed by the broker to the insured.[1]

The duty of care in tort, which is synonymous with the implied term in contract (save that the duty may extend to third parties), is discharged by the excercise of reasonable skill and care by the broker, which can generally be considered to be that exercised by reasonably competent brokers operating within the same market and holding

---

1 *Mint Security* v *Blair* [1982] 1 Lloyd's Rep 188. The broker's liability in contract and tort is well established *Youell* v *Bland Welch & Co Ltd* (Unreported: Judgment 27 March 1990). Nevertheless, Lord Scarman commented in *Tai Hing* v *Liv Chong Hing Bank Ltd* [1986] 1 AC 80 (Privy Council) that: 'Their Lordships do not believe that there is anything to the advantage of the law's development in searching for a liability in tort where the parties are in a contractual relationship. This is particularly so in a commercial relationship. Though it is possible as a matter of legal semantics to conduct an analysis of the rights and duties inherent in some contractual relationships including that of banker and customer either as a matter of contract law when the question will be what, if any, terms are to be implied, or as a matter of tort law when the task will be to identify a duty arising from the proximity and character of the relationship between the parties, their Lordships believe it to be correct in principle and necessary for the avoidance of confusion in the law to adhere to the contractual analysis: on principle, because it is a

themselves out to have the same expertise in the same specialised area of insurance (if any). Thus if a life broker attempts to place marine insurance, he must adhere to the practices in the marine market. He cannot rely upon usage of a practice which may be acceptable in another market if that practice caused a loss and was less 'onerous'. The standard of care is not to be assessed according to the broker's ability but according to the act that he had agreed to carry out. In *Lanphier* v *Phipos* (1838) 8 Car & P 475 Tindal CJ said:

> Every person who enters into a learned profession undertakes to bring to the exercise of it a reasonable degree of care and skill. He does not undertake, if he is an attorney, that at all events you shall gain your case, nor does a surgeon undertake that he will perform a cure, nor does he undertake to use the highest possible degree of skill. There may be persons who have higher education and greater advantages than he has, but he undertakes to bring a fair, reasonable and competent degree of skill.

Thus personal incompetence resulting from the inexperience of a trainee is not a defence to a claim for failure to produce work of an acceptable professional standard (*Dickinson* v *Jones Alexander* (1989) 139 NLJ 1525). Further, the court is always alive to the fact that a broker following a practice common in a market may not be discharging his duty if such practice is not to be expected from the reasonably competent broker. Brokers' liabilities usually arise in the following ways.

---

relationship in which the parties have, subject to a few exceptions, the right to determine their obligations to each other, and for the avoidance of confusion because different consequences do follow according to whether the liability arises from contract or tort, eg in the limitation of actions'. Lord Scarman's comments were endorsed by May LJ in *The Bank of Nova Scotia* v *Hellemic Mutual War Risks Association (Bermuda) Ltd The 'Good Luck'* [1989] 2 Lloyd's Rep 238, and in *La Banque Financiere* v *Westgate Insurance Co Ltd* [1988] 2 Lloyd's Rep 513 at 563 by Slade LJ. The problem was considered obliquely in *Iron Trades Mutual Insurance Co Ltd* v *JK Buckenham Ltd* [1989] 2 Lloyd's Rep 85 where the reinsured was uninsured as a result of their broker's non-disclosure, the date of the broker's breach of contract being the date of such non-disclosure. The reinsured tried to claim in tort after the limitation period had expired on the basis that the limitation period for torts was extended by the Latent Damage Act 1986 which introduced s 14A of the Limitation Act 1980 to apply a starting date for limitation purposes to the date when the necessary knowledge to bring an action accrued ie when the avoidance occurred. The important date in claims in tort is the date of damage; in contract the breach occurs when the defective service is rendered or completed. The court found that as a matter of construction the time-barred claim was not assisted by the LDA. The court confirmed that the Limitation Act expressly preserved the distinction between actions based in tort and contract, so that the claim remained time-barred.

[handwritten margin notes:]
Upheld by CA
Re ERAS EIL
Appeals 1990
2 AER 82

Dispute this part:
Ct held:
i) S. 14A did to Tort
ii) Burden was on Pb
prove L. fell wh S14A
iii) Case was to continue
to trial on that, as
a preliminary issue.

FAILURE TO OBTAIN PROPER INSURANCE

Failure to obtain any insurance

The most obvious item under this head is a failure to obtain any insurance at all (*Smith v L Smith v Price* (1862) 2 F & F 749). Such a failure gives rise to liability unless the broker can show that he took all reasonable steps to effect the insurance but that it was unobtainable, and that he informed his principal accordingly, or took all reasonable steps to do so (*United Mills Agencies Ltd v RE Harvey Bray & Co* (1951) 2 Lloyd's Rep 631 and by the fastest method of communication (*Proudfoot v Montefiore* (1867) LR2 QB 511). The rationale behind this additional obligation is to allow his principal to attempt to obtain insurance elsewhere (*Jameson v Swainstone* (1809) 2 Camp 546 Note 3).

Failure to obtain requisite insurance

Where details of the risk are clearly specified by the client, a failure to obtain the requisite insurance may give rise to liability. The duty is not absolute, since the broker cannot guarantee that insurance will be available on the terms specified, and is merely to use reasonable skill and care (*Youell v Bland Welch & Co Ltd* Unreported: Judgment 27 March 1990). Failing to obtain insurance requested for several vessels, and limiting the insurance to one is a clear breach of specific instructions and a failure to exercise reasonable skill and care (*Dickson & Co v Devitt* (1917) 86 LJKB 313). Where such instructions are unclear the broker will be under a duty to resolve any ambiguity, since if the uncertainty of the instructions is obvious to the broker, he will, in placing the insurance, be making a value judgment which he has not been asked to make and which should result in liability if he errs (*Youell v Bland Welch & Co Ltd* Unreported: Judgment 27 March 1990). Such liability will depend upon the circumstances; the broker may not be liable if, for example, the insurance must be concluded within a specified time and it is not possible to obtain instructions clarifying the position from his principal. In such circumstances it seems better to place the insurance than risk a claim for failing to do so, as long as he selects the option which a reasonably competent broker would bona fide choose in similar circumstances (*Weigall & Co v Runciman & Co* (1916) 115 LT 61). An incorrect decision does not automatically render him liable for negligence. Presumably it is possible for a broker to agree with an insurer that the insurance will be placed to cover both aspects of any ambiguity and confirm it later. Non-marine insurance, however, cannot be ratified after loss.

The courts used to lean towards the broker in cases of ambiguity. In *Waterkeyn* v *Eagle Star & British Dominions Insurance Co Ltd/Price Forbes & Co* (1920) 4 Ll L Rep 178 and (1920) 5 Ll L Rep 42 the insured requested his broker to insure against the collapse of the Russian Bank for Foreign Trade in the light of the Russian Revolution in 1917, since he rightly feared the expropriation of the bank's funds, which included his own. The broker obtained insurance for loss 'directly due to damage or destruction of the premises and contents of the said banks through riots, civil commotion, war, civil war [etc]', which was worthless. The physical collapse of the bank would not alter its liability to the insured. Upon its construction of the wording the court held that the broker was not liable since he had only 'acted prudently in carrying out his activities'. This case is interesting not only because the Belgian insured pointed out to the broker that the subject matter of the risk for which cover was required was not tangible, but was that of credits owed to them by the bank being rendered worthless by the vicissitudes of revolution, but also because the court held that the risk could have been covered by the addition of an 'extremely simple clause' so that the policy provided for 'insolvency caused by rioters, civil commotions, war, civil war [etc]'. A more obvious reason to hold the broker liable would be difficult to find. Nevertheless, the court held that this was the only insurance that the broker could have obtained in the circumstances, which is a considerably better reason for excluding the broker's liability, but should not validate the broker's failure to obtain proper insurance. Obtaining one form of insurance because another is not available is an absurdity, if the insurance obtained clearly fails to meet the insured's requirements. It is considered that a court would have to struggle to uphold the 'only insurance available' reason for this decision today, unless the insurance obtained broadly reflected the insurance requested but contained 'unavoidable' clauses which the insured would prefer not to have. This rationale is also subject to the probable extension of a broker's duties that a broker must not blithely place the insurance requested by his principal, but must attempt to ensure that the insurance properly meets the principal's real requirements. The broker should inform the insured so that he can reiterate his instructions, or has an opportunity to obtain the insurance elsewhere, and so that he can decide whether he wishes to pay premiums for inferior insurance. A broker today may be unable to refute liability by adhering rigidly to specifications made by the insured, which are clearly wrong and would be seen to be wrong by a reasonable broker, without initially questioning his instructions.

Investigating and confirming incomplete instructions

Thus incomplete instructions from the insured (if capable of putting a reasonably competent broker on notice that they do not accurately reflect the insured's requirements) must not pass without investigation and confirmation, and the insurance placed must adhere to the real requirements of the insured. Instructions to a broker to obtain insurance for a voyage from London to Liverpool, when the broker knows or has good reason to believe that the voyage will be to Calais, should result in a duty on the broker to verify the details of the intended insurance. If the principal confirms that Liverpool is the correct intended destination, the broker has discharged his duty of skill and will be under no liability if, having obtained insurance as requested, a loss occurs. This reasoning has been adopted in other jurisdictions. A broker arranging property insurance which excluded business use is liable when he knows that part of the property was used for business purposes (*McCann v Western Farmers Mutual Insurance Co* (1978) 87 DLR (3d) 135). A broker would be liable for failing to obtain property insurance from damage caused by the sea in a location liable to sea flooding, where instructions to obtain insurance against storm, tempest and flood should have been understood to include damage caused by the sea (*Mitor Investment Pty Ltd* v *General Accident Fire & Life Assurance Corporation Ltd* (1984) WAR 365). Failing to ascertain whether the principal fell within the category of excluded persons whose part-time occupations made them uninsurable with a particular company will also give rise to liability. The fact that the broker had requested details of the principal's full-time occupation was insufficient to avoid liability (*McNealy* v *The Pennine Insurance* [1978] 2 Lloyd's Rep 18). Similarly, an answer such as 'no convictions so far as I know' to a question in a proposal form may give rise to an obligation upon the broker to obtain the relevant information (*Warren* v *Henry Sutton & Co* (1976) 2 Lloyd's Rep 276).

Broadly defined scope of insurance

In many cases the principal will broadly define the scope of the insurance required and leave it to the broker to effect such insurance in his discretion. Such latitude enables the broker to weigh all the terms of a proposed contract of insurance and decide which most favours his principal and represents the best possible deal (*Moore* v *Mourgue* (1776) 2 Cowp 480). The cheapest policy may not always be the best suited to the principal's requirements; for a broker to discard on renewal an insurer with whom the insured has had a good relationship in order to obtain a cheaper policy may even be negligent, unless full disclosure has been made to the insured. Indeed, the cheapest policy may indicate an overriding desire on the part of the insurer to obtain premium income now and dispute any claim later. Thus a more expensive policy with a reputable company may well be in the insured's best interests. Liability, however, will not lie on the broker who has not obtained the cheapest policy unless the principal can show that the same insurance was reasonably available elsewhere at a cheaper price, or that the broker unreasonably attributed too much to one factor or term and not enough to another. A wider geographical coverage for the risk at a higher premium may not be reasonable if the insured does not require such wide coverage. Nevertheless, such an error will not necessarily give rise to liability if the broker can show that he exercised reasonable skill, care and judgment. He cannot be expected, for example, to visit every possible insurer to obtain a quotation; he need only visit a reasonable number, which may be ascertained by reference to the current market practice. It should be noted, however, that the quotation facilities now readily accessible on networks of computers will move the burden of proof more substantially onto the broker.

BREACHES OF DUTY IN THE APPLICATION PROCESS

(a) Non-disclosure of facts material to the risk

An insurer will be entitled to avoid the contract at any time if he learns that a fact material to the risk has not been disclosed to him prior to the date the contract was completed. A fact is material if a prudent insurer would take it into account when considering the risk or if it would influence a prudent insurer when considering whether to take the risk or the amount of premium to be charged. The insured may consider that he has provided all relevant information, but he has approached the broker with a view to obtaining his professional expertise and the courts have placed an obligation on the broker to ensure that the insured fully appreciates the extent of his duty of disclosure, and that all such information is passed to insurers.

Thus in *McNealy* v *The Pennine Insurance Co Ltd* the Court of

Appeal stated that the brokers should have obtained all relevant information from the insured by taking positive steps to do so rather than acting only as scribes or messenger boys. In *Ogden & Co Pty Ltd* v *Reliance Fire Sprinkler Co Pty Ltd* [1975] 1 Lloyd's Rep 52 an Australian court stated that the brokers should collect all information that the underwriters may require and should pass it to them. The broker is, of course, subject to a duty of good faith as regards the insurer, and must ensure that his insured's obligations are properly discharged.

In *Coolee Limited* v *Wing Heath & Co* (1930) 47 TLR 78 Rowlett J held that producing and Lloyd's brokers were liable for their negligence in failing to notice on renewal that the insured was using explosives in its operations, having stated on the original application form that it did not. This highly material fact was not disclosed to the insurer who later avoided the policy.

As the duty imposed upon brokers is one to exercise reasonable care, there must be a limit to the exercise that the brokers have to perform, and the placing of liability by the court will depend on the circumstances in each case. The aspect of reasonableness cannot be precisely quantified and there is therefore considerable latitude in its definition, which must also be determined according to market practice. Thus, although a broker should disclose any criminal record of the insured or his staff, he need not delve into the history of each employee of a company to ascertain whether there may be a criminal element that should be disclosed to underwriters, unless he is put on notice to do so (*Fanhaven Pty Ltd* v *Bain Dawes Northern Pty Ltd* (1982) 2 NSWLR 57).

(b) All relevant information must be included in the proposal form

All relevant information should be included in the proposal form. The broker usually completes this with the assistance of the insured, who then signs it. The broker's duty is to ensure that all answers written down by him accurately represent the information provided by the insured (*O'Connor* v *BDB Kirby & Co* [1972] 1 QB 90). The broker is not responsible for the correctness or truth of the answers, except in circumstances where he has a greater knowledge than the insured, as a result of handling previous insurances for that insured even though the insured may also have the relevant· information

(*Dunbar* v *AB Painters Ltd* [1985] 2 Lloyd's Rep 616).[2] The broker is better placed to provide the requested information, and will be liable if he does not do so properly.

Problems often arise out of inadequate information, or ambiguous or evasive answers contained in the proposal form. Where information is provided in a form where it is clearly inadequate, an obvious example being 'not known to brokers', and that actually is the case, then the insurer may accept the risk on that basis and may not later avoid. They are on notice, and need not provide insurance; they can request further information and should do so in such circumstances. Where, however, the broker states that he is unaware of previous claims where a record of claims existed, an Australian court has held that the policy could be avoided for misrepresentation and non-disclosure of a material fact. The broker was, or ought to have been, possessed with knowledge of prior claims and was liable to the insured for failing to exercise reasonable skill and care (*Ogden & Co Pty Ltd* v *Reliance Fire Sprinkler Co Pty Ltd* [1975] 1 Lloyd's Rep 52). Similarly, where a broker is informed by the insured that he is not aware of a particular fact, such as another's driving convictions, and the broker translates that information into a positive statement that there are no convictions, he will be liable to the insured (*Warren* v *Henry Sutton & Co* [1976] 2 Lloyd's Rep 276).

(c) Insured unable to claim against broker in respect of information confirmed by the insured

However, where the insured examines a proposal form or other document completed by the broker on his behalf and confirms that it is correct, he will have no claim against the broker for any information contained therein which later gives rise to a dispute. In *O'Connor* v *BDB Kirby & Co* the Court of Appeal held that the insured's failure to notice the broker's mistake was the proximate cause of his loss. An attempt to avoid such liability by the broker should not succeed in the situation considered in (b) above, as to the extent of the duty of disclosure. The fact that the insured checks the proposal form does not show that the broker, as agent of the

---

2 The judge did not discuss *O'Connor* v *BDB Kirby* in his decision and *Dunbar* runs contrary to the view in that case that the insured is solely responsible for the accuracy of the proposal form. However, *Dunbar* is good law, particularly in cases where the insured relies substantially on the broker for guidance.

insured, has discharged his duty of ensuring that all material facts are made known to underwriters, and that the insured appreciates the extent of his obligations. The broker may therefore be liable if the insured provides him with relevant information which is not requested in the proposal form, and the broker fails to record it on the documentation sent to the insurer, after it has been examined by the insured. The courts have drawn a fine distinction between a failure to notice an error and failing to notice that some information supplied but not requested on the proposal form has not been recorded (*Commonwealth Insurance Co of Vancouver* v *Groupe Sprinks SA* [1983] 1 Lloyd's Rep 67). These comments, however, were obiter and may not be followed if the insured were to read and confirm the contents of the proposal immediately after completion by the broker. Even then the insured could argue that he gave the broker the relevant information and assumed that the absence of potentially relevant information was a consequence of the broker's specific decision to delete it, and that the broker had exercised his duty of reasonable care and competence. Where the information is obviously relevant to an insurer, and the insured must be taken to know this, such an argument may not succeed.

The courts usually try to prevent any hiving-off of responsibility and Phillips J said in *Youell* v *Bland Welch & Co Ltd* (Unreported: Judgment 27 March 1990) at that if the insured inadequately checked his cover at the request of the broker, ' . . . a broker who has undertaken a contractual duty to exercise skill and care for his client can transfer to the client the duty of checking that such care has been exercised by the expedient of sending such a letter, with the result that if both broker and client fail to exercise care the loss falls on the client'. He held (at p 67) that this argument failed because he could see ' . . . no justification for imposing on the client a duty owed to the broker to check the suitability of the cover obtained with a degree of care similar to that which the broker is paid to employ when obtaining it'.

Brokers duties applicable to renewal of a policy

The duties incumbent upon a broker during the application process also apply during the renewal of a policy, and during the claims process. It is not settled in English law that the broker must inform his client that the policy is due for renewal; he has discharged his duty in arranging the insurance and the insured ought to be aware of the date his policy lapses, since he must originally have specified the period of risk. The broker has discharged his contractual duties in the absence of further agreement, or clear market practice relied upon by the (re)insured eg where insurance has been obtained to follow the primary insurance, the broker should attempt to renew the reinsurance if it expires before the primary insurance (*Youell* v *Bland Welch & Co Ltd* (Unreported: Judgment 27 March 1990)). However, brokers usually inform their clients prior to renewal because it is good marketing practice to do so, because they want the premium payable on renewal and because it may be a custom of the market that they do so. Whether a failure to inform the insured that a renewal is due is a breach of an implied term (because it is market custom) has been tested in Canada, where the court held the broker liable in negligence (*Morash* v *Lockart & Ritchie Ltd* (1979) 95 DLR (3d) 647).

Upon renewal the broker must discharge his usual duties, and inform the insured if the renewed contract does not replicate the expired policy. This duty arises from his duty to exercise reasonable skill and care towards the insured, and from his duty to inform the insured of all factors relevant to the contract. There are, however, conflicting authorities. In *Michaels* v *Valentine* (1923) 16 Ll L Rep 244 a broker failed to inform the insured that the premium was to be paid immediately, and not at any time within the grace period allowed in the expired policy. The broker was not held liable because the particular insurance was no longer obtainable with grace days. The new policy was sent to the insured and the court considered that this was sufficient. It is unlikely that this approach towards a broker's duty would be confirmed in today's commercial and legal climate. One would assume that a broker would take every step to ensure that the insured could comply with any new contractual term, particularly where such failure is likely to avoid the policy and in respect of which the insured has no knowledge, and can have no such knowledge except as provided by the broker (eg *Cherry* v *Allied Insurance Brokers Ltd* [1978] 1 Lloyd's Rep 274).

The only saving grace in the broker's favour in *Michaels* v *Valentine* was absent from *Mint Security Ltd* v *Blair* [1982] 1 Lloyd's Rep 188. Lloyd's brokers failed to inform the insured via his producing brokers that the policy of insurance included by reference warranties on a proposal form completed 2½ years earlier. The insurer was not liable because the insured had altered his procedures since the completion of the old proposal form, but before the new form was completed ie on the basis of breach of warranty. Staughton J held the broker liable for failing to inform the insured that the terms of the original proposal form were included. The broker failed to inform the insured of the terms of the new policy.

Unauthorised cancellation of a policy

Similarly, unauthorised cancellation of a policy by the broker will result in his liability for any loss until the date the policy would have expired (*Xenos* v *Wickham* (1867) LT 2 HL 296), unless the insurer knew or ought to have known that the broker was not authorised to cancel and was therefore acting outside his authority, in which case the policy continues or the insurer is liable for breach of contract.

Unauthorized Destruction of Docs - Johnston v L+G 1995 LRLR

FAILURE TO EXERCISE DUE CARE AND ATTENTION GENERALLY

Failure to inform the insured of all relevant matters

It will be clear from the duties outlined above that the broker must keep his client informed as to all relevant matters where he has assumed or is under a duty to do so, particularly in respect of matters known only to the broker. Thus a failure to obtain insurance, or the imposition of a new or onerous term in the policy (*King* v *Chambers & Newman* [1963] 2 Lloyd's Rep 130), are both important matters which will give rise to a liability on the broker if he fails to inform the insured as to their nature and extent, or at least takes every reasonable step to do so (*Youell* v *Bland Welch & Co Ltd* Unreported: Judgment 27 March 1990). He need not, however, take this duty to extremes, provided that any relaxation in his business standards does not affect the insured, and the duty may be assessed less stringently by a court where the insured is a business, rather than a layman unversed in the practice of insurance. Thus a broker is entitled to expect that exporters conduct their business prudently and, when asked to obtain export insurance, could assume that he need not obtain insurance for risks prior to the inception of export (*United Mills Agencies Ltd* v *RE Harvey & Co* [1951] 2 Lloyd's Rep 631).[3] Although the receipt by the insured of the cover note should have alerted them to their lack of insurance whilst the goods were at the packers, the broker was not liable for failing to send them details of the insurance or a cover note immediately. The information was delivered to the insured 3 days after it had been obtained. However, it could still be argued that there is

---

3 Subject to any possible duty to enquire that the policy requested matches the insured's needs, and to advise accordingly.

a custom to the effect that a cover note is sent on the day the insurance is obtained or on the next day, since this is usually what happens. Customs are, however, difficult to prove, particularly in non-marine insurance.

Certainly, if the insured becomes uninsured, the broker must inform him immediately, in clear and unambiguous terms (*London Borough of Bromley* v *Ellis* [1971] 1 Lloyd's Rep 97). It may be that the broker is under a duty to arrange alternative insurance in the event that he cannot contact the insured, but it seems unlikely. The broker is not there to take business decisions for his client, but rather to advise and to carry out his instructions with regard to specified contracts of insurance. The broker is not under any agency of necessity since the principal's property or interests are not in direct, imminent danger, and the insurance is not necessary to preserve those interests. There may, however, be a market custom to obtain insurance or reinsurance in certain circumstances (*Youell* v *Bland Welch & Co Ltd* (Unreported: Judgment 27 March 1990).

Broker advising his client on matters outside his expertise

In the course of his business the broker will not only exercise his discretion but will invariably advise his client, often concerning matters not within his expertise. If the broker chooses to do this, he is subject to the same duty to exercise reasonable skill and care not of a broker who considers himself knowledgeable in that particular area, but of a practitioner in that field. Thus a broker giving legal advice (without reservation) to a client may find himself straying from his own expertise into a mess of liability, whether or not client is aware that the broker is not qualified to give legal advice. The leading case is *Sarginson Bros* v *Keith Moulton & Co* (1942) 73 Ll L Rep 104 in which a broker advised that some timber was uninsurable against war risks, after consulting an insurance company to consider various partially relevant wartime regulations. The timber was insurable, was not insured and was subsequently burnt. The broker was liable. Hallett J stated that the broker should have said that such advice was:

> . . . a matter for a solicitor, not me . . . No-one is under obligation to give advice on those difficult matters. If they are going to give advice, they can always qualify their advice and make it plain that it is a matter which is doubtful or upon which further investigation is desirable; but if they do take it upon themselves to express a definite and final opinion, knowing, as they must have known in this case, that their clients would act upon

that, then I do think they are responsible if they give that information without having taken reasonable care to furnish themselves with such information, of whatever kind it be, as will render it reasonably safe, in the view of a reasonably prudent man, to express that opinion.

The brokers contributed to their downfall by giving positive and definite advice 'in the most categorical way, and in such a way as to deter [the insured] from making any further enquiries . . . '

However, a broker is expected to understand the general principles of insurance law and its application to his own and his clients' business, and any contracts which he negotiates and completes. Thus a broker would be liable if he effected insurance which failed to attach properly to his client's goods because the broker failed to consider the relevant law which was neither arcane nor difficult to ascertain (*Park* v *Hammond* (1816) 6 Taunt 495), or to draw any unusual or unwanted but unavoidable clauses or conditions precedent to the attention of the insured (*Youell* v *Bland Welch & Co Ltd* Unreported: Judgment 27 March 1990). Such insurance may become the subject of litigation, and the fact that a court may not deem it applicable to the loss does not of itself prove that the broker has failed in his duty to exercise reasonable skill, care and judgment. If, however, a reasonably competent broker would have questioned the applicability of such insurance (on legal rather than factual grounds), it may be that he will be liable to the insured. Certainly a wilful misstatement of law is actionable (*Harse* v *Pearl Assurance* [1904] 1 KB 558, 563).

Similarly, where the client expresses concern as to the nature and extent of his cover, the broker should not respond on his own behalf, but should ask the insurer. He must, however, raise the matter clearly and obtain a clear, positive and unequivocal answer (*Melik & Co* v *Norwich Union* [1980] 1 Lloyd's Rep 523) so as to justify a plea of estoppel by the insured should the insurer later decide to the contrary.

The broker ought also to be aware of any vagaries or fluctuations in the market, and in particular to know which insurers are sound, which always dispute claims or take an unduly long time to pay out, or other factors which may be relevant to obtaining a contract of insurance best suited to his client's needs. A broker who knows or ought reasonably to know that a particular insurer is in financial difficulties, and places insurance with them after which they become insolvent, will be liable to the insured for such negligence (*Osman* v *J Ralph Moss Ltd* [1979] 1 Lloyd's Rep 313). The broker will also be in breach of Example 7 of the IBRC Code of Conduct.

Broker must act with reasonable speed

Any failure by the broker to act with reasonable speed which occasions loss to his client will render him liable (*London Borough of Bromley* v *Ellis* [1971] 1 Lloyd's Rep 97). Reasonable speed must be determined according to the circumstances, and relevant factors will include the size and nature of the proposed insurance contract, its availability, its necessity to the client, whether the client is uninsured etc (*Cock, Russell & Co* v *Bray, Gibb & Co Ltd* (1920) 3 Ll L Rep 71). The broker should, however, deliver any information to the insured as quickly as possible (*Proudfoot* v *Montefiore* (1867) LR 2 QB 511).

DAMAGES

Generally

The general principle is that the insured should be placed in the same position as if the act giving rise to non-payment by the insurer had not occurred. In contract this means that the insured should be compensated as if the contract had been properly performed; in tort it is as if the tortious act occasioning the loss had not taken place, so that a valid contract of insurance existed. This principle can, however, only be applied where the broker's error was sufficiently proximate to cause the loss, and that the loss that occurred was sufficiently foreseeable. The concept of foreseeability is applicable to claims founded in tort or contract but is rarely in dispute since the loss is usually a clear and inevitable consequence of the broker's action. Usually the broker's defences consist broadly of an allegation that the insured would not have been insured in the circumstances irrespective of any failure on the part of the broker, or that the insured was uninsurable in any event, or that the insured was responsible for or had contributed to the lack of suitable insurance. These defences usually incorporate a form of contributory negligence by the insured to some degree.

In each case the broker must satisfy the court that the insurer would have responded to the insured's claim by refusing to pay (in full or in part) under the contract. In *Fraser* v *Furman* [1967] 3 All ER 56 the broker failed to renew a liability policy and alleged that the insured had broken a condition which would have enabled the insurer, Eagle Star, to repudiate liability. The Court of Appeal stated that the condition had not been broken but in any event the court should take into account its assessment of ' . . . the chances that an insurance company of the highest standing and reputation, such as Eagle Star Insurance Co Ltd, notwithstanding their strict legal rights, would, as a matter of business, have paid up under the policy' (ibid at p 60). However, this decision is based upon the court's own assessment of the commercial position; no evidence was adduced from Eagle Star as to the course they would have followed.

Similarly, in *Everett* v *Hogg, Robinson & Gardner Mountain (Insurance) Ltd* [1973] 2 Lloyd's Rep 217 the brokers wrongly told the insurers that plastic was not used in the insured's products, which of course it was, and the insured failed to disclose its adverse claims record, both of which amounted to breaches of the duty of utmost good faith.

Distinguishing between avoidance and voidability

Kerr J distinguished between total avoidance as a result of the insured's breach, and voidability where the insurer could elect to treat the policy as void. In cases of avoidance ab initio the insured had to prove that he would have been paid, effectively on an ex gratia basis since no obligation to pay could exist, whilst in cases of voidability the broker had to prove that the insurer would have elected to avoid the policy and refuse to pay all or part of the claim to the insured (ibid p 223). Factors to be considered in both instances would include the amount involved and its importance against the amount of business between insurer and insured, their friendly relationship (or not), and whether a compromise would be likely in the overall circumstances of their business relationship based on 'intelligent guesswork'. ' . . . a fair and reasonable assessment' of the outcome by Kerr J resulted in payment of two thirds of the claim by the brokers. However, where the insurance is void eg for 'ppi' or 'tonner' policies which fall foul of s 4 of the Marine Insurance Act 1906, the court will inflict its version of morality as a matter of public policy and conclude that the insured is not entitled to any substantial damages, irrespective of whether or not the insurer would have paid (*Thomas Cheshire & Co* v *Vaughan Bros & Co* [1920] 3 KB 240).

A similar approach is adopted by the courts in claims against brokers who then allege that their conduct or action was of no relevance since the insured would not have been able to obtain insurance in any circumstances, or perhaps limited cover only, and therefore that the broker caused no (or limited) loss. The courts are not sympathetic to such allegations and prefer to believe that 'some accommodation would have been reached between the [insured] and their insurers' such as charging an additional premium (*Mint Security* v *Blair* [1982] 1 Lloyd's Rep 188).

Thus the courts try to imply or impose an optimistic attitude upon the relationship between insurers and insureds. The position is less clear when the insured contributes to his own loss, and the attitude of the insurer is of little relevance.

The insured may not be obliged to use his care and skill in checking the cover note

As has been considered, a failure by the insured to check his cover note or policy may not vitiate any error of the broker. In *General Accident Fire & Life Assurance Corp Ltd* v *JH Minet & Co Ltd* (1942) 74 LlL Rep 1 Goddard LJ at least implied agreement that there was no duty of any kind upon the insured to read the cover note. It is not the insured's duty to use his own care and skill to confirm that the broker has carried out the job that he was employed to do, and the insured is entitled to rely upon the presumption that the broker has carried out his instructions, and that the policy reflects the insurance requested (*Dickson & Co* v *Devitt* (1916) 86 LJKB). Mr Justice Paull wryly commented in *King* v *Chambers & Newman (Insurance Brokers) Ltd* [1963] 2 Lloyd's Rep 130 at 137 obiter that 'I am the last person ever to think that any insured ever reads his policy through from end to end. I am quite satisfied that it is only the very, very exceptional person who ever does'. Nevertheless, he found it 'almost inevitable that a businesswoman like [the insured] should just open it to check it to see that all the items were there . . . '. In fact he found for the insurer on other grounds but the possibility exists that an insured who actively considers the cover note or policy and fails to notice a patent error will have been contributorily negligent and that damages should be reduced accordingly. It had earlier been commented that 'It may very well be that if the defect is so obvious that it springs to the eye and had indeed been observed by the [insured], use might be made of the point' (*General Accident Fire & Life Assurance Corp Ltd* v *JH Minet & Co Ltd* (1942) 72 LlL Rep 49 at 62. A failure by the insured to notice a mistake on the proposal form during checking will serve to discharge the broker's liability, unless the insured was totally or partially illiterate (*O'Connor* v *BDB Kirby & Co* [1971] 1 Lloyd's Rep 454).

Such a reduction may depend upon the commercial awareness of the insured, who must appreciate that the insurance obtained was not as requested, and who must ratify it to discharge the broker's liability completely (*General Accident Fire & Life Assurance Corporation Ltd* v *JH Minet & Co Ltd* (1942) 74 LlL Rep 1 CA). The broker must prove that the insured 'understood that it did not represent the protection they desired and always desired'. It may not be enough to discharge the broker's liability that the insured ought to have been aware of the error, even where the insured was an underwriter specialising in another area of insurance. However, in *Youell v Bland Welch & Co Ltd* (Unreported: Judgment 27 March 1990) Phillips J said that:

Dickson v *Devitt* and *General Accident* v *Minet* were cases decided on their own facts and do not lay down some inflexible rule of law as to what a broker's client can properly be expected to do in the exercise of reasonable care to protect his own interests. In the present case those clients were Lloyd's agents. The personnel involved were marine underwriters of great experience. They admitted that they should have read carefully the terms of the cover on the three separate occasions when they received it. . . . In my judgment an insurer who was exercising reasonable skill and care in relation to the business he was conducting would have noticed the 48 month clause and would have queried its presence and effect with the brokers. . . . The insurers were guilty of a failure to exercise reasonable care in carrying out what they accepted were customary checks on the manner in which the brokers had performed their duty.

Even though the broker cannot hive off his obligations onto the insured, the insured may himself notice that the insurance is inadequate. In *Youell* v *Bland Welch & Co Ltd* (Unreported: Judgment 27 March 1990) Phillips J commented (obiter):

It may be, though I think it unlikely, that it is an implicit incident of the relationship of insurance broker and client that if the client knows that the cover that his broker has obtained falls short in some particular respect of the cover that he requires he has a duty to point this out to the broker. But that is not this case.

He failed to consider this aspect further. It is submitted that such a duty does exist, if only as part of the duty of the insured to mitigate his potential loss.

The Law Reform (Contributory Negligence) Act 1945 statutorily applies an apportionment of liability, so that damages recoverable by the insured as a result of the broker's error will be reduced as the court considers just and equitable, having regard to the insured's share in the responsibility for the damage suffered. This has been applied in reinsurance to apportion liability where the broker's liability in contract is the same as his liability in the tort of negligence independently of the existence of any contract (*Forsikringsaktielskapet Vesta* v *Butcher* [1988] 1 Lloyd's Rep 19). 'Apportionment of damages under the 1945 Act is not an exercise which is susceptible of that degree of precision. The correct approach is to decide the extent to which the insurers' recovery, calculated according to the first alternative, should be reduced to reflect their contributory negligence and its consequences. In my judgment the appropriate reduction is one of 20 per cent. The brokers must pay 80 per cent of the insurers' claim (*Youell* v *Bland Welch & Co Ltd* Unreported: Judgment 27 March 1990). Certainly, negligent conduct of the insured which does not affect and is irrelevant to his claim cannot be used by the broker to reduce the award of damages against him where his own error has been the sole cause of the loss (*Mint Security Ltd* v *Blair* [1982] 1 Lloyd's Rep 188).

Liability toward third parties

The broker's contract is with the insured, and is one of agency. He can, however, be liable to third parties, either under an additional or collateral contract, or as a result of a failure to discharge his duty of care, or pursuant to statute. For example, the wilful misrepresentation of a material fact to the insurer may render the broker liable for the consequences of this fraud, although the policy will be voidable on the basis that he is the agent of the insured.

A clear example of statutory liability exists under s 53 of the Marine Insurance Act 1906 which states that the broker is personally liable to the insurer for the premium under a marine policy, and the insurer need not even look to the insured for the premium. Section 54 provides that an acknowledgement of receipt of premium in the policy will estop the insurer from denying receipt as against the insured, even though the insured may not have paid and the insurer has not actually received it.

Another situation of broker's liability could arise where he does not make it clear to the insurer that he is acting as agent. This clarification is usually effected by a qualification of his signature by words such as 'for and on behalf of the assured' or 'as agent only', and its absence will render him liable, eg for premiums due (*Transcontinental Underwriting Agency* v *Grand Union Insurance Co Ltd* [1987] 2 Lloyd's Rep 409),[4] when he would not otherwise be liable.

---

4 In fact Transcontinental managed a retrocession pool and was the named retrocedant on two agreements, without any interest in the pool. Hirst J held that Transcontinental could sue and be sued as it had signed without qualification and was deemed to have contracted personally. Transcontinental could recover the loss in full, holding it as fiduciary agent for the pool members, although each member could sue concurrently as unnamed principal. It is a surprising case, standing on the wording of the agreement in question, but is still an authority for the proposition that a broker signing his own name (without any qualification or any contrary indication) will be liable. See *Provincial Insurance Co of Canada* v *Leduc* (1874) LR 6 PC 224, considered at p 177.

Conflict between duties of care owed by broker to principal and to a third party

The above exemplifies a voluntary assumption of liability by the broker on his own behalf. Such an assumption can only be effected where it does not engender a conflict between the duties owed by the broker to his principal and those purportedly owed to a third party, except where the principal is fully informed as to the position and freely consents to the conflict. However, a broker may act for a third party where no potential conflict can arise (*Stockton* v *Mason* [1980] 2 Lloyd's Rep 430).

A conceptual problem results. Why should a broker owe any duty of care to any third party if it could affect his duty of care to his principal in any way, however small? The short answer is that a court will imply a duty of care if there is no possibility of conflict (*Eagle Star Insurance Co* v *Spratt* [1971] 2 Lloyd's Rep 116, 133), but then it has the benefit of 20/20 hindsight and theoretically as good a view of the circumstances as can be obtained. Thus the court has held that the intended beneficiary of a will, who became unable to inherit as a result of the solicitor's negligence in its preparation, was able to claim damages from the solicitor (*Ross* v *Caunters* [1980] Ch 297). However, the court is always alive to the possibility of conflict and will not award damages where a conflict could exist (*Clarke* v *Bruce Lance & Co* [1988] 1 All ER 364, 370). This duty to an intended beneficiary of the policy was not extended in *Macmillan* v *Knott Becker Scott Ltd* [1990] 1 Lloyd's Rep 98 despite the fact that the intended beneficiary would clearly suffer harm if the broker was negligent, and no apparent conflict existed. The facts were that a Lloyd's syndicate tried to claim against a Lloyd's broker (KBS) who had gone into liquidation. The Lloyd's syndicate therefore tried to claim under the Lloyd's broker's errors and omissions cover, which was assumed by the court to have been placed negligently by another Lloyd's broker (NHM). It was therefore of no use. They therefore tried to leapfrog the liquidator by directly pursuing the broker who had arranged the Lloyd's broker's errors and omissions cover. Thus the question was whether the second broker (NHM) could be liable towards the first broker's clients in negligently placing insurance on behalf of the first broker, which was intended to benefit the first broker's clients.

The court formulated the test as being 'Was it fair, just and reasonable that a duty of care having the proposed scope should be held to exist?' (p 205). It concluded that 'a duty of care which was undertaken by contract might be owed to other persons not parties to the contract, if the necessary 'close and direct' relations existed between those persons and the [2nd broker]'. The existence and extent of any duty depended upon the degree of proximity, upon which must be inflicted policy considerations which here were evenly balanced; allowing the intended beneficiary of the policy (the Lloyd's syndicate) to sue the second broker (NHM) direct had much to recommend it as a matter of convenience. However, the Lloyd's syndicate still had a claim against the first broker in liquidation, which could be pursued by the liquidator against the 2nd broker. Evans J said that he would disturb this contractual structure to allow a 'leapfrog' or 'cut through' action if the loss were foreseeable, the parties were sufficiently proximate, and the requirements of justice or commercial convenience so required. In *Ross* v *Caunters*, this was the situation: the beneficiary would have no claim unless he could sue the negligent solicitor direct. In *Macmillan* v *Knott Becker Scott Ltd* no such compelling reason existed to permit direct recovery. Evans J preferred the contractual approach of the second broker, stating that 'Insurance brokers, I am sure, would accept professional instructions on the basis that their liability for financial or economic loss arising from negligence in the performance of those instructions was restricted to their clients. If asked about the possible insolvency of clients, they would assume that their liability was towards the liquidator and towards no-one else' (ibid p 110).[5]

Clearly, however, brokers can owe a duty to a third party. Further, the result of the decision is that the proceeds of the liquidator's action against the second broker (NHM) would be payable by the liquidator to the first broker's creditors, and the aggrieved clients would receive a portion only, so it is certainly arguable that justice required instituting direct action against the second broker (NHM).

It remains open, therefore, for a third party to sue the broker, if:

(a) that is his only remedy;
(b) it was foreseeable that he would suffer loss if the broker were negligent; and
(c) there can be no conflict of interest arising out of the duty of care owed by the broker to the third party, which could affect the broker's relationship with his principal.

In *London Borough of Bromley* v *Ellis* [1971] 1 Lloyd's Rep 97 it was held that the person who would benefit from the successful

---

5 *Macmillan* v *KBS* was decided on the basis of the Court of Appeal decision in *Caparo Industries plc* v *Dickman*, and is therefore a stronger authority after the House of Lords' decision.

assignment of a policy could sue the broker for breaking his duty to use reasonable care in failing to assign the policy properly.

Court may restrict duties of care in contract or tort The courts appear to be following a trend towards restricting duties of care in contract and in tort. In *Huxford* v *Stoy Hayward, The Times* 11 January 1990, the court suggested that it was not possible for a professional adviser to owe a duty of care to a third party whose interests were not substantially coterminous with those of his principal. There was, however, no voluntary assumption by the adviser to third parties and the relationship was not sufficiently proximate to found liability.

In *Caparo Industries* v *Dickman* [1989] 2 WLR 316 a majority Court of Appeal evinced a three part test of the existence of a duty of care owed by a professional adviser involving reasonable foreseeability of harm, the closeness and directness of the parties' relationship ('proximity') (including any voluntary assumption of responsibility), and whether the imposition of a duty is just and reasonable. However, the House of Lords has rejected the application of a universal test to establish the existence of any duty of care in *Caparo Industries plc* v *Dickman* (above) where Lord Bridge endorsed the traditional categorisation of liabilities, preferring the development of novel categories of negligence incrementally rather than under a single general principle. This approach is formulated around various factors including:

(a) whether it is just and reasonable (*Governors of the Peabody Donation Fund* v *Sir Lindsay Parkinson & Co Ltd* [1985] AC 210; *Curran* v *Northern Ireland Co-ownership Housing Association Ltd* [1987] AC 718). 'Justice' and 'reasonableness' are euphemisms for public policy. Thus exposing an adviser 'to a liability in an indeterminate amount for an indeterminate time to an indeterminate class' (Cardozo CJ in *Ultramares Corporation* v *Touche* (1931) 174 NE 441) would refute the imposition of a duty, but it will more readily be found if the adviser is exercising a professional skill for reward, if the lack of a duty prevented the victim from obtaining redress, if the duty alleged followed naturally from an existing duty or if the duty promoted a socially desirable objective. This approach appears to have been adopted by the House of Lords in *Caparo Industries plc* v *Dickman*, in which Lord Bridge considered the salient feature of many previous cases to be that specific reliance by specific people would be placed upon the advice or information given, which was different to reliance being placed upon a statement put into general circulation;

(b) any contractual relationship (*Candlewood Navigation Corporation* v

Mitsui OSK Lines Ltd [1986] AC 1); *Leigh & Sillivan Ltd* v *Aliakmon Shipping Co Ltd* (1986) AC 785); confirmed by Slade LJ in *La Banque Financiere* [1988] 2 Lloyd's Rep 513 at pp 557, 561 and 562);

(c) a close and direct relationship of proximity (*Yeun Kun Yeu* v *A-G of Hong Kong* [1988] AC 175);

(d) any voluntary assumption of responsibility whether as to mis-statements, acts or omissions, upon which the other party relies (*La Banque Financiere* [1988] 2 Lloyd's Rep 513) affirming at pp 558, 559 *Hedley Byrne & Co Ltd* v *Heller & Partners* [1963] 1 Lloyd's Rep 485; [1964] AC 465).

It is relatively easy to accept that a broker could be held liable to a third party who is the intended ultimate beneficiary. It is less easy to accept that a broker could be held liable to the party with whom he is in direct conflict, the insurer. The existence of an 'established business relationship' between the broker and insurer will not operate by itself to engender any legal obligations on the broker (*La Banque Financiere de la cité SA* v *Westgate Insurance Co Ltd* [1988] 2 Lloyd's Rep 513). Their interests cannot be the same, since each competes for the best terms, and what is better for one is usually necessarily detrimental to the other. A higher premium obviously benefits the insurer and not the insured. The primary rule of insurance broking must therefore hold good: the broker is the agent of the party seeking insurance, and nothing must conflict with the proper execution of his duties to that party.

Nevertheless, the courts have held that the broker can be the agent of the insurer, eg when he issues a cover note, and would owe any corresponding duties.

The extent of a broker's liability towards (re)insurers was discussed in *General Accident Fire & Life Assurance Corp* v *Tanter, The 'Zephyr'* [1985] 2 Lloyd's Rep 529. In essence a broker informed the lead reinsurer that his liability would be two thirds less than the amount subscribed on the slip. In fact it was 88.48 per cent of the amount subscribed. As the contract is contained solely in the slip, at least prior to the issue of the policy, the lead reinsurer was liable in that sum. The broker, however, was held liable as principal under a collateral contract with the reinsurer for failing to use his best endeavours to ensure that the slip would sign down as indicated (ibid, Mustill LJ at p 537). The broker may also have been subject to a concurrent duty of care in tort. The court refused to extend any liability beyond the lead underwriter and limited it to an express signing indication to the legal underwriter, given by the broker. Following underwriters who inferred that the lead underwriter must have signed after and in reliance upon a signing indication but did not confirm this with the broker could not claim against the broker. One wonders whether a specific enquiry of the lead underwriter would have given rise to any liability on the part of the broker to the following underwriter who made such an enquiry, and who then relied on the lead underwriter's answer to his detriment, or whether this is not sufficiently foreseeable to give rise to liability. The categories of tort have been said to be never closed and nor, presumably, is the ambit of any category, subject only to any policy considerations that the courts may impose to limit the liability of professional advisers to a particular level.[6]

Crime

Any broker effecting a policy for a party without any *bona fide* insurable interest, or expectation of such an interest, is guilty of an offence under the Marine Insurance (Gambling Policies) Act 1909. The broker could also be liable if he acts fraudulently in any way eg under the Theft Act 1978, Trade Descriptions Act 1976, Prevention of Corruption Act 1906 and Financial Services Act 1986. As a general rule, an agent cannot impose criminal liability on his principal through his actions, unless authorised by or connived in by the principal (*R* v *Stephens* (1866) LR1 QB 702). The principal can also be criminally liable if he ratifies the criminal acts of his agent (*Bedford Insurance Co Ltd* v *Instituto de Resseguros do Brazil* [1985] QB 966).

---

6 Whilst 'Precedents are not exhaustive of duty situations but merely illustrations of cases where the courts have held a duty to exist' (Steyn J in *La Banque Financiere* at p 70), public policy will continue to play a strong role in determining any duty of care: *Candlewood Navigation Corp* v *Mitsui OSK Lines Ltd* [1986] AC 1. The high water mark of professional liability appears to have been passed, and the lines of liability are now being retracted: see eg the House of Lords decision in *Caparo Industries plc* v *Dickman, The Times,* 12 February 1990.

Chapter 13

Insurance at Lloyd's of London

OBTAINING INSURANCE AT LLOYD'S OF LONDON

Insurance may be obtained on the 'company market' or at Lloyd's of London. The company market means exactly that: a company will grant insurance upon the same terms, rules of contract and agency law, and at similar rates to Lloyd's, but the insured must bear the risk that the company's liabilities will be limited, by definition. There will be little recourse beyond the company's assets after a liquidation has been untangled, except perhaps against its directors for offences under the Companies Acts and any attendant civil liabilities.

A policy of insurance effected at Lloyd's, on the other hand, entitles the insured (after properly establishing a valid claim) to obtain all the assets of those members of Lloyd's who have subscribed to the contract through their authorised agent, the 'active underwriter'. The contract is between the insured and many members, each of whom is individually liable for his own agreed share, but not the shares of others. Lloyd's is a singular institution with a plurality of liabilities. Section 8(1) of the Lloyd's Act 1982 states that a member 'shall only be a party to a contract of insurance underwritten at Lloyd's only if it is underwritten with several liability'.

There are three tiers of recourse after the insured has proved that the other contracting parties are liable to him for a claim, and payment is not forthcoming:

(a) the amount retained by Lloyd's as security for those members who have contracted with the insured. Every member has to pay a percentage of the premium income level allocated to him into the central fund held by Lloyd's, which is held in trust to protect the insured;

(b) after exhaustion of the security in (a), the Lloyd's member is liable to the limit of his personal assets, subject to statutory controls. Section 283 of the Insolvency Act 1986 leaves him 'such tools, books, vehicles and other items of equipment as are necessary to the bankrupt for use personally by him in his employment, business or vocation' and 'such clothing, bedding, furniture, household equipment and provisions as are necessary for satisfying the basic domestic needs of the bankrupt and his family'; and

(c) any deficit after (a) and (b) have been exhausted will be met by the Lloyd's central fund.

A Lloyd's insurance policy is not a contract with the Corporation of Lloyd's, but with individual members who are grouped into numbered syndicates. The syndicate is not a partnership, and has no corporate personality, identity or existence separate from the names of which it is comprised. It is not a legal fiction behind which liabilities cannot penetrate.[1] Each syndicate is represented in the Lloyd's market — 'the Room' — by an active underwriter, who is a salaried employee without personal liability (unless also a member of the syndicate for which he underwrites), who operates in one of four areas: marine, non-marine, motor and aviation.[2] The active underwriter deals from a 'box' in the underwriting room with representatives of parties seeking insurance, who are approved by the Committee of Lloyd's and are accredited as 'Lloyd's brokers'.

---

1 Whilst this is factually and legally correct, in most cases the Lloyd's accounting requirements ensure that the syndicate underwriting year of account is closed 36 months after expiry. The underwriter usually purchases 'reinsurance to close' the year but the rights and liabilities of parties to the original policy remain unaffected; it is only the source of ultimate payment that differs.

2 Marine underwriters may write 10 per cent 'incidental non-marine' business, and non-marine underwriters can write some marine. Both marine and non-marine can write aviation business. However, long term life policies are not written at Lloyd's per se, since a separate Lloyd's company exists to deal with this business. These market divisions may be removed from the 1991 year of account, and any syndicate will be able to write any business. The intention behind the demolition is to attract more business to Lloyd's, whose standards will be maintained by an enhanced role of the managing agents in the supervision of their underwriters. The managing agent is responsible for the underwriter, at least to the extent that he must ensure that the underwriter is not incompetent.

The role of the Lloyd's broker in placing insurance

Section 8(3) of the Lloyd's Act 1982 provides that no contract with a Lloyd's member can be arranged without a Lloyd's broker, who actually 'places' the insurance and is sometimes called the 'placing broker'. The insured's broker, if not accredited at Lloyd's or able to operate under an 'umbrella' relationship, will have to contact a Lloyd's broker to obtain the insurance at Lloyd's, sharing the commission. Each of course will be liable to the other for any negligence or other breach of duty. He therefore produces the proposal to the Lloyd's broker and is called the 'producing broker'.

The principles of this monopoly are sound. A prospective Lloyd's broker must satisfy the Council of Lloyd's that they are a suitable partnership or body corporate to negotiate business at Lloyd's, through their integrity, financial status and market experience and ability. Solvency margins must be maintained and a deposit placed in trust as security against any failure to pay premiums. The privileged position of Lloyd's brokers was examined by Sir Henry Fisher in 1980 who concluded that they should be entitled to retain their monopoly as a result of:

(a) their specialised knowledge and experience;
(b) the additional financial capacity required to discharge their strict liability to Lloyd's underwriters for premiums;
(c) the additional administrative infrastructure required to enable them to fulfil the additional duties which do not usually fall upon non-Lloyd's brokers, such as the preparation of a policy;
(d) the personal relationships that are built between underwriters and brokers which would be diluted by opening the Room to all brokers; and
(e) the commitment that the Lloyd's broker has to Lloyd's and his central role there, in particular his crucial part in the marketing of Lloyd's around the world.

Umbrella arrangements

There are two ways of avoiding the mandatory use of a Lloyd's broker. One is an umbrella agreement, colloquially known as a 'piggyback' or 'flag of convenience', which is 'an arrangement between a Lloyd's broker and a non-Lloyd's broker whereby business is transacted at Lloyd's by the directors, partners or employees of the non-Lloyd's broker acting as if they were the directors, partners or employees of the Lloyd's broker itself, using the Lloyd's broker slips' (*Johns v Kelly* [1986] 1 Lloyd's Rep 468). Its purpose is to enable a non-Lloyd's broker to offer its clients the benefits of

Lloyd's without having to pay commission to a Lloyd's broker as sub-agent, by placing an employee with the Lloyd's broker.

The decision in *Johns* v *Kelly* to the effect that Lloyd's brokers were negligent in their failure to exercise proper control over non-Lloyd's brokers under an umbrella agreement, together with non-disclosure of the fact that an umbrella agreement existed, thereby leading to the entitlement of professional indemnity insurers of the Lloyd's brokers to avoid liability, led to Lloyd's Byelaw No 6 of 1988.

The main provisions of Lloyd's Byelaw No 6 of 1988 are that any umbrella agreement must be registered at Lloyd's before any business is transacted (s 2), such agreement being valid for 3 years under s 8 but subject to the provisos that the non-Lloyd's broker must be registered under the Insurance Brokers (Registration) Act 1977 (which he would have to be anyway in order to qualify for the appellation 'broker') under s 9(1)(a), the non-Lloyd's broker must intend to apply for registration as a Lloyd's broker within 3 years from the start of the umbrella arrangement, and he must appear capable of meeting the relevant requirements to become a Lloyd's broker (s 9(1)(b)). The Lloyd's broker must give an undertaking to the Council to supervise the conduct of the non-Lloyd's broker and the non-Lloyd's broker must not be registered under another umbrella arrangement (s 9(2)), or a managing agent of a syndicate (s 9(3)). Although the Council of Lloyd's is clearly taking steps to regulate umbrella agreements, it is in fact hiving off its responsibility onto the Lloyd's broker, who must be directly responsible to any underwriter for payment of premiums under s 15(1), unless the Lloyd's broker and underwriter have effected different arrangements, although of course the Lloyd's broker is entitled to reimbursement from the non-Lloyd's broker (s 15(3)). The Lloyd's broker must take over responsibility for servicing the business under s 16 if the non-Lloyd's broker becomes unable to do so and the Lloyd's broker must ensure that the net brokerage derived under umbrella agreements does not exceed 25 per cent of its net brokerage for any one year (s 20). Under s 17 it must be made clear to the underwriters that the non-Lloyd's broker is not a Lloyd's broker and slips must clearly indicate this. The non-Lloyd's broker must also ensure that records are kept as though he were a Lloyd's broker (s 18), he must also notify any relevant changes to the Council of Lloyd's on a regular basis (s 26), and the Council has the power to ensure that a director of a Lloyd's broker must also be a director of the non-Lloyd's broker (s 10(3)). Subsidiaries of Lloyd's brokers are exempt from certain provisions under s 29.

The Umbrella Arrangements Byelaw also requires all 'officers' of the non-Lloyd's broker to undertake to submit to the jurisdiction of Lloyd's and to comply with Lloyd's Byelaws, the most relevant of which will be:

(a) Inquiries & Investigations Byelaw (No 3 of 1983);
(b) Information & Confidentiality Byelaw (No 4 of 1983);
(c) Misconduct Penalties & Sanctions Byelaw (No 5 of 1983);
(d) Misconduct Penalties & Sanctions Byelaw (No 11 of 1989);
(e) Disciplinary Committees Byelaw (No 6 of 1983);
(f) Appeal Tribunal Byelaw (No 7 of 1983);
(g) Council Stage of Disciplinary Proceedings Byelaw (No 8 of 1983); and
(h) Review Powers Byelaw (No 5 of 1986).

Direct dealing

In the absence of a negotiated, reduced commission, the other method of avoiding payment of the full commission to a Lloyd's broker is to place insurance with an underwriting syndicate which has been allowed to deal direct with non-Lloyd's brokers, although such non-Lloyd's brokers have to be sponsored by a Lloyd's broker who remains liable to the underwriters, and who is paid an overriding commission. Such a practice was developed to meet the needs of clients who do not congregate in any one market but may require immediate cover, and in particular for motor insurance which will be offered direct to the public through newspaper and media advertisements as from 8 March 1990, although enquiries will be routed to the participating syndicates through the associate company of a Lloyd's broker. Temporary cover notes meet the demand for such cover and the relaxation of the 'Lloyd's broker rule' enables Lloyd's to compete effectively with other insurers, whilst maintaining the standards of Lloyd's through the Direct Motor Committee of the Committee of Lloyd's for those Lloyd's brokers for whom such motor business will exceed 60 per cent of their annual premium income, or who will rely on any one non-Lloyd's broker for more than 5 per cent of their annual premium income. The Committee must authorise such dealings and may impose such conditions as it sees fit. The non-Lloyd's broker acts as the agent of the underwriter with authority to act given to him through a Lloyd's broker (*Praet* v *Poland* [1960] 1 Lloyd's Rep 416, 428). The underwriter must still receive a proposal form prior to extending the cover beyond expiry of the cover note.

Placing insurance at Lloyd's

The method of obtaining insurance at Lloyd's commences with the proposed insured's instructions to the Lloyd's broker, who should both prepare an attendance note of any initial instructions and obtain confirmation in writing to avoid later dispute. Once the instructions have been accepted and confirmed or clarified, the broker prepares one of the two key documents: the slip. The slip is a document which must be in standard form[3] for the Lloyd's market[4] and contains various administrative details. On the obverse side is typed sufficient information to enable the underwriter to understand precisely the contract he is being asked to enter into, and in particular to assess the nature and extent of the risk involved. Standard terms may also be included, such as leading underwriter agreements. Various aspects of the proposed contract are abbreviated on the slip, but these should be in common use and capable only of one meaning if later dispute or liability of the broker for negligence are to be avoided. Any non-standard provision which the broker wishes to incorporate into the contract should be attached in full to the slip, but standard clauses or wordings need only be identified by title, number and date of issue (especially if the broker intends to use an old wording which may have been superseded).

The leading underwriter

Having prepared the slip to reflect the insurance required, the broker will then submit it to those underwriters in the Room whom he considers likely to subscribe, and/or to suitable insurance companies. The broker could spend considerable time approaching various underwriters to whom he has to market the risk, but more often he will select a brand leader to endorse his wares: 'the leading underwriter'. The 'leader' is accepted by the other underwriters as one whose judgment is good, and whose negotiated terms will be followed without the need for renegotiation, and later subscription is made considerably easier when an accepted leader is at the head of the slip.

---

3 The marine, non-marine and treaty reinsurance markets each have their own standard slip.
4 The promissory or placing slip originated to avoid the need to issue a formal policy of marine insurance, which attracted stamp duty, and was treated as satisfactory evidence of the contract.

The underwriters who follow the lead may agree to accept any minor amendments or additions to the policy without the need for their specific approval or authority, as long as the leader has agreed to the alteration. This is commonly called a 'leading underwriter agreement' and is clearly an efficient way of effecting changes to the contract without renegotiating with every subscribing underwriter; it is, therefore, usually printed on the broker's slip. It effectively constitutes the leading underwriter as the agent of the following underwriters with specified and limited authority to amend their contracts with the insured. In the absence of such agreement, every later amendment must be agreed by every underwriter before it can bind him. Following underwriters may also refuse to be bound by the leader, or request that they be advised of all amendments.

A leading underwriter clause binding all underwriters to abide by the decisions of the leading underwriter entitles an insured to bring a representative action against the lead as representing all the insurers, even though the insured's claim is against each insurer severally for its proportion of the loss, and some are resident outside the jurisdiction (*Irish Shipping Ltd* v *Commercial Union Assurance Co plc (The 'Irish Rowan')* [1989] 2 Lloyd's Rep 144).

However, the leader's authority must be limited to prevent a following underwriter discovering that the risk that he agreed to write has not metamorphosed into something quite different as a result of any changes agreed between the broker and leader. The broker must know of the relevant restrictions, since if he purports to obtain the leader's agreement to an alteration which should have been agreed with all underwriters because it falls outside the leader's authority, he may be liable to the insured who will believe that he is covered by a different insurance and may act accordingly, subject to any claim against the leader for breach of warranty of authority. Such a claim will be rare because the broker is or should be aware of the extent of the leader's authority, but it could occur if the leader were to misrepresent the position.

Thus the leader cannot agree to a material alteration of the risk, such as an increase in the total sum insured or of any other line on the policy, and it is a question of fact as to what constitutes such a material alteration, although this is usually decided by the leader. In *Barlie Martine Corporation* v *Mountain, The 'Leegas'* [1987] 1 Lloyd's Rep 471, an argument that the leading underwriter clause could be 'pumped up' to permit infinite variation was rejected by Hirst J, partly upon a construction of the clause and its application to the amendment in question, and partly on the basis that 'any notion that it [a marine policy] could be converted into, say, an aviation policy is fanciful in the extreme. Equally fanciful is the notion that the following underwriters could be saddled willy-nilly with indefinite extension without their knowledge, since they would continue to receive premium and could, in any event, have recourse, if they wished, to the termination clause. Underlying the whole relationship between the leading underwriter and the following underwriters, furthermore, is the former's manifest duty of care. An allusion to such a duty had been made in the Savonita Report (Lloyd's List 8 December 1978) in which it was said that: ' . . . the duty of any leading underwriter, when informed of suspicions of fraud in connection with a claim, is to ensure that all following underwriters are aware of the circumstances. In any event, the board would not expect a leading underwriter to settle a claim in such circumstances without an investigation into the allegations'.

In the event of dispute the extent of the leading underwriter's authority will fall to be adduced by objective 'expert' evidence. If in doubt the leader may either request the broker (by crossing out 'Show' as printed on the slip) to obtain the agreement of the other underwriters, indicated by their initials next to the alteration, or addendum containing it, or alternatively to advise the other underwriters of the change, so that they can object if they so wish. Any failure to object after such advice will render them estopped from denying their agreement to the change.

However, leading underwriter agreements usually require the agreement of two or three underwriters to the change, so that Lloyd's and the company market are represented, as the company market will not necessarily agree to be bound by decisions of the Lloyd's leader.

Generally, the leading underwriter agreement will authorise the leader(s) to agree:

(a) any item which is stated in the slip 'to be advised' or 'to be agreed', such as the attachment date or premium; (see below);
(b) additional premiums where the insured is held covered ie where cover can be continued or widened under the contract;
(c) settlements of claims (*Insurance Co of the State of Pennsylvania v Grand Union Insurance Co* [1990] 1 Lloyd's Rep 208, 224), or not;
(d) amendments of an administrative nature, or similar to those possible under RSC Ord 20, which need not be agreed by the subscribing market.

Terms to be agreed

The terms of the agreement will usually be followed in the slip by the abbreviation 'tba l/u' ie 'to be agreed by leading underwriter'. The phrase usually means that a contract has been concluded and that the underwriters will be liable if a loss occurs before the term has been finally agreed, provided that the contract is not void for uncertainty. In the case of premium, for example, a reasonable premium will be deducted which will be agreed between the parties, or by a court or arbitrator in the absence of such agreement (s 31 of the Marine Insurance Act 1906).

However, it may be clear from the circumstances that the insurer intended that no agreement should exist until the term had been agreed. In *American Airlines/Banque Sabbaq SAL v Hope* [1972] 1 Lloyd's Rep 253; [1973] 1 Lloyd's Rep 233; [1974] 2 Lloyd's Rep 301) additional war risks cover was stated on an aviation risks slip 'to be agreed by the leading underwriter' at an additional premium and after the geographical limits had been determined. Before either agreement was reached or a policy issued, the 'insured' aircraft were destroyed by perils falling within the additional war risks cover. The Court of Appeal held that the additional cover did not apply because the geographical limits had not been established with sufficient accuracy to enable the insured to specify the area covered, and there was an assumption that agreement as to both premium and geographical limits had to be reached before any liability could attach. This case does not provide grounds for stating that any part of a contract remaining to be agreed renders that particular part ineffective. However, it should be appreciated that any term not settled may well be ineffective if there is any doubt as to the precise construction of that term ie where different versions exist, the insured will have to prove that the version he relies on would have been included. Premium is capable of objective verification since evidence of market practice can be adduced to show with some accuracy what would have been agreed; other terms are less susceptible to such easy or accurate verification. The leader may have insisted upon a particular version and a court would be hard pressed to disagree, as proof that another term would have been included may be difficult to obtain, since the choice remains subjectively with the underwriter.

Information　The heading 'information' is sometimes introduced into the slip, perhaps in connection with the name of a vessel under a marine cargo policy, or in reinsurance where the reinsured is passing on information given to him by the insured to attempt to protect the reinsured from any error in the information given to him. Whilst the information may not then have the status of a warranty, it may constitute an unqualified representation that the information is true, which will give rise to a right to avoid if it is untrue, as happened in *Highland Insurance Co v Continental Insurance Co* [1987] 1 Lloyd's

Rep 109. The test of the 'caveat' is 'an objective one: what would the words have conveyed to a prudent underwriter in [that] position?' (ibid p 111). The London market custom is that 'reinsurers [do] place reliance on a broker's presentation of "Information" as recording statements of fact unless qualifying language or the context indicates that a particular statement falls in a different category'. Words such as 'Information not warranted' or 'Subject to checking/confirmation' should be used to avoid liability for the information presented.

Subjectivities The underwriter may agree to be bound after certain conditions stipulated by him have been fulfilled, by indorsing the slip with the words eg 'subject to reinsurance'. The broker must advise the insured immediately of any action required to be taken by the insured, or must comply with the requirement if it applies to him eg by obtaining reinsurance for that insurer's portion of risk.

Subscribing the slip

After the relevant details have been disclosed to the following underwriter, and he agrees to accept a portion of the risk, he will underwrite an amount, shown on the slip as a percentage of the total risk. This percentage is his 'line' and is represented by the impression of the underwriter's line stamp on the slip, which contains the percentage taken, the underwriter's initials and the date.

The variations on this theme include the following.

(a) A quotation slip is a standard slip upon which the broker obtains pencilled lines from possible underwriters and may be used by the broker to obtain as many quotations as possible, and return to the most suitable underwriters in order to contract 'firm'. The broker may be trying to demonstrate his ability to his client, or obtain a better rate 'on spec' to show a prospective client that he can obtain a better deal, or because the client has instructed several brokers. The underwriter will usually limit the period for acceptance. In legal terms, such a quotation represents an invitation to treat.

(b) More than one slip — this practice may facilitate earlier completion of the contract, since more brokers can trawl the market, or to avoid conflicts of a political or competitive nature eg Israeli and Arab insurers prefer not to see each other on the slip, as do some underwriters at Lloyd's, or because they contain different terms and the broker is simply testing the market.

(c) An off slip is a copy of the original placing slip and is used by the broker either for reference purposes or for policy signing and accounting purposes. In the latter case it must be authenticated by the signature of the first underwriter on the slip, who will state that it is a complete copy of the original. An off slip is called a 'signing slip' when used for policy signing and accounting purposes, and may also be called a 'closing slip' (although this should refer to one used for accounting purposes only). 'It is the leader's responsibility to check that the signing slip is in accordance with the original slip' (*General Accident Fire & Life Assurance Corporation plc v Tanter, The 'Zephyr'* [1984] 1 Lloyd's Rep 75, 142).

An off slip is also used to solve the problem of obtaining insurance and reinsurance simultaneously. The broker will obtain the authority of a reinsurer to reinsure original risks accepted by the primary insurer in accordance with the line slip. The contract between the insured and the insurer is contained in the off slip which indicates that it has been 'concluded under the auspices of the line slip and reinsured under the reinsurance policy'. (*Balfour v Beaumont* [1984] 1 Lloyd's Rep 273).

(d) A line slip is also used for administrative convenience when a broker intends to place many similar risks with the same underwriters, and is an arrangement between the broker and the underwriters that the broker need only obtain the initials of specified leading underwriters in relation to a particular type of risk, and the leader's acceptance will bind all those who subscribed the line slip, in their agreed proportions. A line slip does not involve the delegation of underwriting powers to a third party, as does a binding authority, but rather involves the delegation of authority by other underwriters to one or more leaders.

(e) A slip policy takes the place of a formal policy, for which it can be exchanged at any time. Essentially it is a signing slip upon which the broker places a 'slip policy sticker', having agreed with the underwriters that a slip policy will be sufficient, and having obtained the leader's initials as usual. The slip is processed as a policy by the LPSO with the premium advice note and returned to the broker. Slip policies are prevalent in reinsurance, actual policies only being issued where the foreign domiciled insured effectively obtains reinsurance in London via a local insurer, to whom he is forced to go by local legislation.

'Closing'

Was discussed in *Phoenix General Insurance Co of Greece SA v Halvanon Insurance Co Ltd* [1985] 2 Lloyd's Rep 599. Hobhouse J at p 614 stated that:

In theory, unless there is some agreement deferring liability, the liability to pay premiums arises as soon as the risk attaches, but in practice that is not when the premium is paid, nor is it when it is expected to be paid. After an original risk is written, it has to be 'closed'. Closing involves the broker delivering to the underwriter a closing form which contains the final financial details of the cover, including the actual premium payable. This is the point at which, as between placing broker and original underwriter, the former is debited in the account and the latter is credited. When the account between broker and underwriter is settled thereafter will depend on the course of dealing between them; the account will normally include a very large number of items and cross items which will periodically be checked and agreed, and a payment or payments made to clear off outstanding balances. Individual items may be settled separately, as with substantial claims.

Thus the broker prepares the closing document, in order to credit the underwriter with the premium to which he is entitled. This document contains the relevant calculations for each underwriter. Receipt of the 'closing' slip may be the first information of the actual signing obtained by a following underwriter (in the absence of an earlier signing list from the broker). The closings ought to be prepared and sent out within a period of between one and three months after placement, but this does not always occur. The underwriter sometimes does not learn of his signing until close to the expiry of cover, or even when a loss occurs.

Closing is the final stage of the process, and the last before a claim. The Lloyd's Policy Signing Office and its counterparts in the marine and non-marine company market, the Institute of London Underwriters and the Policy Signing and Accounting Centre, effect the necessary administration to ensure that the insured receives his policy in the correct format, via the broker. Slips are registered with them by brokers at the time of placing in the market, to enable them to monitor the signing and accounting procedures initiated by the broker, together with premium payments. The leader is given a registration form by the broker, which he completes and sends to LPSO, who in turn send him reports as to its progress.

Status and legal effect of the slip

The slip is a formal document with legal effect, although it is usually superseded by the policy which reflects the content of the slip and puts flesh on the abbreviations contained therein. The slip generally prevails over the policy and the policy may be rectified where it does not accord with the terms of the slip unless the parties have affirmed the policy by words or conduct, so that it cannot later be rectified. It is, however, possible for the slip itself to fail to record the contract agreed by the parties, so that it can also be rectified

(*Eagle Star & British Dominions Ins Co* v *Reiner* (1927) 27 Ll L Rep 173, 175). Nevertheless, a slip is not a policy and in cases of marine insurance s 22 of the Marine Insurance Act 1906 requires the contract to be embodied in a policy before the insured can bring any action. The underwriters will usually arrange for a policy to be issued if one is not in existence. The slip cannot be used as an aid to construction of the policy in the absence of a claim for rectification of the policy where the text of the policy has been agreed by the leading underwriter (*Youell* v *Bland Welch* Interim Judgment Lloyd's Rep 23 February 1990).

There may be problems in a slip 'twixt cup and lip', since the insured is being put in contact with many contracting parties at Lloyd's. Circumstances may change; so too may underwriting minds. The issue usually revolves around the time the contract is concluded. In *General Reinsurance Corporation* v *Forsikringsaktiebolaget Fennia Patria* [1983] 2 Lloyd's Rep 287, Staughton J held that the broking of the slip to the underwriter constituted an offer by the proposed insured, and initialling by the underwriter an acceptance of that offer. Any amendment by the underwriter to any term constitutes a counter offer which can be accepted or rejected by the broker. Thus a binding contract comes into force from which neither can unilaterally resile and in respect of which the underwriter is liable for his share of any loss. This is so even where the slip is not subscribed as to 100 per cent of the total insurance requested, a point argued in detail in *Fennia* where it was contended that there was a Lloyd's custom that an insured could withdraw from the contract when the slip was not fully subscribed. The Court of Appeal held that no such custom had been proved and that to allow the insured to take such action would conflict with the premise that the slip constitutes a binding agreement. However, a contract will not be binding where the underwriter expressed that it be subject to further action by the insured, or that the initialling does not signify an acceptance, provided this is made absolutely clear. Underlining his initials does not negate his apparent acceptance, even though it is intended to warn following underwriters as to his doubts concerning the contract (*Eagle Star Insurance Co* v *Spratt* [1971] 2 Lloyd's Rep 116). Any market usage relied upon to qualify acceptance must be accepted by the whole market, not just the underwriters on one syndicate (ibid, p 125).

General Reinsurance Corporation v *Forsikringsaktiebolaget Fennia Patria* (above) is an example of loss occurring before the slip has been fully subscribed. In such circumstances the insured will usually want to enforce the contract against underwriters, though he will not recoup the sum intended to be insured unless he had been made aware by the broker that the slip had not been fully subscribed and had obtained insurance elsewhere for the balance. Sometimes, however, the slip will be oversubscribed ie when the broker has obtained lines which exceed 100 per cent in total. This may appear overcautious but in fact operates in the broker's interest, since he can spread the risk more evenly, particularly where it is of poor quality; so that he can approach underwriters with a smaller claim should the need arise; so that he can retain his market profile and appear to provide more business to more underwriters; so that he can reach 100 per cent quickly; so that the slip looks better as a result of the large lines appearing on it in anticipation of signing down, which in turn encourage other large lines; so that it will be easier to increase insured values later or to add further subject matter (vessels, vehicles etc) to the insurance; and so that he can show the insured his apparently unlimited contacts and abilities in the market. The broker may also confirm 100 per cent cover to the insured as soon as it is reached, despite any prior signing indication. Whilst this may or may not be laudable, the excess over 100 per cent is superfluous because the principle of indemnity by definition demands that the insurance cannot exceed 100 per cent. Each underwriter's line must therefore be reduced proportionately until 100 per cent is reached, unless the underwriter has requested that his line is 'to stand' ie that it should not be reduced. The broker may also be able to sign down some lines more than others, depending on the signing indications given to each underwriter. Each reduction technically may be a breach of contract, and therefore the premium for the original figure must be paid, if so desired by the underwriters, even though the insured will not recover the insured sum over 100 per cent.[5] The broker would therefore have to pay the underwriters the additional premium if they refuse to reduce, especially in cases where the underwriter has not agreed to a later reduction by writing 'to stand' next to his line. The underwriters may, however, have accepted that a reduction would be necessary when they signed their lines, in which case the 'signing down' may not constitute a breach of contract.

Thus, the underwriters may realise that some signing down may be necessary, and accept this as a recognised and binding market practice, provided it 'does not occur to an unreasonable extent' (*General Accident Fire & Life Assurance Corporation* v *Tanter, The 'Zephyr'* [1984] 1 Lloyd's Rep 75, [1985] 2 Lloyd's Rep 529). They

---

5 See Insurance Contract Law at A32–20.

are more concerned, however, as to the extent of any such signing down, since an error in any indication given by the broker will give rise to some loss to the underwriter either way. If the slip is signed down more than indicated, the underwriter will have less risk to bear but also less premium, whilst any lesser reduction may force the underwriter to accept more risk than he wanted or anticipated, although with commensurately higher premium.

The underwriter desires certainty, especially when nearing his underwriting limit, and will keep records not only of his ultimate signed line notified on closing but also of the anticipated signing at the time of writing the line. He will therefore not be pleased when the final signed line differs substantially from that indicated by the broker. Several underwriters were less than happy in *General Accident Fire & Life Assurance Corporation* v *Tanter, The 'Zephyr'* in which the broker indicated that the (lead) underwriter's lines would sign down to one third of his line written at the time of the indication. However, the oversubscription did not go according to the broker's plan and it was oversubscribed by only 13 per cent, leaving underwriters with 88.48 per cent of their 'original line'. Allegations of liability were then scattered. Three arguments were put forward to Hobhouse J, who rejected them all. These were as follows:

(a) the broker was the agent of the underwriters (who were reinsurers) and the signing limitation was an effective limit on his authority, specifically preventing him from binding them to more than a third. This was negated by the clear rule that the broker acts for the insured in negotiating and placing insurance on his behalf;

(b) the signing indication formed part of the contract and therefore allowed the underwriters to terminate the contract for breach. Hobhouse J held that this theory did not accord with Lloyd's practice or the rule that the slip formed the contract. Where a contract is reduced to writing, the incorporation of oral terms is never easy, particularly where they conflict with what is written; a signing indication of one third clearly contradicts the written line and as such cannot be binding; or

(c) in the absence of any finding that the slip was not conclusive by itself, the signing indication constituted a promissory estoppel, or a misrepresentation. Hobhouse J considered that the doctrine of estoppel did not apply, since the indication was not of existing fact, but of future expectation or belief. Section 20(5) of the Marine Insurance Act 1906 endows such a representation with truth if made in good faith. The indication could not have contractual power or found any promissory estoppel also on the ground that a broker simply could not warrant the eventual written line, since it would not be within his ability to do so; it would depend on the reaction of the remaining market.

The liabilities then fell into two parts: those of the broker to the leading underwriter, and to the following market. Initially Hobhouse J held the broker liable to both in tort as a result of his breach of duty of care. He stated (at p 85) that:

In the present case the giving of a signing indication by a broker to an underwriter is a voluntary act by the broker as a result of which the underwriter to the knowledge of the broker is placed in a situation of reliance upon the broker exercising his professional function with reasonable skill and diligence as a professional man. It is this element of reliance by one person on another arising out of the voluntary assumption by the latter of a relationship to the former, that is of the essence of the duties of care which have been held to exist in the *Junior Books* case and the cases it followed.

The matter then went to the Court of Appeal who, in skirting the wreck of The *'Zephyr'*, had to decide whether a signing indication occasions an enforceable obligation on the broker to the party to whom the indication is given, or any other party following that indication to whom it is not expressly made, and the nature, extent and characterisation of any such obligation. Mustill LJ opined that such an indication clearly gave rise to liability if not complied with, and characterised the obligation as contractual. The broker had impliedly promised that the line would be signed down in return for the underwriter's subscription of the slip, whereby the broker could earn his remuneration, and had entered into a contract collateral to the main insurance contract. Mustill LJ did not consider that the liability was founded in tort, because the broker's promise was gratuitous, and that a representation to use 'best endeavours' could not give rise to liability for failing to do so in the absence of any contract, unless it could be construed as a representation of present fact (at p 538). However, he did comment that a duty in tort *could* arise independently of contract where the co-existence of a contractual bargain means that the relationship is not gratuitous (ibid), but held that a broker could not be liable to any underwriter to whom he had not expressly given a signing indication, despite any inference by that underwriter that such an indication must have been made to the leader. In *Youell v Bland Welch & Co Ltd* (Unreported: Judgment 27 March 1990) Phillips J stated that:

A broker who seeks to persuade an insurer to write a line of original insurance by informing him that specific reinsurance cover is available is, in my judgment, in a relationship with the insurer which gives rise to a duty of care in tort — see *The 'Zephyr'* at p 538 per Mustill LJ.

Three other protrusions from the wreck were also beaten flat. The court rejected the possibilities that the leader acted as agent for the following underwriters, that any misrepresentation made to the leader which entitled him to avoid imbued the following underwriters with the same right, and that there was a custom at Lloyd's to the effect that all underwriters were mutually dependent.

The concept of severability and its effect on the contract of the insured

Lloyd's is essentially a market in which a proposed insured can be put in touch with many syndicates prepared to insure him, each of which is sub-divided into members, each of whom could be individually liable to him. However, many insureds will not be aware of the status or workings of Lloyd's, and need not be aware provided they hold one policy of insurance which reflects their needs, rather than a handful of policies in respect of one subject matter. In reality, however, the insured has a contract with each member, which is entered into by the member's representative, the active or authorised underwriter of his syndicate.

The fact that there are several contracts between the insured and underwriters has not unduly worried the administration of Lloyd's, who will issue one policy of insurance, rather than several. Of course this works to everyone's benefit; neither Lloyd's nor the insured would wish to hold a bundle of policies, all dealing with the same risk. However, the possibility exists that each contract could be on different terms to the others, particularly where the duty of disclosure (and good faith) ensures that facts not existing or immaterial at the date upon which the early underwriters initialled the slip may need to be disclosed to later underwriters if the contract is not later to be avoided, owing perhaps to a change in circumstances, or perhaps because later underwriters insist on different terms.[6]

In *Jaglom* v *Excess Insurance Co Ltd* [1972] 1 All ER 267 Donaldson

---

6 A practice which occasioned a letter from Lloyd's Underwriters Non-Marine Association in January 1989 to its members to the effect that any broker who became unable to complete on the terms agreed with the leader should reapproach him to renegotiate terms for the whole slip. In reality it is rare for the following market to alter the slip.

LJ expressed this concept as being 'absurd' and circumvented it by characterising the slip as an invitation to treat. In fact, the system used to operate in this way until it was agreed that a single policy could be effected to include all lines on a slip, which lead to the formation of the Lloyd's Policy Signing Bureau in 1918. In *General Reinsurance Corporation* v *Forsikringsatiebolaget Fennia Patria* [1983] 2 Lloyd's Rep 287 Staughton J retained the ability of the slip to bind but to entitle previous underwriters to adopt later changes in the slip into their contracts, subject to the insured's right to cancel if an underwriter refuses so to adopt, so that the insured can insist on a 'single' policy wording. It is thought unlikely that the previous underwriters could so insist. The insured has complied with his obligations prior to formation of the contract; that should be enough. The Court of Appeal in *Fennia* did not accept that an insured could cancel a contract because it contained differing terms, but it did not adopt a specific position as to whether an alteration made by any underwriter which was contained in the slip could benefit all, save to say that the slip constitutes the binding contract.

Leading underwriter agreements go some way to resolving part of this problem, since a later underwriter can request the leader to alter the slip to reflect the contract he requires (if within the leader's authority), but the leader may not agree in which case different contracts may result. Further, the insured may not agree to a variation, so that the same result ensues.

Binding Authorities

Under a 'binding authority' an underwriter may authorise a broker to rate and accept specified risks on his behalf without reverting to the underwriter to obtain his approval in each case, unless the authority is limited to issuing the insurance documentation and such approval is required. The broker therefore becomes the agent of the underwriter and the process enables routine risks to be placed at Lloyd's without the need for individual negotiation of each risk, thereby saving time and avoiding excessive administration. The broker deals with the negotiation of terms, although these are not usually capable of much argument, and issues the necessary documentation to the insured. He cannot delegate his duties, as a matter of agency law. Binding authorities do not include marine open covers or non-marine contracts in the form of line slips.

The broker is called the 'coverholder' and the authority must be registered at the LPSO in a standard form according to Lloyd's Byelaw No 4 of 1985 (Binding Authorities).

Binding authorities evidence an accepted practice at Lloyd's in which the broker acts in a dual capacity. On the one hand he is arranging insurance for the insured on the best possible terms, and yet on the other he is obtaining business for his other principal, the underwriter, and obtaining further commission for himself. The issue may be resolved in cases of 'consumer' or 'domestic' insurance eg motor, since the member of the public obtaining insurance should appreciate that the agent giving him insurance without demur or delay must have the insurer's authority to do so,[7] but in commercial insurance the broker is specifically instructed by the insured to obtain the best possible insurance for that insured, and he will believe that the broker is doing exactly that, free from considerations of personal gain or other motive. Thus any failure by the broker to comply with the dictum of Megaw LJ in *Eagle Star Insurance Co v Spratt* [1971] 2 Lloyd's Rep 116 that 'an agent for one party should not act for the opposite party in connection with the same transaction without the latter's informed consent' may lead to liability for breach of his duties as agent (*Fireman's Fund v Excess* [1982] Lloyd's Rep 599), provided damage can be proven eg where the insured can show alternative and better forms of security or terms. One method of avoiding any dispute as to the broker's actions would be to separate within the broking organisation the broking function from the underwriting function, so that both aspects are considered independently. The only area of dispute removed by the operation of a 'binder' is that any information given to the broker will be imputed to the underwriter, so that avoidance for non-disclosure cannot later be attempted by the underwriter in respect of such information if the broker has not passed it on.

The granting, operation and maintenance of binding authorities are regulated by the Binding Authorities Byelaw (No 4 of 1985), the Binding Authorities Regulation (No 1 of 1985) and the Approval of Correspondents Regulation (No 2 of 1985). The last Regulation imposes the approbation of the Correspondents' Approval Committee upon the Lloyd's broker's selection of 'producing brokers' in foreign jurisdictions, a process known as 'tribunalisation', such approval depending upon the fitness and propriety of the applicant taking into account any apparent conflict of interest, its financial

---

7 Actually he is unlikely to consider either his rights and liabilities, or those of the broker, a view held in 1976 by the British Insurance Brokers' Council in their Consultative Document which stated that 'The private individual . . . is likely to have little understanding of insurance or the way in which it is organised'.

resources, its own professional liability insurance and its banking and operating procedures.

There is also a Code of Practice relating to the operation of binding authorities.

The policy

The policy will usually supersede the slip, and provides the flesh for its bones. In theory it should govern the contract, since it is the last 'contractual' document which purports to set out all relevant terms of the agreement,[8] and is intended to reflect that agreement and to have legal effect (*Youell* v *Bland Welch & Co* Interim Judgment Lloyd's List 23 January 1990). However, if it does not accurately reflect the slip, it can be rectified, unless the underwriters have elected to continue the contract upon the terms of the policy rather than the slip, provided they are in possession of all relevant information at the date of election. The slip therefore is effectively the contract; any later terms in the policy which are not contained in the slip are of no consequence unless affirmed (*General Accident Fire & Life Assurance Corporation* v *Tanter, The 'Zephyr'* [1984] 1 Lloyd's Rep 75, at 142). Information in the slip which is not repeated in full in the policy will remain a pre-contractual misrepresentation ie where it is described in the slip as 'information not warranted', and the wording will not affect the rights of the underwriter in reliance thereon. Similarly, the correction of a warranted state of affairs or misrepresentation between the slip and policy will not affect the underwriter's rights, unless the underwriter positively elects to go on with the contract or prejudice is caused to the insured by the insurer's failure to affirm or elect (*Morrison* v *Universal* (1873) LR 8 Ex 197). The issue of the policy is essentially a ministerial act. Where the policy varies considerably from the slip, so that it is really a new contract, the duty of disclosure will continue until the underwriter elects to be bound by the policy. Waiver of a less significant item will not necessarily discharge the insured's duty of disclosure, since the underwriter must be in possession of all material facts.

The problems that arise usually stem from the practice of using abbreviations or shorthand terms in the slip, and inappropriate or ‚

---

8 *Morrison* v *Universal* (1873) LR 8 Ex 197; *Butler Machine Tool Co Ltd* v *Ex-Cell-O Corporation (England) Limited* [1979] 1 WLR 401; *Chichester Joinery Ltd* v *John Mowlem & Co plc* (42) BLR 103.

inconsistent clauses in the policy,[9] or clauses thought to be hallowed but still capable of argument (*Dino Services Ltd* v *Prudential Assurance Co Ltd* [1989] 1 Lloyd's Rep 379).

Lloyd's Facilities

The broker does not operate in a vacuum but rather within a network of interconnecting facilities, the most important of which are:

Lloyd's Underwriters Claims and Recovery Office

The claims section is divided into Hull, Cargo and Reinsurance, and deals specifically with marine claims although it can handle other claims covered by policies subscribed to by the marine underwriters, such as non-marine, aviation and oil exploration. As soon as the broker is notified by the insured that there may be a claim, the broker should inform Lloyd's Underwriters Claims and Recovery Office ('LUCRO') of the details of any casualty or damage to a vessel belonging to the insured and LUCRO will instruct him as necessary. LUCRO will deal with problems concerning the minimising of the loss or in the presentation of the claim, and in connection with the preservation of any rights of recovery against third parties.

The recovery section acts on a 'no cure no pay' basis and works closely with the cargo claims section and the salvage association. Recoveries are pursued on behalf of underwriters against various parties causing loss, such as bailees of cargo or other third parties, and it will protect cargo interests in connection with general average and salvage.

In respect of the authorisation of claims, marine underwriters are categorised as A, B or C. The A category means that the marine underwriters have authorised LUCRO to deal with claims on their behalf absolutely, whilst those in B have given authority to LUCRO to act but still require sight of the claims files in respect of total losses and large cargo claims. Category C underwriters require sight of all claims files, which must be directly submitted to them in the Room. It is therefore important for the broker to know which underwriters fall within category C, so that he can comply as necessary.

---

9 For example *ICA* v *Scor* [1985] 1 Lloyd's Rep 312; *Forsikringsaktielskapet Vesta* v *Butcher* [1988] 1 Lloyd's Rep 19; *Abrahams* v *Mediterranean Insurance & Reinsurance Co Ltd* (Unreported: Judgment given 29 July 1988); *Highlands Insurance Co* v *Continental Insurance Co* [1987] 1 Lloyd's Rep 109, 117.

Lloyd's Underwriters Non-Marine Claims Office

The broker must first prepare a claims file, which must include a synopsis sheet, and then advise the leading underwriter before Lloyd's Underwriters Non-Marine Claims Office ('LUNCO') can deal with a non-marine claim, which it will pursue after checking the claim against the policy details.

LUNCO also produces a claims outstanding list to brokers which details the claims outstanding from underwriters, and underwriters will receive a tabulated list each quarter showing their outstanding losses, divided into the settlement currencies of account.

Lloyd's Aviation Claims Centre

The Centre handles all aviation claims from first advice to conclusion, and is run and financed entirely by its member underwriters, using the name 'Lloyd's' with the approval of the Council & Corporation of Lloyd's.

Lloyd's Policy Signing Office

The Lloyd's Policy Signing Office ('LPSO') has actual and apparent authority to bind underwriters, given to them by each syndicate (*Eagle Star Insurance Co* v *Spratt* [1971] 2 Lloyd's Rep 116). The LPSO functions to provide both a check on the activities and business written by underwriters, a check on the Lloyd's brokers, and a record of the business written, and it performs a vital function in the overall method of operation of Lloyd's, as part of the organisation necessary to administer business of the vast size and complexity that insurance written at Lloyd's produces. Once the broker has concluded the contract of insurance on the slip, it will be passed to his policy department for the preparation of a policy. A reinsurance broker will have a contract wording department, but the purpose of both is the same: to interpret and elaborate on the abbreviations contained in the placing slip, which, with the addition of grammar (and sometimes imagination), will become a policy. The policy is necessary for the collection of a claim, which should be indorsed on its reverse, but it is capable of retention by the broker under his lien until payment of any outstanding premium from the insured.

On completion the policy will be forwarded to the LPSO, who are authorised to check the policies prepared by the brokers, and to provide the relevant information to underwriters thereafter. The Corporation took over the administration of the predecessor of the LPSO, the Lloyd's Underwriters Signing Bureau, in 1921 and in 1924 it became mandatory for Lloyd's policies with a sum insured greater than £100 to bear the LPSO seal. The LPSO then extended its activities to the provision of a central accounting system. The roles of the LPSO can therefore be summarised as checking documents and fulfilling associated functions on behalf of Lloyd's underwriters, operating central accounting, and undertaking various functions on behalf of the Committee or Council of Lloyd's such as the provision of statistical information or monitoring for regulatory purposes. The main departments of the LPSO include the following.

(a) The Marine and Non-Marine Departments are responsible for the processing of policies and indorsements, a function which includes checking that the provisions advised are those intended by the parties, that the provisions conform with all requirements of the Committee of Lloyd's, that they are legal and conform with public policy, that the syndicates are current and valid for the business written, and that the premium calculations are correct. They will also check the Premium Advice Note provided by the broker with each policy and indorsement, which is then transmitted to their computer services department.

(b) The Special Schemes Department investigates any problems arising out of work processed by the Computer Services Department and contains a records and amendments section which deals with all entries that have been incorrectly processed. It also deals with inputs of aviation and non-marine claims, and outward reinsurance debit and credit notes, and contracts.

(c) The Technical Services Department researches any intended new schemes insofar as they affect the LPSO and is also concerned with maintaining the standard of work carried out by LPSO. It also provides an advisory liaison service for brokers and in particular maintains the relevant technical documentation, such as the Lloyd's Policy Signing and Central Accounting Manual.

(d) The LPSO London Group provides a liaison service between the LPSO and the Lloyd's Market, and in particular registers binding authorities.

Procedure It is the responsibility of the Lloyd's broker who has placed the risk to produce the relevant documentation to the LPSO, which comprises a policy (which they usually draft) and a Premium Advice Note, which must be transmitted with the slip to the LPSO. The LPSO will check it, sign it, emboss the policy with the relevant seal and return it to the broker. Lloyd's policies differ from those issued elsewhere in that they are not signed by the insurers themselves, but by LPSO on behalf of all participating underwriters (*Eagle Star Insurance Co* v *Spratt* [1971] 2 Lloyd's Rep 116). The list of syndicate numbers is attached to the policy to show which underwriters are on risk, and an Attestation Clause is included in the policy which specifies that each underwriter's commitment is severable.

The terms and conditions to a large degree reflect those already in use throughout the Market, and in respect of which standard wordings have been in use for some considerable time. These general conditions are common to the class of insurance and will rarely be altered, and they are printed on the policy form, to which reference may be made by the parties during negotiations. In addition there may be specific conditions, inclusion of which may be insisted upon by the parties, which are typed directly onto the policy or attached to the policy as an indorsement. These override the general conditions under the normal rules of construction and the broker must therefore be aware as to the variety and content of the standard forms available for each class of business, the nature of the coverage provided by each printed form, and whether the insured in question will require additional specific conditions in order to ensure that the insurance provided is adequate.

The Non-Marine Association will prepare standard forms for use in the non-marine market and if a different wording is required by the insured, reference must be made to it on the slip. There is also a Special Wordings Scheme in order to simplify the checking and revision of policies for risks not covered by standard wordings, and these essentially comprise wordings agreed between the party requiring the wording and the LPSO, which are then available to the market bearing a LPSO logo and a reference number. These wordings can be used for an indefinite period but any wordings used privately by brokers or underwriters which have not been brought within the Special Wordings Scheme may be used providing the wording is specifically referred to in the slip and is attached to the slip.

Slip policies These are often used by the reinsurance market for marine and non-marine facultative risks where a formal policy is not required. The signing slip is transformed into a slip policy by the addition of a LPSO sticker and form, after agreement between the broker and the underwriters, the initialling of the slip by the leading underwriter as usual and submission to the LPSO who process it as a policy, for which it can be exchanged at any time.

Lloyd's Insurance Brokers Committee

The Lloyd's Insurance Brokers Committee is elected by Lloyd's brokers in BIIBA to provide an executive committee of 16 members for the classes of insurance at Lloyd's, together with sub-committees to examine and discuss specialist aspects of insurance and any problems that may face the broking market. These sub-committees have no powers but can make recommendations, and LIBC representatives serve on various Lloyd's and other committees to ensure that the brokers' views are fully represented. LIBC was originally the Lloyd's Insurance Brokers' Association and played a prominent role in the conception and inception of the Insurance Brokers (Registration) Act 1977, thereafter becoming LIBC, one of BIIBA's regional committees.

Lloyd's Underwriters Associations

These include the following: Lloyd's Underwriters' Association; Lloyd's Underwriters' Non-Marine Association; Lloyd's Motor Underwriters' Non-Marine Association; and Lloyd's Aviation Underwriters' Non-Marine Association. These bodies represent the interests of marine, non-marine, motor and aviation underwriters respectively, collecting and implementing the views of their members, as well as circulating all relevant information. The LUNMA drafts standard policy forms and clauses.

Chapter 14

Types of reinsurance

The size of the insurer and its attitude towards risk management will determine the amount of the risk that the insurer will retain, together with a proportionate amount of premium, and the balance will be reinsured. Reinsurance is divisible into three generic groups: facultative, proportional, and non-proportional, facultative being an individual submission of each risk to the reinsurer on a one-off basis, proportional being divisible into quota share and surplus reinsurance and non-proportional being divisible into excess of loss and excess of ratio.

PROPORTIONAL REINSURANCE

Quota share

An insurer will agree to cede a fixed proportion of all risks within a particular class of insurance, subject to an upper limit of indemnity. The cedant must reinsure a specific proportion of every risk, as agreed beforehand and stated in the treaty wording, and cannot retain the risk in its entirety. The advantages of quota share reinsurance is that the reinsurer obtains an equitable share of risks, in that its administrative costs are lower and there is no freedom of choice. It is particularly useful where the reinsured has limited underwriting experience in any market, or the reinsured's surplus reinsurance claims experience is below the standard required by the reinsurer.

Surplus

The insurer reinsures the difference between his retention and the risk insured, within specified limits, and the cedant has a choice as to how much it will retain for its own account. There is therefore a high degree of value judgement and it is possible for the reinsured to funnel to the reinsurer business which may be high risk or low premium. The reinsured will have to prepare *bordereaux* to take into account the differing amounts from risk to risk, which will usually involve the broker.

NON-PROPORTIONAL REINSURANCE

Excess of loss

The reinsurer will only pay out to the reinsured where a claim exceeds the amount of the loss retained by the cedant, subject to a specified limit of indemnity. Premium for excess of loss business is usually charged at a percentage of the cedant's premium income and excess of loss is popular because it is easy to operate since details of individual risks do not have to be given to the reinsurer.

Excess of loss ratio

This is also known as stop loss reinsurance and is designed to prevent wide fluctuations in any one year by specifying that reinsurance cover will be available if the reinsured's gross loss ratio for a specified period exceeds a prearranged percentage.

THE ROLE OF THE REINSURANCE BROKER

The role of the reinsurance broker is dictated by the type of reinsurance in question. In facultative reinsurance he does little more than he would during 'normal' insurance; in treaty reinsurance he continues to play an active part throughout the subsistence of the contract and maintains a regular dialogue with the parties. He is much more the intermediary as defined in European terms than the English broker, although he continues to act primarily on behalf of the reinsured, in whose success the reinsurance broker may be a key factor. He must understand the essential character and business of the reinsured company and assist it in preparing an effective reinsurance programme to protect it from bad underwriting or bad fortune. His relationship with the parties effectively governs their relationship, and he must be well versed in 'public relations', knowing when to advise the parties to insist upon or concede an issue. The parties' best interests in treaty reinsurance lie in a long-term relationship, out of which the reinsured obtains security for the future and the reinsurer hopes to achieve a modest profit. Such a relationship depends on trust, gained through good faith and fair play. The broker can assist the business expansion of the reinsured by providing reinsurance to complement increased underwriting, or to test new areas. He must therefore obtain the best match between the parties to their mutual advantage.

In legal terms his role is substantially similar to that of an insurance broker but the fact that reinsurance broking is a separate business, carried out by a specialist department or company, indicates that it has a distinctive nature, the skills and tools of which can only be acquired by long experience. Thus he must prepare a fair and substantially accurate picture of the reinsured so that the reinsurer can assess the risk properly by disclosing all material facts within his knowledge, consider the financial position of the reinsurer, and often arrange the preparation of the wording, particularly for a new treaty. In facultative reinsurance a policy usually remains a 'slip policy', and actual policies are only issued where a foreign reinsured is required by local legislation to obtain insurance from a state owned insurer, who then reinsures in the London Market. Usually these follow the terms of the original insurance. In treaty reinsurance the broker may provide his own policy wording for adaptation, or use wordings prepared by either of the parties. As treaty reinsurance is a continuing process, the regular accounting as to the state of the reinsured is conducted by itemising claims or details of the policies allocated to the treaty on *bordereaux*, the extent of which are determined by the policy. In reality accounting problems occupy most of the broker's time because each party's view of the position differs, owing to delay in processing the subject matter, differences in exchange rates at the relevant dates, different interpretations of accounting methods, and problems caused by other parties involved in the transaction. Into these the broker must fit suitable operating systems to ensure that all terms of trade and credit between the parties themselves and the broker are observed, whilst developing suitable management information to enable him to continue assessing the financial position of the parties for the purposes of security and claims recovery, and to apply internal policies such as a dictat not to fund.

The reinsurance broker must maintain a thorough knowledge of markets throughout the world, based upon his dealings and perceptions of leading companies in each country, and in particular their suitability for and compatability with the reinsured's requirements. He must know the main aspects of each country's laws, and in particular the local requirements concerning the carrying on of insurance. His knowledge is specialised and requires constant updating, with a view to advising reinsureds on reinsurers in any jurisdiction, and reinsurers upon contracts with reinsureds similarly.

In summary his functions are to advise the reinsured as to a suitable reinsurance programme and ways of improving its current programme, to obtain suitable reinsurers for a long term relationship on the best terms, to negotiate the terms of the reinsurance and to prepare the contract wording, or to ensure that any wording prepared by the reinsurers conforms to the agreed terms, to arrange the collection of claims and payment of premiums, to prepare any records or documentation for use by the reinsured for his accounting requirements or for renewal, and to assist the reinsured generally by using his relationship between the parties to fulfil their agreement to their mutual advantage.

One feature peculiar to reinsurance is the fact that a primary insurer may ask the broker, who has placed the risk with him, to obtain reinsurance for that risk if it cannot be fitted into his existing reinsurance arrangements. The broker therefore will act as the agent of the insured in placing the insurance, and the agent of the insurer-/reinsured in placing the reinsurance. This is acceptable provided that the broker's duties to his principal, the insured, do not give rise to any potential conflicts of interest. An anomaly which may arise is that the broker may approach a reinsurer before the primary insurance has been broked, so as to prepare a complete 'package'. However, the reinsured is not identified on the reinsurance slip at this stage. Of course the reinsured cannot be so identified, because it is not known whether the primary insurance will be written, or by whom, or whether the primary insurers will require reinsurance, and if they do, whether they will accept the reinsurance terms offered by the broker, or whether the participating reinsurers will be acceptable security to the reinsureds (*Wace* v *Pan Atlantic Group Inc* [1981] 2 Lloyd's Rep 339, 349). The reinsurance contract is therefore created by the offer of the reinsurer and the acceptance by the reinsured/insurer falling within the category of persons anticipated by the reinsurer as offerees, who requests reinsurance after he has initialled the slip. This gives effect to the commercial intention of the transaction, the general requirement of notification of acceptance being waived by the parties (*General Accident Fire & Life Assurance Corporation* v *Tanter, The 'Zephyr'*, [1984] 1 Lloyd's Rep 58, 80).

JURISDICTION

Foreign insurance ceded to London for reinsurance will emanate from a foreign broker, who will proceed via a correspondent broker in London, who will in turn pass the business to Lloyd's reinsurance underwriter via a Lloyd's broker, or onto the company market. In the absence of any agreement between the parties as to choice of law or jurisdiction, the primary insurer's relationship with his broker will be governed by the foreign law, but the sub-agency will probably be governed by English law. An English court will take into account various factors weighted differently to determine which law applies, such as the location of the operation of the sub-agency and reinsurance agreements, and where these agreements were concluded. English law will probably govern the rights of the foreign broker against the English broker(s), so that the English broker may not have any privity of contract with the foreign insurer, depending upon the authority given by the insurer to his reinsurance broker, and does not owe any fiduciary duties (save as to secret profits). The relationship between the foreign insurer and the English reinsurer will probably be subject to English law. However, in the absence of privity of contract the English broker may still be liable to the foreign insurer in tort if the English broker's negligent act gives rise to a foreseeable loss of the foreign insurer, or the English reinsurer agrees with the foreign insurer that the broker will transfer funds to him, and the broker confirms it, thus becoming liable under the principle reiterated in *Shamia* v *Joory* [1958] 1 QB 438.

Reinsurance disputes do not fall within the ambit of the special rules contained in arts 7-12A in the Civil Jurisdiction & Judgments Act 1982 (*Arkwright Mutual Insurance Co* v *Bryanstone Insurance Co Ltd* (1970) *Financial Times*, 26 February 1990). However, the broker who has placed reinsurance with an English insurer in England but is sued by his principal reinsured, who is also domiciled in a country which is a signatory to the Brussels Convention 1968 and therefore subject to the Civil Jurisdiction & Judgments Act 1982, will probably be subject to English law and jurisdiction in any dispute concerning his operations as an agent because he will fall somewhere within art 5 of the Act. Article 5 states that

(1) in matters relating to a contract, in the courts for the place of performance of the obligation in question [ie contract of agency];
(3) in matters relating to tort, delict or quasi-delict, in the courts of the place where the harmful event occurred [ie concurrent duties in tort];
(5) as regards a dispute arising out of the operations of a branch, agency or other establishment, in the courts for the place in which the branch, agency or other establishment is situated;

or under art 6 'where he is one of a number of defendants, in the courts for the place where any one of them is domiciled'.

FORMATION OF A REINSURANCE CONTRACT

The reinsurance contract is formed in the same way as any contract of insurance; in correspondence or by slip, but not usually by proposal form. Often a line slip is used to enable a leading underwriter to insure risks on behalf of following underwriters, so that those following can obtain reinsurance in advance on off-slips against those risks written under the line slip (*Balfour* v *Beaumont* [1984] 1 Lloyd's Rep 272). The subject matter of the reinsurance is the primary contract of insurance, whilst the insurable interest is the reinsured's potential liability to indemnify the insured. These items are coterminous in liability insurance.

Duties

Good faith, materiality and disclosure

The duty of good faith exists between the parties; any breach by the reinsured entitles the reinsurer to avoid *ab initio*.

The duty of disclosure is the same as that in primary insurance. The reinsured must disclose all material facts to the reinsurer, in a manner which is fair and substantially accurate (*Container Transport International Inc* v *Oceanus Underwriting Association (Bermuda) Ltd* [1984] 1 Lloyd's Rep 476). Whilst the reinsurer is deemed to be prudent, he need not apply information received at another time in a disinterested capacity and is not considered aware of circumstances peculiar to certain parties in the market (*North British Fishing Boat Co* v *Starr* (1922) 13 Ll L Rep 206); (*London General Insurance Co* v *General Marine Underwriters Assoc* [1921] 1 KB 104).

In treaty insurance the reinsured is clearly subject to this duty prior to the formation of the treaty, but it seems conceptually difficult to extend it beyond the conclusion of the treaty, since the reinsurer has no option but to accept the risks properly ceded — the absence of choice renders the materiality of any fact otiose. In treaty reinsurance the acceptance of risks is automatic and the reinsurer is effectively reinsuring the ability of the reinsured to write risks successfully, instead of weighing up the attributes and disadvantages of any one risk. Where the reinsurer is able to refuse a risk the duty will continue.

Thus, in facultative reinsurance, where the reinsurer can refuse the risk, those facts which would affect the reinsured's decision in setting the premium or accepting the risk will be equally material to the reinsurer. The reinsured's retention is material (*Traill* v *Baring* (1864) 4 De GJ & S 318), as are any terms of the primary insurance which are not usual or expected (*Property Insurance Co v National Protector Insurance Co* (1913) 108 LT 104), or perhaps the absence of a clause usually present. The duty of good faith will of course extend to all reinsurance claims (*The 'Litsion Pride'* [1985] 1 Lloyd's Rep 437).

Terms of the reinsurance contract

The usual rationale of the contract of reinsurance is that it sits back to back with the primary insurance, and therefore incorporates identical terms. The broker must ensure that the reinsurance wording does not produce any ambiguity or inconsistency with the original, particularly where he is responsible for drafting the reinsurance wording *Youell v Bland Welch and Co Ltd* (Unreported: Judgment 27 March 1990). The court will amend the terms as necessary to give business efficacy to the contract and to effect the intentions of the parties, but only up to a point; the contract will not be rewritten since to do so would constitute speculation by the court.

The reinsurance contract may attempt to incorporate standard terms, some of which may only apply to primary insurance, as happened in *Forsikringsaktielskapet Vesta v Butcher* [1989] 1 Lloyd's Rep 331. Or the primary insurance may contain a term which is unusual, thereby enabling the reinsurer to deny liability on the basis that he would not have seen the original insurance and that such a term should have been disclosed as material.

In either case the contract remains one of indemnity of the reinsured's liability. The reinsurer need not pay if the reinsured paid out without liability, eg under an 'honour' policy (*Re London County Commercial Reinsurance Office* [1922] 1 Ch 67), or if the payment was in excess of liability (*Traders & General Insurance Association v Bankers & General Insurance Co* (1921) 9 LlL Rep 273 or if the underlying contract of insurance is void or unenforceable for illegality (*Phoenix General Insurance Co of Greece SA v ADAS* [1986] 2 Lloyd's Rep 55).

Subject to express wording in the contract of reinsurance to the contrary, the reinsurer's liability to indemnify the reinsured commences not upon the occurrence of an event which may render the reinsured liable to the insured, but when the reinsured's liability is established by a court or by arbitrator or by agreement (*Versicherungs und Transport AG Daugava v Henderson* (1934) 39 Com Cas 312); (*Post Office v Norwich Union Fire Insurance Society Ltd* [1967] 2 QB 363).

Implied terms

Reinsurance law moved forward considerably in *Phoenix General Insurance Co of Greece SA* v *Halvanon Insurance Co Ltd* [1985] 2 Lloyd's Rep 599, in which Hobhouse J held that a facultative/obligatory treaty required an implied term that the reinsured would not channel less profitable or more risk-laden insurance into a contract of reinsurance, and that the reinsured 'would conduct their business in accordance with the ordinary practice of the market and exercise due care and skill. . . . '. The reinsured must (at p 613):

(a) keep full and proper records and accounts of all risks accepted or premiums received and receivable and all claims made or notified; (b) investigate all claims and confirm that they fell within the terms of the contract and were properly payable before accepting them; (c) properly investigate risks offered to them before acceptance and closings relating thereto subsequently; (d) keep full and proper accurate accounts showing at all times the amounts due and payable by the plaintiffs to the defendants and by the defendants to the plaintiffs under the contracts; (e) ensure that all amounts owing to them were collected promptly when due and entered forthwith in their accounts, and all balances owing to the defendants were likewise paid promptly when due; (f) obtain, file or otherwise keep in a proper manner, all accounting claims and other documents and records and make these [reasonably] available to the defendants.

This term is described as 'innominate', the effect of which is that the rights of the parties depend upon the nature of any breach.

The other key to reinsurance control (by reinsurers) is that the reinsured retains for his own account a proportion of the business ceded, so that the reinsured suffers along with the reinsurer if primary contracts prove more onerous than originally anticipated. However, Hobhouse J held in *Phoenix General Insurance Co of Greece SA* v *Halvanon Insurance Co. Ltd.* [1985] 2 Lloyd's Rep 599 that a term need not be implied that a retention would be kept by the reinsured, that the element of retention was not an essential part of the reinsurance contract, that there was no inconsistency between the concept of reinsurance and a nil retention, and that a retention would usually be expressly specified in conjunction with other provisions, such as excess of loss reinsurance. In this case the amount of the retention was not completed in the space provided in the agreement for a retention; Hobhouse J held that agreement as to a retention was not reached because the reinsurers never chose to stipulate a retention and Kerr LJ in the Court of Appeal (1986) Lloyd's Rep 552, 573 held that that part of the clause alleged to require a retention was inserted as part of the Full Reinsurance Clause and that the retention was never addressed. Thus if a retention is required, it must be specified in the slip, and the broker should obtain specific instructions from his clients as to their requirements. However, in *Great Atlantic Insurance Co* v *Home Insurance Co* [1981] 2 Lloyd's Rep 219, 225 Lloyd J held that a clause requiring the reinsured to retain a net percentage was not a warranty, apparently because it was the reinsured who insisted that it should retain a percentage. He accepted that such a clause could constitute a warranty in other cases.

Insurance Company of Africa v Scor

There have been many important reinsurance cases, arising out of the stricter reliance placed upon contractual clauses in recent years. *Insurance Co of Africa* v *Scor* [1983] 1 Lloyd's Rep 541; [1985] 1 Lloyd's Rep 312 CA[1] is a particularly important case which defines the insured's obligations in respect of claims made against it, which appears to restrict the liability of reinsurers to the agreed contractual limit of their indemnity, and which deals with the interaction of two commonly used clauses. Had the reinsurance policy been settled by brokers, a successful claim could probably have been brought against them.

The facts
The African Trading Co (Liberia) Limited ('ATC') insured a warehouse in Monrovia for fire in the sum of $3,500,000 with the Insurance Company of Africa, who reinsured 98.6 per cent with Scor as leading reinsurer. The policy contained a 'claims co-operation' clause and a 'follow the settlements' clause. The warehouse burned down, the water supply having been turned off, and the Liberian army then levelled the site within two days. The only loss adjuster (unqualified) in Liberia watched the fire and was appointed by ICA, whose parent company sent out another adjuster who approved the local adjuster's work, and concluded that:

(a) the loss of stock and cost of rebuilding would exceed $3,500,000; and
(b) that ATC was not responsible for the fire.

ATC claimed under its policy of insurance and other insurers

---

1 The rationale of ICA v Scor is sufficiently important to merit detailed comment, because it both opens and closes doors, and purports to clarify two central premises of most reinsurances: the obligation of the reinsured to settle the primary claim properly, and the obligation of the reinsurer to pay.

paid their proportion, pursuant to a contractual clause specifying payment within 60 days. The plot then thickened considerably.

Scor received anonymous letters alleging that the fire had been started deliberately, that ICA's senior executive had been bribed to say nothing, that the army were involved, and that the local loss adjuster would receive 10 per cent of any insurance payment. Scor therefore refused to authorise the claim, without any explanation, and sent its own loss adjusters to Monrovia, whose job in reality was to investigate the veracity of these allegations. They did so in a secretive manner which annoyed ICA, who had no reason to know of the allegations, and who consequently withdrew their co-operation. Scor refused to pay, on the ground that fraud was suspected. ATC sued ICA, who could only put ATC to proof of their claim, since ICA did not possess the information obtained by Scor, who refused to assist them. Judgment was given against ICA for the policy limit, $3,500,000, together with $600,000 additional 'general' damages and $58,000 costs. ICA sued Scor for an indemnity.

Leggatt J held that Scor was liable to follow ICA's settlement unless Scor could show lack of good faith or collusion or failure by ICA to take all proper and businesslike steps to have the amount of the loss fairly and carefully ascertained. The appointment of a competent loss adjuster was sufficient to discharge the obligation concerning the adjustment of the loss; the reinsured did not have to supervise it. Scor therefore had to pay $4,158,000. Not surprisingly, Scor appealed.

The Court of Appeal upheld Leggatt J's interpretation of the 'follow the settlements' clause but considered by majority that the 'claims co-operation' clause was paramount and emasculated the 'follow the settlements' clause, so that Scor had only to pay for those settlements which had received their approval. However, the claims co-operation clause was not a condition precedent and although breach would entitle Scor to damages if they could be proven, ICA had properly proved that the loss was payable and were entitled to an indemnity, up to $3,500,000.

'Follow the settlements' versus 'claims co-operation' or 'claims control'
A 'follow the settlements' clause obliges the reinsurer to accept any settlement of the insured which has been honestly, fairly and carefully ascertained. Reinsurers are more wary now of reinsureds, not all of whom are gentlemen, and may require some methods of supervision — the claims control clause — to ensure that the reinsured complies with his obligations. It is clear that these clauses are contradictory. Leggatt J and Stephenson LJ considered that the 'follow the settlements' clause triumphed over the 'claims co-oper-

ation' clause because the reinsured had been forced to defend the insured's claim in court, and had been found liable. Thus, although a judgment against the insured was not a settlement arrived at by the parties under the 'claims control' clause, it was effectively a settlement for the 'follow the settlements' clause, and since a judgment is the most objective and independent form of settlement, the reinsurers must be taken to approve of it.

Robert Goff and Fox LJJ disagreed. Reinsurers need only follow a settlement which had received their approval pursuant to the claims co-operation clause, and as the settlement had not been approved by the reinsurer, the 'settlement'/judgment could not be followed. However, the reinsurer had to pay up to the limit of the policy ($3.5m) because the claims co-operation clause was not a condition precedent and could be ignored where the liability of the reinsured to pay the insured was independently and properly established. If the clause had been a condition precedent, ICA would have had to comply fully with Scor's instructions and could not recover without doing so, even if it could prove its loss. In cases where it is not a condition precedent, the reinsured must proceed with care and attempt to comply with the reinsurer's demands for co-operation, however bizarre. The reasoning for this is derived from the general principle in claims notification cases that strict compliance is necessary whether or not the insurer is prejudiced, and that the question of reasonableness is assessed according to the subjective opinion of the insurer where the policy contained a clause requiring 'such information as may reasonably be required', so that any request for immaterial documentation must be satisfied (*Welch* v *Royal Exchange* [1939] 1 KB 294).

Costs

In the absence of clear provision for the reinsured's costs in the contract of reinsurance, the position may be capable of division into two parts. These are as follows.

Where the costs and claim together do not exceed the policy limit
In *British Dominions General Insurance Co* v *Duder* [1915] 2 KB 394 the Court of Appeal held that the cost of reaching a settlement could be recovered from the reinsurer. In contrast the court refused to award the costs of the reinsured in proving that he was not liable to the insured in *Scottish Metropolitan Assurance Co* v *Groom* (1924) 20 Ll L Rep 44. The reinsured in both cases reduced the reinsurer's potential liability; the only distinguishing feature is that in *Groom*

the reinsured may not have been able to recover anything from the reinsurer if the original payment was one which the reinsured need not pay. The issue to some extent revolves around the construction of 'settlement' in the relevant clause of the reinsurance contract; it seems reasonable that the reinsured should recover his costs where the aggregate does not exceed the policy limit, a possibility reviewed by Stephenson LJ in *ICA* v *Scor* in construing 'settlements' as including 'all sums reasonably paid in the normal course of disposing of the assured's claim' (ibid, p 53), provided these costs relate to the original claim and not to a dispute involving the reinsurance policy; and

Where the costs and claim together exceed the policy limit

The initial problem is that a reinsurer who specifies his maximum liability should not be forced to pay any greater sum. This was the position in *ICA* v *Scor*. Leggatt J implied a term into the contract that the reinsurer would reimburse all expenses incurred by its refusal to authorise payment to the reinsured. Stephenson LJ agreed, pushing the term to include all costs voluntarily incurred in establishing liability. Robert Goff and Fox LJJ again disagreed, on the basis that the maximum liability had been agreed and was inviolate, the implied term was inconsistent with the original agreement, and the claims co-operation clause enabled the reinsurer to refuse to authorise a settlement without becoming liable for the consequences of such refusal. Such an implied term was not necessary to provide business efficacy to the contract, and the reinsured therefore did not recover his costs of $58,000, although the final result seems to be more one of public policy than pure legal analysis.

The effect of extra-contractual liability of the reinsured on the reinsurer

A reinsured who is held liable to the insured in respect of payments which are not covered by the contract of insurance will seek to pass such liability on to the reinsurer. Where the actions giving rise to such liability rest entirely on the reinsured, the reinsurer should not be liable. Thus, where a reinsured ignores a term specifying payment within a fixed period after loss, the reinsurer will not be liable for any damages for which the reinsured becomes liable. Where the reinsured refuses to reach agreement with the insured, with the result that the reinsured is later held liable to pay an additional sum as compensation, is the reinsurer liable?

Clearly, the fault lies with the reinsured and the reinsurer need therefore not pay. What, then, is the position when the actions of the reinsurer prevent the reinsured from reaching an agreement with the insured? In *ICA* v *Scor* additional damages of $600,000 were payable by the reinsured because the reinsurer would not approve any settlement and would not divulge the information which may have assisted the reinsured to refute the claim or reach a compromise. In reality these damages were punitive, although this distinction was not made. Fox LJ felt that payment of any sum above the agreed indemnity would be inconsistent with that agreement, and Robert Goff LJ considered that an implied term for such payment would not sit easily with the claims co-operation clause. This implied term was formulated as (ibid, p 332):

If the reinsurers withhold approval of a settlement which the insurer would otherwise have made and as a result the insurer suffers loss or expense which he would not otherwise have suffered, the reinsurers should indemnify the insurer against such loss or expense.

Robert Goff LJ said that the effect of the claims co-operation clause was that 'if a settlement is made without the approval of the reinsurer, it cannot be relied upon as a settlement authorised by the policy, and so cannot constitute a settlement which the reinsurers are bound to follow under the follow the settlements clause' (ibid, p 332). It is therefore clear that the presence of the claims co-operation clause was an overriding consideration in respect of extra-contractual payments. What is the position in the absence of such a clause? Is an agreement to 'follow the settlements' sufficient to compel a reinsurer to indemnify the reinsured against extra-contractual payments occasioned by the reinsurer's intransigence or other contributing factor? It is thought that a reinsurer would be liable to indemnify the reinsured where the total claimed falls within the reinsurance policy limit. This would satisfy the court's criterion concerning open-ended liability, and seems entirely fair. However, the court may not allow additional liability, in excess of the contract, even though instigated by the default of the reinsurer to prevent such unlimited liability. Is this fair? Both Leggatt J and Stephenson LJ thought not.

Stephenson LJ said (at p 323) that:

There seem to me to be three ways in which Scor may be made liable for the $658,000 as well as the $3,500,000. The first is that 'settlements' in the follow settlements clause means all sums reasonably paid in the normal course of disposing of the assured's claim, and that admittedly shorthand phrase can be expanded to cover the damages and costs awarded in the Liberian proceedings. But that was not argued. It was conceded that they were only recoverable from Scor if some term were implied. The second is that the presumed intention of the parties in making the reinsurance contract requires the implication of a term into that contract that these damages and costs should be recoverable from Scor. That is what ICA pleaded. The third is that Scor's refusal to approve a settlement of the claim necessarily implied a request by Scor that ICA should defend the claim in the Liberian proceedings and a promise to pay sums resulting from that refusal and that defence. This is the alternative way in which ICA's case was pleaded and argued.

He continued (ibid, p 324):

> . . . [the judge] . . . regarded the loss suffered by ICA in having to pay what the jury awarded as the reasonably foreseeable, if not direct and inevitable, result of Scor's refusal to approve their settlement of the claim. A contract of reinsurance is a contract of indemnity and the indemnity must, in my judgment, cover any payments made by the reinsured which are the reasonably foreseeable result, in arriving at a settlement of the insured's claim, of any request or requirement, express or implied, by the reinsurer to the reinsured.

Stephenson LJ also held that the claims co-operation clause imposed a reciprocal duty on the reinsurers, and that their conduct in withholding approval and co-operation took them outside the scope of this clause, thereby negativing its effect and bringing the adjudication within those settlements which Scor had contracted to follow.

The three options above therefore constitute the possibilities where there is no overriding claims co-operation clause. Thus the four judges were split equally on the point. Were Fox and Robert Goff LJJ correct? The following points may be relevant in assessing the validity of the case.

(a) Insurers and reinsurers often share extra expenses over the level of indemnity, although usually by agreement. However, it could be argued that 'business efficacy' required the implication of such a term into the reinsurance contract, and it is by no means certain that the parties would have rejected such a term had it been suggested during the formation of the contract.

(b) Robert Goff LJ said (ibid, p 332) that in the absence of approval to a settlement:

> The insurers have therefore to decide what to do in the circumstances. In effect, they have got to prove a liability under the policy with the assured, in respect of which the reinsurers have agreed to indemnify them. They can attempt to prove this, without going to the expense of defending the claim by the assured in legal proceedings; or they may feel it more prudent to defend the claim, on the basis that they may defeat it or, if they do not, they will be in a better position to establish their claim against reinsurers.

They may well be in a very difficult position. But I cannot see the basis for the implied term formulated by the respondents. Had this implied term been proposed by the officious bystander at the time of the contract, it cannot be predicated that the reinsurers would have assented to it.

Fox LJ said (ibid, p 335):

I see no reason to suppose that the parties can have intended that such expense should fall on the reinsurers merely because they exercised the right which the policy gave to them. And I do not feel able to say the respondents were compelled to take the course which they did. It is quite understandable that they did so but they could, had they chosen, have paid the full amount of the ATC claim and then, if the appellants refused to pay on the reinsurance policy, could have sought to prove that they were in fact liable to pay the claim and, therefore, entitled to recover under the reinsurance policy.

However, an adjudication is far less likely to be impugned than a negotiated settlement, and the latter would render the reinsured capable of criticism to the effect that they had not acted honestly and in a businesslike manner to have the loss properly ascertained. Further, Robert Goff LJ's comment that the reinsured's defence of the claim may have put them in a better position against reinsurers retains some validity up to the level of indemnity, but a negotiated settlement would have precluded an award of punitive damages; defending the claim may actually have placed the reinsured in a worse position.

Finally, there seems to be little point in the reinsured proving a claim which exceeds the policy limit for later indemnification by reinsurers, when the reinsured cannot recover the balance over the agreed limit of indemnity.[2]

The prevailing attitude of the Courts in precluding concurrent duties in tort by enforcing the dominance of the contract would appear to substantiate the judgments of Robert Goff LJ and Fox LJ. However, the three options put forward by Stephenson LJ involved an alternative construction of 'settlement', an implied contractual term, and an implied request from the reinsurer to defend the claim, into which was similarly implied a promise to pay for any

---

2 See Michelle Shadler's comments in (1986) LCMNQ 2, 145. The principle of *ICA v Scor* that the reinsured must take all proper and businesslike steps to evaluate the claim has been endorsed in several cases eg *Vesta v Butcher* [1989] 1 Lloyd's Rep 1933.

consequences of that defence. Tort was not involved and it is submitted that the judgment of Stephenson LJ is correct.

OTHER ASPECTS OF REINSURANCE

Fronting

Where an insurer or reinsurer is unable (owing to a local legal impediment), or does not wish to stand in a direct relationship with an insured or reinsured, a 'front' may be used to circumvent the problem. The fronting company is inserted between the insurer and insured (or reinsurer and reinsured) and the insurance or reinsurance cover granted by the front is then reinsured (or retroceded) 100 per cent to the company who in reality wishes to accept the risk. The fronting insurer is paid a fee or overriding commission to enable the risk-taking insurer to accept the risk, but runs a considerable risk itself in doing so, since the security of the risk-taking insurer may be inadequate, leaving the fronting company liable for 100 per cent of the risk.[3] Brokers will often be involved in arranging and setting up a fronting arrangement, and will act in a dual capacity since they will act as agent for the insurer in placing the reinsurance with the front, and as agent for the front in placing that reinsurance as a retrocession with the actual risk-taking company.

Pools

A pool consists of several insurers who have agreed to place certain defined business into their central organisation and then to divide the business between them in agreed proportions. It is particularly useful for hazardous business or where there is a shortage of market capacity, and works best for companies of the same nature, whose business is similar and conducted according to common underwriting and claims guidelines and at similar rates of premium. Although the underwriting for the pool may be handled by one of its members, often it is the broker who has a binding authority to place business into the pool, which again will place it in a dual capacity

---

3 See generally *Phoenix General Insurance Co of Greece SA* v *Halvanon Insurance Co. Ltd.* [1985] 2 Lloyd's Rep 599 and *Phoenix General Insurance Co of Greece SA* v *ADAS* [1986] 2 Lloyd's Rep 552 at 573 and *Wace* v *Pan Atlantic Group Inc* [1981] 2 Lloyd's Rep 339.

in that it will act as agent for the reinsured, and again for the members of the pool. The broker should therefore remain alive to any possibility of conflict and, should a conflict arise, obtain the informed consent of the parties to his continuing role (*Anglo-African Merchants Ltd* v *Bayley* (1970) 1 QB 311).

Where the broker is acting only for the reinsured, he should be aware that the authority of the pool underwriting agent or manager may be limited, because this is invariably the case. The broker should therefore check the authority of the agent so as to be certain that the intended insurance is properly within the agent's authority. If the broker fails to do so and the pool is not bound by its agent's acts, eg for want of authority, the broker may be liable to the reinsured because he would or should have known that the agent's authority was limited (*Russo Chinese Bank* v *Li Lau Sam* [1910] AC 174).

The broker should also identify the members of the pool to whom he is contractually binding the reinsured. Each pool member will be liable to the reinsured, and the pool itself is nothing more than a grouping of co-insurers. The broker should clarify the jurisdiction and law applicable to the contracts and ensure that any clause increasing the liability of remaining pool members after the demise of another member (ie to absorb the shortfall) is incorporated into their contracts with the reinsured.

Chapter 15

Regulation of insurance brokers

The problems endemic throughout the insurance broking industry were becoming apparent by the mid 1970s and in January 1977 a Government Green Paper appeared, entitled 'Insurance Intermediaries',[1] almost concurrently with a Consultative Document on the Regulation of Insurance Brokers issued by the British Insurance Brokers Council.[2] The result was the Insurance Brokers (Registration) Act 1977 which provided for the self-regulation of insurance brokers through the establishment of the Insurance Brokers Registration Council. The rationale behind the Act was to achieve a 'balance between the interests of insurers in maximising their sales outlets and of consumers in knowing that the intermediaries they deal with are experienced and dependable people'.[3]

THE 1977 ACT

The Insurance Brokers (Registration) Act 1977 does not attempt to define an 'insurance broker', merely the steps that must be taken to obtain that title. In fact a definition had been used in the Government White Paper, which was that also used by the Council of the EEC[4] for the purpose of facilitating 'the effective exercise of freedom and freedom to provide services in respect of the activities of insurance agents and brokers and, in particular, traditional measures in respect of these activities'. Member States were asked to abolish

---

1 HMSO Cmmd 6715.
2 Consultative Document on the Regulation of Insurance Brokers.
3 Green Paper para 19.
4 In Directive 77/92/EEC.

restrictions on the freedom of various activities, including 'professional activities of persons who, acting with complete freedom as to their choice of undertaking, bring together, with a view to the insurance or reinsurance of risks, persons seeking insurance or reinsurance and insurance or reinsurance undertakings, carry out work preparatory to the conclusion of contracts in insurance and reinsurance and, where appropriate, assist in the administration and performance of such contracts, in particular in the event of a claim'.

PROVISIONS OF THE ACT

The important provisions of the Act can be summarised as follows.

Section 1
Section 1 provides for the establishment of a body corporate entitled the Insurance Brokers Registration Council which will consist of 17 members, of whom 12 will represent insurance brokers, nominated by the British Insurance and Investment Brokers Association. Among the five persons not chosen by BIIBA, one must be a barrister, advocate or solicitor, another must be a member of a recognised body of accountants and the third must represent the interests of policyholders.

Section 2
Section 2 obliges the IBRC to establish a register of insurance brokers.

Section 3
Section 3 outlines the requirements for the registration of individuals as insurance brokers, for which the criteria are 5 years' practical experience, or 3 years' practical experience together with another suitable qualification. In addition, any applicant must satisfy the Council as to his character, suitability and practical experience, and that he does or will comply with s 11 of the Act. The right to registration is not automatic and, whatever relevant experience may have been obtained by the applicant, he must still provide evidence to substantiate his experience if so requested. The failure of the applicant in *Pickles* v *IBRC* [1984] 1 All ER 1073 to inform the IBRC of the time devoted to insurance business entitled the IBRC to refuse to register him.

Section 4

Section 4 provides for the establishment of a list of incorporated brokers, each of which must be controlled by a majority of registered individuals, in addition to complying with s 11.

Section 6

Section 6 enables the Council to approve any educational institution or qualifications.

Section 7

Section 7 provides the Council with powers of supervision.

Section 8

Section 8 provides for management of the register of brokers and list of incorporated brokers by the Council, and the authority for fees to be payable to the Council.

Section 10

Section 10 provides for a Code of Conduct to be drawn up and revised by the Council, applicable to all brokers.

Section 11

Section 11 provides for rules to be made concerning the requirements for carrying on business as a corporate body, which include maintaining sufficient working capital of not less than £1,000, ensuring that its assets exceed liabilities by at least £1,000, and the prevention of any broker becoming unduly dependent on any particular insurance company for the placement of its business. Section 11 also provides for certain accounting procedures, the retention of money, and the submission to the Council of balance sheets and profit and loss accounts.

Section 12

Section 12 provides for compulsory professional indemnity insurance in order to protect policyholders from negligence, fraud or dishonesty on the part of insurance brokers, or their failure to account for monies received.[5]

---

5 SI 1496 of 1987.

Section 13

Section 13 provides for the preliminary investigation of disciplinary cases by the Investigating Committee of the Council.[6]

Section 14

Section 14 provides for the determination of disciplinary cases by the Disciplinary Committee, after investigation by the Investigating Committee.[7]

Section 15

Section 15 provides for the erasure of the insurance broker or body corporate from the register or list of brokers if he is convicted of a criminal offence which renders him unfit to act as a broker, or is adjudged by the Disciplinary Committee to have been guilty of unprofessional conduct, or fails to comply with the requirements of s 11 or 12.

Section 16

Section 16 provides for the restoration of names erased as a result of disciplinary cases after 10 months from the date of erasure or last application under s 16.

Section 17

Section 17 provides for the erasure from the register or list on the grounds of fraud or error if any entry in the register or list has been fraudulently or incorrectly made.

Section 18

Section 18 provides for appeals in disciplinary and other cases within specified time limits.

Section 19

Section 19 provides for the procedure of the Disciplinary Committee which may administer oaths, issue writs of subpoena, and make rules as to procedure and rules of evidence to be followed in proceedings before the Disciplinary Committee. Disciplinary proceedings are open to the public.[8]

---

6 SI 1456 of 1978.
7 SI 1457 of 1978.
8 SI 1458 of 1978.

Section 20

Section 20 provides for an assessor who shall be a barrister, advocate or solicitor of not less than 10 years standing to assist the Disciplinary Committee in the resolution of any question of law.

Section 21

Section 21 empowers the Council to set up any committee for any purpose.

Section 22

Section 22 provides a penalty for wilfully pretending to be an insurance broker when a party is not so registered, or implying or otherwise pretending that he is registered, subject to certain exceptions contained in s 23 in the case of death or bankruptcy. The current maximum fine is £2,000 for each offence.

Section 24

Section 24 provides for the punishment of a director of a body corporate where the offence of the body corporate is attributable to any neglect on the part of any director.

Section 25

Section 25 provides for the Council to keep proper accounts and to appoint recognised auditors.

Statutory instruments implementing provisions of the Act

The initial Act was followed by a number of Statutory Instruments, which provide for all areas of the Act to be implemented on or by 1 December 1980. The most important Statutory Instruments are as follows.

Conduct (Code of Conduct) Approval Order 1978.[9] This provides for a code of conduct to be followed by registered brokers, subject to three overriding principles:

(a) Insurance brokers shall at all times conduct their business with utmost good faith and integrity.
(b) Insurance brokers shall do everything possible to satisfy the insurance requirements of their clients and shall place the interests of those clients before all other considerations. Subject to these

---

9 SI 1394 of 1978.

requirements and interests, insurance brokers shall have proper regard for others.

(c) Statements made by or on behalf of insurance brokers when advertising shall not be misleading or extravagant.

Registration   IBRC (Registration and Enrolment) Rules Approval Order 1978 (SI 1978 No 1395). This provides for the register of insurance brokers, deals with applications for registration and removal of entries in the register. Amended by SI 1982 No 1406 and SI 1985 No 1804 as to fees. This supplemented by the IBRC (Registration and Enrolment) (Amendment) Rules Approval Order 1978 (SI 1979 No 490 and the IBRC (Registration and Enrolment) (Amendment) Rules Approval Order 1988 (SI 1988 No 1964).

Accounts   Accounts are regulated by the IBRC (Accounts and Business Requirements) Rules Approval Order 1979 (SI 1979 No 489), (Rule 3 revoked by SI 1979 No 490), and the IBRC (Accounts and Business Requirements) (Amendment) Rules Approval Order 1981 (SI 1981 No 1630).

Constitution of IBRC   The Constitution of IBRC is governed by the Election Scheme Approval Order 1980 (SI 1980 No 62), and the IBRC (Constitution of Investigating Committee) Rules Approval Order 1978 (SI 1978 No 1456).

Disciplinary   Disciplining of insurance brokers is regulated by the IBRC (Constitution of Disciplinary Committee) Rules Approval Order 1978 (SI 1978 No 1457), the IBRC (Procedure of the Disciplinary Committee) Rules Approval Order 1978 (SI 1978 No 1458), and IBRC (Disciplinary Committee) Legal Assessor Rules 1978 (SI 1978 No 1503).

Insurance   The insuring of insurance brokers is regulated by IBRC (Indemnity Insurance and Grants Scheme) Rules Approval Order 1987 (SI 1987 No 1496), and IBRC (Indemnity Insurance and Grants Scheme) Rules Approval Order 1979 (SI 1979 No 408 (superseded substantially by SI 1987 No 1496)).

REGULATION OF INSURANCE BROKERS WHO CONDUCT INVESTMENT BUSINESS

Financial Services Act 1986

The premise behind the Financial Services Act 1986 is that every investor must receive unbiased advice from a party who must subordinate his own interests to those of the investor. That party must be a fit and proper person to provide the service offered, which should be based upon his experience of the alternative services available and the specific requirements of the investor. The Securities and Investment Board took the view that the best way to achieve this result would be to polarise the capacities of the intermediaries, so that they are either completely independent or they are not. An independent intermediary must be authorised to carry on investment business by becoming a member of the appropriate self-regulating organisation. In many cases this will be the Financial Intermediaries, Managers and Brokers Regulatory Association (FIMBRA) which an independent insurance broker must join if he is to be authorised to carry on investment business in excess of 25 per cent of his total income, although any broker deriving less than 25 per cent of his total income from investment business can elect to comply with the rules of the IBRC, which may be less stringent than those of FIMBRA, and are certainly less expensive.

The methods of achieving the intended effect of the Financial Services Act 1986 are as follows:

(a) know your customer. Clearly the broker cannot advise in the absence of a detailed knowledge of the insured's personal and financial circumstances;
(b) suitability of investment. The broker can only recommend investments which he believes to be suitable for the insured;
(c) best advice. The broker must not recommend any investment if he knows that there is a better one available;
(d) best execution. The transaction must be effected on the best terms available; and
(e) disclosure of remuneration. The broker must disclose any commission agreement and his precise status in the transaction.

These tenets apply to all brokers in their provision of investment advice.

Insurance brokers (who must have registered with the IBRC under the provisions of the Insurance Brokers (Registration) Act 1977) must be authorised by one of three routes if they carry on investment business:

(a) certification by the IBRC;
(b) membership of FIMBRA; or
(c) authorisation by the SIB.

The route to be selected depends on the amount of investment advice provided. In reality the only practical alternatives will be the IBRC, where the insurance broker derives only a small percentage of his income from investment business, or FIMBRA where the broker obtains a substantial amount of income from insurance and investment business.

IBRC

The IBRC is a registered professional body and has statutory authority as such through the Insurance Brokers Registration Council (Conduct of Investment Business) Rules Approval Order 1988 (SI 1988 No 950), which enshrines the rule book of the IBRC with statutory force. These rules apply concurrently with the IBRC Regulations, which still have to be observed.

The essential criterion for eligibility is the amount of income derived from investment business, which must not be more than 25 per cent of the total income of the broker within the last accounting period.

IBRC Rule 3 enables the broker to carry out the following relevant investment business: buying; selling; or subscribing for units in an authorised unit trust scheme; or recognised collective investment scheme, including shares in investment companies; any life policies; and any rights and interests falling within these categories.

The main rules are set out as follows.

Description of business
All documents emanating from the broker must state that investment business is subject to regulation by the IBRC.

Dual agency
The broker must act as the agent of the insured after the issue of a life policy to him, except as to forwarding premium or forwarding communications to and from the insured.

Churning
The broker must not obtain excessive commission either by charging large brokerage fees, or recommending unnecessary transactions, or recommending the realisation of units or surrender of life policies without good reason.

Client money
The broker must not hold or retain any money belonging to the insured and monies should be paid direct to the relevant recipient.

Unsolicited calls

Brokers may make unsolicited calls as long as they are connected with the sale of life policies or unit trusts or to an authorised or exempted person or an overseas firm which the broker considers and believes to be carrying on investment business. The conduct of calls is carefully regulated.

Advertisements

The rules for advertisements are stringent, and subject to a require-ment that their contents must be capable of being understood by their intended audience. The broker must take reasonable steps to ensure that the advertisement is not misleading and must contain a risk warning, by drawing attention to any front-end loading, the possibility of any fluctuation of the investment, including changes in exchange rates, and whether the return on the investment is capable of variation by the company managing the investment.

Inducements

The broker is not entitled to receive volume-related commission, gifts or reciprocal facilities, so that the independence of the broker is properly maintained.

Complaints

The broker must promptly and properly investigate any complaint and inform the complainant that he may report the matter to the Council and ask the Council to investigate the complaint.

Compliance

A registered insurance broker must supervise and control all invest-ment business and must inform the Council if any event makes compliance with the investment business rules impossible or impractical.

Know your customer

An investigation of the insured's needs must be completed and the insured must be aware of any risk inherent in any transaction.

Best advice

The broker must reasonably believe that the recommended invest-ment is suitable in the light of the information provided by the insured about his investment requirements and circumstances.

Disclosure of commission

The broker must disclose the basis of his remuneration and the amount of initial and subsequent commissions, or state that the commission that he will receive from the insurer, who is a member of LAUTRO, will be disclosed by the insurer. The broker must in any event provide the insured with a 'Buyer's Guide to Life Assurance Personal Pensions Unit Trust Products' which specifies that the broker will normally be paid by commission.

Best execution

The broker must effect all transactions relating to unit trusts directly with the unit trust manager and the transaction must be completed as soon as practicable.

Custody of insured's investments

The investment must be registered in the name of the insured or alternatively in accordance with his instructions and the documents of title must be sent to the insured as quickly as possible to any address nominated by the insured, subject perhaps to any lien that the broker may have over any policy document.

Records

All transaction records must be properly kept, including all relevant facts concerning the insured's personal and financial situation and competence. Records of the insured's monies must be carefully maintained.

Compliance manual

The broker must maintain a compliance manual at its office which must be available to all employees, officers and appointed representatives, and must contain all regulations and IBRC Practice Directions.

Compliance review

An annual review must be carried out to ensure that the compliance procedures are effective, including a review of a representative sample of clients' files and its investment business.

FIMBRA

If an insurance broker transacts more than 25 per cent of his total income by way of investment business, membership of FIMBRA is almost mandatory in the light of the terms of reference of other self-regulatory organisations. FIMBRA obtained SRO status in December 1987 after a merger between the National Association of Securities Dealers and Investment Managers and the Life Insurance and Unit Trusts Intermediaries Regulatory Organisation. FIMBRA has eight categories of membership, as follows:

A1 *membership*

This provides investment advice on all types of investment. All members are authorised in A1 but firms only authorised in A1 may advise only, and cannot arrange investments or handle clients' monies.

A2 *membership*

This involves arranging and effecting transactions concerning life assurance, pensions, collective investments, and new public share issues (on strict conditions). Clients' monies may not be handled. This category is most prevalent amongst insurance brokers.

B1 *membership*

This involves arranging and effecting transactions relating to investments of any nature authorised by FIMBRA in which the broker does not hold any clients' monies or manage investments on a discretionary basis, and in which transactions are completed through a clearing firm which takes responsibility for the performance of the bargain eg a stockbroker.

B2 *membership*

This is the same as category A2 but with the proviso that clients' monies may be handled for a limited range of investments, life assurance, pensions, collective investments and, again, new public share issues on strict conditions.

B3 *membership*

This is the same as category B2, but also includes the management of collective investments.

C1 *membership*

This involves arranging and effecting transactions relating to investments of any kind authorised by FIMBRA provided investments proceed through a clearing organisation. The broker may hold clients' monies and assets.

C2 membership

This involves managing all types of investments provided the assets are held by and dealt with through a custodian and without handling clients' monies.

C3 membership

This involves executing and managing all types of investments that have not been referred to in any other category and handling clients' monies.

Any member not entitled to handle clients' monies must disclose that fact prominently.

Individuals registered with FIMBRA must be fit and proper to act in the capacity in which they intend to act. Their status as a member of FIMBRA is independent from their employer's status as a member of FIMBRA.

FIMBRA members are subject to the following regulations:

Compliance All members (except category C) must prepare annual financial statements and provide them to FIMBRA within four months of their accounting reference date, together with an auditor's report. Category C members have to prepare quarterly financial statements and monthly statements of their financial resources. Compliance procedures and rules must be established and maintained, and a compliance review carried out at least once a year by the member's compliance officer, who will send a certificate of compliance to FIMBRA annually.

Rules governing FIMBRA members Members of FIMBRA must comply with essentially the same rules incumbent upon insurance brokers who have registered with the IBRC, although the FIMBRA rules are more stringent. Thus the FIMBRA member must know his client and provide the best advice (except where he is a 'execution only' client); disclose his commission as required; execute transactions to the client's best advantage (except in life assurance and pension contracts); can make unsolicited calls according to specified rules; must defer from acting as a principal with a client without the consent of that client (except in relation to life policies, pensions or unit trusts); must take great care in connection with any forecasts or product particulars; issue contract notes to the client detailing the transaction not later than the next business day after the transaction; is subject to rules concerning the influencing of business by benefits or gifts which may influence the judgment of the broker, and to stringent advertising regulations; must disclose the necessary information upon his writing paper or other documentation provided by the broker which must include the fact that it is regulated by FIMBRA; must comply stringently with the accounting records requirements and financial resources requirements; can hold clients' assets or funds pursuant to the SIB client money rules; can deal with complaints along specific lines; is subject to random monitoring of his compliance procedures; is subject to a disciplinary scheme in connection with any allegations of misconduct (again broadly along the same lines as the IBRC under the Insurance Brokers (Registration) Act 1977); and in particular must deliver to the client a letter detailing the broker's terms of business or must enter into a client agreement. Rules 5(2), (3) and (4) set out the relevant contents of the client agreement, although client agreements are not required where the service provided by the broker is limited to life policies, pension contracts or unit trust transactions, unless a broker bond or personal equity plan is involved.

Although an action for damages can be brought by a client under s 62 of the Financial Services Act, FIMBRA has substantial powers of investigation and extensive disciplinary powers which allow it to:

(a) prohibit certain transactions;
(b) prohibit the soliciting of business from specified parties;
(c) prohibit dealing with assets and liabilities other than in a specified manner;
(d) appoint a trustee for the transfer of assets;
(e) require additional assets to meet the financial resources requirements;
(f) pursue legal proceedings;
(g) terminate the business of the FIMBRA member;
(h) terminate the party's registration with FIMBRA;
(i) limit the conditions of membership to investment of a particular type;
(j) reprimand the member; and
(k) require the member to follow a FIMBRA directive.

The first action instituted by the SIB involved a member of FIMBRA. On 6 November 1989 the member, which had limited advisory status and was not entitled to hold clients' money or undertake portfolio management, was ordered by the court to repay £1.29 million to its clients on the basis that the proprietor had wrongly promoted himself as having authority to handle clients' money to invest in unit trusts and to manage their portfolios.

Lloyd's brokers

In 1981 the working party of Sir Henry Fisher commented that:

We are satisfied that it is only the maintenance of a privileged class of Lloyd's brokers, with the correlative sanction of exclusion from the privileged class, that enables the Committee of Lloyd's to insist on maintenance by the brokers of the standards required.

Such standards involve protecting the policyholder, ensuring uniform standards for all Lloyd's brokers, having a good working relationship with Lloyd's underwriters, and protecting the Lloyd's name from being brought into disrepute by the activities of the Lloyd's broker. These objectives are achieved by the Council of Lloyd's predetermining and monitoring the financial stability of Lloyd's brokers, and ensuring that all relevant administrative work is efficiently and properly carried out. Thus it was that the Lloyd's Brokers Byelaw (No 5 of 1988) came to pass, divided into the following sections:

(a) interpretation;
(b) registration, review, renewal and withdrawal of registration;
(c) ownership and control;
(d) conduct of business;
(e) financial provisions:
    (i) financial resources;
    (ii) insurance broking accounts;
    (iii) accounting records;
    (iv) accounts and other reports;
    (v) audit;
    (vi) returns;
    (vii) professional indemnity insurance;
(f) records;
(g) notification and information;
(h) protection of insurance creditors;
(i) scheme to provide for run-off costs;
(j) fees;
(k) transitional provisions; and
(l) miscellaneous and supplementary.

The most important items are as follows.

Registration, review, renewal and withdrawal of registration
No person may broke insurance business at Lloyd's unless registered as a Lloyd's broker, such registration to be controlled by the Council of Lloyd's. The criteria for registration include enrolment

in the Insurance Brokers Registration Council List maintained under s 4 of the Insurance Brokers (Registration) Act 1977. The applicant must be fit and proper to be a Lloyd's broker, which will be assessed on the basis of the character and suitability of the directors or partners of the applicant, their experience of the conduct of business at Lloyd's, the reputation, character and suitability of any person who controls the applicant, the character and suitability of the compliance officer, the adequacy of the capital of the applicant, whether the applicant is unduly dependant on a particular insurer or source or kind or class of business, the staff of the applicant, any other relevant matters in the opinion of the Council, and whether or not the Lloyd's broker is subject to any arrangement that might enable it to influence the policy or business of a managing agent or vice versa.

Ownership and control

In accordance with the Lloyd's Act 1982 no Lloyd's broker can be a managing agent or associated with a managing agent unless the Council otherwise agrees. No person can be a director of a Lloyd's broker if he is also a director or partner of an insurance company which underwrites insurance business as an agent for an insurance company.

Conduct of business

Lloyd's brokers can only carry on business as insurance brokers if authorised by the Council, and shall appoint a responsible person for compliance with the Lloyd's Acts 1871 to 1982, the relevant byelaws and regulations, and to ensure that the Lloyd's broker pays due regard to the codes of practice, market circulars or other advice issued by or under the authority of the Council or of the Committee. The Lloyd's broker must, where it is obtaining insurance with an insurance company from which it has connections, deliver to the proposer or agent a written statement stating the nature of the connection except in certain circumstances. Lloyd's brokers must observe the provisions of the Codes of Practice, issued by the Council.

Financial provisions

The byelaw contains several provisions which entitle the Council or Committee of Lloyd's to make conditions or requirements relating to the assets or other financial provisions concerning Lloyd's brokers, including a requirement to maintain an Insurance Broking Account with an approved bank into which will be paid (without delay) all monies (including brokerage) relating to insurance transactions of any kind, and out of which payments to insureds will be paid. The Lloyd's broker must ensure that no insurance broking account (or any approved insurance broking account asset) is subject to any lien or charge of any nature, except those granted to an approved bank by way of security for repayment of temporary advances in connection with duly authorised payments, or by way of security for indemnification of the approved bank against expenses incurred in connection with any Letter of Credit at the request of the Lloyd's broker to be used only for the payment of monies due to an insured, provided an undertaking has been received from the insurer to reimburse the Lloyd's broker in respect of monies paid by the Lloyd's broker.

Every Lloyd's broker who is not subject to ss 221 and 222 of the Companies Act 1985 must hold such accounting records. Every Lloyd's broker must also establish and maintain an adequate system of control over its transactions and records, including the preparation of accounts at the end of every financial year containing information to which, if the broker were a company, Part VII of the Companies Act 1985 would apply.

Lloyd's brokers must also report breaches of any condition or requirement imposed by the Council, or of circumstances which make it likely that such a breach will occur, or any circumstances which materially prejudice its ability or likely future ability to comply.

Every Lloyd's broker must also prepare a statement showing its connections with companies or persons carrying on business related to insurance business in any way, the manner of the dealings, and the operation of binding authorities.

Every Lloyd's broker must ensure that all relevant accounting documentation is examined by an authorised Lloyd's auditor, who shall give such undertakings as may be required by the Council.

Every Lloyd's broker shall file the relevant annual returns, as required by the Council.

Lloyd's brokers shall comply with any conditions prescribed by the Council relating to professional indemnity insurance.

Every Lloyd's broker shall maintain records of all matters which are necessary for the proper recording of each contract of insurance which it arranges to show the identity of all participating insurers and the amounts of their respective participations, full particulars of the relevant contractual terms and conditions, a copy of the policy or other document, the broker's slip, any indorsements or waivers after the contractual completion, together with all relevant documentation relating to contracts made under the Umbrella Arrangements Byelaw (No 6 of 1988) or any binding authority.

Notification and information

Every Lloyd's broker shall notify the Council in writing of any change of interest or membership, together with details of the appointment of any person as a director or partner or compliance officer. Additional information to be reported includes the discharge or cessation of office of directors or partners, the appointment of auditors, the discharge or vacation of auditors, any material change in the location or adequacy or suitability of the staff of the Lloyd's broker, any material change which may affect the Lloyd's broker's ability or willingness to supervise and service its activities, a material change in the location of the books or other records, a change in the date to which the accounts of the Lloyd's broker or its ultimate holding company are prepared, or any cessation of business, whether of insurance broking or any other ancillary business.

Protection of insurance creditors

The Council is empowered to require every Lloyd's broker to execute deeds or other instruments in favour of creditors of Lloyd's brokers.

Scheme to provide for run-off costs

The Lloyd's Council may ensure that a trust fund is established in connection with the continuing discharge of the function of a Lloyd's broker who is unable to discharge his functions.

Insurance Brokers (Registration) Act 1977 c 46

ARRANGEMENT OF SECTIONS

Committees of the Council

Restriction on use of titles and descriptions

Miscellaneous

SCHEDULE — Constitution, etc, of Insurance Brokers Registration Council

An Act to provide for the registration of insurance brokers and for the regulation of their professional standards, and for purposes connected therewith

[29 July 1977]

The Insurance Brokers Registration Council

1. Establishment of Insurance Brokers Registration Council
(1) There shall be established a body to be called the Insurance Brokers Registration Council (hereinafter referred to as 'the Council') which shall be a body corporate with perpetual succession and a common seal and shall have the general function of carrying out the powers and duties conferred on them by this Act.

(2) The Council shall be constituted in accordance with the Schedule to this Act and the supplementary provisions contained in that Schedule shall have effect with respect to the Council.

Registration and training of insurance brokers

2. The insurance brokers register
The Council shall establish and maintain a register of insurance brokers (hereinafter referred to as 'the register') containing the names, addresses and qualifications, and such other particulars as may be prescribed, of all persons who are entitled under the provisions of this Act to be registered therein and apply in the prescribed manner to be so registered.

3. Qualifications for registration
(1) Subject to subsection (2) below and to section 16 of this Act, a person shall be entitled to be registered if he satisfies the Council —

(a) that he holds a qualification approved by the Council under section

6 of this Act, being a qualification granted to him after receiving instruction from an institution so approved; or

(b) that he holds a qualification recognised by the Council for the purposes of this paragraph, being a qualification granted outside the United Kingdom; or

(c) that he has carried on business as an insurance broker, or as a whole-time agent acting for two or more insurance companies in relation to insurance business, for a period of not less than five years; or

(d) that he holds a qualification recognised by the Council for the purposes of this paragraph and has carried on business as mentioned in paragraph (c) above for a period of not less than three years; or

(e) that he has been employed by a person carrying on business as mentioned in paragraph (c) above, or by an insurance company, for a period of not less than five years; or

(f) that he holds a qualification recognised by the Council for the purposes of this paragraph and has been employed by a person carrying on business as mentioned in paragraph (c) above, or by an insurance company, for a period of not less than three years; or

(g) that he has knowledge and practical experience of insurance business which is comparable to that of a person who has carried on business as an insurance broker for a period of five years; or

(h) that he holds a qualification recognised by the Council for the purposes of this paragraph and has knowledge and practical experience of insurance business which is comparable to that of a person who has carried on business as an insurance broker for a period of three years.

(2) A person shall not be entitled to be registered in the register by virtue of subsection (1) above unless he also satisfies the Council —

(a) as to his character and suitability to be a registered insurance broker; and

(b) in a case falling within paragraph (a), (b), (e) or (f) of subsection (1) above, that he has had adequate practical experience in the work of an insurance broker; and

(c) if he is carrying on business as an insurance broker at the time when the application is made, that he is complying with the requirements of rules under section 11(1) of this Act.

(3) Subject to section 16 of this Act, a person shall be entitled to be registered in the register if he satisfies the Council that he or a partnership of which he is a member is accepted as a Lloyd's broker by the Committee of Lloyd's.

(4) The Secretary of State may, after consulting the Council, by order provide that any of the paragraphs in subsection (1) or (2) above shall be omitted or shall have effect subject to such amendments as may be specified in the order.

4. List of bodies corporate carrying on business as insurance brokers

(1) The Council shall establish and maintain a list of bodies corporate carrying on business as insurance brokers (hereinafter referred to as 'the list') containing the names, principal places of business and such other particulars as may be prescribed of all bodies corporate which are entitled

under this section to be enrolled therein and apply in the prescribed manner to be so enrolled.

(2) Subject to subsection (3) below and to section 16 of this Act, a body corporate shall be entitled to be enrolled in the list if it satisfies the Council —

(a) that a majority of its directors are registered insurance brokers; or

(b) in the case of a body corporate having only one director, that he is a registered insurance broker; or

(c) in the case of a body corporate having only two directors, that one of them is a registered insurance broker and that the business is carried on under the management of that director.

(3) A body corporate shall not be entitled to be enrolled in the list by virtue of subsection (1) above unless it also satisfies the Council that it is complying with the requirements of rules under section 11(1) of this Act.

(4) Subject to section 16 of this Act, a body corporate shall be entitled to be enrolled in the list if it satisfies the Council that it is accepted as a Lloyd's broker by the Committee of Lloyd's.

5. Appeals against refusal to register or enrol

(1) Before refusing an application for registration under section 3 of this Act or an application for enrolment under section 4 of this Act, the Council shall give the person by whom or the body corporate by which the application was made an opportunity of appearing before and being heard by a committee of the Council.

(2) Where the Council refuse any such application, the Council shall, if so required by the person by whom or the body corporate by which the application was made within seven days from notification of the decision, serve on that person or body a statement of the reasons therefor.

(3) A person or body corporate whose application is so refused may within twenty-eight days from —

(a) notification of the decision, or

(b) if a statement of reasons has been required under subsection (2) above, service of the statement,

appeal against the refusal of the Court.

(4) The Council may appear as respondent on any such appeal and for the purpose of enabling directions to be given as to the costs of any such appeal the Council shall be deemed to be a party thereto, whether they appear on the hearing of the appeal or not.

(5) On the hearing of any such appeal the Court may make such order as it thinks fit and its order shall be final.

6. Approval of educational institutions and qualifications

(1) The Council may approve for the purposes of this Act any institution (hereinafter referred to as 'an approved educational institution') where the instruction given to persons being educated as insurance brokers appears to the Council to be such as to secure to them adequate knowledge and skill for the practice of their profession.

(2) The Council may approve for the purposes of this Act any qualification (hereinafter referred to as 'an approved qualification') which appears to the Council to be granted to candidates who reach such a standard of proficiency at a qualifying examination as to secure to them adequate knowledge and skill for the practice of their profession.

(3) Where the Council have refused to approve an institution of qualification under this section as suitable for any purpose, the Secretary of State, on representations being made to him within one month of the refusal, may, if he thinks fit, after considering the representations and after consulting the Council, order the Council to approve the institution or qualification as suitable for that purpose.

(4) The Council shall publish before the day appointed for the coming into operation of section 3(1)(a) of this Act, and from time to time thereafter, a list of approved educational institutions and approved qualifications.

7. Supervision of educational institutions and qualifying examinations

(1) It shall be the duty of the Council to keep themselves informed of the nature of the instruction given by any approved educational institution to persons being educated as insurance brokers and of the examinations on the results of which approved qualifications are granted.

(2) For the purposes of their duty under subsection (1) above the Council may appoint persons to visit approved educational institutions and to attend at the examinations held by the bodies which grant approved qualifications.

(3) It shall be the duty of visitors appointed under subsection (2) above to report to the Council as to the sufficiency of the instruction given by the institutions visited by them, or of the examinations attended by them, and as to any other matters relating thereto which may be specified by the Council either generally or in any particular case, but no visitor shall interfere with the giving of any instruction or the holding of any examination.

(4) Where it appears to the Council (as a result of a report under subsection (3) above or otherwise), —

   (a) that the instruction given by any approved educational institution to persons being educated as insurance brokers or the examinations taken by such persons are not such as to secure the possession by them of adequate knowledge and skill for the practice of their profession; and

   (b) that by reason thereof the approval of the institution or qualification in question should be withdrawn,

the Council shall give notice in writing to the institution or body of their opinion, sending therewith a copy of any report on which their opinion is based.

(5) On the receipt of the notice the institution or body may, within such period (not being less than one month) as the Council may have specified in the notice, make to the Council observations on the notice and any report sent therewith or objections to the notice and report.

(6) As soon as may be after the expiration of the period specified in the notice under subsection (4) above the Council shall determine whether or not to withdraw their approval of the institution or qualification, as the case may be, taking into account any observations or objections duly made under subsection (5) above.

(7) The Council shall give notice in writing of any decision under this section to withdraw approval of an institution or qualification to the institution or body concerned and the decision shall not take effect until the expiration of one month from the date of the giving of the notice or, if during that time the institution or body makes representations with respect

to the decision to the Secretary of State, until the representations are finally dealt with.

(8) Where the Council have decided to withdraw approval of an institution or qualification, the Secretary of State, on representations being made to him within one month from the giving of notice of the decision, may, if he thinks fit, after considering the representations and after consulting the Council order the Council to annul the withdrawal of approval.

(9) The Council may pay to visitors appointed under this section such fees and such travelling and subsistence allowances as the Council may determine.

8. Supplementary provisions as to the register and list

(1) The register and list shall be kept by the registrar of the Council who shall be appointed by the Council.

(2) The Council may make rules with respect to the form and keeping of the register and list and the making of entries and alterations therein and, in particular —

> (a) regulating the making of applications for registration or enrolment and providing for the evidence to be produced in support of any such applications;
> (b) providing for the notification to the registrar of any change in the particulars required to be entered in the register or list;
> (c) prescribing a fee to be charged on the entry of a name in, or the restoration of a name to, the register or list;
> (d) prescribing a fee to be charged in respect of the retention in the register or list of any name in any year subsequent to the year in which that name was first entered in the register or list;
> (e) providing for the entry in the register of qualifications (whether approved qualifications or not) possessed by persons whose names are registered therein and for the removal of such qualifications from the register, and prescribing a fee to be charged in respect of the entry;
> (f) authorising the registrar to refuse to enter a name in, or restore it to, the register or list until a fee prescribed for the entry or restoration has been paid and to erase from the register or list the name of a person who or body corporate which, after the prescribed notices and warnings, fails to pay the fee prescribed in respect of the retention of that name in the register or list;
> (g) authorising the registrar to erase from the register or list the name of a person who or body corporate which, after the prescribed notices and warnings, fails to supply information required by the registrar with a view to ensuring that the particulars entered in the register or list are correct;
> (h) prescribing anything required or authorised to be prescribed by the provisions of this Act relating to the register or list.

(3) Rules under this section which provide for the erasure of a name from the register or list on failure to pay a fee shall provide for its restoration thereto on the making of the prescribed application in that behalf and on payment of that fee and any additional fee prescribed in respect of the restoration.

(4) Rules under this section prescribing fees may provide for the charging of different fees in different classes of cases and for the making of arrange-

ments for the collection of fees with such body or bodies as may be prescribed.

9. Publication of register and list

(1) The Council shall cause the register and list to be printed and published within one year of the establishment of the Council and as often thereafter as they think fit.

(2) Where the register or list is not published in any year after the first publication thereof, the Council shall cause any alterations in the entries in the register or list which have been made since the last publication thereof to be printed and published within that year.

(3) A copy of the register or list purporting to be printed and published by the Council, shall, as altered by any alterations purporting to be printed and published by the Council, be evidence in all proceedings that the individuals specified in the register are registered therein or, as the case may be, that the bodies corporate specified in the list are enrolled therein; and the absence of the name of any individual or body corporate from any such copy of the register or list shall be evidence, until the contrary is shown, that he is not registered or, as the case may be, that it is not enrolled therein.

(4) In the case of an individual whose name or a body corporate the name of which does not appear in any such copy of the register or list as altered as aforesaid, a certified copy, under the hand of the registrar, of the entry relating to that individual or body corporate in the register or list shall be evidence of the entry.

Regulation of conduct

10. Code of conduct

(1) The Council shall draw up and may from time to time revise a statement of the acts and omissions which, if done or made by registered insurance brokers or enrolled bodies corporate, or by registered insurance brokers or enrolled bodies corporate in particular circumstances, constitute in the opinion of the Council unprofessional conduct.

(2) The statement shall serve as a guide to registered insurance brokers and enrolled bodies corporate and persons concerned with the conduct of registered insurance brokers and enrolled bodies corporate, but the mention or lack of mention in it of a particular act or omission shall not be taken as conclusive of any question of professional conduct.

11. Requirements for carrying on business

(1) The Council shall make rules requiring registered insurance brokers who are carrying on business as insurance brokers (hereinafter referred to as 'practising insurance brokers') and enrolled bodies corporate to ensure —

(a) that their businesses have working capital of not less than such amount as may be prescribed;

(b) that the value of the assets of their businesses exceeds the amount of the liabilities of their businesses by not less than such amount as may be prescribed; and

(c) that the number of insurance companies with which they place insurance business, and the amount of insurance business which they place with each insurance company, is such as to prevent their businesses from becoming unduly dependent on any particular insurance company.

(2) The Council shall also make rules requiring practising insurance brokers and enrolled bodies corporate —

(a) to open and keep accounts at banks for money received by them from persons with whom they do business;

(b) to hold money so received in such manner as may be prescribed;

(c) to keep such accounting records showing and explaining the transactions of their businesses as may be prescribed; and

(d) to prepare and submit to the Council at such intervals as may be prescribed balance sheets and profit and loss accounts containing such information as may be prescribed for the purpose of giving a true and fair view of the state of their businesses.

(3) Without prejudice to the generality of subsections (1) and (2) above, rules under this section may empower the Council —

(a) to require practising insurance brokers and enrolled bodies corporate to deliver at such intervals as may be prescribed reports given by qualified accountants and containing such information as may be prescribed for the purpose of ascertaining whether or not the rules are being complied with; and

(b) to take such other steps as they consider necessary or expedient for the purpose of ascertaining whether or not the rules are being complied with.

(4) Subject to subsections (5) and (6) below, an accountant is qualified to give reports for the purposes of the rules if he is a member of a recognised body of accountants or is for the time being authorised by the Secretary of State under section 389(1)(b) of the Companies Act 1985 or, in Northern Ireland, by the Department of Commerce for Northern Ireland under section 155(1)(b) of the Companies Act (Northern Ireland) 1960.

(5) An accountant shall not be qualified to give such reports —

(a) in relation to a practising insurance broker, if he is an employee or partner of, or an employee of a partner of, the practising insurance broker;

(b) in relation to an enrolled body corporate, if he is not qualified for appointment as auditor of the enrolled body corporate.

(6) A Scottish firm of accountants shall be qualified to give such reports if, but only if, all the partners are so qualified.

(7) Rules under this section may make different provision for different circumstances, and may specify circumstances in which persons are exempt from any of the requirements of the rules.

12. Professional indemnity, etc

(1) The Council shall make rules for indemnifying —

(a) practising insurance brokers and former practising insurance brokers, and

(b) enrolled bodies corporate and former enrolled bodies corporate,

against losses arising from claims in respect of any description of civil liability incurred by them, or by employees or former employees of theirs, in connection with their businesses.

(2) The Council shall also make rules for the making of grants or other

payments for the purpose of relieving or mitigating losses suffered by persons in consequence of —

    (a) negligence or fraud or other dishonesty on the part of practising insurance brokers or enrolled bodies corporate, or of employees of theirs, in connection with their businesses; or

    (b) failure on the part of practising insurance brokers or enrolled bodies corporate to account for money received by them in connection with their businesses.

(3) For the purpose of providing such indemnity and of enabling such grants or other payments to be made, rules under this section —

    (a) may authorise or require the Council to establish and maintain a fund or funds;

    (b) may authorise or require the Council to take out and maintain insurance with authorised insurers;

    (c) may require practising insurance brokers or enrolled bodies corporate or any specified description of practising insurance brokers or enrolled bodies corporate to take out and maintain insurance with authorised insurers.

(4) Without prejudice to the generality of the preceding subsections, rules under this section —

    (a) may specify the terms and conditions on which indemnity or a grant or other payment is to be available, and any circumstances in which the right to it is to be excluded or modified;

    (b) may provide for the management, administration and protection of any fund maintained by virtue of subsection (3)(a) above and require practising insurance brokers or enrolled bodies corporate or any description of practising insurance brokers or enrolled bodies corporate to make payments to any such fund;

    (c) may require practising insurance brokers or enrolled bodies corporate or any description of practising insurance brokers or enrolled bodies corporate to make payments by way of premium on any insurance policy maintained by the Council by virtue of subsection (3)(b) above;

    (d) may prescribe the conditions which an insurance policy must satisfy for the purposes of subsection 3(c) above;

    (e) may authorise the Council to determine the amount of any payments required by the rules, subject to such limits, or in accordance with such provisions, as may be prescribed;

    (f) may specify circumstances in which, where a registered insurance broker or an enrolled body corporate for whom indemnity is provided has failed to comply with the rules, the Council or insurers may take proceedings against him or it in respect of sums paid by way of indemnity in connection with a matter in relation to which there has been a failure to comply with the rules;

    (g) may specify circumstances in which, where a grant or other payment is made in consequence of the act or omission of a practising insurance broker or enrolled body corporate, the Council or insurers may take proceedings against him or it in respect of the sum so paid;

    (h) may make different provision for different circumstances, and may specify circumstances in which practising insurance brokers or enrolled bodies corporate are exempt from any of the rules;

(i) may empower the Council to take such steps as they consider necessary or expedient to ascertain whether or not the rules are being complied with; and

(j) may contain incidental, procedural or supplementary provisions.

Disciplinary proceedings

13. Preliminary investigation of disciplinary cases

(1) The Council shall set up a committee, to be known as the Investigating Committee, for the preliminary investigation of cases in which —

(a) it is alleged that a registered insurance broker or enrolled body corporate is liable to have his or its name erased from the register or list on any ground specified in section 15 of this Act; or

(b) a complaint is made to the Council by or on behalf of a member of the public about a registered insurance broker or an enrolled body corporate or an employee of a registered insurance broker or an enrolled body corporate.

Any such case is hereinafter referred to as 'a disciplinary case'.

(2) A disciplinary case shall be referred to the Investigating Committee who shall carry out a preliminary investigation of it and, unless they are satisfied that there is insufficient evidence to support a finding that the registered insurance broker or enrolled body corporate is liable to have his or its name erased from the register or list, the Committee shall refer the case, with the results of their investigation, to the Disciplinary Committee set up under the next following section.

(3) The Council shall make rules as to the constitution of the Investigating Committee.

14. The Disciplinary Committee

(1) The Council shall set up a committee, to be known as the Disciplinary Committee, for the consideration and determination of disciplinary cases referred to them under the last foregoing section and of any other cases of which they have cognizance under the following provisions of this Act.

(2) The Council shall make rules as to the constitution of the Disciplinary Committee, the times and places of the meetings of the Committee, the quorum and the mode of summoning the members thereof.

(3) Rules under this section shall secure that a person, other than the Chairman of the Council, who has acted in relation to any disciplinary case as a member of the Investigating Committee does not act in relation to that case as a member of the Disciplinary Conmittee.

15. Erasure from the register and list for crime, unprofessional conduct, etc

(1) If a registered insurance broker or enrolled body corporate —

(a) is convicted by any court in the United Kingdom of any criminal offence, not being an offence which, owing to its trivial nature or the circumstances under which it was committed, does not render him or it unfit to have his or its name on the register or list, or

(b) is judged by the Disciplinary Committee to have been guilty of unprofessional conduct,

the Disciplinary Committee may, if they think fit, direct that the name of the insurance broker or body corporate shall be erased from the register or list.

(2) If it appears to the Disciplinary Committee that a registered insurance broker or an enrolled body corporate has contravened or failed to comply with any rules made under section 11 or section 12 of this Act and that the contravention or failure is such as to render the insurance broker unfit to have his name on the register or the body corporate unfit to have its name on the list, the Disciplinary Committee may, if they think fit, direct that the name of the insurance broker or body corporate shall be erased from the register or list.

(3) Where —

(a) the name of a director of an enrolled body corporate is erased from the register under subsection (1) above; or

(b) a director of any such body corporate is convicted of an offence under this Act, or

(c) the name of a registered insurance broker employed by any such body corporate is erased from the register under subsection (1) above and the act or omission constituting the ground on which it was erased was instigated or connived at by a director of the body corporate, or, if the act or omission was a continuing act or omission, a director of the body corporate had or reasonably ought to have had knowledge of the continuance thereof,

the Disciplinary Comittee may, if they think fit, direct that the name of the body corporate shall be erased from the list:
Provided that the Disciplinary Committee shall not take a case into consideration during any period within which proceedings by way of appeal may be brought which may result in this subsection being rendered inapplicable in that case or while any such proceedings are pending.

(4) If the Disciplinary Committee are of opinion as respects an enrolled body corporate that the conditions for enrolment in section 4 of this Act are no longer satisfied, the Disciplinary Committee may, if they think fit, direct that the name of the body corporate shall be erased from the list.

(5) Where a registered insurance broker dies while he is a director of an enrolled body corporate, he shall be deemed for the purposes of subsection (4) above to have continued to be a director of that body until the expiration of a period of six months beginning with the date of his death or until a director is appointed in his place, whichever first occurs.

(6) When the Disciplinary Committee direct that the name of an individual or body corporate shall be erased from the register or list, the registrar shall serve on that individual or body a notification of the direction and a statement of the Committee's reasons therefor.

16. Restoration of names erased as a result of disciplinary cases, etc

(1) Where the name of an individual or body corporate has been erased from the register or list in pursuance of a direction under the last foregoing section, the name of that individual or body corporate shall not again be entered in the register or list unless the Disciplinary Committee on application made to them in that behalf otherwise direct.

(2) An application under subsection (1) above for the restoration of a name to the register or list shall not be made to the Disciplinary Committee

(a) within ten months of the date of the erasure; or

(b) within ten months of a previous application thereunder.

17. Erasure from register and list on grounds of fraud or error

(1) If it is proved to the satisfaction of the Disciplinary Committee that any entry in the register or list has been fraudulently or incorrectly made, the Disciplinary Committee may, if they think fit, direct that the entry shall be erased from the register or list.

(2) An individual may be registered or a body corporate enrolled in pursuance of this Act notwithstanding that his or its name has been erased under this section, but if it was so erased on the ground of fraud, that individual or body corporate shall not be registered or enrolled except on an application in that behalf to the Disciplinary Committee; and on any such application the Disciplinary Committee may, if they think fit, direct that the individual or body corporate shall not be registered or enrolled, or shall not be registered or enrolled until the expiration of such period as may be specified in that direction.

(3) Where the Disciplinary Committee direct that the name of an individual or body corporate shall be erased from the register or list under this section, the registrar shall serve on that individual or body a notification of the direction and a statement of the Committee's reasons therefor.

18. Appeals in disciplinary and other cases

(1) At any time within twenty-eight days from the service of a notification that the Disciplinary Committee have under section 15 or section 17 of this Act directed that the name of an individual or a body corporate be erased from the register or list that individual or body corporate may appeal to the Court.

(2) The Council may appear as respondent on any such appeal and for the purpose of enabling directions to be given as to the costs of any such appeal the Council shall be deemed to be a party thereto, whether they appear on the hearing of the appeal or not.

(3) Where no appeal is brought against a direction under section 15 or section 17 of this Act or where such an appeal is brought but withdrawn or struck out for want of prosecutions, the direction shall take effect on the expiration of the time for appealing or, as the case may be, on the withdrawal or striking out of the appeal.

(4) Subject as aforesaid, where an appeal is brought against a direction under either of those sections, the direction shall take effect if and when the appeal is dismissed and not otherwise.

19. Procedure of Disciplinary Committee

(1) For the purpose of any proceedings before the Disciplinary Committee in England or Wales or Northern Ireland the Disciplinary Committee may administer oaths, and any party to the proceedings may sue out writs of subpoena ad testificandum and duces tecum, but no person shall be compelled under any such writ to produce any document which he could not be compelled to produce on the trial of an action.

(2) The provisions of section [36 of the Supreme Court Act 1981] or of the Attendance of Witnesses Act 1854 (which provide a special procedure for the issue of such writs so as to be in force throughout the United Kingdom) shall apply in relation to any proceedings before the Disciplinary Committee in England or Wales or, as the case may be, in Northern Ireland as they apply in relation to causes or matters in the High Court or actions or suits pending in the High Court of Justice in Northern Ireland.

(3) . . .

(4) The Council shall make rules as to the procedure to be followed and the rules of evidence to be observed in proceedings before the Disciplinary Committee; and in particular —

(a) for securing that notice that the proceedings are to be brought shall be given, at such time and in such manner as may be specified in the rules, to the individual or body corporate alleged to be liable to have his or its name erased from the register or list;

(b) for securing that any party to the proceedings shall, if he so requires, be entitled to be heard by the Disciplinary Committee;

(c) for enabling any party to the proceedings to be represented by counsel or solicitor or (if the rules so provide and the party so elects) by a person of such other description as may be specified in the rules;

(d) for requiring proceedings before the Disciplinary Committee to be held in public except in so far as may be provided by the rules;

(e) for requiring, in cases where it is alleged that a registered insurance broker or enrolled body corporate has been guilty of unprofessional conduct, that where the Disciplinary Committee judge that the allegation has not been proved they shall record a finding that the insurance broker or body corporate is not guilty of such conduct in respect of the matters to which the allegation relates;

(f) for requiring, in cases where it is alleged that a registered insurance broker or enrolled body corporate is liable to have his or its name erased from the register or list under section 15(2) of this Act, that where the Disciplinary Committee judge that the allegation has not been proved they shall record a finding that the insurance broker or body corporate is not guilty of the matters alleged.

(5) Before making rules under this section the Council shall consult such organisations representing the interests of insurance brokers and bodies corporate carrying on business as insurance brokers as appear to the Council requisite to be consulted.

(6) In this section and in section 20 of this Act 'proceedings' means proceedings under this Act, whether relating to disciplinary cases or otherwise.

[*Note*: Section 19(3) amended by Sched 5 of the Supreme Court Act 1981.]

20. Assessors to Disciplinary Committee

(1) For the purpose of advising the Disciplinary Committee on questions of law arising in proceedings before them there shall be in all such proceedings be an assessor to the Disciplinary Committee who shall be a barrister, advocate or solicitor of not less than ten years' standing.

(2) The power of appointing assessors under this section shall be exercisable by the Council, but if no assessor appointed by them is available to act at any particular proceedings the Disciplinary Committee may appoint an assessor under this section to act at those procedings.

(3) The Lord Chancellor or, in Scotland, the Lord Advocate may make rules as to the functions of assessors appointed under this section, and, in particular, rules under this subsection may contain such provisions for securing —

(a) that where an assessor advises the Disciplinary Committee on any question of law as to evidence, procedure or any other matters specified in the rules, he shall do so in the presence of every party, or person representing a party, to the proceedings who appears thereat or, if the advice is tendered after the Disciplinary Committee have begun to deliberate as to their findings, that every such party or person as aforesaid shall be informed what advice the assessor had tendered;

(b) that every such party or person as aforesaid shall be informed if in any case the Disciplinary Committee do not accept the advice of the assessor on any such question as aforesaid,

and such incidental and supplementary provisions, as appear to the Lord Chancellor or the Lord Advocate expedient.

(4) Subject to the provisions of this section, an assessor under this section may be appointed either generally or for any particular proceedings or class of proceedings, and shall hold and vacate office in accordance with the terms of the instrument under which he is appointed.

(5) Any remuneration paid by the Council to persons appointed to act as assessors shall be at such rates as the Council may determine.

(6) The power to make rules conferred by this section shall be exercisable by statutory instrument.

Committees of the Council

21. General power to appoint committees

(1) The Council may set up a committee for any purpose (other than a purpose for which the Council are required to set up a committee under this Act) and may delegate to a committee set up under this section, with or without restrictions or conditions, as they think fit, any functions exercisable by them except the following —

(a) the power to make rules under this Act,

(b) any functions expressly conferred by this Act on any committee set up under any of the foregoing provisions of this Act, and

(c) subject to any express provision for delegation in the rules, any functions expressly conferred on the Council by rules under this Act.

(2) The number of members of a committee set up under this section and their term of office shall be fixed by the Council.

(3) A committee set up under this Act may include persons who are not members of the Council, but at least two-thirds of the members of every such committee shall be members of the Council.

(4) Every member of a committee set up under this Act who at the time of his appointment was a member of the Council shall, upon ceasing to be a member of the Council, also cease to be a member of the committee:

Provided that for the purposes of this subsection a member of the Council shall not be deemed to have ceased by reason of retirement to be a member thereof if he has again been nominated or elected a member thereof not later than the day of his retirement.

Restriction on use of titles and descriptions

22. Penalty for pretending to be registered, etc

(1) Any individual who wilfully —

(a) takes or uses any style, title or description which consists of or includes the expression 'insurance broker' when he is not registered in the register, or

(b) takes or uses any name, title, addition or description falsely imply-ing, or otherwise pretends, that he is registered in the register,

shall be liable on summary conviction to a fine not exceeding [the prescribed sum] or on conviction on indictment to a fine.

(2) Any body corporate which wilfully —

(a) takes or uses any style, title or description which consists of or includes the expression 'insurance broker' when it is not enrolled in the list, or

(b) takes or uses any name, title, addition or description falsely imply-ing, or otherwise pretends, that it is enrolled in the list,

shall be liable on summary conviction to a fine not exceeding [the prescribed sum] or on conviction on indictment to a fine.

(3) References in this section to the expression 'insurance broker' include references to the following related expressions, that is to say 'assurance broker', 'reinsurance broker' and 'reassurance broker'.

23. Exceptions from section 22

(1) Where a practising insurance broker dies, then, during the period of three months beginning with his death or such longer period as the Council may in any particular case allow, the last foregoing section shall not operate to prevent his personal representatives, his surviving spouse or any of his children or trustees on behalf of his surviving spouse or any of his children from taking or using in relation to his business, but in conjunction with the name in which he carried it on, any title which he was entitled to take or use immediately before his death.

(2) Where a practising insurance broker becomes bankrupt, then, during the period of three months beginning with the bankruptcy or such longer period as the Council may in any particular case allow, the last foregoing section shall not operate to prevent his trustee in bankruptcy or, in North-ern Ireland, the assignee in bankruptcy, from taking or using in relation to his business, but in conjunction with the name in which he carried it on, and title which he was entitled to take or use immediately before the bankruptcy.

24. Offences by bodies corporate

Where an offence under this Act which has been committed by a body corporate is proved to have been committed with the consent or connivance of, or to be attributable to any neglect on the part of, any director, or any person purporting to act in any such capacity, he as well as the body corporate shall be guilty of that offence and shall be liable to be proceeded against and punished accordingly.

Miscellaneous

25. Accounts of Council

(1) The Council shall keep proper accounts of all sums received or paid by them and proper records in relation to those accounts.

(2) The Council shall appoint auditors to the Council who shall be mem-bers of a recognised body of accountants.

(3) The Council shall cause their accounts to be audited annually by the

auditors to the Council and as soon as is practicable after the accounts for any period have been audited the Council shall cause them to be published and shall send a copy of them to the Secretary of State together with a copy of any report of the auditors thereon.

26. Service of documents
Any notice or other document authorised or required to be given under this Act may, without prejudice to any other method of service but subject to any provision to the contrary in rules under this Act, be served by post; and for the purpose of the application to this section of section 26 of the Interpretation Act 1889 (which relates to service by post) the proper address of a person or body corporate to whose registration or enrolment such a document relates shall be his or its address in the register or list.

27. Rules etc made by Council
(1) Rules made by the Council under sections 8, 11, 12, 13, 14 or 19 of this Act, the statement drawn up by the Council under section 10 of this Act or any revision of that statement made by the Council under that section shall not come into operation until approved by order of the Secretary of State.

(2) The Secretary of State may approve rules made under section 19 of this Act either as submitted to him or subject to such modifications as he thinks fit; but where the Secretary of State proposes to approve any such rules subject to modifications he shall notify the modifications to the Council and consider any observations of the Council thereon.

(3) The Secretary of State may, after consulting the Council, by order vary or revoke any rules made under section 8, 11 or 12 of this Act or revise the statement under section 10 of this Act.

28. Orders
(1) The power to make orders under this Act shall be exercisable by statutory instrument; and any order made under this Act may be varied or revoked by a subsequent order so made.

(2) Any statutory instrument by which that power is exercised, except one containing an order under section 30(3) of this Act or any such order as is mentioned in subsection (3) below, shall be subject to annulment in pursuance of a resolution of either House of Parliament.

(3) An order under section 3(4) or section 27(3) of this Act, an order under paragraph 2 of the Schedule to this Act approving a scheme subject to modifications or an order under paragraph 10 of that Schedule shall not be made unless a draft of the order has been approved by resolution of each House of Parliament.

29. Interpretation
(1) In this Act, unless the context otherwise requires —

'approved qualification' and 'approved educational institution' have the meanings respectively assigned to them by section 6 of this Act; 'authorised insurers' means a person permitted under the Insurance Companies Act [1982] . . . to carry on [insurance business of class 13 or of classes 1, 2, 14, 15, 16 and 17 in Schedule 2 to the Insurance Companies Act [1982]];

'the Council' means the Insurance Brokers Registration Council established pursuant to section 1 of this Act;

'the Court' means the High Court, or, in relation to Scotland, the Court of Session or, in relation to Northern Ireland, a judge of the High Court of Justice in Northern Ireland;

'disciplinary case' has the meaning assigned to it by section 13 of this Act;

'employee' in relation to a body corporate, includes a director of the body corporate and 'employed' shall be construed accordingly;

'enrolled' means enrolled in the list and 'enrolment' shall be construed accordingly;

'functions' includes powers and duties;

'insurance business' means insurance business [other than industrial assurance business (within the meaning of section 1(2) of the Industrial Assurance Act 1923 or Articles 2(2) and 3(1) of the Industrial Assurance (Northern Ireland) Order 1979)], and 'insurance broker' shall be construed accordingly;

'list' means the list of bodies corporate carrying on business as insurance brokers;

'practising insurance broker' means a registered insurance broker who is carrying on business as an insurance broker;

'prescribed' means prescribed by rules under this Act;

'recognised body of accountants' means any one of the following, namely —

the Institute of Chartered Accountants in England and Wales;

the Institute of Chartered Accountants of Scotland;

the Association of Certified Accountants;

the Institute of Chartered Accountants in Ireland;

any other body of accountants established in the United Kingdom and for the time being recognised for the[purposes of section 389(1)(a) of the Companies Act 1985]by the Secretary of State;

'register' means the register of insurance brokers and 'registered' and 'registration' shall be construed accordingly;

'registered insurance broker' means a person who is registered in the register;

'the registrar' means the registrar of the Council appointed under section 8(1) of this Act.

(2) References in this Act to any other enactment (including an enactment of the Parliament of Northern Ireland and an Order in Council under the Northern Ireland Act 1974) shall be construed as references thereto, as amended, and as including references thereto as extended, by or under any subsequent enactment.

[*Note*: Section 29 amended by Sched 4 of the Insurance Companies Act 1981; by Sched 5 of the Insurance Companies Act 1982; by Sched 2 of The Companies Consolidation (Consequential Provisions) Act 1985. Repealed in part by Sched 5 of the Insurance Companies Act 1980.]

30. Short title, extent and commencement

(1) This Act may be cited as the Insurance Brokers (Registration) Act 1977.

(2) This Act extends to Northern Ireland.

(3) Subject to subsection (4) below, this Act shall come into operation on

such date as the Secretary of State may by order appoint and different dates may be appointed for different provisions and for different purposes.

(4) The day appointed for the coming into operation of section 22 of this Act shall not be earlier than the expiration of a period of two years beginning with the day appointed for the coming into operation of section 1 of this Act.

SCHEDULE

Section 1

CONSTITUTION ETC, OF INSURANCE BROKERS REGISTRATION COUNCIL

1. The Council shall consist of —
    (a) twelve persons chosen to represent registered insurance brokers of whom one shall be Chairman of the Council;
    (b) five persons nominated by the Secretary of State of whom one shall be a barrister, advocate or solicitor, another shall be a member of a recognised body of accountants and a third shall be a person appearing to the Secretary of State to represent the interests of persons who are or may become policyholders of insurance companies.

2. (1) The persons chosen to represent registered insurance brokers in the first instance shall be nominated by the British Insurance Brokers' Association.

(2) The persons chosen to represent registered insurance brokers after the retirement of those nominated under sub-paragraph (1) above shall be elected by registered insurance brokers in accordance with a scheme which —

    (a) shall be made by the Council;
    (b) shall not come into operation until approved by order of the Secretary of State; and
    (c) may be varied or revoked by a subsequent scheme so made and so approved.

(3) The Secretary of State may approve a scheme either as submitted to him or subject to such modifications as he thinks fit; but where the Secretary of State proposes to approve a scheme subject to modifications he shall notify the modifications to the Council and consider any observations of the Council thereon.

(4) The Council shall submit a scheme to the Secretary of State for approval before the expiration of a period of two years beginning with the day appointed for the coming into operation of section 1 of this Act.

(5) In the exercise of any functions under this paragraph due regard shall be had to the desirability of securing that the Council include persons representative of all parts of the United Kingdom.

3. Nominations of the first members of the Council shall so far as practicable be made before the day appointed for the establishment of the Council in time to enable the persons nominated to assume membership on its establishment.

4. (1) The term of office of —

    (a) members nominated by the British Insurance Brokers' Association shall be such period, not exceeding four years, as may be fixed by the scheme;

(b) members elected by registered insurance brokers shall be such period as may be fixed by the scheme;

(c) members nominated by the Secretary of State shall be such period, not exceeding three years, as may be fixed by the Secretary of State.

(2) In this paragraph 'the scheme' means the scheme or schemes under paragraph 2 above which are for the time being in operation.

5. A member of the Council may at any time, by notice in writing addressed to the registrar, resign his office.

6. (1) A person nominated or elected to fill a casual vacancy among the members of the Council shall hold office during the remainder of the term of office of the person whose vacancy he has filled.

(2) Any vacancy other than a casual vacancy in the membership of the Council shall be filled before the date on which the vacancy occurs.

7. A person ceasing to be a member of the Council shall be eligible to be again nominated or elected a member.

8. (1) The Council shall have power to do anything which in their opinion is calculated to facilitate the proper discharge of their functions.

(2) The Council shall, in particular, have power —

(a) to appoint, in addition to a registrar, such officers and servants as the Council may determine;

(b) to pay to the members of the Council or their committee such fees for attendance at meetings of the Council or their committees and such travelling and subsistence allowances while attending such meetings or while on any other business of the Council as the Council may determine;

(c) to pay to their officers and servants such remuneration as the Council may determine;

(d) as regards any officers or servants in whose case they may determine to do so, to pay to, or in respect of them, such pensions and gratuities, or provide and maintain for them such superannuation schemes (whether contributory or not), as the Council may determine;

(e) subject to the provisions of section 1 of the Borrowing (Control and Guarantees) Act 1946 or, in Northern Ireland, of section 2 of the Loans Guarantee and Borrowing Regulation Act (Northern Ireland) 1946 and of any order under those provisions for the time being in force, to borrow such sums as the council may from time to time require for performing any of their functions under this Act.

(3) The powers of the Council and any of its committees may be exercised notwithstanding any vacancy, and no proceedings of the Council or of any of its committees shall be invalidated by any defect in the nomination or election of a member.

9. The Council may make standing orders for regulating the proceedings (including quorum) of the Council and of any committee thereof:

Provided that orders shall not be made under this paragraph with respect to the proceedings of the Disciplinary Committee.

10. The Secretary of State may, after consulting the Council, by order so amend the provisions of this Schedule as to vary the number of members and the manner in which they are chosen or appointed.

Insurance Brokers Registration Council (Code of Conduct) Approval Order 1978

(SI 1978 No 1394)

1. This Order may be cited as the Insurance Brokers Registration Council (Code of Conduct) Approval Order 1978 and shall come into operation on 20th October 1978.

2. The Code of Conduct drawn up by the Insurance Brokers Registration Council pursuant to section 10 of the Insurance Brokers (Registration) Act 1977 is hereby approved as set out in the Schedule to this Order.

SCHEDULE

CODE OF CONDUCT DRAWN UP BY THE INSURANCE BROKERS REGISTRATION COUNCIL PURSUANT TO SECTION 10 OF THE INSURANCE BROKERS (REGISTRATION) ACT 1977

Words and expressions used in this Code of Conduct shall have the same meaning as are ascribed to them in the Act except that:

'insurance broker' means registered insurance broker and enrolled body corporate;

'insurer' means a person or body of persons carrying on insurance business;

'advertisements' or 'advertising' means canvassing, the offer of services or other methods whereby business is sought by insurance brokers.

1. This Code of Conduct shall serve as a guide to insurance brokers and other persons concerned with their conduct but the mention or lack of mention in it of a particular act or omission shall not be taken as conclusive of any question of professional conduct.

In the opinion of the Council the objective of the Code is to assist in establishing a recognised standard of professional conduct required of all insurance brokers who should, in the interests of the public and in the performance of their duties, bear in mind both this objective and the underlying spirit of this Code.

Matters which might relate to acts or omissions amounting to negligence will be dealt with, if necessary, by the Courts but the Council acknowledges that gross negligence or repeated cases of negligence may amount to unprofessional conduct.

2. The following are, in the opinion of the Council, the acts and omissions which, if done or made by registered insurance brokers or enrolled bodies corporate constitute unprofessional conduct: namely any acts or omissions that breach the fundamental principles governing the professional conduct of insurance brokers set out in paragraph 3 below.

3. The principles mentioned in paragraph 2 above are as follows:

    A.   Insurance brokers shall at all times conduct their business with utmost good faith and integrity.

    B.   Insurance brokers shall do everything possible to satisfy the insurance requirements of their clients and shall place the interests of those clients before all other considerations. Subject to these requirements and interests, insurance brokers shall have proper regard for others.

    C.   Statements made by or on behalf of insurance brokers when advertising shall not be misleading or extravagant.

The following are some specific examples of the application of these principles:

(1) In the conduct of their business insurance brokers shall provide advice objectively and independently.

(2) Insurance brokers shall only use or permit the use of the description 'insurance broker' in connection with a business provided that business is carried on in accordance with the requirements of the Rules made by the Council under sections 11 and 12 of the Act.

(3) Insurance brokers shall ensure that all work carried out in connection with their insurance broking business shall be under the control and day-to-day supervision of a registered insurance broker and they shall do everything possible to ensure that their employees are made aware of this Code.

(4) Insurance brokers shall on request from the client explain the differences in, and the relative costs of, the principal types of insurance which in the opinion of the insurance broker might suit a client's needs.

(5) Insurance brokers shall ensure the use of a sufficient number of insurers to satisfy the insurance requirements of their clients.

(6) Insurance brokers shall, upon request, disclose to any client who is an individual and who is, or is contemplating becoming, the holder of a United Kingdom policy of insurance the amount of commission paid by the insurer under any relevant policy of insurance.

(7) Although the choice of an insurer can only be a matter of judgment, insurance brokers shall use their skill objectively in the best interests of their client.

(8) Insurance brokers shall not withhold from the policyholder any written evidence or documentation relating to the contract of insurance without adequate and justifiable reasons being disclosed in writing and without delay to the policyholder. If an insurance broker withholds a document from a policyholder by way of a lien for monies due from that policyholder he shall provide the reason in the manner required above.

(9) Insurance brokers shall inform a client of the name of all insurers with whom a contract of insurance is placed. This information shall be

given at the inception of the contract and any charges thereafter shall be advised at the earliest opportunity to the client.

(10) Before any work involving a charge is undertaken or an agreement to carry out business is concluded, insurance brokers shall disclose and identify any amount they propose to charge to the client or policyholder which will be in addition to the premium payable to the insurer.

(11) Insurance holders shall disclose to a client any payment which they receive as a result of securing on behalf of that client any service additional to the arrangement of a contract of insurance.

(12) Insurance brokers shall have proper regard for the wishes of a policyholder or client who seeks to terminate any agreement with them to carry out business.

(13) Any information acquired by an insurance broker from his client shall not be used or disclosed except in the normal course of negotiating, maintaining, or renewing a contract of insurance for that client or unless the consent of the client has been obtained or the informtion is required by a court of competent jurisdiction.

(14) In the completion of the proposal form, claim form, or any other material document, insurance brokers shall make it clear that all the answers or statements are the client's own responsibility. The client should always be asked to check the details and told that the inclusion of incorrect information may result in a claim being repudiated.

(15) Advertisements made by or on behalf of insurance brokers shall comply with the applicable parts of the Code of Advertising Practice published by the Advertising Standards Authority and for this purpose the Code of Advertising Practice shall be deemed to form part of this Code of Conduct.

(16) Advertisements made by or on behalf of insurance brokers shall distinguish between contractual benefits, that is those that the contract of insurance is bound to provide, and non-contractual benefits, that is the amount of benefit which it might provide assuming the insurer's particular forecast is correct. Where such advertisements include a forecast of non-contractual benefits, insurance brokers shall restrict the forecast to that provided by the insurer concerned.

(17) Advertisements made by or on behalf of insurance brokers shall not be restricted to the policies of one insurer except where the reasons for such restrictions are fully explained in the advertisement, the insurer named therein, and the prior approval of that insurer obtained.

(18) When advertising their services directly or indirectly either in person or in writing insurance brokers shall disclose their identity, occupation and purpose before seeking information or before giving advice.

(19) Insurance brokers shall display in any office where they are carrying on business and to which the public have access a notice to the effect that a copy of the Code of Conduct is available upon request and that if a member of the public wishes to make a complaint or requires the assistance of the Council in resolving a dispute, he may write to the Insurance Brokers Registration Council at its offices at 15 St Helen's Place, London EC3A 6DS.

Lloyd's Act 1982

8. Insurance Business

(1) An underwriting member shall be a party to a contract of insurance underwritten at Lloyd's only if it is underwritten with several liability, each underwriting member for his own part and not one for another, and if the liability of each underwriting member is accepted solely for his own account.

(2) An underwriting member (not being himself an underwriting agent) shall underwrite contracts of insurance at Lloyd's only through an underwriting agent.

(3) An underwriting member shall in the course of his underwriting business at Lloyd's accept or place business only from or through a Lloyd's broker or such other person as the Council may from time to time by byelaw permit.

(4) Breach of any of subsections (1) to (3) above shall constitute an act or default in respect of which disciplinary proceedings may be brought in accordance with byelaws made under section 7 (The Disciplinary Committee and the Appeal Tribunal) of this Act.

Financial Services Act 1986

138.—(1) Rules made under section 8 of the Insurance Brokers (Registration) Act 1977 may require an applicant for registration or enrolment to state whether he is an authorised person or exempted person under Part I of this Act and, if so, to give particulars of the authorisation or exemption; and an individual shall be treated as satisfying the requirements of section 3(2)(a) of that Act (applicant for registration to satisfy Council as to his character and suitability) if he is an authorised person or a member of a partnership or unincorporated association which is an authorised person.

(2) In drawing up any statement under section 10 of that Act or making any rules under section 11 or 12 of that Act after the coming into force of this section the Insurance Brokers Registration Council shall take proper account of any provisions applicable to, and powers exercisable in relation to, registered insurance brokers or enrolled bodies corporate under this Act.

(3) In section 12(1) and (2) of that Act (which requires the Council to make professional indemnity rules) for the words 'The Council shall' there shall be substituted the words 'The Council may'.

(4) In section 15 of that Act (erasure from register and list for unprofessional conduct etc) after subsection (2) there shall be inserted —

'(2A) The Disciplinary Committee may, if they think fit, direct that the name of a registered insurance broker or enrolled body corporate shall be erased from the register or list if it appears to the Committee that any responsible person has concluded that the broker (or a related person) or the body corporate has contravened or failed to comply with —

(a) any provision of the Financial Services Act 1986 or any rule or regulation made under it to which he or it is or was subject at the time of the contravention or failure; or

(b) any rule of any recognised self-regulating organisation or recognised professional body (within the meaning of that Act) to which he is or was subject at that time.

(2B) In subsection (2A) above —

(a) 'responsible person' means a person responsible under the Financial Services Act 1986 or under the rules of any recognised self-regulating organisation or recognised professional body (within the meaning of that Act) for determining whether any contravention of any provision of that Act or rules or regulations made under it or any rules of that organisation or body has occurred; and

(b) 'related person' means a partnership or unincorporated association

300

of which the broker in question is (or was at the time of the failure or contravention in question) a member or a body corporate of which he is (or was at that time) a director.'

(5) The Insurance Brokers Registration Council shall cooperate, by the sharing of information and otherwise, with the Secretary of State and any other authority, body or person having responsibility for the supervision or regulation of investment business or other financial services.

(6) For the purposes of the said Act of 1977 'authorised insurers' shall include —

    (a) an insurance company the head office of which is in a member State other than the United Kingdom and which is entitled to carry on there insurance business corresponding to that mentioned in the definition of 'authorised insurers' in that Act; and

    (b) an insurance company which has a branch or agency in such a member State and is entitled under the law of that State to carry on there insurance business corresponding to that mentioned in that definition.

SCHEDULES

Investment business is described in Schedule 1 of the Financial Services Act 1986 as including:

(1) dealing in investments

(2) arranging deals in investments

(3) managing investments

(4) investment advice

(5) establishing collective investment schemes except market making or establishing or operating any authorised unit trust scheme.

The following categories of investment may be dealt in:

(1) shares

(2) debentures

(3) government and public securities

(4) units in collective investment schemes

(5) any instruments entitling their holders to shares, certificates representing securities, options, or rights and interests in investments.

(6) Longterm insurance contracts, defined in s 10 Part 1 as follows.

Long term insurance contracts

10. Rights under a contract the effecting and carrying out of which constitutes long-term business within the meaning of the Insurance Companies Act 1982.

Notes

(1) This paragraph does not apply to rights under a contract of insurance if —

    (a) the benefits under the contract are payable only on death or in respect of incapacity due to injury, sickness or infirmity;

    (b) no benefits are payable under the contract on a death (other than a death due to accident) unless it occurs within 10 years of the date on which the life of the person in question was first insured under the contract or before that person attains a specified age not exceeding 70 years;

    (c) the contract has no surrender value or the consideration consists of a single premium and the surrender value does not exceed that premium; and

    (d) the contract does not make provision for its conversion or extension in a manner that would result in its ceasing to comply with paragraphs (a), (b) and (c) above.

(2) Where the provisions of a contract of insurance are such that the effecting and carrying out of the contract —

    (a) constitutes both long-term business within the meaning of the Insurance Companies Act 1982 and general business within the meaning of that Act; or

    (b) by virtue of section 1(3) of that Act constitutes long-term business notwithstanding the inclusion of subsidiary general business provisions,

references in this paragraph to rights and benefits under the contract are references only to such rights and benefits as are attributable to the provisions of the contract relating to long-term business.

(3) This paragraph does not apply to rights under a reinsurance contract.

(4) Rights falling within this paragraph shall not be regarded as falling within paragraph 9 above. [Contracts for differences.]

Lloyd's Byelaws and Regulations — Chronological Index

5 January 1983
(1) Interpretation
[Amended: 24 October 1983]
[Amended: 19 December 1983]
[Amended: 9 April 1984, p 9]

(2) Administrative Suspension
[Amended: 18 July 1984, pp 3, 4]
[Revoked: 3 June 1987 by Byelaw No 7 of 1987]

(3) Inquiries and Investigations

(4) Information and Confidentiality
[Amended: 14 May 1984 by Byelaw No 4 of 1984]
[Amended: 6 July 1988 by Byelaw No 5 of 1988]
[Amended: 6 July 1988 by Byelaw No 6 of 1988]

(5) Misconduct, Penalties and Sanctions
[Amended: 19 December 1983, pp 8–9]

(6) Disciplinary Committees
[Amended: 5 December 1983, p 1]
[Amended: 13 January 1986 by Byelaw No 1 of 1986]
[Amended: 4 November 1987 by Byelaw No 12 of 1987]

(7) Appeal Tribunal
[Amended: 5 August 1986 by Byelaw No 5 of 1985]

(8) Council Stage of Disciplinary Proceedings
[Amended: 18 July 1983, p 14]

(9) Promulgation of Byelaws and Regulations

(10) Ordinary and Extraordinary General Meetings
[Amended: 4 March 1987 by Byelaw No 3 of 1987 pp 21–22]

17 January 1983
(11) Quorums and Appointments of Committees and Sub-Committees
[Amended: 7 February 1983, p 20]
[Amended: 4 March 1987 by Byelaw No 2 of 1987]

(12) Direct Motor Business

7 February 1983
(13) The Council and Committee
[Amended: 9 April 1984, p 10]
[Revoked: 4 March 1987 by Byelaw No 1 of 1987]

(14) Maintenance of Byelaws and Regulations

(15) Miscellaneous Matters

(16) Suspension from Membership of the Council, the Committee, and any Sub-Committee

(17) Deputy Chairman and Chief Executive of the Society
Amendment to Byelaw No 11 of 1983

6 June 1983
(18) Issue of Proceedings by Council

18 July 1983
(19) Suspension: Supplementary and Consequential Matters

(20) Substitute Agents
Amendment to Byelaw No 8 of 1983

(21) Disclosure by Direction

24 October 1983
Amendment to Byelaw No 1 of 1983

5 December 1983
Amendment to Byelaw No 6 of 1983

19 December 1983
(22) The Register of Members
Amendment to Byelaw No 5 of 1983

9 January 1984
(1) Information relevant to the operation of Sections 10, 11, and 12 of Lloyd's Act 1982

13 February 1984
(2) 1983 Annual Reports of Syndicates
[Revoked: 4 November 1987 by Byelaw No 11 of 1987]

9 April 1984
(3) Disclosure of Interests
[Amended: 4 November 1987 by Byelaw No 11 of 1987 para 2]
Amendment to Byelaw No 1 of 1983
Amendment to Byelaw No 13 of 1983

14 May 1984
(4) Underwriting Agents
[Amended: 1 July 1987 by Byelaw No 8 of 1987]
[Amended: 8 June 1988 by Byelaw No 4 of 1988]
[Amended: 10 May 1989 by Byelaw No 6 of 1989]
[Amended: 7 June 1989 by Byelaw No 9 of 1989]
[Amended: 1 November 1989 by Byelaw No 14 of 1989]
[Amended: 7 March 1990 by Byelaw No 2 of 1990]
[Amended: 4 April 1990 by Byelaw No 4 of 1990]

18 July 1984
(5) Recovery of Monies paid out of Lloyd's Central Fund or the Funds and Property of the Society
[Revoked: 15 April 1985 by Byelaw No 2 of 1985]
Amendment to Byelaw No 2 of 1983

6 August 1984
(6) Syndicate Premium Income
[Amended: 6 May 1987 by Byelaw No 5 of 1987]
[Amended: 7 March 1990 by Byelaw No 3 of 1990]

Reg 1 of 84: The Syndicate Premium Income (Monitoring) Regulation
[Amended: 6 May 1987 by Regulation No 1 of 1987]

8 October 1984
(7) The Syndicate Accounting Byelaw
[Amended: 10 March 1986 by Byelaw No 2 of 1986, para 10]
[Revoked: 4 November 1987 by Byelaw No 11 of 1987]

(8) Underwriting Agents (Interim Provisions)
[Duration expired: 23 July 1987]

12 November 1984
(9) Membership
[Amended: 10 March 1986 by Byelaw No 3 of 1986]
[Amended: 4 March 1987 by Byelaw No 4 of 1987]
[Amended: 2 December 1987 by Byelaw No 15 of 1987]
[Amended: 11 May 1988 by Byelaw No 3 of 1988]
[Amended: 7 June 1989 by Byelaw No 10 of 1989]

10 December 1984
(10) Syndicate Audit Arrangements
[Amended: 17 June 1985 by Byelaw No 3 of 1985]
[Amended: 7 June 1989 by Byelaw No 7 of 1989]

11 March 1985
(1) Agency Agreements

15 April 1985
(2) Recovery of Monies paid out of Lloyd's Central Fund or the Funds and Property of the Society
[Revoked: re-enacted in Byelaw No 4 of 1986, paras 8 & 10]

17 June 1985
(3) Syndicate Audit Arrangements (Amendment)

5 August 1985
(4) Binding Authorities
[USA General Cover Conditions: amended by letter dated 25 November 1985]
[Amended: 11 May 1988 by Byelaw No 1 of 1988]

Reg 1 of 85: The Binding Authorities Regulation
[Amended: 11 May 1988 by Regulation No 1 of 1988]
[Amended: 15 February 1989 by Regulation No 2 of 1989]

Reg 2 of 85: The Approval of Correspondents Regulation
[Amended: 3 September 1986 by Regulation No 1 of 1986]
[Amended: 11 May 1988 by Regulation No 2 of 1988]
[Amended: 15 February 1989 by Regulation No 1 of 1989]

Code of Practice Operation of Binding Authorities

(5) Appeal Tribunal (Amendment)

9 December 1985
(6) Reinsurance to Close

(7) Multiple Syndicates
[Revoked: 10 May 1989 by Byelaw No 5 of 1989]
Code of Practice For Underwriting Agents and Active Underwriters: Multiple Syndicates
(8) Lloyd's Introductory Test

13 January 1986
(1) Disciplinary Committees (Amendment)

10 March 1986
(2) Related Parties

(3) Membership (Amendment)

12 May 1986
Code of Practice
New paras 768 to Multiple Syndicates Code of Practice

14 July 1986
(4) Central Fund
[Amended: 7 October 1987 by Byelaw No 10 of 1987]
[Amended: 7 December 1988 by Byelaw No 9 of 1988]

3 September 1986
Reg 1 of 86: The Approval of Correspondents (Amendment) Regulation

13 October 1986
(5) Review Powers
[Amended: 6 July 1988 by Byelaw No 6 of 1988]

8 December 1986
(6) Nominated Members of the Council (Remuneration)

4 March 1987
(1) Council and Committee
[Amended: 2 December 1987 by Byelaw No 16 of 1987]
[Amended: 7 December 1988 by Byelaw No 10 of 1988]
[Amended: 6 June 1990 by Byelaw No 5 of 1990]

(2) Quorums and Appointments of Committees and Sub-Committees (Amendment)

(3) Ordinary and Extraordinary General Meetings (Amendment)

(4) Membership (Amendment No 2)

6 May 1987
(5) Syndicate Premium Income (Amendment)

Reg 1 of 87: The Syndicate Premium Income (Monitoring) (Amendment) Regulation

3 June 1987
(6) PCW Syndicates (Exemptions and Miscellaneous Provisions)

(7) Administrative Suspension

1 July 1987
(8) Underwriting Agents (Amendment)

7 October 1987
(9) Membership (Entrance Fees and Annual Subscriptions)

(10) Central Fund (Amendment)

4 November 1987
(11) Syndicate Accounting
[Amended: 1 February 1989 by Byelaw No 2 of 1989]

(12) Disciplinary Committees (Amendment)

2 December 1987
(13) Members' Ombudsman

(14) Modified Arbitration Procedure

(15) Membership (Amendment No 3)

(16) Council and Committee (Amendment)

11 May 1988
(1) Binding Authorities (Amendment)

(2) Council Members (Indemnification)

(3) Membership (Amendment No 4)

Reg 1 of 88: The Binding Authorities (Amendment) Regulation

Reg 2 of 88: The Approval of Correspondents (Amendment No 2) Regulation

8 June 1988
(4) Underwriting Agents (Amendment)

6 July 1988
(5) Lloyd's Brokers
[Amended: 7 June 1989 by Byelaw No 8 of 1989]
[Amended: 4 October 1989 by Byelaw No 13 of 1989]
[Amended: 6 June 1990 by Byelaw No 6 of 1990]

Code of Practice Lloyd's Brokers

(6) Umbrella Arrangements
[Amended: 6 June 1990 by Byelaw No 7 of 1990]

7 September 1988
(7) Members' Agents (Information)
[Amended: 1 March 1989 by Byelaw No 4 of 1989]

7 December 1988
(8) Agency Agreements

(9) Central Fund (Amendment No 2)

(10) Council and Committee (Amendment No 2)

11 January 1989
(1) Insurance Ombudsman Bureau

1 February 1989
(2) Syndicate Accounting (Amendment)

Code of Practice: Syndicate Expenses

(3) Members' Ombudsman (Amendment)

15 February 1989
Reg 1 of 89: Approval of Correspondents (Amendment No 3)

Reg 2 of 89: Binding Authorities (Amendment No 2)

1 March 1989
(4) Members' Agents (Information) (Amendment)

10 May 1989
(5) Multiple Syndicates
[Amended: 2 August 1989 by Byelaw No 12 of 1989]

(6) Lloyd's Market Certificate

7 June 1989
(7) Syndicate Audit Arrangements (Amendment No 2)

(8) Lloyd's Brokers (Amendment)

(9) Underwriting Agents (Amendment No 3)

(10) Membership (Amendment No 5)

(11) Misconduct (Reporting)

(12) Multiple Syndicates (Amendment)

(13) Lloyd's Brokers (Amendment No 2)

(14) Underwriting Agents (Amendment No 4)

(15) Members' Compensation Scheme

(16) Membership (Amendment No 6)

(17) Run-Off Years of Account

(18) Underwriting Agents (Amendment No 5)

1990
(1) Syndicate Accounting (Amendment No 2)

(2) Agency Agreements (Amendment)

(3) Syndicate Premium Income (Amendment No 2)

(4) Underwriting Agents (Amendment No 6)

(5) Council & Committee (Amendment No 3)

(6) Lloyd's Brokers (Amendment No 3)

(7) Umbrella Arrangements (Amendment)

Reg 1 of 90: Following Year Underwriting (Amendment)

Reg 2 of 90: Personal Stop Loss

Reg 3 of 90: Insurance Intermediaries

26 July 1989
Reg 3 of 89: Following Year Underwriting

27 September 1989
Reg 4 of 89: Financial Guarantee Insurance

Lloyd's Code of Practice for Lloyd's Brokers

Issued by The Council of Lloyd's on 6 July, 1988 Under Paragraph 20 of the Lloyd's Brokers Byelaw (No 5 of 1988)

This Code of Practice comes into force on 1 November, 1988

INTRODUCTION TO CODE OF PRACTICE FOR LLOYD'S BROKERS

1. The intention of Lloyd's in promulgating codes of practice is to assist in establishing a recognised standard of professional conduct for all members of the Lloyd's community who should, in discharging their duties as such, bear in mind both the provisions and the underlying spirit and intent of these codes.

2. The Code of Practice for Lloyd's brokers is intended as an explanatory statement of the principles which are expected to apply to the conduct of Lloyd's brokers.

3. Lloyd's brokers and their partners, directors and employees who are individually registered under the Insurance Brokers (Registration) Act 1977 are also subject to the Code of Conduct drawn up under that Act. The three fundamental principles of that code are:

   A. Insurance brokers shall at all times conduct their business with utmost good faith and integrity.

   B. Insurance brokers shall do everything possible to satisfy the insurance requirements of their clients and shall place the interests of those clients before all other considerations. Subject to these requirements and interests, insurance brokers shall have proper regard for others.

   C. Statements made by or on behalf of insurance brokers when advertising shall not be misleading or extravagant.

4. Under the terms of the Lloyd's Brokers Byelaw (No 5 of 1988) the Council must be satisfied on the registration or the review of the registration of a Lloyd's broker that the Lloyd's broker is a 'fit and proper' person. In making that assessment the Council may have regard to the observance by the Lloyd's broker of any relevant Lloyd's codes of practice.

5. Lloyd's brokers are the agents of their clients and, as such, they are subject to the general law as it applies to agents. The provisions of the Code of Practice are not intended in any way to derogate from that general law.

6. It is recognised that the practice described in this Code may be at variance with the law or legally established custom or practice applicable elsewhere than in England and Wales. In such circumstances, departure from the Code may be appropriate.

7. This Code applies only to the insurance activities of Lloyd's brokers. A Lloyd's broker is a partnership or body corporate permitted by the Council to broke insurance business at Lloyd's.

6 July 1988

CODE OF PRACTICE FOR LLOYD'S BROKERS

Unless the context otherwise requires, for the purpose of this Code of Practice the term 'Lloyd's broker' includes the individuals engaged in the insurance activities of the Lloyd's broker as well as the partnership or body corporate permitted by the Council to broke insurance business at Lloyd's.

The paragraphs inset in italics are the examples given in the IBRC Code of Conduct of the application of the three fundamental principles of that Code. These examples are relevant in this Lloyd's Code because Lloyd's brokers and their partners, directors and employees who are registered insurance brokers in the UK are subject to the IBRC Code.

1. Relationship with Client

1.1 When a Lloyd's broker establishes a relationship with a client, he should take appropriate steps to see that the client understands the Lloyd's broker's role.

1.2 A Lloyd's broker should understand the type of client with which he is dealing (including whether the client is a private individual, a business, another insurance intermediary or a reassured) and the extent of the client's awareness of risk and insurance and take that knowledge into account in his dealings with the client. A Lloyd's broker should take appropriate steps to see that the client is aware that local law may affect his insurance requirements.

> *(1) In the conduct of their business insurance brokers shall provide advice objectively and independently.*
>
> *(4) Insurance brokers shall on request from the client explain the differences in, and the relative costs of, the principal types of insurance which in the opinion of the insurance broker might suit a client's needs.*

1.3 Misunderstandings as to the scope of authority and instructions are far less likely to arise where they are set down in writing. Therefore, in the absence of accurate written instructions from a client as to coverage sought, a Lloyd's broker should, where it is reasonably practicable, confirm instructions in writing promptly, including appropriate reference to recommendations made by the Lloyd's broker but declined by the client.

1.4 A Lloyd's broker should not act for one client if he is aware that by so doing he could materially prejudice the performance of his obligations to another client.

2. Remuneration

2.1   A Lloyd's broker should, if requested by a client, disclose the amount of brokerage and the nature and where practicable the amount of commission or other remuneration he receives as a result of effecting an insurance for that client.

2.2   A Lloyd's broker will have to consider whether he is likely to receive any brokerage by effecting reinsurances of an original insurance. This type of remuneration will not normally be received by a Lloyd's broker in his capacity as agent of the original client and will not, therefore, normally be disclosable if the original client enquires. This will, however, depend on the circumstances of the particular transaction.

> (6) *Insurance brokers shall, upon request, disclose to any client who is an individual and who is, or is contemplating becoming the holder of a United Kingdom policy of insurance the amount of commission paid by the insurer under any relevant policy of insurance.*

> (10) *Before any work involving a charge is undertaken or an agreement to carry out business is concluded, insurance brokers shall disclose and identify any amount they propose to charge to the client or policyholder which will be in addition to the premium payable to the insurer.*

> (11) *Insurance brokers shall disclose to a client any payment which they receive as a result of securing on behalf of that client any service additional to the arrangement of a contract of insurance.*

2.3   A Lloyd's broker should deduct and retain any commission from the amount of a claim collected for a client only where this is the recognised practice for the type of insurance concerned and if the Lloyd's broker intends to deduct and retain any such commission the proportion should be disclosed to the client prior to the Lloyd's broker undertaking to effect the insurance.

2.4   Where it is the normal practice to return commissions *pro rata* to any return premiums, any intention on the part of a Lloyd's broker to depart from this practice should be advised to the client when the Lloyd's broker accepts his instructions to place the risk.

3. Confidentiality of Client Information

> (13) *Any information acquired by an insurance broker from his client shall not be used or disclosed except in the normal course of negotiating, maintaining, or renewing a contract of insurance for that client or unless the consent of the client has been obtained or the information is required by a court of competent jurisdiction.*

3.1   A Lloyd's broker may wish to compile statistics or otherwise use information gained from the operation of the accounts of various clients, in order to broke a risk for a particular client to insurers. In each case, the Lloyd's broker should consider what information he may properly use and great care must be taken that a client about whose account information is being used is not adversely affected by it. Although calling upon his general knowledge and experience of other clients' affairs would normally be permissible, the disclosure by a Lloyd's broker of information revealing the identities of clients and specific details of their affairs without their informed consent is not permissible, unless such information is already available to the market generally.

3.2   The duty to maintain the confidentiality of information can be overridden in certain limited and specific circumstances. For example, the

Lloyd's Information and Confidentiality Byelaw (No 4 of 1983) empowers the Council of Lloyd's (or other person acting under its authority) to require Lloyd's brokers to produce information including that relating to the affairs of their principals and clients. That provision thus permits confidential information to be legitimately imparted by a Lloyd's broker in circumstances other than those set out in the IBRC code.

3.3   A Lloyd's broker should take appropriate steps to maintain the security of confidential documents in his possession.

4. Choice of Insurers

(5) *Insurance brokers shall ensure the use of a sufficient number of insurers to satisfy the insurance requirements of their clients.*

(7) *Although the choice of an insurer can only be a matter of judgment, insurance brokers shall use their skill objectively in the best interests of their client.*

4.1   A Lloyd's broker should not allow any shareholding or other connections which he has with any insurance company, non-Lloyd's underwriting agent, coverholder or Lloyd's syndicate to prejudice the performance of his duties to his clients. In this context, connections with a Lloyd's syndicate would include the participation by partners, directors or employees of the Lloyd's broker in the syndicate as Members of Lloyd's or the placing of Members of Lloyd's on the syndicate by a Members' Agent which is connected with the Lloyd's broker.

4.2   Except for certain compulsory classes of insurance, it is not illegal under English law for an insurance for a client based in the UK to be effected outside the UK with an insurer which is not authorised to carry on insurance of the class concerned in the EEC. If, however, a Lloyd's broker suggests to such a client that such an insurance should be placed with such an insurer, he should, if he believes that it would be appropriate having regard to the client's experience of insurance, advise the client in writing that:-

(a) the management and solvency of the insurer are not supervised by the appropriate authority in any EEC member country;

(b) notwithstanding that the client may be an individual who would otherwise fall within the protection of the Policyholders Protection Act 1975, in the event of the failure of the insurer, no protection would be afforded to the client by that Act if the insurer was not suitably authorised in the UK; and

(c) the client may have difficulties in bringing proceedings and/or executing a judgment against the insurer.

The client's written acknowledgement of such advice should be sought.

4.3   Where a client's instructions concerning the choice of an insurer override a Lloyd's broker's advice, the Lloyd's broker should inform the client that this is contrary to the Lloyd's broker's advice and seek the client's written acknowledgement thereof.

5. Disclosure to Insurers

5.1   It is the duty of the Lloyd's broker and his client to disclose all material circumstances within their knowledge and to give a fair presentation of the risk to insurers.

5.2   A Lloyd's broker should explain to a client the duty of good faith and the obligation to disclose all circumstances material to the risk which he wishes to insure and the consequences of any failure to make such disclosure.

5.3 Other than in exceptional circumstances, a Lloyd's broker should not complete a proposal form on behalf of a client. If the Lloyd's broker does so complete a proposal form he should disclose that fact to the insurers.

> (11) *In the completion of the proposal form, claim form, or any other material document, insurance brokers shall make it clear that all the answers or statements are the client's own responsibility. The client should always be asked to check the details and told that the inclusion of incorrect information may result in a claim being repudiated.*

5.4 Slips and other placing information presented to insurers should be clear and unambiguous and the Lloyd's broker's relevant personnel should be competent to answer insurers' reasonable questions about the risk. A Lloyd's broker should be prompt to convey insurers' requests for further information to the client.

5.5 If a Lloyd's broker has reason to believe that the disclosure of the material facts by the client is not true, fair and complete, he should request the client to make the necessary true, fair and complete disclosure. In the absence of such agreement, the broker should consider whether he should decline to continue acting for the client and what obligations he has to insurers or any regulatory authority.

5.6 In cases where two Lloyd's brokers act jointly on a placing, they should each take appropriate steps to see that there is a clear mutual understanding of their respective duties to the client. Both Lloyd's brokers should also take appropriate steps to see that the client and insurers know each Lloyd's broker's responsibilities.

6. Documentation

> 9 *Insurance brokers shall inform a client of the name of all insurers with whom a contract of insurance is placed. This information shall be given at the inception of the contract and any changes thereafter shall be advised at the earliest opportunity to the client.*

6.1 Cover notes and other written evidence of cover issued by a Lloyd's broker should be signed by suitably senior personnel. It is good practice for such documents to be signed by someone of seniority who was not involved in the placing but who has checked that the placing has been properly effected instead of or as well as the person responsible for the placing. This latter practice will not normally need to be followed in respect of temporary motor insurance cover notes.

6.2 A Lloyd's broker should only advise a client that any proportion of an insurance has been effected when that proportion has been accepted by insurers.

6.3 A Lloyd's broker should provide his client with prompt written confirmation that an insurance has been effected and the terms thereof. If the full wording is not included with the confirmation, the Lloyd's broker should forward it as soon as possible.

6.4 Subject to any lien that he may legitimately exercise, a Lloyd's broker should pass on promptly to a client any written evidence or documentation relating to a contract of insurance arranged for that client which the client may reasonably require. Where the Lloyd's broker exercises a lien and withholds documents, he should inform the client accordingly.

> (8) *Insurance brokers shall not withhold from the policyholder any written*

evidence or documentation relating to the contract of insurance without adequate and justifiable reasons being disclosed in writing and without delay to the policyholder. If an insurance broker withholds a document from a policyholder by way of a lien for monies due from that policyholder he shall provide the reason in the manner required above.

7. Accounting

7.1   At an early stage in the business relationship, a Lloyd's broker should advise a client of his obligations to the Lloyd's broker and insurers concerning the timely payment of premiums.

7.2   Any insurance monies handled by a Lloyd's broker have to be kept in Insurance Broking Accounts. The operation of these accounts is the responsibility of the Lloyd's broker and he receives and retains any interest or investment income earned on them. A Lloyd's broker should apply due diligence to the collection and payment of all insurance monies.

7.3   A Lloyd's broker should have proper regard for the settlement due date agreed with the insurers for any contract of insurancec.

7.4   A Lloyd's broker should remit money received and due to clients promptly. Where a risk is placed with a number of insurers, and claims monies are remitted to the Lloyd's broker at different times, the Lloyd's broker will need to consider whether, having regard to the amount received and the time when the balance will be received, and any other relevant factors such as amounts owed by the client to the Lloyd's broker, he should pass on to the client such proceeds as he has received as soon as possible rather than await the balance and make payment in full.

8. Binding Authorities

(NB In this section, 'binding authorities' does not include limited binding authorities where reference has to be made to one or more leading insurers before a risk is bound.)

8.1   It is insurers' practice, particularly in certain classes of business, to grant underwriting authority to a Lloyd's broker under a binding authority. The primary purpose of this practice is to facilitate prompt and efficient acceptance of business. If a Lloyd's broker is in a position to place business from his own clients under the binding authority, that Lloyd's broker has a potential conflict of interest. A Lloyd's broker should not accept business from a client under a binding authority granted to him if to do so would not be in the client's best interests.

8.2   Where a Lloyd's broker accepts his own client's risk on behalf of insurers under a binding authority granted to him, he should disclose this to the client. Where the client so requests, a Lloyd's broker should inform him of all financial advantages to the Lloyd's broker of the use of the binding authority.

8.3   At the time of accepting a binding authority a Lloyd's broker should remind the insurers who are granting that authority that the Lloyd's broker's first duty will be to his existing and future clients rather than to the insurers granting the authority.

9. Claims

9.1 A Lloyd's broker should explain to his clients their obligations to notify claims promptly and to disclose all material facts.

9.2 If a Lloyd's broker has reason to believe that the notification of the facts of a claim by a client is not true, fair and complete, he should request him to make the necessary true, fair and complete disclosure. In the absence of such agreement, the broker should consider whether he should decline to continue acting for the client and what obligations he has to insurers or any regulatory authority.

9.3 A Lloyd's broker should take appropriate steps in connection with claims notified by clients to see that all information properly required by insurers is promptly provided to them.

9.4 A Lloyd's broker should give prompt advice to his client of insurers' requirements concerning notified claims.

9.5 On receipt of insurers' decision on the settlement or otherwise of a claim, a Lloyd's broker should promptly inform the client.

9.6 A Lloyd's broker should not, without the fully informed consent of both parties, act for both his client and insurers during the claims settling process if by doing so he would be undertaking duties to one principal which are inconsistent with those owed to the other. In any event, a Lloyd's broker who receives or holds on behalf of the insurers concerned an adjuster's report or similar document relating to an insurance claim made by his client should only do so on the basis that the information in the report may be imparted to the client.

9.7 A Lloyd's broker has a potential conflict of interest where he has an insurer's authority to settle claims. If he cannot reconcile the client's best interests with the obligations to the insurer concerned, he should refer the claim to the insurer for instructions.

9.8 In circumstances where the interests of two or more clients of a Lloyd's broker might conflict (eg where one is the first party and one the third party in an accident), the Lloyd's broker should take appropriate steps so that the interests of each can be fairly represented.

10. Renewal

The client should be aware of the date of expiry of his insurance from the insuring documentation. It should nevertheless be normal practice for a Lloyd's broker to seek from his client whose insurance is approaching expiry instructions concerning the renewal of that insurance and to remind the client of the duties of good faith and disclosure.

11. Transfer of Client

> (12) *Insurance brokers shall have proper regard for the wishes of a policyholder or client who seeks to terminate any agreement with them to carry out business.*

On transfer of a client to another Lloyd's broker, the prior Lloyd's broker should if so instructed by the client and subject to the payment of any monies owed by the client to the prior Lloyd's broker make available to the new Lloyd's broker all such documentation to which the client is entitled and which is reasonably necessary for the new Lloyd's broker to discharge his duties to that client.

12. Servicing

A Lloyd's broker should provide any relevant service requested by his client in relation to any insurance placed for that client notwithstanding the expiry of the insurance contract, unless the Lloyd's broker is properly satisfied that the client has instructed a new broker to assume all such obligations and that the new broker has accepted such instruction.

13. Complaints

13.1 A Lloyd's broker should have a procedure so that complaints by clients and insurers are at the appropriate stage dealt with at a suitably senior level and other than by the personnel involved in the matter giving rise to the complaint. Upon receipt of a complaint, a Lloyd's broker should give notification to the client of the complaints procedure which he operates. The notification should incorporate a reference to the right of a complainant to write to the Council of Lloyd's.

> *(19) Insurance brokers shall display in any office where they are carrying on business and to which the public have access a notice to the effect that a copy of the Code of Conduct is available upon request and that if a member of the public wishes to make a complaint or requires the assistance of the Council in resolving a dispute, he may write to the Insurance Brokers Registration Council at its offices at 15 St Helen's Place, London EC3A 6DS.*

13.2 A Lloyd's broking company or partnership should add the following paragraph to the notice required by IBRC Practice Note (No 2) to be displayed in its office and display that notice in a prominent position in the reception area of its office:

> *This Company/Partnership and those described above as 'At Lloyd's' are insurance brokers acting under the statutory authority of the Council of Lloyd's to whom complaints or disputes may be referred.*

14. Supervision of Staff

> *(3) Insurance brokers shall ensure that all work carried out in connection with their insurance broking business shall be under the control and day-to-day supervision of a registered insurance broker and they shall do everything possible to ensure that their employees are made aware of this Code.*

14.1 A broker should either operate his own training programmes or make use of training programmes such as those operated by Lloyd's Training Centre and the Chartered Insurance Institute, participation in which will maintain and improve the competence of all involved in the Lloyd's broking business.

14.2 A Lloyd's broker should take appropriate steps to see that its staff are aware of legal requirements, including the law of agency, affecting their activities.

14.3 A Lloyd's broker should take appropriate steps to see that his staff are aware of the standards expected of them by this Code of Practice.

15. Competence

A Lloyd's broker should not handle classes of business in which he is not competent.

16 Use of Lloyd's name

16. A Lloyd's broker should not permit businesses over which he has control to misuse Lloyd's name.

16.2 A Lloyd's broker should be careful not to do or permit to be done anything that would prejudice the regulatory status of insurers in any jurisdiction.

(2) *Insurance brokers shall only use or permit the use of the decription 'insurance broker' in connection with a business provided that business is carried on in accordance with the requirements of the Rules made by the Council under sections 11 and 12 of the (1977) Act.*

(15) *Advertisements made by or on behalf of insurance brokers shall comply with the applicable parts of the Code of Advertising Practice published by the Advertising Standards Authority and for this purpose the Code of Advertising Practice shall be deemed to form part of this Code of Conduct.*

(16) *Advertisements made by or on behalf of insurance brokers shall distinguish between contractual benefits, that is those that the contract of insurance is bound to provide, and non-contractual benefits, that is the amount of benefit which it might provide assuming the insurer's particular forecast is correct. Where such advertisements include a forecast of non-contractual benefits, insurance brokers shall restrict the forecast to that provided by the insurer concerned.*

(17) *Advertisements made by or on behalf of insurance brokers shall not be restricted to the policies of one insurer except where the reasons for such restriction are fully explained in the advertisement, the insurer named therein, and the prior approval of that insurer obtained.*

(18) *When advertising their services directly or indirectly either in person or in writing insurance brokers shall disclose their identity, occupation and purpose before seeking information or before giving advice.*

The author and the publisher thank Lloyd's for permission to reproduce the Code of Practice for Lloyd's Brokers.

Further Reading

Cockerell & Shaw, *Insurance Broking and Agency: The Law and the Practice*, 1st edn (Witherby 1979).

Hodgin, *Insurance Intermediaries and The Law*, 1st edn (Lloyd's of London Press 1987).

Hodgin, *Protection of the Insured*, 1st edn (Lloyd's of London Press 1989).

Peters, *UK Retail Insurance Brokers Handbook*, 1st edn (Business Books Ltd 1989).

Parkington, Legh-Jones, Longmore and Birds, *MacGillivray and Parkington on Insurance Law*, 8th edn (Sweet & Maxwell 1988).

Merkin and McGhee, *Insurance Contract Law*, Looseleaf, (Kluwer).

Hardy Ivamy, *General Principles of Insurance Law*, 5th edn (Butterworths 1986).

Kiln, *Reinsurance in Practice*, 1st edn (Butterworths 1981).

Golding, *The Law and Practice of Reinsurance*, 5th edn (Witherby 1987).

Birds, *Modern Insurance Law*, 2nd edn (Sweet & Maxwell 1988).

Clarke, *The Law of Insurance Contracts*, 1st edn (Lloyd's of London Press 1990).

Reynolds, *Bowstead on the Law of Agency*, 15th edn (Sweet & Maxwell 1985).

Fridman, *Fridman's Law of Agency*, 5th edn (Butterworths 1983).

Wood, *English and International Set-Off*, 1st edn (Sweet & Maxwell 1989).

Jackson and Powell, *Professional Negligence*, 2nd edn (Sweet & Maxwell 1987).

Dugdale and Stanton, *Professional Negligence*, 2nd edn (Butterworths 1989).

Guest, *Chitty on Contracts*, 26th edn (Sweet & Maxwell 1989).

Treitel, *Law of Contract*, 7th edn (Sweet & Maxwell 1987).

Index

321